Wheeler's Last Raid

Wheeler's Last Raid

by

Lewis A. Lawson

Wingate College Library

The Penkevill Publishing Company
Greenwood, Florida

Acknowledgements

My wife and our children and our families knew that this project meant a great deal to me and for eight years kindly tolerated my disappearance to a library, battlefield, or home of a descendant. I owe a huge debt of appreciation to Miss Betty Baehr, Head of Interlibrary Loan Services, University of Maryland, during the period of my project. Not only was her professional service always prompt and thorough, but Army brat that she was, her knowledge of Kentucky and the Civil War often provided me with valuable leads. I owe great affection to my colleague, Gayle E. Wilson, who suffered me when I had nobody else to talk to.

I owe my sincere thanks to the following people, who are either librarians or descendants of one of the participants. The librarians were invariably competent and considerate; the descendants were invariably sympathetic to my inquiries. My experience confirms the fact that the nation is still populated by fine people.

Ms Virginia M. Adams, Special Collections, Public Library, Providence, Rhode Island; Mr. Richard W. Alexander, San Francisco, California; Mr. Bayard Antle, Columbia, Kentucky; Mr. Douglas Arm-

strong, Mansfield, Ohio; Mr. Clinton I. Bagley, Mississippi Department
of Archives and History, Jackson, Mississippi; Mr. R. P. Baker, Arkansas History Commission, Little Rock, Arkansas; Mrs. Bonnie Ball,
Haysi, Virginia; Mrs. Helen Ball, Special Collections, Miami University
Library, Oxford, Ohio; Mr. LeRoy Barnett, Michigan History Division,
Michigan Department of State, Lansing, Michigan; Mrs. Ursula S. Beach,
Director, Montgomery County Historical Society, Clarksville, Tennessee; Mrs. Margaret J. Bedle, Reference Librarian, Public Library, Beaumont, Texes; Miss Marylin Bell, Archivist, Manuscripts Section, Tennessee State Library and Archives, Nashville, Tennessee; Mr. James R.
Bentley, Secretary of the Filson Club, Louisville, Kentucky; Mr. James
D. Birchfield, Tallahassee, Florida; Mr. Carey S. Bliss, Curator of
Rare Books, the Huntington Library, San Marino, California; Mrs.
Joe Bowman, Williamson County Historian, Franklin, Tennessee;
Ms Rebecca A. Bowman, Public Library, Cleveland, Tennessee; Ms
Lucile Boykin, Genealogy Division, Public Library, Dallas, Texas;
Mr. Roger D. Bridges, Director of Research, Illinois State Historical
Library, Springfield, Illinois; Ms Virginia Bridges, Reference Department, South Georgia Regional Library, Valdosta, Georgia; Miss Eleanor
S. Brockenbrough, Assistant Director, The Museum of the Confederacy,
Richmon, Virginia; Mr. David W. Brown, Manuscripts Department,
Duke University Library, Durham, North Carolina; Mr. and Mrs. Kenneth Brown, Alcoa, Tennessee; Mr. Frank Bugbee, New Albany, Indiana; Dr. Jacqueline Bull, Head of Special Collections, University
of Kentucky Libraries, Lexington, Kentucky; Ms Carol M. Burke, Administrative Assistant to the Chairman, The Sperry and Hutchinson
Company, New York, New York; Mrs. Helen Burress, Dutch Valley,
Clinton, Tennessee; Mr. Orin Cain, Niles, Michigan; Mrs. Marie T.
Capps, Map and Manuscripts Librarian, United States Military Academy
Library, West Point, New York; Ms Jean Carefoot, Archivist, Texas
State Library, Austin, Texas; Dr. Gordon T. Chappell, Department of
History, Huntingdon College, Montgomery, Alabama; Mr. Franklin
G. Chestnut, Jr., Assistant Librarian, Bethel College, McKenzie, Tennessee; Mr. Alexander P. Clark, Curator of Manuscripts, Princeton
University Library, Princeton, New Jersey; Mr. Brian Cockhill, Archivist, Montana Historical Society, Helena, Montana; Mr. Richard
C. Cohan, Hinesville, Georgia; Mrs. Nellie W. Coile, Public Library,
Cuthbert, Georgia; Mr. Howson W. Cole, Librarian of the Virginia
Historical Society, Richmond, Virginia; Dr. James H. Colgin, Waco,

Texas; Mr. William H. Combs, Director, Michigan State University Archives, East Lansing, Michigan; Mr. John B. Conger, President, Lincoln County Historical Society, Fayetteville, Tennessee; Mrs. Estelle Cosby, Goodspring, Tennessee; Mr. Hubert Covington, Moderator of the General Assembly of the Cumberland Presbyterian Church, Nashville, Tennessee; Mrs. Kermit F. Crippen, United Daughters of the Confederacy, Richmond, Virginia; Mr. Jere M. Dabbs, Special Collections Librarian, University of Alabama, University, Alabama; Mrs. Alice C. Dalligan, Chief, Burton Historical Collection, Public Library, Detroit, Michigan; Dr. William C. Davis, Editor, *Civil War Times Illustrated,* Harrisburg, Pennsylvania; Mr. James A. Dean, President, Albion Historical Society, Albion, Michigan; Mr. Ronald F. Deering, Librarian of the Southern Baptist Theological Seminary, Louisville, Kentucky; Mr. Rodney G. Dennis, Curator of Manscripts, Houghton Library, Harvard University, Cambridge, Massachusetts; Mr. Charles W. Deweese, Director of Editorial Services, The Historical Commission of the Southern Baptist Convention, Nashville, Tennessee; Mr. David Eden, Reference Department, Public Library, Savannah, Georgia; Mrs. Elizabeth Ellsberry, Chillicothe, Missouri; Mr. Richard T. Eltzroth, Archivist, Atlanta Historical Society, Atlanta, Georgia; Ms Katherine Embury, Public Library, Memphis, Tennessee; Mr. David E. Estes, Curator, Special Collections, Emory University Library, Atlanta, Georgia; Mrs. Ruth A. Estes, Public Library, Oneonta, Alabama; Ms Mary B. Fleischer, Barker Texas History Center, Universit of Texas Library, Austin, Texas; Mrs. Charles D. Gallaher, President, Wayne County Historical Society, Waynesboro, Tennessee; Mrs. William J. Garrett, Franklin, Tennessee; Mrs. Patricia B. Gatherum, Ohio Historical Society Library, Columbus, Ohio; Mr. Paul F. Geier, Delphos, Ohio; Mr. Charles G. Gibbons, Hillsdale, Michigan; Mr. F. O. Gibbs, War Memorial Public Library, Franklin, Tennessee; Mrs. Olive Gill, Public Library, Galion, Ohio; Mrs. Gray Golden, Austin, Texas; Mrs. G. E. Goodyear, Hastings, Michigan; Ms Alberta Graham, Abingdon, Virginia; Mr. Richard B. Graham, Columbus, Ohio; Ms Frances Greathouse, College Grove, Tennessee; Ms Patricia A. Green, Washington, D. C.: Mr. Richard Greenwalt, Alliance, Ohio; Mrs. Blanche Grigsby, Hawkins County Historian, Rogersville, Tennessee; Mrs. J. M. Hafner, Owensboro, Kentucky; Mr. Edward H. Hahn, Pittsburgh, Pennsylvania; Mrs. Holloway Haines, Maceo, Kentucky; Ms Martha M. Haines, Detroit, Michigan; Ms Dianna Hallford, Southwest Collection, Texas

Tech University, Lubbock, Texas; Dr. Josephine L. Harper, Reference Curator, State Historical Society of Wisconsin, Madison, Wisconsin; Ms M. J. Harper, Montgomery County Public Library, Clarksville, Tennessee; Mr. Dennis I. Harris, Curator of Manuscripts, Western Reserve Historical Society, Cleveland, Ohio; Mr. Mark Harris, Kentucky Division, Louisville Free Public Library, Louisville, Kentucky; Miss Carroll Hart, Director, Georgia Department of Archives and History, Atlanta, Georgia; Dr. Thomas H. Hartig, The Ohio Historical Society Archives, Columbus, Ohio; Mrs. Virginia R. Hawley, General Reference Supervisor, The Western Reserve Historical Society Library, Cleveland, Ohio; Mrs. Jesse T. Heard, Putnam County Historian, Algood, Tennessee; Mr. Bruce Henry, Huntington Library, San Marino, California; Mrs. Thomas Hillman, The Ohio Genealogical Society, Mansfield, Ohio; Ms Vickie L. Hocker, Archives Department, Rosenberg Library, Galveston, Texas; Mrs. Pat Hodges, Kentucky Library and Museum, Western Kentucky University, Bowling Green, Kentucky; Mrs. Lelia F. Holloway, Special Services, Oberlin College Library, Oberlin, Ohio; Mr. Hubert T. Holman, Fayetteville, Tennessee; Mr. Milo B. Howard, Jr., Director, Alabama Department of Archives and History, Montgomery, Alabama; Mrs. Oliver Howard, State Historical Society of Missouri, Columbia, Missouri; Mr. James S. Irvine, Speer Library, Princeton Theological Seminary, Princeton, New Jersey; Dr. Charles A. Isetts, The Ohio Historical Society Archives, Columbus, Ohio; Mrs. Virginia Fitzhugh Jeffery, Batesville, Arkansas; Mr. Charles S. Jones, San Antonio, Texas; Mr. Kent Keeth, Archivist of the Texas Collection, Baylor University, Waco, Texas; Mr. DeForest B. Kelley, Amherst, Ohio; Mr. John R. Kemp, Curator of Manuscripts, Louisiana State Museum, New Orleans, Louisiana; Mrs. Reginald A. Kenney, Blacksburg, Virginia; Mr. Arthur M. Kent, Wytheville, Virginia; Mr. Chester V. Kielman, Archivist, Barker Texas History Center, University of Texas, Austin, Texas; Mr. Leon E. Kingsley, Reading, Michigan; Mr. Max Kingsley, Hudson, Michigan; Mrs. C. M. T. Kirkman, Helena, Arkansas; Mrs. Mary Jane Knisely, Orlando, Florida; Mrs. Sam Knutson, Interlibrary Loan Service, University of Texas Library, Austin, Texas; Ms Betty R. Kondayan, Cyrus Hall McCormick Library, Washington and Lee University, Lexington, Virginia; Mrs. Henrietta Krause, Manuscripts Librarian, The State Historical Society of Missouri, Columbia, Missouri; Ms Marcia LaFranc, The Rhode Island Historical Society Library, Providence, Rhode Island; Mrs. R. M. Larimer, Supervisor of Special Collections, Carol M. Newman Library, Virginia Polytechnic Institute, Blacksburg, Virginia; Miss Florence Lathrop, Pasadena, California; Mrs. Robert Lauer, Amherst, Ohio; Mr. D. W. Lawler, Curator of the Wilson County Museum, Lebanon, Tennessee; Mr. Arthur Lawson, Public Library, Lexington, Kentucky; Mr. Charles Lawson, Rogersville, Tennessee; Mrs. Sally Leach, Humanties Research Center, University of Texas Library, Austin, Texas; Ms Eve Lebo, Manuscripts Specialist, University of Washington Library, Seattle, Washington; Ms Phyllis Leech, Allen County Historical Society, Lima, Ohio; Mrs. Lillian M. Lewis, Special Collections Librarian, Atlanta University, Atlanta, Georgia; Ms Mary Lou Livesay, Carroll County Public Library, Carrollton, Kentucky; Ms Therese Logue, Mississippi Department of Archives and History, Jackson, Mississippi; Mrs. Gertrude M. Long, Pontiac, Michigan; Mrs. Ann G. Lowe, Hardeman County Public Library, Quanah, Texas; Mrs. I. J. Lunsford, Cuthbert, Georgia; Mr. William J. MacArthur, Jr., Head, McClung Historical Collection, Knoxville-Knox County Public Library, Knoxville, Tennessee; Mr. J. Porter McCall, Sarasota, Florida; Mr. William S. McCarroll, Hopkinsville, Kentucky; Mrs. Sharon Brown McConnell, Supervisor, Townsend Room, Eastern Kentucky University Library, Richmond, Kentucky; Mrs. Ethel J. McCutcheon, Curator, Texas Confederate Museum, Austin, Texas; Mr. Alan R. MacDougall, Barker Texas History Center, University of Texas Library, Austin, Texas; Ms Elaine McEver, City Department of Personnel, Atlanta, Georgia; Ms Patricia McPeak, United Methodist Publishing House, Nashville, Tennessee; Mr. Donald Mackey, Addison, Michigan; Ms. Harriet McLoon, Assistant Curator, Americana Manuscripts, Huntington Library, San Marino, California; Professor Richard M. McMurry, Department of History, Valdosta State College, Valdosta, Georgia; Mr. William McNitt, Reference Archivist, Bentley Historical Library, University of Michigan, Ann Arbor, Michigan; Mr. David I. McWhirter, Director of the Library and Archives, Disciples of Christ Historical Society, Nashville, Tennessee; Mrs. John M. Manley, Homewood, Alabama; Mr. Wayne C. Mann, Director of the University Archives, Western Michigan University, Kalamazoo, Michigan; Miss Bill March, Singletary Memorial Library, Rusk, Texas; Ms Hazel L. Marlow, Foard County Library, Crowell, Texas; Mr. William J. Marshall, Jr., Acting Head, Special Collections, Unversity of Kentucky Libraries, Lexington, Kentucky; Mr. James C. Martin, Barker Texas History Center, University of Texas, Austin, Texas; Mrs. Will C. Martin, Baton

Rouge, Louisiana; Ms Linda M. Matthews, Emory University Library, Atlanta, Georgia; Mrs. Mary L. Meyer, Reference Division, Public Library, Nashville, Tennessee; Mr. William Miles, Bibliographer, Clarke Historical Library, Central Michigan University, Mount Pleasant, Michigan; Mrs. W. L. Ming, The Texas Collection, Baylor University, Waco, Texas; Ms Eden Moseley, Public Library, San Marcos, Texas; Mr. Archie Motley, Manuscripts Department, Chicago Historical Society, Chicago, Illinois; Miss Adah Mullendore, Sevierville, Tennessee; Mrs. Ben Nail, Crawford, Texas; Mrs. Doris B. Nave, Kentucky Historical Society Library, Frankfort, Kentucky; Mrs. Clarence Neufeld, Perryton, Texas; Mrs. Josephine M. Newberry, Wytheville, Virginia; Mr. Jack C. Northrup, Hilldale, Michigan; Mr. Jeff Northrup, Public Library, Birmingham, Alabama; Ms Juanita Ziegler Oas, Public Library, Sturgis, Michigan; Professor Matthew O'Brien, Department of Englihs, Georgia Institute of Technology, Atlanta, Georgia; Mr. Walter W. Ogilvie, College Grove, Tennessee; Miss Nell Orr, LaFayette, Alabama; Mr. R. Bruce Parham, Manuscripts Curator, University of Arkansas Library, Fayetteville, Arkansas; Ms Karen Dawley Paul, Manuscripts Department, Alderman Library, University of Virginia, Charlottesville, Virginia; Mrs. H. J. Perrin, Hillsdale, Michigan; Mrs. Arlene J. Peterson, The Ohio Historical Society Library, Columbus, Ohio; Mrs. Winifred E. Popp, Huntington Library, San Marino, California; Ms Kay H. Powell, Special Collections Division, Howard-Tilton Memorial Library, Tulane University, New Orleans, Louisiana; Ms Nancy Presley, Public Library, Santa Monica, California; Public Library, Goliad, Texas; Public Library, Wise, Virginia; Ms Mary Jo Pugh, Reference Archivist, Bentley Historical Library, University of Michigan, Ann Arbor, Michigan; Mrs. Louise Purvis, Public Library, Stephenville, Texas; Mrs. Hubert A. Quillen, Kingsport, Tennessee; Professor James Z. Rabun, Department of History, Emory University, Atlanta, Georgia; Mr. Tom Ramsey, Kingsport, Tennessee; Ms Nancy Jo Rankin, Kentucky Historical Society Library, Frankfort, Kentucky; Ms Charlotte Ray, Georgia Department of Archives and History, Atlanta, Georgia; Mrs. Alvaretta K. Register, Statesboro, Georgia; Mrs. Ann Reinert, Nebraska State Historical Society, Lincolsn, Nebraska; Mrs. Agnes Riley, Lexington, Kentucky; Mrs. Sterling Robertson, Executive Director, Central Texas Area Museum, Salado, Texas; Mr. Willard L. Rocker, Genealogical and Historical Room, Washington Memorial Library, Macon, Georgia; Ms Marsha Trimble Rogers, Manuscripts Department, Alderman Library, University of Virginia, Charlottesville, Virginia; Mrs. William H. Rosier, President, Liberty County Historical Society, Midway, Georgia; Mr. Julius Ruff, Southern Historical Collection, University of North Carolina Library, Chapel Hill, North Carolina; Mr. Frank B. Sanders, Saltville, Virginia; Mr. A. J. Sargenti, Amesville Ohio; Ms Gertrude Saylors, Sparta, Tennessee; Ms Beth Schneider, Archives for the American Southwest, Texas Tech University, Lubbock, Texas; Ms Linnet Shade, Public Library, Smithville, Texas; Mr. Richard A. Shrader, Southern Historical Collection, University of North Carolina Library, Chapel Hill, North Carolina; Mr. John P. Siemer, Chief of Division, Adjutant General's Department, State of Ohio, Columbus, Ohio; Colonel Harold B. Simpson, The Hill Junior College History Complex, Hillsboro, Texas; Ms Marlene T. Sipes, The Southern Caroliniana Library, University of South Carolina, Columbia, South Carolina; Ms Judith A. Sketoe, Public Library, Chattanooga, Tennessee; Mr. Everard H. Smith, III, Southern Historical Collection, University of North Carolina Library, Chapel Hill, North Carolina; Mrs. Fannie Rhea Smith, Public Library, Sweetwater, Tennessee; Ms Hannis S. Smith, Supervisor of Library Services, Library of American Samoa, Pago Pago, American Samoa; Dr. Richard J. Sommers, Archivist, U. S. Army Military History Research Collection, Carlisle Barracks, Pennsylvania; Mr. Joe C. Sparks, Gradyville, Kentucky; Ms Margaret Sparks, Public Library, Spring Hill, Tennessee; Mrs. Bernice C. Sprenger, Chief, Burton Historical Collection, Public Library, Detroit, Michigan; Mrs. Frances H. Stadler, Missouri Historical Society, St. Louis, Missouri; Mr. Thomas P. Stamps, Emory University, Atlanta, Georgia; Mr. Lee Stanton, New York State Library, Albany, New York; Mr. William C. Stark, Sheffield Lake, Ohio; Mrs. Merrily Gayle Steiner, Montgomery, Alabama; Mrs. Connie L. Stephenson, Assistant Director, Georgia Historical Society, Savannah, Georgia; Mrs. Edna Sullivan, Mt. Zion, Illinois; Ms Ann Swainn, Archivist, Radford College Library, Radford, Virginia; Mrs. Susan B. Tate, Special Collections, University of Georgia Library, Athens, Georgia; Miss Mataina Te'o, Senior Librarian, Nelson Memorial Public Library, Apia, Western Samoa; Ms Saundra M. Thomas, Hernando, Mississippi; Mrs. Rita A. Thompson, Brandenburg, Kentucky; Mr. Robert A. Tibbetts, Curator of Special Collections, The Ohio State University Library, Columbus, Ohio; Mr. Charles M. Trowbridge, Niles, Michigan; Mr. Everette Truly, Natchez, Mississippi; Mrs. Walton R. Tucker, Fayetteville, Tennessee; Ms Virginia Turkal, Hastings, Michigan; Mrs. Dewey Turner, Bakerton, Kentucky; Mrs. Pamela S. Ujvari, Public Library, Mansfield, Ohio; Mr. Gibson Vance, Abingdon, Virginia; Mrs. Sidney B. Waite, Columbus, Ohio; Ms Viola Waite, Public Library, Perryton, Texas; Mrs. Edith Walden, Assistant Manuscripts Librarian, Indiana State Library, Indianapolis, Indiana; Mrs. Carolyn A. Wallace, Manuscripts Curator, Southern Historical Collection, University of North Carolina Library, Chapel Hill, North Carolina; Professor Robert J. Wallace, Prestonsburg Community College, Prestonsburg, Kentucky; Mrs. John B. Walton, Barry County Historical Society, Hastings, Michigan; Major Daniel C. Warren, Fort Leavenworth, Kansas; Ms Doris Terry Welch, County Clerk of Freestone County, Fairfield, Texas; Mrs. Alice U. Woolf, Demopolis, Alabama; Mr. Larry J. Wygant, Archivist, Rosenberg Library, Galveston, Texas; Mr. Daniel A. Yanchisin, Public Library, Memphis, Tennessee.

Acknowledgments for Illustrations

CONTENTS

List of Illustrations

Introduction

The story of the Confederate cavalrymen under General Joe Wheeler who rode north from the Atlanta defenses in August of 1864 is a story of failure. Their raid did not accomplish any of the objectives that General John B. Hood, their commander, had envisioned. It did not cause General William T. Sherman to lift the siege of Atlanta, did not even seriously disrupt the flow of supplies to his army or cause him to send back a part of his force to strengthen his lines of communication. It did not cause serious confusion in the Union-occupied South, and it did not draw off any pressure being applied to any other Southern field force. Nor did it affect any political decision made by the Republican administration or the Democratic opposition. The movement was, in short, an exercise in futility, so recognized by Sherman from the moment of the first sketchy reports to his headquarters.

The effect of the raid upon Wheeler's cavalry and upon the defense of Atlanta was disastrous. There were too many needless casualties. Wheeler's subordinates, Generals Will T. Martin and John S. Williams, were disgraced and relieved, while another, General John Kelly, simply sacrificed his life. The brilliance of Wheeler's personal bravery was overshadowed by his inability to discipline his men, many of whom simply decided to remain at home or were, without supervision, too easily captured. And while Wheeler's cavalry was, in effect, destroying itself as an offensive force, the besieging Union cavalry was able to operate on Hood's flanks pretty much at will, cutting his few remaining routes of supply and reinforcement. Small wonder that Sherman was delighted with Hood's plan.

Militarily, then, the raid was unimportant. Yet it was by no means insignificant to the men who rode north or those who opposed them along the way. A surprising number of both Southern and Northern participants later tried to recall their experiences and organize them in personal narratives and regimental histories. For one thing, many of the Southern raiders were just happy to be relieved from the trenches and out taking a trip, so that they found the time memorable, while many of their Yank opponents remembered the raid as a welcome break in the monotony of garrison duty. For another thing, the loose and fluid nature of cavalry raiding made each man think his particular experience was somewhat different and therefore worthy of interest.

Yet, perhaps because the campaign played no role in the ultimate outcome of the war, or even because there was no account by an officer famous in other actions, there has been no extended or detailed historical presentation of the events of the raid. This admittedly small gap in the general history of the war I wanted to fill. I scoured the newspapers of the time, unpublished letters, diaries, and memoirs, regimental histories and county histories. I advertised in county newspapers and rode down country roads reading mailboxes, in my search for descendants. These materials, reflecting both Southern and Northern sources, frequently yielded what might be considered historically trivial information, for example, that often a man could not reduce his experience to words in a letter and ended up talking about the weather or his weight. But, then, a moment's reflection reveals that these two data are not nearly so trite or perfunctory as might be thought. They both reveal a man's intensely personal experiencing of his environment: living on a horse, one discovers just how variable and direct the weather is; living on the land, one takes comfort that he has been able to prowl enough food to maintain his weight.

What is personally important, in other words, may not be collectively, militarily, or even historically important. But to describe an event without conveying the trivial, human responses of the viewer of the event is to falsify the event. For events do not occur, pure in their historical essence, while tiny, insignificant, subjective responses also derivatively occur, like so many Instamatics popping at the Grand Old Opry. Without the viewer, no view — therefore history ought to acknowledge the element of the random, the distractive, the mistaken, the contradictory, the repetitious. If it includes these impurities, it many be less eloquent, but more truthful.

One might counter that the truth would then be boring, that the significant would be lost among the subjective, that the lesson of history would not be so easily apprehended. But that lesson is not to be found in some long-past event, but rather in the responses that people have made to the event. Of course, specialists may concentrate upon the particularities of an event, the more to establish exactitude and order of occurrence. Still, though, when every inherent structure has been discovered, the meaning will still be an interpretation. The original layer of interpretation is, to labor the obvious, the interpretation made by the participants in the action, such as the Confederate cavalrymen under General Joe Wheeler who rode north. . .

I wanted to create a narrative that is sound, solid history. I did not attribute a thought or an action to any character without a primary source to support me. At the same time I wanted to use some of the techniques of fiction — allusion and reference, imagery, irony and counterpoint — to endow the material with more than just a day-to-day chronological organization. Still, I refrained from selecting just that material which would support some thesis provided by a modern, "omniscient" analysis. I wanted to stress the randomness of the events as the ordinary participants experienced it. I included the hopes they expressed that proved to be unrealized, the conclusions they drew that proved to be premature. History may indeed be the supreme fiction — so I tried to use fictional technique to restore an unconsecutive quality to a stream of time.

The voice of the narrative is presumed to be a participant in all of the activities, describing them at some later time. He is limited in his knowledge to those events recorded in genuine historical documents. He is reporting those experiences which would have been a shared, collective observation, rather as "we" — the town — becomes a character in some of Faulkner's work. Referring to himself as "we," instead of "I," asserts that his description is a consensus. There are violations of the restricted point of view, in that private letters or diary entries are sometimes quoted in their entirety, but these violations seem safely within the conventions established for this technique. A few actions are purely fiction, but these actions are not attributed to any historical persons. Huckleberry Finn complimented Mark Twain, author of *The Adventures of Tom Sawyer* by saying, ". . . he told the truth, mainly. There was things which he stretched, but mainly he told the truth." I could ask for no better conclusion about my work.

Wheeler's Last Raid

I

Newnan, Georgia: "a Kilkenny cat fight"

(July 22-31, 1864)

*T*hat summer of 1864 was rough on us boys in Wheeler's cavalry. General Johnston had conducted a masterful campaign of withdrawl from north Georgia, and his Army of Tennessee was perky with good morale. The infantry and the artillery occupied one good position after another and punished old Sherman every time he came up to them. But that meant that Joe Wheeler's boys had to stay behind to cover those withdrawals and contend with folks who were apt to be angry at being euchred one more time.

Then in July the army was on a line with its back to Atlanta, and the cavalry was ordered to the flanks, W. H. Jackson on the left and Wheeler on the right, to stretch and give, so that old Sherman, with his huge army, couldn't extend his lines and outflank us. To do this, though, the cavalry was spread thin, about as spotty and stunted as grass in a schoolyard.

And besides the enemy in front of us, Wheeler had the press behind him to watch out for! It's a good thing that he and the rest of us in his outfit were armed, for, like the Psalmist says, our enemies were lively, and they were strong: and they that hated us wrongfully were multiplied. The press attacked him for not raiding old Sherman's line of supply back up to Chattanooga and thus compelling a halt to the Yank advance. But the papers ought to have known that Wheeler took his orders from Johnston and then from Hood, when Johnston got the sack. Wheeler got testy, we learned from camp talk, and complained to Bragg, who sat at the right hand of Jeff Davis: "You may have heard from the papers that my command was inactive and a burden. It is hardly necessary for me to tell you that this all started by some members of General Forrest's staff who still think that his elevation can be facilitated by my detraction. They seem bent upon carrying out their ends but I am happy to state that their efforts have as yet had but little if any detrimental influence upon my command."[1]   Then he added, "I told General Johnston on yesterday that if he would order Forrest here with his command and would order me to Forrest's place or into Middle Tennessee I would certainly give a good account.

1.   Letter, Joseph Wheeler to Braxton Bragg, July 1, 1864, Container 2, Folder 5, Wheeler Papers. Western Reserve Historical Society.

"Forrest has more men than I, and the army of Tenn. would have more cavalry, and fat horses in place of mine which are worn down by constant service on scant forage since last August."

"With a command disciplined like mine now is, raiding could be done without demoralization."

The reporter for the *Southern Confederacy* led the pack in chasing our little Joe, so he must have been one of Nate Forrest's supporters. His articles got so bad that he charged Wheeler with "sluggish inactivity" — a claim so wild that "Ora" defended Wheeler in an article in *The Montgomery Daily Advertiser* that went just as far in the other direction, by calling Wheeler our "young Marat."[2] "Mooraw," indeed.

Since we were tied to the flanks, often having to file into the works like infantry, and were getting bullyragged by the papers, old Sherman must have got the idea that we were played out. So he decided to use his cavalry to break the railroads into Atlanta, thinking that there would be no opposition to speak of. First he sent Garrard out, on July 22, to Covington, to burn the place and tear up the Augusta tracks. Then, on the 27th, he sent out Garrard and Stoneman down our right flank to work on the Central tracks. At the same time he sent McCook down our left flank, to operate on the Atlanta and West Point road. Our Joe Johnston had warned Wheeler that he should expect such raids,[3] before he left Atlanta on the 18th when Bragg and Davis fired him, but we were still tied by a short leash.

2.   "Ora," Montgomery *Daily Advertiser,* June 27, 1864.
3.   John F. Stegeman, *These Men She Gave* (Athens: University of Georgia Press, 1964), p. 114.

COVINGTON
JULY 22

Garrard rode into town with just as much ease as if he had signed a note for it and even put something down. We had a few boys behind Stone Mountain, on the lookout, and on the night of the 21st, they reported that Garrard was moving out,[4] but General Hardee told Wheeler not to pursue them, for the attack that he was about to make, at Decatur, would pull them back. But it didn't; the Yanks moved north, for a few miles, then turned southeast and struck the Augusta tracks at Conyers. They burned that enterprising community, which really wasn't much to begin with, then moved on down the ten miles of track to Covington. They arrived just in time to disturb everybody's dinner at the army hospital. Naturally the male nurses lit out for the pine thickets, rather than get gobbled up, and this left Grandma Smith, the chief matron, to serve up all the meals. The Yanks told her she'd either have to take the oath or they'd have to banish her North, but she said, "Nary time will you do either,"[5] and they went off to fight somebody they could whip.

They lined up the wounded from the wards that could walk and started toward their headquarters with them. The only person who disputed with them was an old cit by the name of Press Jones.[6] He was plowing when he heard

4. *The War of the Rebellion: A Compilation of the Official Records of the Union and Confederate Armies* (Washington: Government Printing Office, 1880-1901), I, 38, pt. 3, p. 953. Wheeler's Report. Hereafter referred to as *ORR.*

5. A. A. Hoehling, *Last Train from Atlanta* (New York: Thomas Yoseloff, 1958), p. 135.

6. Augusta *Southern Watchman,* August 3, 1864.

that the Yanks had come, but he quit right quick and got his squirrel rifle and went over to the court house, and when the first squad of the captured Reb wounded came by, old Jones lifted the guard right out of his saddle. Then he reloaded and ran to another street and took another one. Then he reloaded again and in a few minutes fired into a crowd that came riding up, wounding two. This provoked them, for they shot him dead and smashed his head up pretty good with their gun butts. Then they found a quarter-master home on furlough, named George Daniel, who had been out bird hunting, and stood him up before a firing squad. They started to put a handkerchief over his eyes, but he said, "No, a Confederate soldier can face death without being blindfolded."[7]   This made two, evened up the score, and they didn't require any boot.

The hospital rats that could run, did. The Yanks didn't chase them, though; they set to work with torches. They burned two thousand bales of cotton, "the SNOW OF SOUTHERN SUMMERS,"[8] as the poet Timrod calls it. And they burned the thirty new hospital buildings and all the refugees' piled-up furniture at the depot, items which nobody has celebrated in a poem, as we have heard tell. Most of the cits loaded up what they could and stampeded out towards the Social Circle,[9] where they warned the folks there to parcel everything out to the servants and get them to hide it.[10] A good many of the Covington cits had gotten smooth at fleeing, they'd done it so many times. Since there

7.   Walter Clark, *Under the Stars and Bars* (Augusta: Chronicle Printing Company, 1908), p. 150.

8.   "Ethnogenesis"

9.   *ORR*, I, 38, pt, 2, p. 809. Garrard's Report.

10.   James I. Robertson, ed., *The Diary of Dolly Lunt Burge* (Athens: University of Georgia Press, 1962), pp. 92-92.

was no place to get refuge for long, they'd become "run-nagees," as Bill Arp called such folks as himself.[11]

The Yanks didn't tarry long in Covington, just raised the temperature some, which, if you know Georgia in July, was-n't needed, much less asked for. Then they moved on to Oxford, which was also a hospital town. They say that the Rebs lit out of that locality like the times when a country girl would come in looking for a pa for the baby she was going to have. But the Yanks didn't chase them — had busi-ness to attend to, just like Yanks. Oh, they took the ones they found, like you'd take wind-fall apples, even if you didn't have time to shake the tree. They told their prisoners to stick around, that they'd be lodging at the Camp Douglas hotel, up in Illinois, soon enough. One fellow said he sat around two or three hours reading Miss Evans' *Macaria*,[12] that story book the Yanks have been burning as contraband ever since Chattanooga.[13] It must have protected him, like they say it has protected others, stopping bullets and such, for the Yanks clean overlooked him when they left. It is generally agreed that books can be edifying in most singular ways — though there is seldom such powerful testimony as that here given.

The Yanks came right back, though, because they had gone through a Reb mail bag they'd picked up and found a letter to Hood sent by a girl spy, who had snuck around the Yank camps. But the girl hid in an attic, and her pa had some folks lower him down a well rope,[14] so the Yanks

11.   Charles H. Smith, *Bill Arp, So Called* (New York: Metro-politan Record Office, 1866), p. 109.

12.   Clark, pp. 144-147.

13.   Louise Manly, "Augusta Evans Wilson," p. 5842, in *Library of Southern Literature,* ed. E. A. Alderman and J. C. Harris (Atlanta: Martin and Hoyt Company, 1907).

14.   Clark, pp. 150-151.

DECATUR
JULY 22

All this time most of us in Wheeler's cavalry were too close to infantry to be easy. We were ordered to attack Decatur, as a part of Hardee's attack on the Yank left. Hardee had said that there would only be some Yank cavalry in the town,[15] and we figured that if they were Garrard's boys we could chase them around and around the hen house. But it was a division of intrenched infantry, as well, and Wheeler dismounted us and charged us right against their right. The scouts said that Garrard's wagon train had been left in town, and that information was cheering and very motivating. For a while it was just a blur; when the Yanks started pulling out, all the women and children came out of their houses to jubilate and then got caught in the open between the Yanks and us, so it was a royal mix-up, with us running into town, the Yanks running out of town, and the women and children running around in circles. Most of the cits finally ran into the yard of Mary Ann Gay, who was standing by her gate waving her kerchief at us as we went by. Several of the boys took a kiss from her hand as they went by, but when General Allen, of the Alabama Brigade, came up, he told Miss Gay: "Go in your cellar and lie down, the Federals are forming a line of battle, and we, too, will form one that will reach across these grounds, and your home will be between the two lines. Go at once."[16]

Miss Gay was a perky one, and she wasn't about to miss the first battle that had come her way, so she watched the whole shebang, which she later described: "Shot and shell

---

15. John Witherspoon DuBose, *General Joseph Wheeler and the Army of Tennnessee* (New York: Neale Publishing Company, 1912), p. 373.

16. Mary Ann Gay, *Life in Dixie During the War* (Atlanta: Foote and Davies, 1894), p. 128.

flew in every direction, and the shingles on the roof were following suit, and the leaves, and the limbs, and the bark of the trees were descending in showers so heavy as almost to obscure the view of the contending forces. The roaring of cannon and the sound of musketry blended in harmony so full and so grand, and the scene was so absorbing that I thought not of personal danger, and more than once found myself outside of the portals ready to rush into the conflict. . . ." If she had looked down the street a little, she might have seen a little less profound scene of war: a young trooper running to his company with a pone of hotel egg bread under each arm,[17] like young Ben Franklin entering Philadelphia.

By then our advance was out of town, through the graveyard, where somebody yelled at a Yank corpse, "Well, my friend, you are a long way from home to find a graveyard."[18] The Alabama Brigade still led the way, with the Twelfth Alabama Battalion right up at the head, like they were racing for the swimming hole. One of the Alabamians was Lieutenant Murphy, of Company B, Twelfth Alabama, who got within ten feet of the prepared works that the Yanks had scrambled behind; he turned to yell, "Forward my brave boys to victory,"[19] and went down like a tree. We would have gone over those works, for we hadn't forgotten those wagons. But Hardee sent for us, and we had to mount up and move out, with just the usual number of skulkers to plunder the prisoners and the dead.

One fellow who neither went nor stayed was "Butter-

17.   O. P. Hargis, "A Georgia Farm Boy in Wheeler's Cavalry," *Civil War Times Illustrated*, VII (November, 1968), 40.

18.   DuBose, p. 374.

19.   "12th Alabama Cavalry Regiment," manuscript in Military Records Department, State of Alabama Archives.

milk,"[20] who wrote home to the Montgomery *Daily Advertiser* about his part in the festivities:

"*Mr. Editor*: Our operations on the extreme right for two weeks past have so completely absorbed my time, that I found it impossible until the present moment to continue my series of edifying communications.

"There is a fatality attendant on the movements of our command, for wherever we go, we find ourselves in proximity to gentlemen of miscegenating proclivities. With a persistence worthy of a better cause, they have thrust their marine-tinted abdomens before our enraptured gaze until we are tired of them; we acknowledge that they have succeeded in *entertaining* us, and would now suggest that they cease their affectionate endearments, lest we become enervated with satiety. Within the last week they have isolated us from the main army, flanked us, enfiladed us, surrounded us, cut us off and endeavored to capture us; whenever our little command took a position to check their advance, we found ourselves flanked on both sides; whenever we attempted to fall back, we found the enemy in our rear. There are fifty distinct roads on every square mile of Georgia soil, leading in one hundred different directions; I hardly know whether to attribute it to skill, good luck, or Providence, but it is an undeniable fact, that if our ubiquitous foe gets possession of forty-nine of these roads, we always manage to leak out safely on the fiftieth. It has become popular to designate the days of our first revolution as the 'days that tried men's souls,' but our recent movements have tried their *soles* in such an increased ratio, that I no longer marvel at the enhanced value of boots; the demand is much greater than the supply; the shoemakers are public benefactors and I shall pay them $500 for my next pair with pleasure, es-

20. "Buttermilk," Montgomery *Daily Advertiser*, August 8, 1864.

pecially if they will take my note for the amount. To a man
drawing the magnificent salary of $24 per month, the price
of clothing is no object. I am not writing with my nether man
encased in a pair of $290 breeches, and would inform Mr. W.
of Montgomery that I am well satisfied with the investment;
the unmentionables fit elegantly, and the beautiful white
cord down the sides has rendered the wearer irresistible to
those of the fair sex who ruminate in North Georgia, and of
whom I get an occasional glimpse. Although removed from
the society of the ladies, I still hold them in affectionate
remembrance, and the possession of anything calculated to
recommend me to their favor, is a source of inexpressible
gratification.

"I regret to state, however, that many of our ci-devant
beaux have become so demoralized by the war as to ignore
the very existence of women; one would imagine from their
general appearance and behavior that they had been weaned
very early in life and had known no female influence since.
Do the ungrateful wretches forget who first contracted their
primitive trousers to render an attack in the rear with the
corrective rod more effective? Do they forget who, in later
years, monopolized all their pocket money, by necessitating
monetary transactions with ice cream vendors and livery
stable proprietors? Do they forget the anticipatory enjoyment of liquidating the resources of milliners and dress-
makers? If they do, they are lost, irretrivably lost. The vision
of *that prospective cradle* of their own will hardly work
their salvation, if they are already indifferent to the neat
little slippered foot and decked ankle, formerly pictured by
their vivid imaginations as rocking that cradle.

"I hope my remarks will open their eyes to a sense of
their unfortunate condition; I hope they will remember that
they owe all they ever had to their mothers and all they ever

expect to have to their wives, and I hope the reader will forgive this digression. I have been thinking so long of a pair of magnificent black eyes I saw yesterday that I have grown callous to every other subject but the ladies.

"For the sake of variety, we had turned the tables on the Yankees and were chasing them in a style unheard of since Mrs. Potiphar's celebrated love-chase. We chased them out of their breastworks, out of the woods, out of the fields and out of Decatur, until out of very weariness we stopped. My own mad career was checked, just before reaching Decatur by a crack on the jaw with a spent ball; bleeding at every pore, I went to a house in the rear to get washed and bandaged, and having been suffering with a sick head ache all day, I gracefully extended myself on the porch to sleep. My slumbers were interrupted by a sweet voice inquiring if I wouldn't have a pillow, and on opening my eyes to see from whence the fairy sounds had issued, I was entranced by a vision of a feminine loveliness that entirely obliterated all further idea of sickness. I expressed my assent to her query and the young lady hastily prepared me a couch, when with a look of unutterable love, I threw myself on it and sighed; she probably thought the sigh was the result of bodily pain, as she murmured her sympathy and sat down beside me to brush off the flies.

"I told her that a head ache was my inducement to seek the shelter of her roof, and that I should ever feel grateful to the inventor of head aches for the pleasure I was then deriving from her society. She immediately procured a wet towel to spread over my temples, and while adjusting our eyes met:

'Oh magic of love, unembellished by you,
Has the garden a blush, or the herbage a hue?

Or blooms there a prospect in nature of art,
Like the vista that shines through the eye to the heart!'

"Words cannot express the feeling of *all overishness* that took possession of me at this moment, suffice it to say I fainted; a more matter of fact narrator would have modified this expression; he would probably have stated that, judging from the sound, I slept.

"On recovering, (or awaking) I still saw my attentive friend at her post, and she commenced a conversation by saying that my face was very much swollen, and inquiring if I suffered much from my wound. I attempted to reply, but found that while there was nothing to apprehend, the wound had enlarged my jaw to an extent that rendered talking very difficult. I therefore remarked that I suffered more mentally than physically; that it was painful in the extreme to be obliged to leave my kind nurse; that I should ever entertain sentiments of the warmest gratitude towards her; that it would, hereafter, be the one object of my life, to resume at the first opportunity an acquaintance so agreeable; and that as it was getting late, I had better start for camp. When I clasped her hand and bid her good bye, she told me I would find some difficulty in eating for a while. I had never thought of this before, and the idea of subsisting on spoon victuals completely prostrated me. I was unable to reply, to think that a notorious gourmand like myself would have to come to mush, rendered me speechless. I only recovered my senses by hearing the voice of my charmer utter in accents of heavenly sweetness, 'I reckon you ens had better get some nice gal to chaw your vituals for you.' I left. . . ."

When "Buttermilk" got back to camp, he found everybody in a sweat to go off after the Yanks under Garrard, who had moved out on the night of the 21st, heading for Covington.

But it wasn't until noon the next day, the 23rd, that Wheeler was turned loose to chase them.[21] By midnight we had gone forty miles and got nothing but the exercise, for Garrard's men had vamoosed. The cits thereabouts were not that pleased to see us; they seemed to think that we'd steal what the Yanks had missed in their hurry. It seemed to be a settled and dismissed truth that summer that Wheeler's Cavalry never got a horse honestly, when there was a dishonest way to accomplish same. As one cit, Bill Arp, put it, in painting the character of both Yanks and his Southern brethren: "Betwixt the one and the other a poor runnagee had as well be among the Turks and wild Arabs of the African desert."[22]

DECATUR
JULY 27

Back we came, if anything lighter than when we left — when you have to sit at the second table for other cavalry, you can't count on getting fat. We hung about Hardee's skirts for the next day or so, then were ordered to take the place of Hardee's corps in the trenches, at 3:00 a.m., on July 27th.[23] Now taking their horses away didn't set well with our boys; they feel like something's missing, as the drunk said when he saw his finger on the chopping block. It's one thing to dismount for a little set-to and trust your horse to the fourth man to hold for a while; but it's another thing altogether to leave him behind and go into a ditch. So at dawn we welcomed pushing out as a skirmish line — that at least was moving along over ground, not just jumping

21. *ORR*, I, 38, pt. 3, p. 953. Wheeler's Report.
22. Smith, p. 109.
23. W. C. Dodson, *The Campaigns of Wheeler and his Cavalry* (Atlanta: Hudgins Publishing Company, 1899), p. 217.

you head out of a hole every once in a while, like a ground hog.

We shoved them back across the railroad during the morning.[24] Then they went to earth in their trenches. It was almighty hot out in that sun, so we just lazed around like lizards, only firing every now and then at anybody over there that got curious. In the meantime, a steady stream of scouts coming in signaled something was up. We found out that a large Yank cavalry force had moved out east that morning with five days' rations.[25] It sounded like they were going back to Covington, to see if maybe they had missed anything that would burn.

Wheeler decided pretty quick, though, that the Yanks had something more ambitious in mind, for the scouts said that Stoneman, not Garrard, was running the show. All morning long, Hood was peppered with reports, requests to follow the Yanks, and requests for reinforcement by Humes, who was stationed with Jackson, over on the left flank, at East Point. But Hood had the notion that Sherman was getting ready to lift the siege, and he wanted his cavalry ready to attack the retreat.[26] It took him a while to get it through his head that Sherman wasn't backing off. Finally, at supper time, Wheeler got permission to send after the Yanks what force he could spare.[27] He said that he couldn't spare *any,* but that he would send 1,500,[28] the least that could be expected to provide the Yanks with any distraction at all. Kelly, Iverson, Allen, and Breckinridge left at once. One of Allen's boys, Wilbur Mims, of the Prattville Dragoons, Com-

24.   *ORR,* I, 38, pt. 3, p. 953. Wheeler's Report.

25.   Dodson, p. 218.

26.   DuBose, p. 376,

27.   Typewritten "Manuscript," p. 3, in Wheeler Papers, State of Alabama Archives.

28.   *ORR,* I, 38, I, p. 3, p. 953. Wheeler's Report.

pany H, Third Alabama spoke for all the boys in welcoming the turn of events: "we entered into this chase like school-boys in a game. . ."[29] Anything was better than being teth-ered: "Being entrenched in the city was a tedious experience with our regiment. No fresh buttermilk, no fresh pork, no hot cornbread or biscuits." So out they came. The boys hadn't seen their horses in four days, Raymond Cay, Liberty Independent Troop, Fifth Georgia, reflected, as his regiment got its orders: "at midnight, in the pouring rain, we file out of the boggy ditches."[30]

FLAT SHOALS
JULY 28

Later that night, Hood must have seen that the whole thing was planned to cut his roads, not mask a retreat, for he ordered Humes along and told Wheeler to go in person to squelch the raid. About 3:00 a.m., on the 28th, just about the time when the birds stretch and hawk and spit, Wheeler caught up with Iverson, Allen, and Breckinridge, who had been skirmishing with the Yank pickets at Snapping Finger Bridge.[31] When Kelly came up from Tucker's Cabin about daylight, the whole command, about fifteen hundred men, was ordered forward, to hit the Yanks on the flank at Flat Shoals.[32] We charged them as Wheeler liked to do: inde-pendent brigade attacks in quick succession.[33] If you had

29. Captain Wilbur F. Mims, *War History of the Prattville Dra-goons* (Thurber, Texas: Journal Printery, n.d.), p. 13.

30. "The Last General Officer," *Confederate Veteran,* XXXVI (October, 1928), 365-366.

31. "The End of Stoneman's Raid," Atlanta *Intelligencer,* August 21, 1864.

32. Dodson, p. 220.

33. DuBose, p. 373; Joseph A. Vale, *Minty and the Cavalry* (Har-risburg: Edwin K. Meyers, Printer, 1886), p. 327.

been an early morning crow flying over, it would have re-
minded you of a string of squibs popping off and jerking
around at a Fourth of July barbecue. The attack confused
the Yanks, and they hustled across South River and started
backing up the road toward Latimar's. They were all acting
like they were short-timers who wanted to get home alive;
we kept on pestering them, overtook three of their wagons,
and rounded up a number of prisoners, Seventh Pennsylvania and Fourth Michigan mostly. Kelly's Division would
have run right up their backs, but Wheeler came up and
told him that we didn't have the force to deal with them.[34]
It was just another time when that war didn't make a hell
of a lot of sense.

From the prisoners we discovered why the Yanks were
acting so timid, though they numbered about four thousand;
one, it was Garrard's command, and, two, they were just
teasing us, while Stoneman took about two thousand men
and headed off toward McDonough, to join up with another
Yank force coming around Atlanta from our left. We eased
up and let them back off without us. Instead, we prowled
those wagons and tried to get a little breakfast before the rain
started, for it was a cloudy morning. Wouldn't you know
that just when we got a little slab of bacon hung on a stick,
the call came to mount up.   Kelly was to stay and keep
Garrard honest, while Iverson, Allen, and Breckinridge were
to take off after Stoneman.[35] At about that time, a courier
rode in from Hood, after traveling all night, to tell Wheeler
that W. H. Jackson, over on the left, below Atlanta, wouldn't
be able to check that new raid, and that Wheeler personally

34.   Letter, George Knox Miller to his wife, August 1, 1864.
Miller Papers, Southern Historical Collection, University of North
Carolina.
35.   ORR, I, 38, pt. 3, p. 953. Wheeler's Report.

had better attend to it. So Wheeler sent word to Humes not
to come to Flat Rock, but to turn south towards Jonesborough. He left Kelly with only Dibrell's Tennessee Brigade
and ordered Kelly to send the boys in Anderson's Confederate Brigade, including our new issue regiment, the Fifth
Georgia,[36] spruce in their new uniforms, on after him on
the road to Jonesborough. You know, it was like a malish
drill around there for a while: men running to the bushes
for a little business before a long ride, camp negroes trying
to get their truck all together, and different outfits sailing
out in all directions.

Wheeler kept just his staff with him, counting on picking
up enough of a force along the way to worry the Yanks
coming east from the Chattahoochee. He overtook Humes,
with about five hundred men, mostly Ashby's Tennessee
Brigade, and they rode into Jonesborough about 4:00 p.m.[37]
The gals and their ma's were out along the road with pitchers
of water for the heat of the afternoon,[38] and it was just like
the wonderful old days in Middle Tennessee, when the war
was a lot younger. The day before these selfsame cits would
have been cussing us for horse thieves; now they honeyed the
Rebs and wanted them please to ride six miles down the line
to Lovejoy's Station and vanquish the cursed invader, Mc-
Cook's Cavalry.

There wasn't much left of Lovejoy's when Wheeler got
there — just a lot of smouldering cotton and tobacco that
had been piled up at the depot, as if waiting for the Yanks.

36. "Osceola," of Kelly's Division, refers to the "new issue"
Fifth Georgia, a regiment just up from Florida, in the Memphis *Appeal*,
June 25, 1864.

37. *ORR*, I, 38, pt. 3, p. 953. Wheeler's Report.

38. Robert Franklin Bunting, *Letters of Robert Franklin Bunting*, Vol. II (Naples, Florida: Typescript, 1944), unpaginated.

Damn the cotton, it got us Southerners into this fix in the
first place, but a smoke's a smoke. The folks there said that
a good many of the Yanks were drunk[39] and dressed up like
a tacky party, had on all kinds of clothes, such as Odd Fellows' and Masons' aprons that they had prowled from one
of our wagon trains at Fayetteville.[40] They said that the
Yanks bragged that they had sabered two thousand mules
at the wagon train and that that ought to give every buzzard
in Georgia a square meal, for a change. Naturally the Yanks
were gone, back toward Fayetteville, when Wheeler got
there, but he did get word from Jackson, with a proposition
that if Wheeler would nag at the Yanks from the rear, he
would get in front and head them.[42]

At Lovejoy's the boys with Wheeler learned what had been
going on with Jackson, on the left of the Atlanta defenses.
Early on the 28th, scouts brought back word that a Yank
force was using a pontoon bridge to come across the Chattahoochee at Riverton. Once they got across, about 3:00
p.m.,[43] most of them cut out directly for the Macon and
Western, by way of Fayetteville, but the First Wisconsin
headed up the river toward Campbellton.[44] Two and a
half miles east of there, on the Fairburn road, they ran into
Colonel "Iron Sides" Harrison, with the "Joshes"[45] of the

39. Dodson, p. 238.

40. "The Raid on the Macon Railroad," New York
Times, August 12, 1864.

41. ORR, I, 38, pt. 2, p. 783. Lamson's Report.

42. ORR, I, 38, pt. 3, p. 954. Wheeler's Report.

43. ORR, I, 38, pt. 2, p. 769. Croxton's Report.

44. ORR, I, 38, pt. 2, p. 791. Smith's Report.

45. Mamie Yeary, Some Recollections of the Boys in Gray
(Dallas: Smith and Lamar, 1912), p. 374. James C. Ivey remembered
the nicknames.

Third Arkansas and the "Chums"[46] of the Eleventh Texas of his own brigade, and the Fifth Tennessee of Ashby's Brigade. The Yank commander, a Major Paine, First Wisconsin, was a brave man, you'll have to grant him that, for he brought his advance of about fifty men up to within fifty yards of Harrison's advance, the Fifth Tennessee, boosting up his men by yelling, "They will give way soon." Adjutant Allen ordered Captain Dave Blevins' Company C to pour it to the Yanks, and several Yanks fell out of their saddles.[47] One of them was the Major, who yelled as he went down, "I am shot dead — *forward!*"[48] But the Yanks must have got their directions mixed up, for they skedaddled. Then Harrison's whole command moved up, whipped the Yanks at Elliott's Mill, and sent them packing.

That Major Paine sure had tough luck with us. He had been captured by the Eighth Texas, Terry's Rangers, at Varnell's Station, back in May, after his horse fell on him. When they pulled the dead horse off his leg, he said, "Boys, the worst I hate about this is being captured by Wheeler's men. I knew him at West Point."[49] This time he was dying in a tent in an oak grove in the Georgia darkness. He would have done well to have stayed captured.

By 9:15 p.m., General Sul Ross' Texas Brigade had caught up, having been ordered to leave its position at Lick Skillet in order to support Harrison. The boys were allowed to

46.   W. H. Davis, "Cavalry Service Under Gen. Wheeler," *Confederate Veteran*, XI (August, 1903), 353, remembered that the Eleventh Texas was nicknamed the "Chums."

47.   William Gibbs Allen, "War Reminiscence," manuscript, William Gibbs Allen Papers, State of Tennessee Archives.

48.   Letter, Stanley E. Lathrop, August 1, 1864. State Historical Society of Wisconsin.

49.   W. P. Witt, "After M'Cook's Raid Below Atlanta," *Confederate Veteran*, XX (March, 1912), 115.

dismount and rest, bridle in hand, until daylight, on the 29th.[50] Then the whole command moved out, like the Children of Israel, going toward a pillar of smoke that could be seen in the southeast. Some of the boys in the advance had been lucky enough to get something to eat along the way; the girls and their ma's reached up pieces of fresh fruit pie still warm from the oven,[51] so that the boys went riding along with happy, smeary faces, licking pie juice off their fingers. It was thoughtful of the Yanks to go raiding just as fruit came in season. Most of the boys hadn't eaten since the night before, though, so when the whole command stopped, the messes began to start fires for boiling water and branched out into the corn fields for roasting ears. Before the water got hot, though, Jackson rode up and sent the advance forward to Rock River. The Yanks had burned the planks of the bridge, but the sills hadn't burned, so the boys stripped the rails from some nearby fences and fixed the bridge in two shakes of a sheep's tail. The boys said that they would have slaughtered that old sheep and roasted him, if they'd had five minutes more.

But Jackson pushed them on, and now they reached the section of the road that was covered by trash everwhere:[52] wagon boxes that were mostly ashes, scattered papers, dead mules with the green flies already beginning to descend on them. Then, from the top of a hill they saw the Yanks coming toward them. That was peculiar, for the Yanks should have been heading the other way, toward the railroad. The boys figured that the Yanks had got to the railroad and done their business, but that some Reb outfit, maybe Wheeler, had flushed them out and was pushing them back. When Jackson

50. *ORR*, I, 38, pt. 3, p. 963. Ross' Report.
51. Witt, p. 115.
52. *ORR*, I, 38, pt. 3, p. 963. Ross' Report.

came up, he decided to hit them at once from the front, where they weren't expecting it. He yelled, "Charge them, boys!"[53] The Rebs started down the lane, right toward the two Yank regiments that were charging with their sabers flashing in the evening sun.

Colonel Jones' Ninth Texas hit them first and gave them a volley with their shotguns, but then, since the Texans didn't have pistols or sabers, they began to waver.[54] At that minute Jackson's escort and the boys in Company H, Fifth Tennessee, sailed in;[55] only two dozen or so, they went on, thinking that they were going to get run down and stomped right there in that lane. Finally, though, Captain Mullendore ordered them to halt, pull down the rail fences on both sides of the lane and get out of the way. The lane was so narrow that one horse tripped up would plug it, so a boy named Witt, from Company H, stayed there by the fence to see if he could do the trick. Pretty soon his horse was shot by a homemade Yank in the First Tennessee Cavalry, and Witt was afoot between the two lines. Look out! Right then, he heard a bugle behind him, and there came Colonel Pete Ross and his bugler, just the two of them charging right up the lane toward the Yanks. The sheer gall of Ross had its effect, for the front Yanks reined in and the others got jammed up behind them. The lead Yank went right between the two Rebs and on down the road, but the others didn't even have enough room to take a slice at the Colonel. By then the Sixth Texas, following Colonel Ross, had come up and dismounted. They were raring to get at the Yanks, so that each captain had to wave his hands and dance around,

53. Witt, p. 115.
54. *ORR*, I, 38, pt. 3, pp. 963-964. Ross' Report.
55. Witt, p. 115.

like he was trying to keep a cow out of the bean patch, just
to calm his company down, until the whole line got formed.
Then they charged with a yell, and Witt noticed that he was
still standing there in a kind of hot silence, now joined by
a horse holder from the Sixth Texas. The Texas boy was
cussing, so mad that he had been left that he tried to get off
a shot up the lane and wound up shooting his own knee..
Witt thought that the knee would be smashed all to flinders,
but the Texas boy was still so put out that he just turned
around and started walking back to where the doctor ought
to be, like he had done exactly what he'd aimed to do.
Witt went with him and picked up the lead Yank in the
lane, lonesome because he couldn't find anybody to surrender to.

"Yank, have you come on a visit?"

"Yes, my mule brought me in."

"He was bringing you some when you passed me."[56] The
Yank was cheered up a right smart, to be spoke to.

General Jackson must have figured that he had the Yanks
completely boxed in. Their column was stretched out for
miles, with prisoners, pack animals, and ambulances in the
middle, as sluggish in the hot late evening sun as a snake
that had swallowed a barnyard rat. Ross' other regiments,
the Third and the Twenty-seventh Texas, had come up, and
the brigade was dismounted and formed in line,[57] while,
to the west, Harrison's Brigade was sitting on the road near
Fayetteville. The Yanks seemed stuck in their tracks, for
they dismounted and sent out their pickets.[58] It seemed
only a matter of time until they'd send out the white flag and
get their tickets to Andersonville.

56.   Witt, p. 116.
57.   *ORR*, I, 38, pt. 3, p. 964. Ross' Report.
58.   *ORR*, I, 38, pt. 2, p. 770. Croxton's Report.

But, instead, as darkness fell and the bullbats started swooping around, Ross' Brigade heard firing off to the right, and it appeared that the Yanks had roused up after a nap and were trying to push through Harrison. So Ross' Brigade was ordered to their horses and pointed west, stopping after a few hours to roast some green corn and rest for a few hours, for by then some of them had been in the saddle for twenty-eight hours.[59]   Harrison was still waiting for the attack that never came, with a good deal of grumbling by the boys about not getting to go out after the Yanks.[60] Actually, what had happened was that the Yanks changed course and turned off on the road to Newnan.[61] This meant that both Harrison and Ross were off the scent and that Wheeler, back at Lovejoy's, became the lead dog of the pack.

At Lovejoy's, Wheeler's boys had stopped for about an hour to feed and gossip with the stragglers and about fifty prisoners brought in from the fights that Jackson had had with the Yanks.[62] The prisoners were hopping mad about getting gobbled up. They said they were supposed to get to Lovejoy's last night, but had been delayed six hours waiting for the pontoon train that crossed them over the Chattahoochee.[63] Even so they had gotten to Lovejoy's by 7:00 a.m., torn up jack, and waited around until 2:00 p.m for

59.   Samuel Benton Barron, *The Lone Star Defenders* (New York: Neale Publishing Company, 1908), p. 200.

60.   Witt, p. 116.

61.   "Citizen," "The McCook Raid," Macon *Daily Telegraph,* August 9, 1864.

62.   Bunting; Letter, Joseph Wheeler to Braxton Bragg, August 6, 1864, Container 2, Folder 5, Wheeler Papers. Western Reserve Historical Society.

63.   Henry H. Belfield, "My Sixty Days in Hades," in *Military Essays and Recollections,* MOLLUS — Illinois, Volume III (Chicago: The Dial Press, 1899), p. 449.

Stoneman[64] They should have been there and gone, like a hired hand courting an Irish washerwoman, they said, but now they were off to Andersonhell. They said that the Yanks were loaded down with prisoners of their own. That morning, before daylight, the Yanks had lined up in the courthouse square at Fayetteville,[65] then had spread out, to go from door to door, bagging fat Reb commissary officers still on the roost, like plucking fat pullets out of a line of chicken houses. And even before that, outside of Fayetteville, they had snatched both sanctified and sinner from a wagon train, the Chaplain of the Third Texas Cavalry[66] and that bunch of idlers that always manages to stay with a train. Well, if they had to be gobbled, it's a good thing they both were, for the one provides employment for the other. All told, the Yanks had about three hundred Rebs out ambling in the Georgia sunshine.[67]

WHITE RIVER
JULY 30

Then it was dark, and Wheeler's boys turned west toward Fayetteville, which they reached by midnight without seeing either Yanks or Harrison. They did find out that the Yanks had veered off to the left, and Wheeler sent word to Jackson to hustle up and try again to head them.[68] Then the boys again took up their gallop, the gait that they had been using all day,[69] which had become so punishing that

64.   *ORR*, I, 38, pt. 2, p. 770. Croxton's Report.
65.   *ORR*, I, 38, pt. 2, 786. Purdy's Report.
66.   Barron, p. 200.
67.   *ORR*, I, 38, pt. 2, p. 786. Purdy's Report.
68.   Dodson, p. 224.
69.   DuBose, p. 337.

riders were dropping out of the column at a pretty steady rate. About 1:30 a.m., this would be July 30th, the front boys slowed down as they hit a cool, damp wave of air that hinted water was just ahead; bridges were always likely spots for ambushes. They rode slowly down through an oak barren, maybe two hundred yards wide.[70]

It turned out to be the White River, and sure enough, the Yanks were across there, beyond a thirty-foot high bridge.[71] The Yanks caught the boys bunched up and let them have it, and then when the boys backed off, the Yanks fired the piles of rails that they had placed on the bridge.[72] At least that gave a little light, and Wheeler moved the boys to the side, so that they had a flanking fire on the Yank side of the river. We snuck down below the bridge, where the river made an abrupt bend, and lined the bank, then on the command, we poured it into the other side; when there was no reply we charged onto the bridge to put out the fire.[73]

Then the Yanks fired again; they were lying across the road at the rise, about seventy-five yards away.[74] It was hot and heavy for a while; every so often somebody would groan, as one of our boys would drop onto the bridge or fall off into the water, and a couple of times a Yank cussed and a rifle would come flying down the road. We found out why, later, when we captured some of these boys: the Fourth Kentucky Mounted Infantry, which this was, had Ballard rifles, which burst or jammed, almost if you looked

70. John B. Vaughter, *Prison Life in Dixie* (Chicago: Central Book Concern, 1880), p. 23.

71. Dodson, p. 224.

72. *ORR,* I, 38, pt. 2, p. 779. West's Report.

73. Vaughter, p. 27; D. M. Guthrey, "Wheeler's Cavalry Around Atlanta," *Confederate Veteran,* XIII (June, 1905), 267.

74. Dodson, p. 225.

at them.[75] In a while the Yanks could be heard leaving, and the boys managed to rebuild the bridge in about an hour.

Then it was time to mount up and head on down the road. A little moonlight would have helped, but it was the wrong time of the month, so the boys just had to blunder along, hoping that the worst thing to hit them would be a bat or owl or even a low-hanging tree branch. Since they were expecting an ambush every minute, it seemed forever before they ran into firing. Actually they did go about three miles and were hit about 3:00 a.m. At once Wheeler's boys tried to ride right over the piled-up fence rails, tried to several times, as a matter of fact.[76] Then the boys tried to take them on the left flank, but discovered that the Yanks had mounted companies stretched back along both sides of the road, like streamers flying on the wind behind a flag pole. Talking about frustration! The right flank was hit, then, by Colonel Paul Anderson's Fourth Tennessee and a part of the Eighth Texas, and just at dawn they came out about two hundred yards behind the barricades. Chaplain Bob Bunting, of the Eighth Texas, said that the road was littered with dead, wounded, and discarded equipment.[77] Again it was the Fourth Kentucky Mounted Infantry the Rebs were facing, and, you'll have to hand it to them, they didn't shirk. They kept on firing, as exposed as they were, and were gunned down or overcome, one by one. It was a game show. Something like two hundred Yanks were captured here, with forty more lying twisted and dead among the horse and mule shit.[78] That morning the flies had a choice for breakfast.

75.   *ORR*, I, 38, pt. 2, p. 780. West's Report.
76.   *ORR*, I, 38, pt. 2, p. 779. West's Report.
77.   Bunting.
78.   *ORR*, I, 38, pt. 3, p. 955. Wheeler's Report.

By then Wheeler's boys had been on the road for seventy ass-numbing hours.[79] But the column moved out again, with a slower gait, as it became a struggle just to keep going. More and more horses were going lame, more and more men going to sleep and falling out of the saddle. About that time Colonel Gus Cook, with the rest of the Eighth Texas, and General Ross, with two of his regiments, caught up. The boys weren't too happy about the shape of things — the Yank advance was up to Newnan, on the Atlanta and West Point Railroad. Newnan was a hospital town, with plenty of supplies, dry forage that would perk up their animals, shelter. The Yanks could hole up there for a while, eat, feed their stock, cut the road, while Wheeler's small command, broke down and gut-growling, would have to hang back, for fear of harming the helpless Reb wounded housed there, or, if they did attack, have to take on a much larger force snug in an infantry postion.

NEWNAN
JULY 30

The faint toot of a train whistle, followed by a burst of gunfire, could only mean that the Yanks had ridden right into Newnan,[80] that a Reb engineer was trying to get up steam for a last-minute escape, or that the Yanks had it, to use it for whatever devilment they could dream up. Wheeler's boys were almost in sight of McCook's column now, but they thought that that old horse had made it to the barn. Gradually, though, the racket increased toward town, and the Yanks appeared to be milling around. Their artillery had

---

79.   ORR, I, 38, pt. 3, p. 955. Wheeler's Report.
80.   Richard B. Harwell, ed., *Kate: The Journal of a Confederate Nurse* (Baton Rouge: Louisiana State University Press, 1959), p. 214.

been unlimbered, but not pointed toward Wheeler, and now those artillery boys were dragging their teams back and limbering up, while other troopers were slapping pack animals with the flat of their sabers to get them off the road and out of the way.

Then the Yanks began to move, like a coil of rope playing out, heading south, for some reason, glancing by Newnan to the right. Wheeler figured out that they would try to come out on the LaGrange road, so he sent Colonel Henry Ashby, on his big horse Bayard,[81] with Lieutenant-Colonel Lewis and about eighty boys of the First Tennessee and Major Aiken and about the same number from the Ninth Tennessee Battalion, straight through Newnan, to try to get ahead of the point of the Yank column.[82] You can just feature how flabbergasted they were to ride right into a perfect mob of Rebs lined up along the tracks and on the depot platform. Well, who in hell are you, and who's that gent over there riding around bareback,[83] like a Dunkard's hired hand? Go to hell, Tennessee, and that's General Phil Roddey. It turned out that Roddey's cavalry had been going up to Atlanta on the cars, but had laid over the night before because of the trouble up the tracks at Palmetto. Scouts had been sent out by the Post Commander early in the morning to see if any Yanks were about,[84] but, blind as they were, they probably had a hard time finding their way back to town. They told Roddey the coast was clear,

81. James P. Coffin, "Col. Henry M. Ashby," *Confederate Veteran,* XIV (March, 1906), 121.

82. James H. Lewis, "History of the First Tennessee Cavalry," in *Military Annals of Tennessee,* ed. John Berrien Lindsley (Nashville: J. M. Lindsley Company, 1886), pp. 890-891.

83. Harwell, p. 215.

84. Montgomery *Daily Advertiser,* August 11, 1864. Typescript copy in State of Alabama Archives.

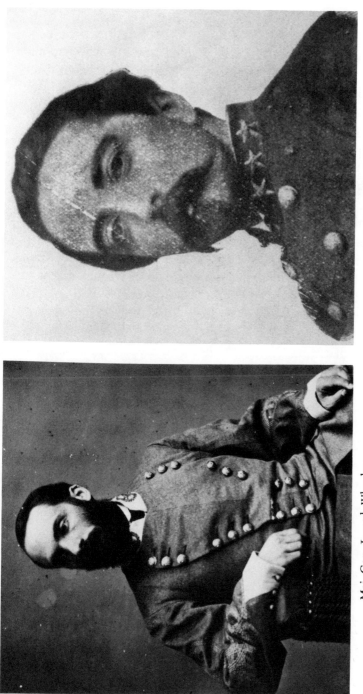

Maj.-Gen. Joseph Wheeler

Col. Henry M. Ashby

Col. Thomas Harrison

Lt.-Col. Paul F. Anderson

so his boys loaded up, the engine tooted — and there stood the Yanks thirty yards down the track, demanding a surrender. Roddey yelled that he didn't come into Georgia to surrender and ordered his boys to fire. The Yanks scooted off, and Roddey rousted his Alabamians off the cars and into a battle line. Then they pushed forward, while the Yanks came up to meet them. Their little set-to had lasted a couple of hours when Wheeler's boys began to come up behind the Yanks.

When the Yanks broke off the fight and started to slide off to the left of Roddey's men, Roddey figured that they were going to try to make it to the river. So he took a part of his command, got the train, and headed south to try to head them off. But the Yanks had taken the time to tear up the tracks, so he brought the train back to Newnan. Just as we got into Newnan, he had borrowed a horse to round up his command and all the walking wounded out of the hospitals. As we started to ride out of town, he got off the horse and started walking at the head of his column. It must have been that he recognized that all of his men, dismounted as they were, were just as uncomfortable about walking as he was, so, although he was lame in one ankle, he started out to march with his troops.

BROWN'S MILL
JULY 30

When Colonel Ashby led his men in, Roddey's men pitched up what bread they had in their pockets, and the little force from Wheeler's command tore on out of town. They got four miles below town, near Brown's Mill, before the Yank column came out on the road.[85] The Rebs found a

85. *ORR,* I, 38, pt. 2, p. 762. McCook's Report.

perfect place for their ambush, woods with plenty of undergrowth, and when the Yank advance rode up, the Rebs
played the bluff game the whole way — they charged, yelling
and screaming like haints.[86] The Yanks must have been
entirely spooked by now, for the advance, which we later
found out was the Second Kentucky, broke for the rear,
yelling that they had been hit by infantry.[87] They ran
right through their second line, the Fourth Indiana, which
charged. Then both lines settled down to snipe at each
other, Reb and Yank, but the task had been done, for Ashby
had tricked the whole Yankee column into stopping.

By the time Wheeler had gotten up the right flank of
the Yank advance, and when he got word from Ashby that
the Yanks were stalled and dismounted, he decided to hit
them at once, even though the odds must have been well
over five to one.[88] But hit he did, with the Eighth Texas
and the Fourth Tennessee, maybe sixty Texas Rangers
and twice as many Tennesseans.[89] W. H. Davis, of the Fourth
Tennessee, remembered that moment: "At this juncture we
marched to within fifty yards of their line, when a shot
from a vedette's rifle killed the horse of one of the advance
guard. My regiment . . . filed to the right, and wheeled into
line, confronting the enemy."[90] The Fourth Tennessee would
have received the distinctly unmilitary, but unmistakable
orders from Paul to his People: "Attention, Cedar-Snags!
Line up on Jim Britton! Charge!"[91] Private Davis remembered that the Fourth had some help: "The remaining

86.   Lewis, p. 890.
87.   *ORR,* I, 38, pt. 2, p. 787. Purdy's Report.
88.   *ORR,* I, 38, pt. 3, p. 955. Wheeler's Report.
89.   Bunting, n.p.
90.   W. H. Davis, "Cavalry Service Under Gen. Wheeler," 353.
91.   Dudley G. Wooten, *Comprehensive History of Texas* (Dallas:
W. G. Scarff, 1898), p. 686.

regiments dismounted and, obliquing to the right, took up their respective positions, aligning on the 4th Tennessee. All this was accomplished in a few minutes. The line being formed, our bugler sounded, 'Forward.' We were then within fifty yards of the enemy. The underbrush was very dense and rendered our advance very difficult. We were within twenty-five yards of their line, and yet could not see them when they poured a volley into us. Thereupon we let fly a volley at them, raised a yell and charged."[92] The surprising charge enabled Wheeler to push that mass of Yanks about a hundred yards, but then the Yanks got a little shape, in a depression out in a hundred-acre field, and they pushed back. At that moment Ross' Brigade arrived, dismounted, and charged, linking up with Wheeler and Ashby. Sam Barron, of the Third Texas, took part in that charge: "We were moved rapidly into the timber and ordered to dismount to fight. As many of our men were behind, instead of detailing the usual number of horse-holders, we tied the horses, leaving two men of the company to watch them. Almost immediately we were ordered into line, and before we could be properly formed were ordered to charge, through an undergrowth so dense that we could only see a few paces in any direction. As I was moving to my place in line I passed John Watkins, who was to remain with the horse, and on a sudden impulse I snatched his Sharpe's carbine and a half dozen cartridges. On we went in the charge, whooping and running, stooping and creeping, as best we could through the tangled brush. I had seen no enemy in our front, but supposed they must be in our front, or beyond it. Lieutenant Sim Terrell, of Company F, and myself had got in advance of the regiment, as it was impossible to maintain a line in the brush, Terrell only a few paces to my right. Terrell was

92. W. H. Davis, "Cavalry Service Under Gen. Wheeler," 353.

an ideal soldier, courageous, cool, and self-possessed in battle. Seeing him stop I did likewise, casting my eyes to the front, and there, less than twenty-five yards from me, stood a fine specimen of a Federal soldier, behind a black jack tree, some fifteen inches in diameter, with his seven-shooting Spencer rifle resting against the tree, cooly and deliberately taking aim at me. Only his face, right shoulder, and part of his right breast were exposed. I could see his eyes and his features plainly, and . . . at least two feet down his gun barrel. As quick as thought I threw up the carbine and fired at his face. He fired almost at the same instant and missed me. Of course I missed him, as I expected I would, but my shot had the desired effect of diverting his aim and it evidently saved my life.

"Directly in front of Terrell was another man, whom Terrell shot in the arm with his pistol. The Federals both turned around and were in the act of retreating when two or three of Terrell's men came up and in less time that it takes to tell it two dead bodies lay face downwards where, a moment before, two brave soldiers had stood. I walked up to the one who had confronted me, examined his gun, and found he had fired his last cartridge at me. Somehow I could not feel glad to see these two brave fellows killed. Their whole line had fallen back, demoralized by the racket we had made, while these two had bravely stood at their posts. I have often wondered what became of their remains, lying away out in the brush thicket. . . ."[93]

All along the line, as the bugles blared, the Rebs charged, first yelling, then grunting, finally just sweating and wheezing, not even bothering to smack the mosquitoes in the sultry gloom. There was light ahead, then through the sumac and sassafras at the edge of the woods, across an open field,

93.   Barron, pp. 200-202.

which became a rise that the Yanks hid behind in confusion.[94] In about forty-five minutes, we had killed or wounded over two hundred, had captured over three hundred, including two brigade commanders.[95]

Whoopee! Dress-up day for Wheeler's boys. But wouldn't you know it, even before we could size up a single pair of boots from a prisoner, firing broke out back down in the woods. Another bunch of Yanks, the Eighth Iowa and the First Tory Tennessee, had turned Wheeler's left and gotten among Ross' horses. So back down through the woods Wheeler took the boys at a run,[96] for it wouldn't do for a cavalryman to lose his legs. It was give and take down there for the best part of an hour, with both sides pulling each other off horses, aiming at each other, instead of at each other's horses, for a change, in a general mix-up. W. H. Davis, with the Fourth Tennessee, said it was a "Kilkenny cat fight." His Colonel, Old Paul Anderson, was captured three times, but rescued by his men each time, and after the third such rescue, he said, "Boys, it looks like the Yankees were determined to have me, anyhow."[97] But finally the Yanks pulled back, and the boys paused to get their breath.

Which they didn't get. The Yanks who had been chased up the rise now came back across the open field, into the sassafras and sumac, then into the woods, where by now it was beginning to get dark. They were led by McCook himself, for T. J. Towles, Company G, Third Texas, had a little confab with him: "As I was sitting, with my back to a tree

94. *ORR*, I, 38, pt. 2, p. 783. Lamson's Report.

95. Dodson, p. 227.

96. Typewritten "Manuscript," p. 12, in Wheeler Papers, State of Alabama Archives.

97. W. H. Davis, "Cavalry Expeditions in Georgia," *Confederate Veteran*, XVI (June, 1908), 251.

for support, my clothing saturated with blood, from the loss of which I was very faint and weak, General McCook, accompanied by some members of his staff, halted in front of me, and the General remarked: 'Major, you appear to be suffering.' I replied that I thought I was mortally wounded and requested surgical aid. The General replied that he could not give his own wounded the necessary attention, and said apologetically: 'You have been a soldier long enough to know how these things are, and you must not think hard of me.' He wished to know what forces were opposing him on the immediate field. I replied that he could form as correct an estimate of their numerical strength as I could, as the divisions of Jackson, Wheeler, and Roddey were present, whereupon he remarked to his staff: *We must get out of this!* and immediately rode away."[98]

By now McCook must have felt the see-saw tip against him, for there seemed to be Rebs everywhere. In their return to the woods, the Yanks had even gotten rattled and shot a Holy Joe, Chaplain Edward Hudson, of the Sixth Texas,[99] as he was helping the wounded, and a lot of the Yanks must have seen the bad luck of that action. Down there, too, they had captured General Humes and tried to get him to the rear, if a rear could be found. Before this could be done, though, Wheeler sent two mounted squadrons out into the field as they were going back across, and Humes was swooped right away from the bumfuzzled Yanks, like a pretty girl at a picnic.[100]

McCook must have felt a little panicky when he pulled back up the rise and quickly formed his exhausted men behind a rail fence. It wasn't getting dark fast enough to

98.   Victor M. Rose, *Ross' Texas Brigade* (Louisville: Courier-Journal, 1881), pp. 112-113.

99.   Rose, p. 120; Bunting, n.p.

100.   Dodson, p. 228; "Citizen."

suit him, for more and more Rebs were finding their way to
the front. By this time we had been joined by the boys in
Anderson's Confederate Brigade, about four hundred strong,
which had finally come up and were getting in line.

Sergeant John Ash, Company A, Fifth Georgia, was keeping a diary, and he recorded later what the Confederate
Brigade had been up to for the last little while. On Friday,
July 29th, they had had it pretty easy: "Remained in bivouac, the Yankees having moved from our front, untill 1 p.m.
when orders came for us to march to the West Point R.R.
and attack a raiding party from the left of our army, which
has cut the Western & Macon R.R. and now making its
way back across the Chattahoochee with main army.
Marched all day and about 10 p.m. halted this side of Jonesboro." They rested for two hours, then moved out again,
trying to catch up with Wheeler: "We resumed the march,
passing thru and beyond Jonesboro. At 3 a.m. halted on
the road from Jonesboro, and laid down by our horses till
day light, and then started on the march again. Soon we
passed 5 dead and one wounded Yankee on the road where
our men fought the Yankees beyond Fayetteville. This side
of Fayetteville we saw where the enemy burned and destroyed some of our wagons, taking the men who were with
the prisoners. And on we went, galloping a part of the
way; and reached Newnan . . . After halting a few moments,
we galloped thru the town, just beyond which our troop
— 10 priv. 2 noncoms and Lt. Blois were sent forward to
reconnoiter, and find out the position of the enemy. We
galloped several miles untill we came in view of our men
skirmishing with the enemy. We then returned to our command."[101]

101. Diary Entry for July 30, 1864, John H. Ash Papers, Emory
University Library.

The Confederate Brigade got to the field while the Yanks and the Texans were fighting over the horses, so General Anderson ordered his men who were still in the saddle to move out in support of the Texans. Some of the boys in the Fifth Georgia said that the Eighth Confederate refused to charge, so that Liberty Troop of the Fifth had to go it alone. After they had cleared the Yanks out, one Georgian wrote home, they were complimented by the colonel of the Eighth and by General Anderson.[102] But there had been bad blood between the two regiments ever since they had been brigaded together, and the "new issue" Georgians would have been tempted to blow up any action by the Eighth that might be questioned. Good general that he was, Dick Anderson immediately made a public announcement that any comparison was bound to slight somebody and that all troops under his command had acted with great gallantry.[103] The whole thing just shows you, though, that genuine Rebs were never really extended by just Yanks and needed another enemy at all times.

The Yanks must have been curious about the new arrivals, for they cut General Anderson down at once,[104] while he was forming his men, got him just above the knee, so that Colonel Bird, of the Fifth Georgia, had to take over the command. At about the same time, General Roddey, with somewhere between six hundred and a thousand boys,[105] his dismounted cavalry and the walking wounded from the hospitals of Newnan, had come the six miles from

102. "The Fifth Georgia Cavalry at Newnan," Savannah *Republican,* August 18, 1864.

103. "The Eighth Confederate Cavalry at Newnan," Savannah *Republican,* August 20, 1864.

104. *ORR,* I, 38, pt. 2, p. 956. Wheeler's Report.

105. Wheeler says six hundred; "Citizen" says one thousand.

town on foot and said that they had enough energy left to take a little walk up through that field. Roddey had even brought his brass band with him, and as soon as they had caught their breath and fanned themselves, they set up in a locust grove and gave a little concert.[106] Too bad he didn't have a lemonade stand, as well, and we could have a real social.

Everybody was ready to go, to get this thing done with before dark. And, after a long delay, so long that the ranks were beginning to break and go back into the woods to relieve themselves, the order was given to move out. Some speculated that the delay was because McCook was expected to surrender,[107] if he had a little time to meditate upon it, but if that was the case, it didn't pan out. The boys must have been out of range for small arms, they thought, for there wasn't a shot being fired at them now, and come to think about it, not even any artillery fire. The only sounds were the scuffling, puffy sound made by feet stepping on the dry clods of that plowed field, a sound as familiar to these farm boys as the singing of the crickets and locusts on a late summer evening. They made it to the fence, with not a Yank to be found. Then, carefully, break ranks, cross the rails one by one, and line off again. Face the woods — it'll come now.

But no, the boys advanced, caught up with some stragglers, poured volleys into the dark thickets. Once there was a "cloud-burst of money,"[108] as the Yanks threw away some boxes of Confederate bills that they had prowled from that wagon train that they had burned. Most boys didn't even stop to pick it up; somehow bills fluttering

106. Montgomery *Daily Advertiser*, August 11, 1864.

107. William Andrew Fletcher, *Rebel Private, Front and Rear* (Beaumont: Press of the Greer Printing Company, 1908), pp. 111-112.

108. DuBose, p. 379.

about didn't seem very valuable just then, for it took $500 of that stuff to buy a pound of bacon or lard,[109] if you could find them. They did think, though, about horses, boots, and other truck, and the Yanks still had those things with them. Get the Yanks, get their goods. So on they pushed, looking for the quick, the tender, which they found when they saw the Yank line stretched out along the far side of a deep gulley.[110]

And here it fell totally apart: it seems like some folks just don't know what to do with good fortune. We'd come this far, only to go snipe hunting. Later, Wheeler claimed that Roddey, on the left, advised against charging them.[111] But John Will Dyer, who had walked out of a ward at Newnan to join Roddey's command for the battle, claimed that the Yanks hoisted a flag of truce and that Wheeler allowed McCook to parley him out of daylight because they were both West Pointers and therefore officers and gents.[112] Dyer, who was a member of the First Kentucky Cavalry, allowed that Bedford Forrest or Old Pap Williams, of the Kentucky Brigade, would have "raked in the whole pot." Roddey's boys also claimed that Roddey, who was just a common old stick like Bedford Forrest, had wanted to charge, but that Wheeler wouldn't permit it.[113] The most disgusted were the boys who had been chasing and fighting these particular Yanks for the past twenty-four hours; Chaplain Bunting, of the Eighth Texas, said Wheeler just got

109. Hoehling, p. 253.

110. *ORR*, I, 38, pt. 3, p. 956. Wheeler's Report; *ORR*, I, 38, pt. 2, p. 772. Croxton's Report.

111. *ORR*, I, 38, pt. 3, p. 956.

112. John Will Dyer, *Reminiscences; or, Four Years in the Confederate Army* (Evansville: Keller Printing and Publishing Company, 1898), p. 239.

113. Harwell, p. 217; "Citizen"

scared to strike, that "Wheeler withdrew his force and fled, which gave them an opportunity to spike their two guns, abandon all their ambulances, supplies, &c, and to slip through our lines in the direction of the river. Thus the prize was lost by not striking at the proper moment, and pressing our advantage. They expected to surrender, and had spoken to the prisoners in their hands, asking their interposition in their behalf. But the demand was not made, and the advantage was lost."[114]

The Texas had cut the Yank force in two and stampeded part of them, and the whole bunch was almost surrounded, when Wheeler eased up on them. Everybody seemed to agree with Sergeant Ash, in the Fifth Georgia, that it was just plain bad judgment that let the Yanks get out of the sack and loose down the Corinth road.[115] Wheeler sent Ross around to the left to block any retreat that way, and Ross no sooner reached the Yank lines than the Eighth Iowa and some broken units sent out a flag and surrendered over five hundred.[116] It was that easy. Some of the Yanks, probably from the Second Indiana, who had been guarding the Reb prisoners, turned right around and surrendered to Colonel Worthington, the ranking Reb prisoner.[117] Whoopee, bottom rail on top!

Meanwhile Wheeler ordered up Jackson's command, which had not got to the field until the battle was over, to guard the prisoners, and then tried to mount all of his boys to close the loop.[118] But the horses were just broke down after

114. Bunting, n.p.
115. Diary Entry for July 30, 1864, John H. Ash Papers, Emory University Library.
116. ORR, I, 38, pt. 3, p. 956. Wheeler's Report; ORR, I, 38, pt. 3, p. 965. Ross's Report.
117. Citizen.
118. ORR, I, 38, pt. 3, p. 956. Wheeler's Report.

three days of hard work and green forage, and many just couldn't make it. So Wheeler sent what he could of the Fifth Tennessee and the Third Arkansas toward Franklin to pursue Jim Brownlow's Union First Tennessee. Pretty soon, a wag hauled off a poem for the occasion:

The Raider — An Epic

Brownlow went out to play raider and thief,
He ran against Roddey and soon came to grief.
He fought to catch a train, but was met with a shout,
And in the shortest possible space of time, with
    seven hundred of his men, a good many horses, six
    pieces of artillery, and all of his plunder,
    "went up the spout."[119]

The boys appreciated the sentiments of the poem and were charitable towards the poet — they let him live.

Brownlow was the son of that raving old Knoxville scoundrel Parson Brownlow, and the boys would have liked to clip the wings of such a high-flying tory. His brag was, that a week or two before he and some of his regiment swam the Chattahoochee and captured sixty of our boys and made them strip and swim back with him.[120] It would have been a proper pay-back to strip him and walk him off to the officers' prison pen in Macon; when he got there he could preach, like his hateful old pa, and take for his text, Job I, 21: "Naked came I out of my mother's womb, and naked shall I return thither. . . ."

Brownlow was so popular, in fact, that a lot of the boys in the Eighth Texas "volunteered" to go along after him.

119. Montgomery *Daily Advertiser,* August 8, 1864.

120. *Harper's Weekly,* August 13, 1864.

121. Henry William Graber, *The Life Record of H. W. Graber, a Terry Texas Ranger, 1861-1865* (n.p., n.d.), p. 192.

Colonel Bird, with the Confederate Brigade, which was still a little fresher than the others, was sent after the other party, McCook's. Both parties cleaned up the woods pretty well, for the Yanks didn't have much fight left in them, but they did have plenty of boots, watches, clothes, and such truck. The Confederate Brigade caught three hundred horses and mules, and some prisoners,[122] though the former was preferred, to tell the truth. Sergeant Ash kept a pretty good account of the pursuit to the river. The Confederate Brigade had moved out about dusk, but they just couldn't get their horses to respond, they were so tired. So a halt was ordered, and the horses were tempted with fodder and oats. Then the column was started up again, and the horses had heart enough to last for about five miles. But then both horses and men were so jaded that a halt was ordered, and the men lay down in the road to rest, while the horses fed on long forage.

Before daylight the men moved out again, the force falling away as men and horses simply wore out. After seven miles, those that were left caught up with the Yanks at the Chattahoochee. Sergeant Ash was so weary that he couldn't make it up to the skirmish line, but after a while he recovered enough to go shopping: "I treated myself to a pretty good Yankee horse, bridle, halter, and saddle, turning over my horse and equipment to the government. I rode down to the river and got two good blankets, 2 shirts, and other little things. When we had picked up all the horses, equipment, etc., and a few Yanks, we were marched into bivouac about a mile from the river, remaining there all day and night."[123]

122. *ORR*, I, 38, pt. 3, pp. 972-973. Vaughan's Report.
123. Diary Entry for July 30, 1864, John H. Ash Papers, Emory University Library.

Somehow, though, the larger part of both Yank mobs had got across the Chattahoochee that night, although they were shot at right into the water itself.[124] Some of the boys disregarded Wheeler's order not to cross the river and chased Brownlow right on into Alabama,[125] while others spent the next day, the 31st, sweeping the banks for discarded clothes and diving in the river for those lovely abandoned Yank carbines.[126] Wheeler claimed that the Confederate Brigade was derelict, that Colonel Bird not only allowed it to stop and rest, but went to sleep himself,[127] so that the Yanks got away, but who let the coon out of the sack in the first place?

CHATTAHOOCHEE RIVER
JULY 31

It was good luck for one bunch of Yanks from the Fourth Kentucky that Wheeler was on the scene when they were captured. Some boys from the Third Texas caught a bunch of them when they came crawling out of the swamp like a herd of cooters. They threw up their hands to surrender, but one of them shot a Reb major in charge. The Rebs riddled that one, and another Reb officer yelled, "Kill every ＿＿＿ ＿＿＿ ＿＿＿ ＿＿＿!"[128] But at that moment Wheeler and his staff came up, and the Yanks claimed pro-

124. Letter, George Knox Miller to his wife, August 1, 1864. Miller Papers, Southern Historical Collection, University of North Carolina.
125. Graber, pp. 192-193.
126. Fletcher, p. 112.
127. *ORR*, I, 38, pt. 3, p. 956. Wheeler's Report.
128. Vaughter, pp. 29-30.

tection; Wheeler ordered that their surrender be accepted. It turned out that the Yank was a Reb deserter, who must have figured that he was a dead man the minute he was recognized by a Reb, so he might as well take somebody with him.

Back at Brown's Mill the ordinary cleaning up was going on. Mobs of stragglers appeared from down in the woods where they had been hiding, and pretty soon they could be seen leading horses and carrying bundles taken from the dead and captured Yanks.[129] A rumor swept over the field that some of the Yanks had gotten gold coin, as well as Confederate bills, when they captured our wagon trains, that one Yank alone had buried $8,000,[120] so whole swarms of excited men were running around, turning over logs, rocks, toad stools even, and scooping out any place that looked like it had recently been dug up.

Down the way, a field hospital was being set up,[131] and the Reb and captured Yank surgeons took a drink together and took off their coats and turned back their sleeves. Some were already busy and bloody, for a pile of limbs was growing outside a tent, and one was walking around, like a buyer at a stock show, pointing out which pile the wounded should go in, as they were brought in off the field, for of course not all the wounded were worth working on. The prisoners were being marched off toward Newnan, but one was not so lucky, for he was taken by a Reb captain, who had come out from the hospital suffering from his third wound of the war, and shot down in the woods.[132]

129. "Citizen."

130. Hiram T. Bird, *Memories of the Civil War* (n.p., n.d.), pp. 49-50.

131. Mrs. Fannie A. Beers, *Memories* (Philadelphia: J. B. Lippincott, 1888), p. 152.

132. Harwell, p. 216.

The captain said his act was in revenge for what the Yanks had done to his mother and sister; even so there was a good deal of talk about hanging him, but it remained just that.

To tell the truth, it was just like all the other battles we had seen, so we didn't see much that seemed to be worth talking about. It takes someone seeing it for the first time to be shocked, like Mrs. Beers, a nurse at one of the Newnan hospitals, who came out to assist the doctors:

"Dr. McAllister silently handed me two canteens of water, which I threw over my shoulder, receiving also a bottle of peach brandy. We then turned into a ploughed field, thickly strewn with men and horses, many stone dead, some struggling in the agonies of death. The plaintive cries and awful struggles of the horses first impressed me. They were shot in every conceivable manner, showing shattered heads, broken and bleeding limbs, and protruding entrails. They would not yield quietly to death, but continually raised their heads or struggled half-way to their feet, uttering cries of pain, while their distorted eyes seemed to reveal their suffering and implore relief. I saw a soldier shoot one of these poor animals, and felt truly glad to know that his agony was at an end.

"The dead lay around us on every side, singly and in groups and *piles*; men and horses, in some cases, apparently inextricably mingled. Some lay as if peacefully sleeping; others, with open eyes, seemed to glare at any who bent above them. Two men lay as they had died, the 'Blue' and the 'Gray,' clasped in a fierce embrace. What had passed between them could never be known; but one was shot in the head, the throat of the other was partly torn away. It was awful to feel the conviction that unquenched hatred had embittered the last moments of each. They seemed mere youths, and I thought sadly of the mothers, whose hearts would throb with equal anguish in a Northern and a Southern home. In a corner of the field, supported by a pile of broken fence-rails, a soldier sat apparently beckoning to us. On approaching him we discovered that he was quite dead, although he sat upright, with open eyes and extended arm.

"Several badly wounded men had been laid under the shade of some bushes a little farther on; our mission lay here. The portion of the field we crossed to reach this spot was in many places slippery with blood. The edge of my dress was red, my feet were wet with it. As we drew near the suffering men, piteous glances met our own. 'Water! water!' was the cry.

"Dr. McAllister had previously discovered in one of these the son of an old friend, and although he was apparently wounded unto death, he hoped, when the ambulances returned with the stretchers sent for, to move him into town to the hospital. He now proceeded with the aid of the instruments, bandages, lint, etc., I had brought to prepare him for removal. Meantime, taking from my pocket a small feeding-cup, which I always carried for use in the wards, I mixed some brandy and water, and, kneeling by one of the poor fellows who seemed worse than the others, tried to raise his head. But he was already dying. As soon as he was moved the blood ran in a little stream from his mouth. Wiping it off, I put the cup to his lips, but he could not swallow, and reluctantly I left him to die. He wore the blue uniform and stripes of a Federal sergeant of cavalry, and had a German face. The next seemed anxious for water, and drank eagerly. This one, a man of middle age . . . was badly wounded in the side. A third could only talk with his large, sad eyes, but made me clearly understand his desire for water. As I passed my arm under his head the red blood saturated my sleeve and spread in a moment over a part of my dress. So we went on, giving water, brandy, or soup; sometimes successful in reviving a patient, sometimes able only to whisper a few words of comfort to the dying. There were many more left, and Dr. McAllister never for a moment intermitted his efforts to save them. Later came more help, surgeons, and attendants with stretchers, etc. Soon all were moved who could bear it.

"Duty now recalled me to my patients at the hospital.

"My hands and dress and feet were bloody, and I felt sick with horror.

"As I was recrossing the battle-field accompanied by Dr. Welford, of Virginia, the same terrible scenes were presented to the view. The ground was littered with the accoutrements of soldiers, — carbines, pistols, canteens, haversacks, etc. Two cannon lay overturned, near one of which lay a dead Federal soldier still grasping the rammer. Beneath the still struggling horses lay human forms just as they had fallen. Probably they had been dead ere they reached the ground, but I felt a shuddering dread lest perhaps some lingering spark of life had been crushed out by the rolling animals.

"We had nearly reached the road when our attention was arrested by stifled cries and groans proceeding from a little log cabin which had been nearly demolished during the fight. Entering, we found it empty, but still the piteous cries continued. Soon the doctor discovered a pair of human legs hanging down the chimney, but with all his pulling could not dislodge the man, who was fast wedged and only cried out the louder.

"'Stop your infernal noise,' said the doctor, 'and try to help youself while I pull.' By this time others had entered the cabin, and their united effort at length succeeded in dislodging from the chimney, — not a negro, but a white man, whose blue eyes, glassy with terror, shone through the soot which had begrimed his face. He had climbed up the chimney to escape the storm of shot, and had so wedged himself in that to release himself unaided was impossible. Irrepressible laughter greeted his appearance, and I — I am bitterly a-shamed to say — fell into a fit of most violent hysterical laughter and weeping. Dr. Welford hurried me into the buggy, which was near at hand, and drove rapidly to town. . . ."[133]

Lots of folks were heading into town, ambulances, prison-ers, stragglers, and just plain tired hungry soldiers. Along the way, since the battle with the Yanks was over, some of the boys began to have to fight with the cits again, who began trying to claim their stock. That morning the doctors had told the ladies of the town to prepare food against the time when the battle would be over, so by the time the boys got to the hospitals there was the nearly forgotten smell of hot food coming out of the cook houses.[134] It was mostly corn bread and soup beans and roasting ears, but it was mouth-watering, as the boys stood there in the dark yard while the nurses and blacks got it out to them. Lots of boys sat down to eat where they stood — and fell asleep where they sat.

NEWNAN
JULY 31

The next day, July 31, was a Sunday, and most of us just loafed around Newnan. The pious were off hunting a church, while the wicked went off looking for some liquor, which they mostly didn't find, for it had been sent out of town

133. Beers, pp. 152-155.
134. Harwell, pp. 216-217.

last Thursday, when the Yanks had first been sighted across the Chattahoochee.[135] The culture-hungry and just plain curious went down to the warehouse to see the imprisoned Yank officers, who were allowed out of their two little offices, to take the sun and fresh air. There was a whole slew of them, guarded by a Lieutenant Barron and some boys of the Third Texas; there were twenty-two just from the Eighth Iowa alone, from the colonel on down.[136] The colonel was a sour old cuss, with his mouth puckered up like he had been eating green persimmons out there in the woods, but the other officers were a lively, jovial lot, who got to singing their patriotic songs, like "Down with the traitor, up with the star," and got such a good hand for it that they said that they wouldn't sing any more until they had some food.[137] The boys said that the singing wasn't *that* good, but they were fed anyway. The boys on detail buried the dead of both sides in the town cemetery and guarded the Yank enlisted men in the cotton warehouse that stood between the hospitals and the depot.[138] Every time a new batch of prisoners was pushed into the warehouse, there would be hoots and yells, "What? You, too! I was in hopes that you had escaped."[139] Then there would be a fresh outburst of cussing against McCook, for the Yanks said that a jackass with the blind staggers could have generaled them better than he did.

We found out why that Iowa colonel, Dorr, his name was,

135. Harwell, p. 214.;

136. S. B. Barron, "Wheeler's Cavalry in the Georgia Campaign," *Confederate Veteran*, XIV (February, 1906), 70.

137. Belfield, pp. 454-455.

138. Mrs. Myrtie Candler Long, "Reminiscences of Life in Georgia," *Georgia Historical Quarterly*, XXXIII (December, 1949), 311.

139. Vaughter, p. 35.

looked like a Puritan preacher that had run out of sinners.
The Eighth Iowa Surgeon's Steward, Hi Bird, called "Little
Medicine," said that the Colonel had gotten shot in the side
the day before, and that he had sewed the old turkey up
while the battle was still going on. So the Colonel probably
wasn't breathing any more than he had to, much less singing. That steward was a sharp little Yank. He came up to
one of the Third Texas and asked for a match to light his
candle, like a little boy in a fairy tale. The guard said, "We
have not seen a match or pin since the war commenced, as
we depended on the north for these supplies."[140] So Bird
said to take him to the drug room and he could make some
matches. Sure enough, just like a Yankee, he busied around,
got the clerk to mix him some powder of chlorite of potash,
as he called it, and sugar. Then he swabbed a taper with
nitric acid, touched it to a pinch of his powder, and, poof,
had a blaze. Yanks didn't know about a lot of things, but
somehow, the longer the war went on, what they didn't
know about didn't seem all that important.

There was plenty of plunder to look at that day: the
Yank cannons had been brought into town;[141] so many
small arms had been captured that all of the boys had been
equipped and what was left was taken to the hospitals for
emergencies; and the Yank regimental flags were flaunted,
some of them being cut up, with a patch for anyone who
wanted one.[142] We also watched the blacks and officers'
and doctors' ladies being brought back into town from
their hiding places. We were still steamed up about the
way Wheeler lost us the pot yesterday by not calling, and
and some who were writing home put it right into their

140. Bird, p. 23.
141. Dyer, p. 238.
142. Harwell, p. 217.

letters. Captain Knox Miller, of the Eighth Confederate, Anderson's Confederate Brigade, said it for a good many of us: "Our forces were maneuvered until they almost surrounded the enemy when a hot engagement took place and the enemy driven at all points until they drew up their prisoners and formed themselves preparatory to surrendering when strange to say Gen. Wheeler the 'Belligerent Baby' called off his forces and allowed his enemy to run off leaving their artillery, over two hundred prisoners (among them some 40 of our Qr. Masters), and large amounts of property taken from our citizens."[143]

And don't you know, while we were still fuming about the way that things had fallen out, somebody got hold of this Richmond monthly that had a puff about Wheeler the size of a cloud. That high-toned *Southern Literary Messenger* did lay it on thick: "Little Hero," and "this *favored child of Mars*," and "brave 'Navarre,'" and "the *Young Marat*," and "our gallant cavalier," and topping off with, "Where sobriety, accomplished manners and highly cultivated morals are admired, in every particular, this YOUNG GENERAL is a beautiful model, *sans reproche*!"[144] Whooee! Move over, Chevalier Bayard, and let the "Belligerent Baby" in your pew. Hum. Wonder what old Nate Forrest said when he read that puff? His view of Wheeler was that he was a "clever little fellow but not fit for command."[145]

143. Letter, George Knox Miller to his wife, August 1, 1864. Miller Papers, Southern Historical Collection, University of North Carolina.

144. "Major Gen. Joseph Wheeler, Jr.," *Southern Literary Messenger*, XXXVIII (April, 1864), 222-232.

145. Quoted in a letter from Gen. William T. Martin to Miss Ellen Martin, July 19, 1863, a copy of which was presented to the author by Mrs. Will C. Martin, II, Baton Rouge, Louisiana.

II

Sunshine Church, Georgia: "Boys, that is good news!"

(July 27-31, 1864)

NEWNAN
JULY 31

*T*oward evening on July 31st we began to get the news off the telegraph that the boys who had gone with Iverson on Thursday, the 28th, had caught up with Stoneman and captured him, somewhere near Macon. It seems that Stoneman was slowed up by Howell Cobb's malish and local cits, so that he had to turn around and start back. Then he got boxed in by Iverson and surrendered. They said he just sat down and cried, when he saw how small the Reb outfit was that he surrendered to.[146] And one of our boys standing around down at the depot, observing how Stoneman's raid was like McCook's excepting a few particulars, namely that Stoneman got bagged and McCook didn't, said he'd bet that Stoneman wasn't the only Major General in these parts that cried over the outcome, that the *"favored child of Mars"* probably was pretty low about the whole business — like a fellow that discovers he's married a gal who can't seem to get to bed before he goes to sleep — every night.

We found out more about Stoneman's capture, when we got to the Covington neighborhood Sunday, the 7th of August. We had come by easy stages from Newnan, while Iverson's command was coming up from Macon, where it had gone after the battle at Sunshine Church. The rumor everywhere was that Wheeler was going to be sacked,[147] for he still had part of the press after his scalp, and when that happens, most people throw up their hands and cry for terms. This is the way one paper put it:

" But little transpired at the front since my last, worthy of note. General quiet prevails along the lines this morning. Up to last evening the enemy was supposed to be continuing their movements toward our left. We have reason to believe, however, with less confidence of success in their ultimate purpose of cutting us off from our communications.

"Sherman evidently understands that every inch of the ground will be contested. It is equally evident that he has

146   "Georgia—Stoneman's Capture—Battle of Sunshine Church," Philadelphia *Inquirer,* August 24, 1864.

147.   *ORR,* I, 38, pt. 5, p. 413. Glass' Report.

no thought of testing our breastworks. It becomes, therefore, a work of strategy, in which I have strong hopes he will be defeated by the unsurpassed energy of Gen. Hood and the unequaled gallantry of his troops, unless the problem is worked out by means of his cavalry.

"Praise and censure on the part of editors and army correspondents have been so indiscriminate on the one hand, and so inconsiderate on the other, that it is with hesitancy that I indulge in either. *The inefficiency of the cavalry of this army has been too serious a matter, and is too patent to the commonest understanding to require silence.* If it had been so for a day, or a month, or if it was wanted in a field for simple operations, or was deficient in material for effective service, we might, in a spirit of charity, find excuse in some one of these reasons.

"But I am gratified to know, while I am pained to say, that no such excuse exists. From personal knowledge, I am prepared to say, that the material composing the cavalry, connected with the army, is of the highest order; and I have been assured by various well-informed sources, that, in point of numbers, it is amply able to cope with that of the enemy. And yet, from Fort Donelson on the Cumberland River, to Fayetteville and Macon, *we have had an almost unbroken line of discouraging and ruinous inefficiency in that arm of the service under the special charge of Gen. Wheeler.*

"I am not disposed to disparage the merit of this officer. We have simple assurance of his gallantry and patriotism, and we have heard of no complaint against him from either of the distinguished Generals who have respectively commanded this army.

"We might conclude, therefore, that whatever inefficiency exists has resulted from *their* orders, at least to such an extent as to prevent their complaining. Gen. WHEELER

certainly satisfied Gen. BRAGG. He seems to have satisfied Gen. JOHNSTON, and we have no evidence to the
contrary in the case of Gen. HOOD. I submit, therefore,
that *while this continues,* if the public complain, they should
direct it against the superior and not the subordinate. If
our roads are torn up and our communications cut off; if
our wagon trains and depots are burned; our towns sacked,
our country devastated and our subsistence destroyed; while
the enemy's communications, running for hundreds of
miles through our territory, remain undisturbed, and their
rear is permitted to enjoy the most perfect repose, the
fault, if there is any fault, is with the Commander of the
Army of the Tennessee, who either fails to appreciate the
inefficiency of Gen. WHEELER, or seeing it, is unwilling
to take the responsibility of attempting its correction by
the necessary change.

"I do not make these remarks so much in the spirit of
censure as to fix responsibility. If Gen. WHEELER—however
gallant, however patriotic, however high in rank—is unequal
to the task before him, no one has so good a means of knowing that fact as Gen. HOOD; and, knowing it, upon him
rests the responsibility of a change; and if it is not made,
the conclusion is inevitable that he takes upon himself
whatever of responsibility attaches to that arm of the service
under the present leader, either by approving his management
of the cavalry, or by his unwillingness to make such changes
as will correct the inefficiency, to whomsoever it may be
chargeable.

"It has been a matter of wonder to all military men with
whom I have conversed for weeks past—I give but little
weight to the speculations of citizens—that so little has
been done upon the enemy's rear, in view of the length and
exposed condition of his communications. Scarcely an ex-

periment has been tried in that direction. On the contrary, their cavalry have been permitted to sweep over a wide district of country, extending from Decatur on the Tennessee River to Opelika on the Montgomery and West Point Railroad, thence around to the Georgia Railroad, and last to the Macon and Western Railroad, almost without the show of resistance, in little time and with trifling loss.

"I respectfully submit that this ought not to be permitted, and that the country should look to Gen. HOOD, and not to Gen. WHEELER, to correct it. The latter has shown he cannot. The former can, and such is my faith in his practical energy that I believe he will; and if so, the sooner the better."[148]

Now that's Tennessee journalism; if you could aim that correspondent in Sherman's direction, he could blow up a regiment with every paragraph. It sounded as if Wheeler had left the folks at Macon as dissatisfied as the folks at Newnan, so that made us all the more interested in what the boys with Iverson had done. Those boys said that you never saw such a bunch of sore-headed folks as those Yanks that surrendered to them Sunday evening, July 31st. Stoneman took turns crying and raving that he had been betrayed by Adams' Yank Kentucky Brigade, while everybody else said that Stoneman had acted like a lunatic during the entire raid. They said that they had started out in good order from Decatur on the 27th and that Garrard's command had dropped off at Flat Shoals to block any chase by Wheeler. But, that soon, Stoneman began to act strange. For the Yank camp talk had been that they were going to make a dash south to McDonough, then west to Lovejoy's Station,

148. *Bristol Rebel,* quoted in New York *Times,* August 14, 1864. It is perhaps the Chattanooga *Rebel* instead.

on the Macon and Western Railroad, where they would
link up with McCook's command.[149]

COVINGTON
JULY 28

Stoneman, instead, led them due east, so that they wound
up at Covington about 9:00 a.m. on the 28th.[150] It wasn't
because Stoneman was lost, either, for he had a first-class
guide in "Little Red," George T. Allman, of Cornersville,
Tennessee.[151] A noted mule trader hereabouts before the
war, "Little Red" was apparently repaying folks for all
the hospitality that he had received. For some reason Stoneman determined to cross the Ocmulgee River east at Covington, then go south, and finally to cross the river west at
Planter's Factory.[152] The Yank private must have decided
that they were out for a ramble such as Garrard conducts:
ride for a hundred miles, take pains to avoid the enemy, and
report back when you've seen a half dozen broken-down
home guards picketing a pig pen.

Maybe this was what caused the Yanks to get careless.
The First Yank Kentucky had only about two weeks to
pull and must have figured that this kind of do-less raid
was a fine wind-up for them, for a good many of them got
drunk in Covington, that early in the morning, and Stoneman had a devil of a time trying to get them back into
columns of four.[153] In time the command moved out, a little

149. *ORR,* I, 38, pt. 2, p. 75. Sherman's Report.
150. *ORR,* I, 38, pt. 2, p. 915. Smith's Report.
151. "Escort," "The End of the Stoneman Raid," Atlanta *Intelligencer,* August 21, 1864.
153. Eastham Tarrant, *The Wild Riders of the First Kentucky
Cavalry* (Louisville: R. H. Carothers, 1894), p. 360.

wobbly, toward Monticello. The Yanks were from respectable regiments: Fifth and Sixth Indiana, First and Eleventh
Kentucky, Eighth Michigan, Fourteenth Illinois, and Mc-
Laughlin's Ohio Squadron.[154] But the lack of a clear sense
of what they were about seems to have infected them with a
kind of don't give a damn jauntiness.

They were divided into three bodies to cover more countryside, but this meant less supervision and more looting
and prowling. There was plenty of ripe fruit, peaches, apples,
and melons, and very little resistance, so that the whole day
was pretty much of a lark. One of the bodies left the main
route above Clinton, then passed through Blountsville,
twelve miles west of Milledgeville. Their subsequent behavior was characterized by a correspondent from Sparta:
". . . they impressed a fat old gentleman by the name of
Shoat, to guide them to Gordon—made him ride a bare backed
mule, hard trotting and lean, as the tale goes, by way of
punishment for his implacability. Of course they left him
hors de combat before they reached the place. Thence
they went down the railroad, burning the depots and destroying the Oconee bridge. They then turned up the river,
crossed at Tucker's Ferry, below Milledgeville, passed in a
few miles of the Capital, having one of Tucker's negroes
for a pilot. Several were captured near the bridge at Milledgeville.

"As they passed up the river they obtained the names of
the principal farmers, but seemed in too great a hurry to
visit many of them."[155] But when they did pick a farm to
descend upon, "very grievous *were they*," just like the
locusts in Egypt. At one place, just to give you the picture,

154. Tarrant, p. 359.
155. "Letter from Sparta," Charleston *Daily Courier,* August 8,
1864.

this is how they spread out and did mischief. Some burned the gin house that had nearly two hundred bales of cotton in it. Others butchered the cows and hogs, right in the front yard. They wrung all the pigeons' necks and tied them in strings on their saddles, for later. At the same time they wrecked the smoke house, put dirt in the lard, quick lime in the syrup, and took all the wine that was put up in the casks. Before they left they even killed the handsome peacocks, whose fans swept the gravel of the yard, even though nobody ate the peafowl meat.[156]

Along the way, they burned their bridges behind them,[157] the ones that crossed the Ocmulgee, to keep any Reb force from coming up behind them, even though Stoneman claimed after his surrender that he had been deceived into thinking that there were four bridges, whereas there was none, and that it was the falsity of this information that so disheartened him.[158]

MONTICELLO
JULY 28

At sundown on the 28th, near Monticello, Stoneman told some of his officers that the lack of bridges was forcing him to change his objective, which now would be the Macon and Savannah Railroad.[159] The Yanks spent the

156. Mrs. Oscar McKenzie, "When Sherman Marched Through Georgia," *Reminiscences of Confederate Soldiers and Stories of the War,* Typescript, Volume 3, Georgia United Daughters of the Confederacy Papers, 1940, State of Georgia Archives, pp. 357-358.

157. Tarrant, p. 360.

158. "Georgia—Stoneman's Capture—Battle of Sunshine Church," Philadelphia *Inquirer,* August 24, 1864.

159. *ORR,* I, 38, pt. 2, pp. 919-920. Tompkins' Report.

entire night in camp, then traveled by several different routes again all day on the 29th, getting to the railroad between Gordon and Macon by sundown. Again the various brigades rested most of the night, then, on the morning of the 30th, were ordered to concentrate before Macon for an attack.[160] The damage they did along the railroad was costly, but a good many of the Yanks must have wondered if they were carrying out Sherman's orders: their objective was usually the killing of Rebs, and so far few Rebs had even been seen. The word began to get around that Stoneman intended attacking Macon in order to free the Yank officers imprisoned at Camp Oglethorpe. And attack they did, along about 9:00 a.m.

MACON
JULY 30

But they were about twelve hours too late. The day before Captain Dunlap and his scouts had reported the nearness of the Yanks,[161] and by the next morning Governor Brown and Generall Howell Cobb had about two thousand men armed and in line of battle, two miles from town on the Ocmulgee River. Genral Cobb had organized the town pretty well for the emergency. He ordered a group of transient Yank prisoners onto the cars for Savannah at 4:00 o'clock in the morning and got them through Griffin Station just before Stoneman cut the line, and he ordered the surplus marched down into a swamp and held there.[162] At the

160. *ORR*, I, 38, pt. 2, p. 926. Capron's Report.

161. John Campbell Butler, *Historical Record of Macon and Central Georgia* (Macon: J. W. Banks, 1958), pp. 263-265.

162. Willard W. Glazier, *The Capture, the Prison Pen, and the Escape* (New York: United States Publishing Company, 1868), p. 131.

same time he had his officers search private houses for weapons, and every conceivable kind of weapon could be seen in use by his men, from fowling pieces to bad breath. All in all, the command probably looked about as random as the one that Falstaff was ashamed of, even though they were cheered up by General Joe Johnston, who rode out to the battle line on his bay mare,[163] to show the figure that the whole Army of Tennessee loved. Everybody came — citizens old and young, quartermaster clerks, mechanics from the government shops, the firemen, convalescents from the hospitals, and the Silver Grays, a home guard company of old gents.

Probably the only member of the Silver Grays under the age of fifty was fourteen-year-old Thomas Dabney, Jr., who remembered vividly the events of that morning: ". . . the streets rang with the cry of heralds from the mayor calling upon everyone who could shoulder a gun to run to the railroad bridge to defend it at all hazards.

"Father and I ran to the arsenal and got forty rounds of ammunition apiece, and then ran all the way to the bridge, over a mile distant. We were among the first to arrive, but soon old men and boys began to pour in from all quarters. A considerable number of convalescents from the numerous hospitals located in Macon joined us. We were none too soon, for already could be seen the long lines of the enemy not over a half-mile from the bridge, and every few moments shot and shell whistled over the heads of the defenders of that bridge.

"Father's company was Company A, Findley's battalion, but it generally went by the name of the 'Silver Grays,'

163. Manuscript history of the Fifty-first Alabama Cavalry, by John Witherspoon DuBose, in State of Alabama Archives.

from the color of the hair of the members. I was the only member in it without a gray head.

"Finally the enemy moved his position farther down the river, and General Johnston ordered most of his men across the river, leaving Company A to defend the bridge.

"A furious cannonade was opened upon this point, but as we, according to orders, were lying behind the railroad embankment, none of the Silver Grays were touched until Major Taliaferro placed two cannon on our side of the river and proposed returning the enemy's fire. Volunteers to man the guns were called for. In an instant father and many other old gentlemen were busy loading the two twenty-pounders that were to commit such havoc in those serried blue lines just on the crest of yonder hill. Our shot flew wide of the mark and the blue lines wavered not. Suddenly the enemy ceased firing, and horsemen were seen galloping up and down the long line. We were beginning to feel much encouraged, when suddenly an old solider cried out, 'Look, the enemy is *massing his batteries!*' It was only too true. Cannon seemed to come from everywhere, and a perfect storm of shot and shell burst upon our devoted heads. In a few minutes our guns were silenced, but not until several of the Silver Grays lay dead beside the little brazen guns which brought us nothing but death.

"We were ordered to lie down again. The battle scene shifted, and finally General Stoneman and most of his men were outwitted and captured. A small brigade of Texans under the gallant General Gregg, I think, coming up in the enemy's rear decided the day in our favor."[164]

Young Thomas Dabney was wrong about General Gregg and the Texans capturing Stoneman, but then he was quite

164. Susan Dabney Smedes, *Memorials of a Southern Planter* (New York: Alfred A. Knopf, 1965), pp. 205-206.

young and not present at the capture, which was the day
after the battle at Macon. Dabney ended his part in that
battle with a realization of wonderment: "Father and I did
not fire a gun during the entire day."

Added to the force of home guards were six hundred
Tennesseans and a thousand Georgia militia, both arriving
on the evening of the 29th from Andersonville, heading
toward Atlanta. At Clinton Stoneman had learned that a
flood had carried away the city bridge at Macon and that
General Joseph Johnston was at Macon, so he must have
lost a little more of what nerve he had left. When he saw
the lay of the land at Macon, he must have been dismayed.
The only way across the river was guarded by Fort Hawkins
on the east bank, with batteries that his artillery couldn't
reach.[165]   Some of the Reb artillery was mounted on flat
cars, which were pushed out when the gunners wanted to
fire and then pulled back, like a bulldog on a leash.[166]
And even if Stoneman could have passed that point, there
appeared to be thousands of intrenched infantry to be
contended with.

One of those fierce infantry was Campbell Tracy, who had
been recovering in a Macon hospital from a wound received
in Virginia. He said that he and the other wounded were
treated to the highest style he had received since being in
the army; they were carried out to the field in carriages.
They were positioned with the Silver Grays:
"We went into line of battle in a swamp: deployed as skirmishers and were all posted behind trees. I was well flanked:
the venerable Dr. Wills, pastor First Presbyterian Church,
was on my right; and that good father in Israel, the Rev. Dr.

165. *ORR,* I, 38, pt. 2, p. 916. Smith's Report.
166. Wilbur F. Hinman, *The Story of the Sherman Brigade*
(Alliance, Ohio: Published by the author, 1897), p. 891.

J. E. Evans, Mulberry St. Methodist Church, was on my left;
a veteran soldier having been thus *wisely* placed all along
the line between the citizens! Soon Stoneman came up, and
the firing commenced. His first advance was repulsed, but
he soon got a battery in position, and opened on us with
that. A second charge in our line was driven back, and
everything was going as lively as in old Virginia, when on
their third advance a Yank got a side shot at me as I leaned
against my tree to shoot. His bullet went between my lip
and the bark, the shock knocking me off my crutches. As
I fell the blood flowed freely, my lip having been cut by
pieces of the bark.

"Old Parsons Wills and Evans, quit firing, and ran to my
assistance. I told them I was not much hurt; to help me
up, and go back and keep firing, or the enemy would break
through the line!! But wishing to help me (*thinking I needed
surgical aid*) and *knowing they needed to get off the firing
line!* — they insisted on picking me up, *nolens volens.* They
had me hoisted up as high as their shoulder! — me just *a
kickin' and a cussin'*! Parson Evans said 'Campbell, ain't
you afraid to take the name of the Lord in vain, right here
in the presence of Death, Hell and Destruction?' Just then
a shell bursted close by. They let me drop and *broke for
the rear*! I called to them for God's sake to come back, or
the Yanks would break through the line! I *swore some
more* and they came back, and helped me to my tree. I
said to them, as we resumed the shooting, 'I tell you, boys,
you like to have broke my wounded leg over! Don't you
try that stunt again!' "[167]

Despite Campbell Tracy's statement to the contrary, the
Yank attack was half-hearted at best. They lost seventeen

167. James Cooper Nisbett, *Four Years on the Firing Line* (Chattanooga: The Imperial Press, 1914), pp. 377-378.

killed and twenty-seven wounded, they said. We had about
fifty casualties, about two-thirds of which were inflicted by
our own men.[168]   Most of the Reb casualties occurred in
Nisbet's Tennessee regulars, who charged the Yanks in front
of the pickup Reb force.[169]   Well, that sort of thing is to be
expected when you put guns in the hands of the clergy.

The fight turned into a stand-off, with the artillery of both
sides doing most of the work, noise at least. The Yanks
couldn't get in, and the Rebs sure as hell weren't coming
out. So about 3:00 p.m. Stoneman ordered his command
to withdraw and start south. The Yanks weren't sure why
they were going south: some said that Stoneman was going
to high-tail it to Florida, where there were Yank coastal forts;
others said that this had been his plan all along, that he
planned to free the Yank prisoners at Andersonville and get
all the glory. If getting to Andersonville was the idea, then,
some observed, they needn't worry, for it was beginning
to look as if the whole outfit would end up there.

The Yanks didn't go more than a mile or two, though,
before a Reb cavalry column was reported that would reach
the ferry to be used before they Yanks could. Stoneman
halted the command, therefore, and gave orders to start back
north. Since this was to head right into the face of the Wheeler force that had been trailing them, nearly every officer in
the column disapproved of the decision.[170]   The word was
passed, though, that the route to be taken was east toward
Milledgeville, and the men were somewhat better disposed,
because the ones who had been over that way on the trip

168. "The Stoneman Raid," Charleston *Mercury,* August 8,
1864.

169. Butler, p. 264.

170. James Monroe Wells, *With Touch of Elbow* (Philadelphia:
John C. Winston Company, 1909), pp. 207-208.

down hadn't met any oppostion.[171]

The twelve-mile trip back up to Clinton was accomplished by dark. Leading the way, the men of the Eighth Michigan were told by a negro that a party of about fifty Rebs was in town. So they split up and came in by all different roads: this little trick netted them twenty prisoners. Then they turned about the same number of their brethren out of jail, that had been captured on the march down.[172] If they had been playing swap, they could have put the Rebs in, in place of the Yanks; but instead they paroled the Rebs and burned the jail, then marched out of town by the light of the fire.

It was here that the men expected to turn onto the Milledgeville road. But Stoneman was told that the Rebs had been drawn over that way by the downward raids, whereas the Covington road was fairly clear.[173] So off the Yanks went north into the darkness, soon to run into the challenge, "Who comes there?"

"The Eighth."

"Eighth what?"

"Eighth Michigan. What regiment is that?"

"First Alabama."

"BARROOM!"[174]

The Yanks kept pushing from 9:00 p.m. until 1:00 in the morning, with the Rebs giving way and doubling up. At that time Stoneman stopped thinking like a cavalry officer, if he was thinking at all, for he got defensive; he sent out the Eighth Michigan and the Fourteenth Illinois as skirmishers

171. ORR, I, 38, pt. 2, p. 916. Smith's Report.
172. Wells, p. 211.
173. ORR, I, 38, pt. 2, p. 920. Tompkins' Report.
174. Wells, p. 212.

and ordered the other regiments to build barricades.[175] His brigade officers, even his staff officers, urged him to avoid contact, rather to remain mounted and move off to the east.[176] But the entire night slipped by, while more Rebs gathered for the feast and while the Yanks concluded that their goose was cooked.

SUNSHINE CHURCH
JULY 31

At dawn on the 31st Stoneman pushed his command forward. To some he appeared crazed in his obsession to force his way through the concentrated Rebs.[177] The Yanks moved perhaps two miles, until they got to a little settlement known as Sunshine Church. Just outside the churchyard the two remaining pieces of artillery were planted, and the church itself was arranged for a strange service that Sunday morning — the Yank surgeons set up shop there.[178] Then Stoneman ordered forward a skirmish line on foot, going with it himself. As they advanced, the Yanks could see, all of them but perhaps one, that the Rebs had carefully chosen the field for the battle: the Yanks had to go up a road over open ground to attack, discovering as they went that the fortified Reb lines were like a ∧ , enfilading both flanks with artillery.[180]

General Iverson, commanding the trailing Reb cavalry,

175. "Doctor," "Stoneman's Raid," Detroit *Free Press,* August 16, 1864.

176. Tarrant, p. 363.

177. Tarrant, p. 363.

178. Wells, p. 213.

179. *ORR,* I, 38, pt. 2, p. 916. Smith's Report.

180. "Doctor."

had indeed played patience with Stoneman. Back on the 28th, Wheeler had thought that Stoneman would strike toward McDonough, so he ordered Iverson down that way. When he got to Stockbridge, Iverson was ordered to pause and wait for Stoneman to commit himself.[181]   It wasn't until 11:00 p.m., on the 29th, therefore, that Iverson was released, to engage Stoneman at Covington or wherever he might be found.   But it wasn't that simple, for Stoneman had several different hands he could play: he could be heading for Milledgeville, or he could be heading for Macon and Andersonville, or he could still plan to double-back, cross the Ocmulgee, and hit the Macon and Western Railroad about Griffin.   So Iverson couldn't get up a full head of steam and follow Stoneman directly, only to find all the bridges burned and ferries sunk in front of him.   He told Wheeler that he would move towards Milledgeville, feeling out Stoneman's intentions all the while.

It wasn't until the morning of the 30th, when the Rebs got to Monticello, that Iverson was sure that Stoneman was heading directly for Macon.   Still Iverson didn't bust loose to get there; he reasoned that Macon would have to take care of itself, since he couldn't get there in time, and that his best move was to take it easy, so as to be in good shape when he eventually did hit the tiring Yank command.   That evening, after advancing another fifteen miles, the Rebs learned that Stoneman had been turned back at Macon and was retreating toward them.   Allen's Alabama Brigade was sent forward to stall the Yanks, and the other Rebs went into camp. pretty well sure that they would gobble up the Yanks the next morning.

Although he had a much smaller force, Iverson maintained

181. "Escort."

control over the battle all day. When the Yanks came forward, he withdrew Allen's Brigade, which had been acting as skirmishers, and sent it to the extreme right of the Yanks, to prevent any movement off on the Milledgeville road. This movement must have been misunderstood by the Yanks as a retreat, for they went on that much faster, with that sharp *huzza, huzza* yell that they had. The Kentucky Brigade remained in place, blockading the road in the center. Then Iverson ordered the Georgia Brigade off to the Yank left, with the Fourth Georgia to gain the Yank rear and the First and Third Georgia to attack.

The Fourth Georgia came upon a fellow named Francis Green. The officer in charge asked him if he knew the country, and Green said that he knew every pig path. So the officer asked him to take them around the Yank line to the Clinton road in the Yank rear. Now Green was home wounded and on parole from the Twelfth Georgia Infantry, and if the Yanks captured him and discovered that he had violated his parole, they'd likely kill him. But he said that he'd go, anyhow.

As he remembered it: "They set off at a fast gait, he led them around Ben Green's, by the old Butts place, the Luke Mercer place and came into the Clinton road at Wayside, where Jonathan Holmes lived and there at a well were several Yankees drinking water. The Confederates charged them running up the road to Sunshine Church, as hard as they could go, Green and the others following shooting and yelling. The Yankees believed a large force from the direction of Clinton was coming."[182]

The Yank line of battle was the First and Eleventh Kentucky and Eighth Michigan on the left, McLaughlin's Ohio

182. Carolyn White Williams, *The History of Jones County* (Macon: J. W. Banks Company, 1957), p. 117.

Squadron and Fourteenth Illinois on the right, and Fifth and Sixth Indiana in reserve. As luck would have it, then, the attack by the two Georgia regiments hit the short-timer Yank Kentucky regiments and hit them hard.[183] The Kentuckians stalled, wavered, and began to fall back. Colonel Adams, bareheaded and waving his saber, pushed through the line and tried to rally the men, pleading with them not to smirch their flag now.[184]. But it didn't put any starch in the line, and as it began to drift back, so did the whole Yank defense.

The charge was deadly, as J. A. Wynn, Company A, First Georgia, confirmed: "We charged about 10 o'clock a.m. . . . . Thirty-eight of our boys were killed and wounded in the charge, among them was 1st Lieutenant Jesse Crabb in command of our Company. He had his right thigh broken with a minie ball. He was immediately on my left and came near falling against me. I called Berry Atwood and we carried him off the field and placed him on a stretcher and Berry Atwood stayed and cared for him. I went back where I had left my gun and found Lee Reed of Co. E, Carroll Co., Ga., lying on his back in the broiling hot sun, with his brains oozing out. I called one of Co. B and with his assistance carried Reed in the shade of a scrubby pine, washed his face, crossed his hands and left him dying. A little farther on I found a large Yankee with his thigh broken and two of his comrades lying dead near him. I dragged the poor fellow in the shade of a small pine and I think he died where I left him. As I passed on I found a dead Yankee lying on his face in an old field ditch shot in the back of the head. His name was Dud Sanders, Co. H, 1st Kentucky, U.S. Cavalry. The fellow had on Confederate grey pants and

183. *ORR,* I, 38, pt. 2, p. 927. Capron's Report.
184. Wells, p. 214.

Confederate woven suspenders. My suspenders were worn out and I appropriated his . . . I then followed the sound of guns and caught up with my command, about half a mile farther on."[185]

Back the Yanks went, draggled-assed and refusing to look at their officers, until they could hear the negroes screaming and the mules hee-hawing at the noise of the artillery. On the road back from Macon, so many negroes had trailed the column that the Yanks called them the "Nigger Brigade."[186] Now they were milling around with the led stock, a field full of them. The Yanks had freed them, but were beginning to understand that they couldn't get free of them.

The Yanks might have run farther, if they had had the energy, for they certainly had the inclination. As it was, they fell back on the reserves, in the pine thickets, formed up a passable line, and waited. Many of them went to sleep pretty soon,[187] they were so wrung out from the trip. But to the ones who were awake, the wait was perhaps worse than fighting, for they had too much time to think. Over two hours passed, and the Yanks could only conclude that the force from Macon was coming up behind them to pull the noose tight.[188]

Speaking of nooses, during that long delay Captain Carr, holding the outer line for the First Kentucky, had a woman come up to one of his pickets and ask permission to come through, so that she could be with her mother, who lived nearby, during this awful time. But Carr ordered her to wait and went to check to see if the old lady would own such an

185. J. A. Wynn, Reminiscence, State of Georgia Archives, pp. 58-59.
186. Tarrant, p. 369.
187. Wells, p. 213.
188. *ORR,* I, 38, pt. 2, p. 917. Smith's Report.

ugly daughter. The old lady didn't, so Carr came back and asked the "woman" some questions that trapped "her." Carr arrested the fellow as a spy and took him to Stoneman, who made him keep the dress on all day. When the Yanks fell apart later that day, the provost guards took the fellow with them, saying they thought that they'd have time to stop long enough to hang him.[189] But that night he got away. It turned out to be a fellow named Joe Funderbeck, who had been home on furlough, who had been caught away from home by the Yanks and was trying to get back during the lull in the battle.[190]

Actually Iverson was using the delay to faze the Yanks. His various movements had forced them to stretch their lines for two miles and think of themselves as the defenders. Then he called together his brigade commanders, Allen, Butler, and Crews, and explained his plan of attack. The Yanks had bunched up on their left, where they had been hit earlier. So Crews' Georgians were to demonstrate and fool the Yanks into thinking that they were to be hit again in their sore spot. At the same time Allen's Alabamians, who had been quietly returning to the center, were to charge in double ranks, break the Yank right center, and pivot and enfilade the line to their left. Then in cooperation Butler's Kentuckians were to send their left wing into the opening and pivot and enfilade the Yank line to the right.

At the same time, Stoneman, his staff, and some of his brigade commanders were meeting. Almost everyone wanted to move off to the Yank right rear, which seemed to have the least opposition.[191] But Stoneman refused to order

189. Tarrant, p. 364.
190. W. C. Dodson, "Stampede of Federal Cavalry," *Confederate Veteran*, XIX (March, 1911), 124.
191. *ORR*, I, 38, pt. 2, p. 917. Smith's Report.

the whole command to move; such a movement, he argued, would result in many men getting separated and probably getting bushwhacked. He meant to surrender, if he had to, he said, but he would delay his surrender as long as possible, to cover the escape of any unit which wanted to try to cut its way out.[192]   By now Stoneman seemed to be a broken man, and the brigade and regimental commanders seemed to understand that they were free to do whatever they thought best, if they were over run.[193]

By then it was 4:00 in the hot, silent afternoon. The Rebs had left the Yanks alone for over three hours; only the sweat bees, gnats, and mosquitoes seemed to resent the invasion of their pine thickets. Then, all at once, the woods seemed to erupt, as the Reb artillery cut loose from both flanks and from the front, all on the same point. Almost in a second, a gloom of smoke, dust, and pine needles darkened the Yank position. The accuracy of the artillery was wondrous; shells were landing on top of one another, so that the second sometimes killed men who had run to help the men hit by the first.[194]

And right behind the barrage came the Alabama Brigade, then the Kentuckians. Iverson's plan was working like a Waterbury watch. The Yanks, still stunned from the barrage, after such a long wait, could only run. Capron's Brigade, over on the right, was cut off from Stoneman and chased right back upon its horses.[195]   Before Capron's men could mount, the Fourth Alabama and Twelfth Alabama Battalion caught up and started pulling them off. The "hand-to-hand"

192. "Georgia — Stoneman's Capture — Battle of Sunshine Church," Philadelphia *Inquirer*, August 24, 1864.

193. *ORR*, I, 38, pt. 2, p. 920. Tompkins' Report.

194. Tarrant, p. 364.

195. *ORR*, I, 38, p5. 2, p. 927. Capron's Report.

went on for a full twenty minutes — grunts, screams, wheez-
es, dying falls. Capron's only alternative was to lead his survivors in flight.[196]

Over on the left the Kentucky Yanks got the word that
Stoneman was going to send in the white flag and became
so furious that for the first time all day they were a united
body. Colonel Adams stormed back to Stoneman and raged
against surrender. His men's time was up, he yelled. And
besides that, Major Boyle's battalion of the Eleventh Kentucky contained many men who had once been in the Reb
army. They would never even make it to Andersonville.
But Stoneman still thought that the best thing to do was
to surrender as a group. He said, "If you attempt to get
out, your command will be cut all to pieces and killed."

Here or there, the Yanks figured, it didn't make much
difference. Adams cooly replied, "I will take the responsibility," and hurried back to his command. The Kentuckians
quickly mounted, welcoming others from other regiments
to go with them, for all order had disappeared. Then, to
their astonishment, Adams led them out through gullies so
deep and brushy that not a single shot was fired at them.[197]

The Eighth Michigan had fallen back upon the two Indiana regiments that had been in reserve. The Yanks had
then been pushed another mile, out of the woods, across an
old field of sedge grass and haw bushes, through a creek, to
rest against a hill. Two hours had passed since Capron and
Adams had gone off. As the men of the Eighth caught their
breath and tried to form up, they noticed an officer riding
forward, carrying a stick with a white cloth tied to it. Major
Buck, now in command after the capture of Colonel Weir,

196. "Twelfth Alabama Cavalry Regiment," Manuscript, State
of Alabama Archives.
197. Tarrant, p. 365.

talked to the other officers; then they decided to chance it, so what was left of the Eighth Michigan and much of the Fifth and Sixth Indiana went out, riding off even as the officer crossed the old field.

The remainder of McLaughlin's Ohio Squadron, pushed back from the Yank right center, decided that they, too, ought to be departing, even without ceremony.[198]   They mounted and charged down the hill, only to get bogged down in the quicksand along the creek. Half their number was captured, for as they struggled with their mounts, the Rebs ran up to line the edge of the swale.

Colonel Butler, of the Fifth Indiana, had been persuaded by Stoneman to remain as long as opposition was possible. Now he wanted to be released, so that he could try to take the last organized body out. When he applied to Stoneman, the reply was curious, to say the least: "Be a man and surrender."

Butler was enraged at the deception. He screamed to Stoneman that he was a "liar and a coward." Then Butler ran to his men, formed them up, and started out with them. But the Rebs, who had ceased firing when the flag went in, saw the moving column and riddled it. Butler was killed, and the survivors captured.[199]

That ended the contest. At that point, "after several hours fighting," J. A. Wynn remembered, "I saw a fellow with a white flag, dressed in blue, come galloping down to Col. Crews and I said, 'Boys, that is good news'."[200]

O. P. Hargis, Company I, First Georgia, took part in the surrender:

"The captain of the skirmish line ordered us to cease firing. The officer rode up to our line and asked where our

198. Williams, p. 126.
199. "Doctor."
200. Wynn, p. 59.

Col. Charles C. Crews

Brig.-Gen. Alfred Iverson

Brig.-Gen William W. Allen

commanding officer was. He was told that he was back with the line of battle. He said 'send after him that General Stowman wishes to surrender.' Colonel Cruise was commanding the fight, General Iverson was sick and not on duty, then Colonel Cruise and his staff came riding up to meet the Federal officer. They saluted each other and the officer told Colonel Cruise that General Stowman wished to surrender. Colonel Cruise said 'alright I will go in and receive him.' They rode back together and we followed on.

"When we got over the little hill there the Federals stood in line with their guns stacked in front of them and General Stowman sitting on his horse. Colonel Cruise rode up and saluted General Stowman. Stowman said that he preferred to surrender to General Iverson, but was refused by Colonel Cruise.

"After Colonel Cruise received General Stowman we all formed up in the road. Stowman's Adjutant General saw Colonel Butler, Kentucky Regiment, sitting on his horse, and he said, 'Hello, Colonel Butler, how do you do? I am glad to see you.' They had went to school together. Then the Adjutant went around among the officers and got a pair of fine English navy pistols, and told him he would make a present of them to him. Colonel Butler said, 'Thank you sir, I hope I will do good service with them the next fight I get into.' The Adjutant said 'Don't talk to me that way.' Colonel Butler said, 'I don't mean if you and I come in contest, I mean among your men.' Then he said 'three cheers for Colonel Cruise,' then General Stowman hung his head. Stowman was a fine looking officer. Then we marched all the prisoners back through the battle ground to General Iverson's headquarters and put a strong guard around the prisoners for the night."[201]

201. Hargis, 41.

That Adjutant, a dark-skinned Kentucky major, sure did have a giving nature. Come to think of it, so did Stoneman: he gave us eight hundred Sharp's eight-shooter rifles.[202] But the Adjutant was personal about it, if you known what I mean — when he got to the officer's prison in Macon, on Monday evening, August 1st, he knocked the silver spurs off his heels and gave them to Ed Lathrop, one of the guards.[203] Well, it was in keeping with the Scriptures, where it says that "every man *shall give* as he is able, . . ." Stoneman was still weepy, Lathrop said; he just sat on a stool, like a girl in a fairy tale, with his face in his hands and his elbows on his knees and let the bitter tears flow. He probably was still seeing himself and his six hundred being marched off to General Iverson's headquarters at Joseph White's house by Colonel Crews and his one hundred and eighty-two ragged boys.[204] Why it reminds you of the bard Tennyson's poem:

> Half a mile, half a mile,
>   Half a mile onward,
> All in the valley of Jones
>   Rode the six hundred.
> 'Forward the White Kerchief!
>   Stack up the guns! he said:
> Into the valley of Jones
>   Rode the six hundred.

MACON
AUGUST 1

The next morning the few Rebs that Iverson hadn't sent

202. Charleston *Daily Courier*, August 6, 1864.
203. Edward S. Lathrop, "Gossipy Letter from Georgia," *Confederate Veteran*, XX (November, 1912), 520.
204. "Georgia — Stoneman's Capture — Battle of Sunshine Church," Philadelphia *Inquirer*, August 24, 1864.

after the fleeing Yanks were detailed to take Stoneman and his imps down to Macon. The Rebs had no supplies, so the men, Yank and Reb together, had to go into the corn fields along the way and get roasting ears for their meals.[205] There weren't enough Rebs to mount a satisfactory guard, so some Yanks just went into the corn fields and didn't bother to come back.[206] In their condition they could have gotten work in the neighborhood as scarecrows.

The Yank officers were allowed to ride in and arrived at Camp Oglethorpe late that afternoon, August 1st. Most of the town was there to see Stoneman come across that bridge that had been denied to him a few days before. He seemed to be in command of himself as he came in; up on that saddle that he paid $500 in gold for,[207] he *looked* like a winner. As the reporter for the *Intelligencer* noted on the occasion: "The General is a large, tall, thin man, with a face very much bronzed and rough, somewhat haggard features, sandy whiskers and hair, dark, keen, lowering eyes and look, directing sharp, piercing looks, occasionally, at his interrogators. He bears the appearance of a man who exacts implicit obedience to his commands, and is stern in his decrees. His strong, powerful frame seems capable of enduring any amount of hardship. His every feature, and powerful, wiry motions, indicate the advance of a Hercules, and mark him the leader of desperate enterprises, the character of which has made him his reputation as an inimitable raider."[208]   But when he opened his mouth, Stoneman

205. Hargis, 41.

206. Daniel S. Whitenack, "Reminiscences of the Civil War: Andersonville," *Indiana Magazine of History*, XI (June, 1915), 130-131.

207. Lathrop, 520.

208. "Georgia — Stoneman's Capture — Battle of Sunshine Church," Philadelphia *Inquirer*, August 24, 1864.

let out his true nature. His eyes began to look like those of an old hound, as he confessed that he felt humiliated to have surrendered to such a small force, but, as the Macon *Telegraph* put it, he "says his men were so demoralized and dispirited that they would not fight."[209] How's that for leadership?

Colonel B. W. Frobel, of the Reb army, arrived in Macon just about the time that General Stoneman was brought in. His army eyes caught aspects of meaning in General Stoneman's arrival that the cit reporters failed to mention:

"It was late in the afternoon before I reached the station, but had the good fortune to find a freight train just about leaving for Macon. Having arranged for a car with the agent for our horses, and leaving some directions for Davis, I jumped on the train, and in a hour or so was in the city.

"General Stoneman had just been brought in as a prisoner by the cavalry, and there was, consequently, some excitement and a good deal of rejoicing. . . .

"There had been sharp fighting about Atlanta for some days past, and, consequently, each train from that point brought in a heavy freight of wounded. Hundreds of poor fellows were lying on the platforms at the depot, while the car-sheds were literally crowded with them, patiently waiting to be removed to the hospitals, which were located at Vineville. This is some mile or so from Macon, and as the number of ambulances was limited, the process of removal was very slow."[210]

Colonel Frobel realized that an occasional Stoneman bagged did not outweigh the hundreds of wounded, that maybe the great Reb flaw was a taste for gallantry combined

209. Charleston *Daily Courier,* August 6, 1864.

210. B. W. Frobel, "The Georgia Campaign," *Scott's Monthly Magazine,* V (February, 1868), 39.

with a disinclination to do arithmetic. The next day was a repetition: ". . . the horses having arrived in the meantime, we took the cars at nine A.M. for Atlanta. At short intervals along the whole length of the road, we passed hospital after hospital, until it actually seemed as if a whole army of wounded men were distributed along the route, and these continued to increase as we approached that ill-fated city."

MACON

AUGUST 2

The Yank privates from Stoneman's command got to walk into Macon and didn't arrive until Tuesday morning. The reporter from the Macon *Telegraph* was there to greet them, too: "They appeared in good spirits, and did not look as if they had been caught committing their usual rascalities. They are a very good looking body of men, and informed us that they were picked out for the purpose of destroying our communications. They inquired very anxiously after the military prison at Andersonville, and expressed great fear at being sent there, the officers having told them that the place was very unwholesome, and caused hundreds of their comrades to die daily. When informed that they were deceived, they expressed themselves satisfied to remain there until, as one remarked, Sherman came to relieve them. Sherman may visit Andersonville, but it will only be as Stoneman has visited Macon."[211] It seems like Georgia journalism is determined to be as ferocious as the Tennessee variety.

The "satisfied" prisoners were turned over to the malish for their trip down to the resort at Andersonville. By that

211. Charleston *Daily Courier*, August 5, 1864.

time, the cits were turning to other interests. A reception for General Iverson was planned for Thursday, August 4th, at 5:00 p.m., in the picnic grove behind Wesleyan Female College, and an appeal was made for coffee, milk, and other refreshments.[212]   The event was called off, though, for Iverson had to return to duty, to oversee the round-up of those Yanks that had escaped at Sunshine Church.[213]

There was something of a festivity, though, as J. A. Wynn recalled: "The 1st Ga. Cavalry was detailed to guard the prisoners to Macon . . . The ladies of Macon filled our haversacks with good rations and presented the Regiment with a purse of $700.00 cash. A detail of ten men was sent out and the $700.00 was spent for water melons. Such a water melon feast and such a war with melon rinds I never witnessed before . . . God bless the ladies of Macon."[214]

Once those Yanks that left the field at Sunshine Church decided to go, they had gone like a bunch of bats. J. W. Turk, a Reb horse agent, got to the field just in time to help chase the Yanks: "The first three or four miles of the stampede the men seemed to have bunched pretty well, making a roadway about thirty feet wide. It was almost as clear of bushes, weeds, and everything of that kind as a regular public road. Even the ground rails of fences were torn from their places, and one could scarcely tell that there had been a fence there except by the fences on either side of the newly made road."

Not all the Yanks had good luck in escaping, as Turk observed: "After going about two miles, we came to a gulley in a pine thicket, about eight feet deep and twelve or fifteen wide, in which there were many horses and men,

212. Hoehling, p. 236.
213. Hoehling, p. 240.
214. Wynn, p. 59.

nearly all of which seemed to be dead. Those in front had filled the gulley, and the others passed over the gulley on the men and horses that filled it. One or two men and horses were killed in crossing a small branch on a pole bridge something like two miles beyond the big gulley mentioned."

Turk had seen a good deal of the war and wasn't very curious about it any more. So, since he wasn't under Iverson's command, he dropped out of the chase and made plans for the next day:

"I spent the afternoon and until nine or ten o'clock at night sending word to young ladies in the neighborhood and to two or three young boys to meet me at a designated point the next morning and we would take a horseback ride over the battlefield and trail of the stampeded Federals. The battlefield was a novel sight to the girls. The floor of Sunshine Church was almost covered with wounded soldiers. Horses, guns, pistols, and the like were to be seen all around, with now and then a dead soldier. When we reached the gulley that had been filled with men and horses, the awful sight caused nearly all of the girls to shed tears, and one or two almost collapsed."[215]

The other pursuers, those from Iverson's command, were a bit more persistent. Right after the charge that broke the Yank will, a hundred Kentuckians had fought the Yanks for mounts and then chased the Yanks who had been able to get them.[216] Iverson recalled Allen's Alabama Brigade, mounted it, and sent it north to Hillsboro, there to turn toward Eatonton and block the Yank column. But Allen missed the way and the Yanks. That left only the Kentucky Brigade, which had started directly on the track right after the Alabamians left.

215. W. C. Dodson, "Stampede of Federal Cavalry," 124.
216. "Escort."

With several hours' start, the Yank units had some time
to get a little organization. When Capron inspected his column, he found that he had about three hundred present.
Since many were either without arms or ammunition, they
were placed in the middle of the column. Those without
ammunition for their weapons swung them against trees,
to break them in two at the breech.[217] Then the column
resumed its progress, but at a slower pace, for many men
had ridden their horses to death in the first few miles.[218]
Bearing to the left, Capron's column slid past Eatonton and
Madison.

EATONTON
AUGUST 1

Adams' Yank Kentucky Brigade, with over five hundred
present, had taken another road, one that led right up to
Eatonton. Along about sunrise on Monday, August 1st,
they rode in, dismounted, and got busy burning the depot.
While they were thus occupied, they had a little surprise.
The malish from Hancock and Baldwin, about a hundred
of them, must have decided that Milledgeville was by-passed,
so they took the cars up to Eatonton. They stopped short
of town, sent out scouts, and then walked in. They weren't
very practiced at warfare, so they just demanded the surrender of the Yanks. And the Yanks, worn out and droopy
anyhow, must have figured that the malish out-numbered
them, otherwise they'd never have acted as they were; so
they all took off their hats, to indicate that they were surrendering. But the malish, mind you, being new at the

217. ORR, I, 38, pt. 2, p. 928. Capron's Report.
218. Tarrant, p. 366.

game, didn't know what the sign meant, so they banged away at the Yanks. The Yanks must have decided not to take their chances with such uneducated fools, so they skedaddled to their horses and left, with one wounded Yank remaining as the fruit of the great battle of Eatonton.[219]

These particular Yanks must have been totally frustrated, for they looked around for something else to burn. As one observer put it: "The same rascals would have fired the Eatonton factory but for the ruse of a faithful negro, belonging to Col. Devit, of Wheeler's cavalry, whose family reside near this place, as refugees. The boy in question was driving some cattle of his master's . . ., and a short distance this side of the factory, met a Yankee scout, who pretended to be a member of Wheeler's cavalry, but finally acknowledged himself what the boy took him for, a Yankee. The faithful negro, fearful of the loss of his horse and cows, told him there was a large force of rebel cavalry at the factory. He instantly mounted his stolen mule, and left his jaded horse, bridle and saddle, and two blankets as trophies for the negro. He galloped back, met his approaching comrades, told them that Iverson's forces were just ahead and turned them from their courses. The depot was burning as the negro passed through Eatonton."

They got their wish when they got to Madison — they burned it. Then they moved out, to meet Capron's outfit at Pouder's farm, seven miles northeast of Rutledge, at dusk. The next morning, August 2nd, they rode into Watkinsville. At that point, they decided to attack Athens, destroy the Armory and other government works. They must have felt safe enough from the pursuing Rebs to try to end their raid with a little success. The plan was for

219. "Letter from Sparta," Charleston *Daily Courier,* August 8, 1864.

Adams to go forward and try the approaches to the town, then to send word to Capron, about two miles to the rear. But when the Yank Kentuckians found the town too well fortified for their meager strength, they sent back a guide to lead Capron up behind them as they moved on up the Oconee River toward Jefferson. The guide got them lost, though, and Capron delayed for six hours in the drowsy Georgia heat trying to locate Adams. Finally he decided to strike out on his own. By then his men had ridden over fifty miles in twenty-four hours and were beginning to fall out of their saddles. Sometime after midnight he felt compelled to go into camp for a couple of hours. His arrangements were professional: pickets were put out, Eighth Michigan in front and Fourteenth Illinois behind, the gangs of negroes still following the column like a shadow were sent to the rear, and the men were told to lie by the road and keep their horses saddled.

For two hours or so, the Yanks got the rest that their bodies craved. Then, in the darkness just before dawn, there was a sudden breeze and noise, like a summer storm had crept upon them. But it was Willie Breckinridge's Reb Ninth Kentucky that had slipped up on the pickets and swept them up, then stampeded the negroes right through the main Yank camp. Bedlam! The Yanks had taken off their boots, to favor their swollen feet, and their coats and saddles, to use as pillows, despite Capron's orders.[220] To top that, most of the men who still had guns had already been over-run. So it was a royal mixup of howling negroes, dazed Yanks, and yelling Rebs there in the dark road.

The farthest Yank regiment was the Eighth Michigan, and it attempted to form a line. Major Buck and Captain McDonald got a few men together on their right. Then

220. Wells, p. 218.

McDonald rode over to steady the left, and the Doc of the Eighth Michigan saw what happened next: "Capt. McDonald, seeing that the left was somewhat in confusion, dashed over, dismounted, and ordered the men he met there to form in line. It being still dark, he did not discover that they were rebels, until a rebel officer rode up towards him and asked 'what son of a bitch was giving command to his men?' Ascertaining it was the Captain giving orders, he asked, 'What regiment do you belong to sir?' The Captain cooly answered, 'The Eighth Michigan, sir.' At this the rebel officer drew his revolver, and, without demanding a surrender, discharged it at the Captain, the ball going in close proximity to his head. The Captain then told him he surrendered. The rebel officer now dismounted and came up to the Captain and drew his revolver, but fortunately the cap snapped. He then told the Captain to come with him. Taking him to one side of the road, he said, 'Surrender, do you, you Yankee son of a bitch. We don't give quarter; we intend to shoot every damned one of you,' taking a cap from his cap pouch, and while in the act of putting it on his pistol, said, 'I'll show you how to surrender; what the hell made you run away after Stoneman had surrendered you.' The Captain saw that he intended to shoot him, and would give him no quarter. Pulling a pocket pistol from one of his side pockets, while the rebel was fixing the cap, he brought it within an inch of his head and shot him dead on the spot. Two rebel soldiers hearing the report, came dashing up, but before they had time to revenge the death of their officer, two Yankee bullets laid them out."[221]

For a few minutes it looked as if the Eighth Michigan would not only hold, but would counter-charge and capture the Kentuckians, for the Yanks outnumbered the Rebs

221. "Doctor."

about two to one. About that time, though, Sergeant Phil Pointer, little more than a boy, beardless and with features as fine as a woman's, emerged from the Reb line and urged Colonel Breckinridge to try one more charge. At their leader's command, the Rebs swept forward, and the stunned Yank line broke.[222]

Now the Yanks had a choice: they could crawl through the fences that bordered the road and try to escape across the open fields on foot, or they could try to shoulder a horse down that narrow road ahead of the Rebs. Those who went it on foot were mostly ignored by Breckinridge's boys, for they could be picked up all day, even by the cits. Instead, the forty-odd Kentuckians stayed right behind the Yank horsemen.

A mile or so down the road the Yanks struck the bridge across Mulberry River. The first few must have made it over, but when the mass of Yanks hit it, the whole thing shook like it had the ague. In an instant the cross planks were shattered and punched out; the first wave of horses plunged into the water below, with the successive waves plunging onto them. There seemed to be no way to go — death would come, either by the hurtling bodies, or by the muddy water, or by the balls fired by the Rebs who now lined the southern bank of the river.

There was no resistance, so the Rebs ceased firing and started helping their captives up the muddy bank. One of the prisoners was Willie Breckinridge's Yank brother.[223] When they were all seined out, the Yanks were escorted back up the road, toward Athens, where they could be put aboard the cars for Macon and Andersonville.

222. "Gallant Phil Pointer," *Confederate Veteran*, XI (March, 1903), 110.
223. DuBose, p. 380.

The Rebs were exhausted, but jubilant. They reckoned that they had broken up the only large body of Stoneman's command yet remaining. They were shocked, then, when they ran smack into Adams' advance, charging to rescue Capron's force.[124] Before they knew it, Colonel Breckinridge himself had been captured. But he wasn't recognized, probably because his ordinary jeans shirt made him look like a private, and he slipped away.[225] The Adams men didn't linger, since they had little ammunition, but just bluffed loose what they could of Capron's men, and then headed on for the Chattahoochee.[226]

ATHENS
AUGUST 3

That was the end of the affair, and the Ninth Kentucky, about a hundred strong, turned its attention to bringing their three hundred Yank prisoners into Athens. A reporter of the Athens *Southern Watchman* was on hand to observe the entry into town: "They arrived in this place about 3 o'clock in the afternoon and, of course, there was great excitement, as this was the first squad of Yankees who had visited us since the beginning of the war.

"The prisoners presented a sorry spectacle. Ragged, some of them bareheaded, some barefooted, and all very dirty, we have never seen an equal number of men looking so badly. The great mass of them appeared to be the 'rag, tag and bobtail' of the communities from when they came. We recognized 'the rich Irish brogue and sweet German accent' among them. It is true that now and then a respectable

124. Tarrant, p. 368.
225. Stegeman, p. 123.
226. *ORR*, I, 38, p5. 2, p. 918. Smith's Report.

looking man was to be seen among the officers and men.
The great mass of them, however, looked like 'hard cases.'"[227]

So did their Reb escorts, if the reported had bothered
to look, for dirt seemed somehow to attach to anybody
who went without washing long enough. The Yanks were
penned up on the campus at Franklin College until the
local authorities could find out if the track through Gordon
to Macon had been repaired. The cits all around Athens
regarded the Yanks as a P. T. Barnum show, and they came
to the college to gawk at them. Since it was Wednesday,
lots of ladies made plans to go to prayer meeting that evening — by way of the campus, no doubt to save a Yank soul,
if one could be found whose heart was not too hard. They
found that the Yanks were beginning to get their spirit
back. One of the Yanks told a local belle named Sukie
Daughtery that he had seen a great many girls prettier than
she, saw one the day before, in fact — a yellow girl.[228]

ATHENS
AUGUST 4

A celebration was planned for the next afternoon, August
4th. At that time, Breckinridge's boys were escorted up
Broad Street by a brass band to the campus gate, where they
were met by the mayor and other he-pillars of the community. Then, finally dismounting, they were ushered into
the Chapel, where sat the she-pillars waving their handkerchiefs and clapping their hands. Major Austin, of the Ninth
Kentucky, said that the boys suddenly realized, by looking

227. Athens *Southern Watchman*, August 10, 1864.
228. Kenneth Coleman, ed., *Athens, 1861-1864* (Athens: University of Georgia Press, 1969), 102.

at all those clean people, just how dirty they were and how long they had been that way. So they just sort of slunk into the back rows, like ordinary reprobates, to listen to a speech by the mayor.[229]   A response was given by Captain Campbell, whose company had led the attack the day before at Jug Tavern. Then a banquet was served up to the ragged troopers. Courtesy demanded that a response be made, but none of the Kentuckians wanted that chore. Contrasted with the garrison soldiers, they were filthy and ragged – but finally Jim Black came forward from one of the farthest rows.

Some of the she-pillars were heard to comment that if he spoke like he dressed, then his speech ought to be a disgrace. Major Austin noted the result: "With all these visible defects, the young man braced himself for the conflict, and with one sweeping glance over the sea of faces, he addressed himself to the 'chair' with an ease and grace of manner which showed he was no novice in the part he was called upon to perform. As he warmed up to his subject, every one seemed to lose sight of his outward appearance. His lofty and sublime thoughts, clothed in classically chosen language and expressed in that impassioned eloquence which always commands attention and respect, completely captivated his hearers. The excitement of the crowd at times, when he would round off a beautiful period, became intense, and would only subside after a wild burst of applause. When he told, in gentle cadence, of his home within the enemy's lines, over a thousand miles away, and how he parted with his mother and sister and bade his classmates in college adieu, to take up arms for the struggling South, and of the hardships he had endured, there was scarcely a dry eye in the house. He held the crowd spell-

229. Stegeman, p. 123.

bound for an hour. When he descended from the rostrum the ladies gathered about him, anxious to grasp the hand of the soldier-orator and congratulate him on his magnificent effort."[230]

Jim Black was quite a practitioner of rhetoric. Back up in Kentury, he had written the graduating speech for his class at Georgetown College. The authorities had objected that the speech was too Southern to be given in Yankee territory and had demanded that he write another. He refused, and they refused to graduate him. As soon as possible, he left with a company of other recruits to join General John H. Morgan, but it was captured and sent to Johnson's Island. So he had the pleasure of being a prisoner of war before he had ever gotten to the war. After being exchanged, he finally made it to Morgan's command, about Christmas, 1862. Having been in the field ever since, he could truthfully speak of the hardships.[231]

Well, the action by Breckinridge wound up the McCook and Stoneman Raids. The only thing left was to make the whole thing official with a proclamation, and Wheeler obliged us soon enough:

"Headquarters Wheeler's Cavalry Corps
"Near Atlanta, Ga., Aug. 5, 1864
"SOLDIERS; The Major-General commanding thanks his command for the energy and determined gallantry displayed in their recent operations. The foiling of a most stupendous effort on the part of the enemy to destroy our country is due to your valor and patriotism.

230. Quoted in W. C. Dodson, *Campaigns of Wheeler and his Cavalry*, p. 247.
231. Augusta Bar Association, *Memorial Exercises in Honor of J. C. C. Black* (n.p., n.d.), pp. 3-4.

"During the present campaign you have captured and killed a number of the enemy equaling your own strength. You have defeated him in every action in which you have engaged, capturing his cannon, colors and arms. Your great commander, General Hood, fully appreciates your services. Stand together, my brave soldiers, continue your good conduct, and the lasting gratitude of your country will be your reward."

"Joseph Wheeler"
"Major-General"[232]

Whatever the War Baby really felt about the raid, he put on a good front. He wrote old Bragg, sitting up there in Richmond at the right hand of Jeff Davis:

"I suppose you have heard of the destruction of the raiding parties of the enemy. General Sherman's plan was beautiful.

"When the raid started it found me as usual in the trenches confronted by the enemy.

"We first checked Garrard's Division which was within twelve miles of the Rail Road. Another column having gone further East under General Stoneman I sent Genl. Iverson with three brigades in pursuit. The results you now know. Very few escaped and those who did escape are worthless to the enemy.

"McCook with three brigades (3,000) three thousand strong had crossed near Campbelton and was making for Jonesboro with Jackson after him. I left one brigade to watch Garrard's Division which we had driven back towards Lithonia & with the remainder of my force (1,000) one thousand men started after McCook. Jackson had attacked

232. W. C. Dodson, *Campaigns of Wheeler and his Cavalry*, p. 234.

him near Lovejoys capturing fifty prisoners.

"I communicated with him on arriving and he replied that if I would follow the enemy he would get in their front.

"I followed them with four hundred men fighting them at night and rebuilding the bridges the enemy had destroyed. Jackson failed to get in the enemy's front and went into camp leaving me the contest. Roddey fortunately was at Newnan with his dismounted men which the enemy observed and tried to turn the town. This enabled me to overtake them. I had already captured two hundred prisoners and killed a great many.

"My force was now five hundred strong. I sent two hundred to get ahead of the enemy which was accomplished. I then attacked with the remaining three hundred McCooks Division which was nearly three thousand strong and routed and defeated them.

"The remainder of my force then came up and assisted in gathering up the prisoners now numbering about one thousand. Iverson's command has also captured very nearly that number. The enemy's loss in killed is very heavy.

"McCook's column which I fought near Newnan lost very nearly, if not quite four hundred killed. General Iverson thinks that Stoneman's loss in killed is nearly three hundred. Among the prisoners captured near Newnan were two brigade commanders and four colonels. General Hood has a plan now for the Cavalry from which I hope and trust great good will result."

> "Respectfully Genl,"
> "Your obt Servant & Friend"[233]

'Twas a famous victory, all right, though a little more

233, Letter, Joseph Wheeler to Braxton Bragg, August 6, 1864, Container 2, Folder 6, Wheeler Papers, Western Reserve Historical Society.

credit could be given to the malish at Macon, Roddey, and Jackson. As soon as Hood saw how things were falling out, he telegraphed Davis a proposal to send Wheeler to work on Sherman's railroad line back to Chattanooga. Hood had hopes that the Confederate cavalry in both Alabama and Mississippi would also be sent to attack the railroad between Chattanooga and Nashville.[234] Davis replied that he concurred, though we never did hear any more of that cooperation from the other forces.

234. John B. Hood, *Advance and Retreat* (Bloomington: Indiana University Press, 1959), p. 198.

III

Along the Augusta Railroad, Georgia:
"preparing for a rampage"

(August 5-10, 1864)

*B*eginning on August 5, Wheeler began to put Hood's plan into effect, for the various commands were ordered to congregate around Covington. Dibrell's Brigade remained at Flat Shoals, where it had been since it sent Garrard slinking off. The Confederate Brigade came back from Newnan to the Social Circle; on the way, the prudent Sergeant Ash got permission to do a little business at the Jonesboro depot: "Put in a bag the two Yankee blankets, 2 shirts, some coffee and other little things and expressed them to home."[235] Harrison's boys moved on up to Oxford, while Williams' Kentucky Brigade stayed in Athens, where it was impressing the local cits with its good manners. And Martin's Division began to concentrate at Covington, after dropping Stoneman and his visitors off at Macon.

Pretty quickly the camp talk began to circulate that Wheeler's boys were to go on a little trip themselves. From his camp at Covington, Isaac Ulmer, of the Third Alabama Cavalry, wrote his sister:

"My dear Sister —

"A move of some kind is on hand a few lines before we start would be acceptable. The supposition is that Genl Wheeler is about to go on an extensive raid in the seat of the Enemy as he has concentrated all of his Cavalry at this point on the Augusta R.R. I am glad that we have moved from the Vicinity of Atlanta and a 'something' of this sort is needed to stir us up, and keep us from stagnating in our tracks. Some of the Cavalry, poor fellows, had a hard ride after Stoneman and his crew. They will now have the pleasure of being followed as they did the Yankees."[236]

Nearby, at the Social Circle, a special shipment of salt for the horses arrived,[237] and the boys in the Confederate Brigade guessed that such rations meant a raid. John W. Cotton, of the Tenth Confederate Regiment, decided that he had better inform his wife and seven children:

235. Diary Entry for August 5, John H. Ash Papers, Emory University Library.

236. Letter, Isaac Barton Ulmer to his sister, August 6, 1864. Isaac Barton Ulmer Papers, Southern Historical Collection, University of North Carolina.

237. *ORR*, I, 38, pt. 5, p. 951.

> "Georgia Camps three miles from the
> Social Circle on the Augusta railroad
> and fifty miles from Atlanta. . .

"Most dear beloved wife again I take my pen in hand to try to rite you a few lines to try to let you no that I am well and doing very well I hant any nuse to rite to you I recon Asa has rote to you about the rade that they were after when I got her we are fiting now to make a raid in rear of the yankeys it is thought we will start tomorrow I don't recon you will here from me any more til we come back if I ever come back I will rite again I hope we will be able to pay them back for all the raids they have made on us if we can bee successful in getting in there rear and cut off there supplies it may bee the means of making them fall back from Atlanta there has been two very hard fits here at Atlanta since I left home and reports says our men whiped them badly we still hold Atlanta and I hope we will bee able to still hold it Mariah I hant seen Asa since I got here the rest of the boys says he stoped at his pars but he may be at home for what I no He has been gone over a weak I got a letter for him that nan sent by oneal and read it I was glad to here you were all well it had a letter in it for tony I mailed to him. Asa captured two yankey horses and bridals I hope these few lines may reach you in dieu time and find you well and doing well it is uncertain whether you get this letter or not but you may get it after while nothing more at present I remain your affectionate husband til death"[238]

Over at Flat Shoals, Stephen Jordan, of the Ninth Tennessee Cavalry, noted in his diary: "Fair & pleasant. On picket last night. Rain & very dark. Returned to camp about 11

238. Lucille Griffith, ed., *Yours Till Death: Civil War Letters of John W. Cotton* (University: University of Alabama Press, 1951), pp. 117-118.

o'clock. Orders to have horses shod & 2 extra shoes fitted
& nails. I pulled some green corn today for my horse, the
first I ever took in my life & I hope I may never be forced
to do so again. Preaching this evening at 4 o'clock. . ."[239]
No doubt Jordan wasn't the only trooper who was feeling
guilty because he had had to take some roasting ears that
didn't belong to him, so the chaplain must have seen a good
market for his product. Getting the horses shod told Dibrell's
Tennessee Brigade that something was up, and the chaplain
probably also wanted to inform the Almighty of a forwarding address.

Ashby's Brigade moved over to Covington, where it began
remounting.[240] Adjutant Allen noted that many of the horses
were lame and barefooted, but that there was no lack of
replacements, so much stock had been captured from the
Yanks. But then he observed that many of the Yank horses
were too heavy and not fit for a long march or a charge at
close quarters. So the Fifth Tennessee had to scrounge
around to locate the Tennessee or Kentucky horses that were
preferred.

Harrison's Brigade, which along with Ashby's Brigade
made up Humes' Division, was also at Covington. Like a
good many of the boys, Will Nicholson, of the Eighth Texas
got off a letter home. To his aunt, Mrs. M. A. Crocheron,
of Bastrop, Texas, he wrote:

"Some time has elapsed since I last wrote home. I do not
remember the date of my last letter home. The last I received
from home however was dated May 9th. We understand

239. Stephen Jordan Diary, entry for August 7, 1864, in Jill
Knight Garrett and Marise P. Lightfoot, *The Civil War in Maury County, Tennessee* (Typescript, 1966), p. 31.

240. William Gibbs Allen, "War Reminiscences," manuscript,
William Gibbs Allen Papers, State of Tennessee Archives.

there are a great many letters somewhere in Georgia for us, but owing to the disorganized condition of the roads, occasioned by the recent Yankee raids, we are unable to get them at present. Gen. Hood still holds Atlanta and so far has defeated every attempt made by the enemy to capture the city. Since my last a great many events have transpired. We have seen a good deal of very hard service, been in quite a number of fights. I will first relate the unfortunate occurrence connected with Jesse Billingsley. He with Billy Sayers and several others were sent out to ascertain the position of the Yankee pickets when they ran into an ambuscade. It was night. The Yankees fired a volley at the party and Billingsley fell from his horse, though not until he had killed one of the Yankees who demanded his surrender. His horse came out — no signs if blood on his saddle. It is possible that he was only badly wounded though the chances are that he was killed without uttering a word. Time alone will develop his fate. A short account of the late extraordinary and daring raids of the Yankee cavalry will not be uninteresting. Four different raiding parties have lately been operating in the rear of our army, the most formidable of which were Stoneman's and McCook's.

"Gen. Stoneman succeeded in penetrating our rear as far as Macon, but fortunately he and his whole party were captured. He had destroyed several railroad bridges and depots and committed numerous depredations on the citizens. His force was four thousand. McCook had three thousand with him and operated principally on the Macon road and the West Point road. Our division was engaged with McCook, but did not succeed in capturing him. We captured one thousand of his men and compelled the remainder to retreat across the river in great disorder, leaving most of their horses and arms in our hands. Our Reg. did some very severe fighting near Newnan. Our casualties were 14 — two

killed. Mr. Maxey Co. B — A Maj. Thornton Co. F — Catron
Co. D flesh wound in the leg, the fighting so close and in
such a dense undergrowth that a good many of our regiment
was captured, but all succeeded in getting away. Our Cavalry
is now making preparations to make some kind of a trip.
We all think it a raid in the rear of Sherman and expect to
start in a few days.

"If you have an opportunity please send me some money
as I have been compelled to borrow some which is very unpleasant when money is so scarce in the regiment. The
Government owes me considerable money, but it is uncertain when I can get it. I am well — from your nephew
Wm. Nicholson

"Capt. Kyle & Maj. Christian will be sent to Texas soon
to bring back the deserters from the 8th Texas. W. N."[241]

From the same regiment, Sergeant John W. Hill wrote to
all his relations in Bastrop, to tell all about his relations
in Georgia:

"Camp at Covington Ga Aug 7th 1864
"Miss M. S. Hill

"Bastrop   Dear Sister   As we are in camp this morning
I thought I would drop you a few lines to let you know that
we are all well. We have just ret from the left wing of our
army   We went over there after a Raid by the Enemy. We
first caught up with them at Jonesburough on the Atlanta
& Macon Rail. R where we had a fight with them   They had
done very little damage to the Rail Road   When we came up
withe them.   They with-drew there forces after knight in
the direction of Newman Coweta Co   We caught up withe
there rear Guard at Shake-Rag a little place between Fa-
yettesvill & Newman and captured about one hundred fifty

241. Letter, William Nicholson to his aunt, August 9, 1864,
in the James Nicholson Papers, University of Texas Library.

(150) prisoners and killed several And I am sorry to informe you that in the fight that Major Thornton of Co F was killed He was shot in the face and killed dead I was close to him but did not see him fall but do not think He ever spoke. He was a good soldier and a brave man and ought to have had a good position in the army But He never Sought itt After riding all knight and nearly all of two dayes we came up to them again about three (3) miles from Newman Our Regt & the fourth Tenn was dismounted We drove them a short distance when they gave us sutch a heavey voley that we had to fall back When Rosses Texas Brigade came to our asistance and we drove them from the field. I captured a prisnor And had taken him back & Delivered him to the gard which was near our horses When the Enemy Maid a charge on our Horses which had bin left without an Suport I mounted my horse and with about tenn or twelve others kept them back untill they could get off with the horses We had very few men in the fight as we had riden so hard that a good many of our horses had given out. We had two killed and tenn or twelve wounded in the Regt. V Catron of our Company was wounded in the leg We killed and wounded about one hunred and fiftey 150 of the Enemy and cap-tured about one thousand (1,000) And got nearly all of there horses We got two picies of Artilery Some waggons & Amblances I got a Six Shooter and a Spencer Gun which shoots Seven (7) times But as I had two Six Shooters be-fore I let Bro Tom have the Pistol Bro Tom got him a very good horse

"Bro Bog is at Est Point in the Hosppital We saw Cousin Tom Hill about two weeks ago he was well Cousin Cap got a mule in the fight and went down to Griffen and left his horse and is riding the mule He got back last knight all well down there. Cap got a letter from S Blanton last knight She is down at Uncle Billys they are all well down there

H Williamson is in State Service After the fight was over at
Newman I got a pass and went to See Mrs. Honeycutt Mr
Parks second Wife   She had just got a letter from Cousin
John Parks   he is sick in the Hospittal at Petersburg Va I
stayed one knight withe them   They asked a thousand
questions about you all   She had two daughters one was
married But her husband died in the armey. She has one
child the other is a young Lady a very nice girl She had
two Sons in the armey   one of them is dead I Also called
on John. Hills family in Newman   He is Col of a Regt. of
State troops Burwell Hill lost his arme by a wound received
at Getesburg He was home But I did not get to see him
He lives some distance from town   Frank McGuire got a
letter a few days ago from Cynthia Walker She reports
all well down there She says She will go to Texas withe
us after the war is over iff we will go by after her   But I
am affraid that time will never come. There is a report in the
Regt. that there will two officers bee sent from the Regt.
this winter after the men that have gone home from the
Regt. We are resting at this place for a few dayes I Expect
in less than a week we will turne up in the rear of the Enemy
The Enemy maid a raid to Macon whilest we were after the
other raid   But they did not get off mutch Better than the
ones that we were after as they got Genl Stonemon and
about half of his comand Crops here is fine We have Rosting
Ears for Breakfast Diner & Supper Fruit crop is very good.
But how I long to bee at home and rest where the Sound
of the Bugle will not arouse me nor the sound of Artilery
& musketry will not disturb my repose Scott I feel like I
could write a week iff I knew that this would ever reach you
But I have written so mutch and yet no answer returns that I
almost Dispare of ever hearing from home any more. All
the Boyes are well There is nothing new or strange You
must excuse all mistakes and write often and long letters

for you do not know how mutch I want to hear from home Cousin Geo McGehee has gone withe Lt Black to the rear of the Enemy after horses

    "All join me in mutch love to you all —"[242]

While they were writing their letters and otherwise getting ready for a trip, there was a good deal of singing in camp. One song was the special version of "The Yellow Rose of Texas" that the Rangers used:

Song of the Texas Rangers
Inscribed to Mrs. John H. Wharton

I

The morning star is paling,
  The camp fires flicker low,
Our steeds are madly neighing
  For the bugle bids us go;
So put the foot in stirrup,
  And shake the bridle free,
For to-day the Texas Rangers
  Must cross the Tennessee!
    With Wharton for our leader,
      We'll chase the dastard foe,
    Till our horses bathe their fetlocks
    In the deep blue Ohio.

II

Our men come from the prairies
  Rolling broad, and proud, and free,
From the high and craggy mountains,
  To the murmuring Mexic sea;
And their hearts are open as their plains,
  Their thoughts are proudly brave
As the bold cliffs of the San Bernard,

---

242. Letter, John W. Hill to his sister, August 7, 1864, in the John W. Hill Papers, University of Texas Library.

Or the Gulf's resistless wave.
   Then quick into the saddle,
      And shake the bridle free,
   To-day with gallant Wharton,
      We cross the Tennessee.

III

'Tis joy to be a Ranger;
   To fight for dear Southland;
'Tis joy to follow Wharton,
   With his gallant, trusting band;
'Tis joy to see our Harrison
   Plunge, like a meteor bright,
Into the thickest of the fray,
   And strike with deadly might.
      Oh! who would not be a Ranger,
         And follow Wharton's cry,
      To battle for their country —
         And if it need be — die!

IV

Up with the crimson battle-flag!
   Let the blue pennon fly!
Our steeds are stamping proudly,
   They hear the battle-cry.
The thundering bomb, the bugle's call,
   Proclaim the foe is near,
We strike for God and native land,
   And all we hold most dear.
      Then spring into the saddle,
         And shake the bridle free —
      For Wharton leads thro' fire and blood,
         For Home and Victory![243]

Of course, it was only a song, for Wharton had been gone a
long time — ran afoul of Wheeler.

243. Emily V. Mason, *The Southern Poems of the War* (Baltimore: John Murphy and Company, 1867), pp. 93-95.

In the same vicinity, Captain George Knox Miller, of the Eighth Confederate Regiment, finished making out a half-dozen reports and then sat down to write his wife, who was refugeeing in Anderson County, South Carolina. Refreshed after a good night's sleep and a breakfast of biscuit and honey, with clean clothes on and even with boots blacked, Miller wrote that he had never felt better since he joined the service: ". . . I have been perfectly well for several days past, having recovered entirely from the chills and have been fortunate enough to get plenty to eat, consequently am flourishing. The papers I suppose have told you that the great Yankee raiders Stoneman and McCook have been handsomely thrashed out by Mr. Wheeler's 'entire company' and as usual are heaping praise on the undeserving. Gen. Iverson did not capture Stoneman by any of his skill or generalship but more praise is due to Col. Crews of the Geo. Brigade and Gen. Allen of the Ala. Brig. Gen. Humes & Gen. Ross it seems are the only men that were after McCook. . . . We arrived here yesterday evening and as yet I do not know what is on the carpet, but the indications are that we are preparing for a rampage — having whipped and cut up the Yankee cavalry. It may be contraband news to be put in a private document, but we are concentrating most of our cavalry in the neighborhood of Covington — which evidently means something. Lt. Col. Robinson, an artillery officer of considerable reputation in this army, has been made Brigadier and in the absence of Gen. Anderson has taken command of our Brigade. Many of my Ala. friends & acquaintances have been killed and wounded around Atlanta lately — among them Lt. W. H. Moore, formerly a member of my Co. and without exception the best young man I ever knew.

"I received a letter from Sister Cynthia this morning in which she gave me an account of the raid there but nothing else from home of special interest. Talladega is now virtually within the enemy's lines — there being no force left to protect the country. Pa has written to me for advice as to what to do and I scarcely know what to advise — I have seen so much distress among refugees that I believe it best for him to stay at home and risk the worst. It is beggary almost either way. If the Yankees were to occupy the place I expect they would take my family of negroes — if I were to run them off the trouble would probably exceed their value and I believe I'll let them stay and if they choose to go to the Yankees. I would bring Jake the father of the family in the army if it were not for separating him from his wife and children. I captured another horse from McCook's raid and am now pretty well mounted. I now have one horse with me and two off recruiting for this fall and winter campaigns. Several of my Co. have just returned from home with prest horses and Gen. Kelly said this morning I had the best mounted troop in the Brigade. I mailed a letter to you Thursday at Jonesboro — but not having heard from my Cellie since the 15th ult am becoming very anxious. I expect you have wondered what could have become of Knox — so seldom have I written lately — but it has been beyond my power and you must not become alarmed at any protracted silence for I do not know one week but what I will be in Tenn. or Ky. the next. Give my best respects to all friends — my love to all the family — likewise to the young lady who sent me hers. Write very soon and very often, and still believe me as ever most affectionately your Knox"[244]

Captain Miller didn't quite get the name of his new commander right, nor did he mention, if he knew, that that "ar-

244. Letter, George Knox Miller to his wife, August 7, 1864. Miller Papers, Southern Historical Collection, University of North Carolina.

tillery officer of considerable reputation" was very loyal to Wheeler and to old Bragg. It was enough for Chaplain Bunting, of the Eighth Texas, though, that the "artillery officer" was a Texan, and he was delighted to send the information in a letter he was preparing for the Houston *Daily Telegraph:* "Col. Felix Robertson, son of Brig. Gen. Robertson, of Texas, who so long and ably commanded Hood's old Texas Brigade in Virginia, has been promoted to a Brigadiership, and assigned to duty in the cavalry. He is a young man of distinguished gallantry, and has won for himself much glory in command of artillery. Should his life be spared, a brilliant future awaits him in his new field. . . ." Then the chaplain concluded by mentioning his own field: "Our meetings are held with much interest as circumstances permit. Rev. W. W. Hendrix, of College Grove, Tennessee, Chaplain of the 4th Tennessee, has cooperated with me. He is a most agreeable and devoted co-laborer."[245] With becoming modesty, Chaplain Bunting didn't repeat the claim about his success, that his "command enjoyed a larger spiritual blessing in souls, converted and enrolled for Christ, than any cavalry regiment in the Army of Tennessee."[246] The boys in the command certainly appreciated his efforts, for they had just presented him with a horse "for his zealous labors for their temporal and spiritual good." He may have tempered his pride in the horse by remembering the Scriptures, though; as the Psalmist says: "An horse *is* a vain thing for *safety*: neither shall he deliver *any* by his great strength."

The whole command enjoyed the loll-around. Over at Athens, Jim Black, Ninth Kentucky, noted his activities in his diary: "Answered Miss Addie's letter. Ordered back to the company. Brig. moved on the Gainesville road. Stayed

245. Bunting.
246. *The Encyclopedia of the New West,* p. 391.

in town till almost day, with the Glee Club."[247] Probably most of the Ninth went to town looking for glee — though there would be a rare one who just wanted to read. One was a fellow everybody called the Scholar because he was always working up his Greek from a book he called his *Anabasis*. One day, this other fellow said he'd rather spend his time trying to grab a kiss.

The brief resting spell came to an end, and the commands began to tighten up. Each man was issued four days' rations and fifty to sixty rounds of ammunition.[248] Although there were still men armed with Mississippi and Enfield rifles, many were pleased to be carrying the Spencer seven-shooters that had been captured from McCook's and Stoneman's men.

Then the marching orders came down from corps:

I. In the march about to commence no soldier or officer of any grade whatever will be permitted to carry any article of private property, except one single blanket and one oil-cloth.

II. The troops will be inspected daily while en route, and any additional article found upon the person or horse of any trooper or officer will be immediately destroyed.

III. The ordnance wagons, ambulances, limber-boxes, and caissons will be inspected twice each day, and the officer controlling them will be arrested, and, if practicable, immediately punished if the smallest article of private property is found being thus transported.

J. Wheeler
Major-General[249]

Well, that circular put an end to all the talk about Wheel-

247. Diary entry for August 10, 1864, James Conquest Black Papers, Southern Historical Collection, University of North Carolina.
248. Philadelphia *Inquirer*, August 26, 1864.
249. *ORR*, I, 38, pt. 5, p. 953.
250. *ORR*, I, 38, pt. 5, pp. 950-951.

er's getting the sack. In fact, the word made the rounds of the camps. probably planted by Wheeler's stick people and yellow dogs, that Hood had written to say "that he is not disappointed in the least, . . ."[250] that so much of McCook's command got away. So off we started, still led by a man that most folks thought just couldn't lead. Even in praising the victory over Stoneman and McCook, most papers didn't let up on Wheeler; the Augusta *Chronicle* opined: "The cavalry of General Hood's army has had a fine opportunity to display its mettle during the recent raids, and right well has it been improved. It has exhibited splendid prowess, and high capabilities, which give promise of brilliant achievement in the future. It has shown greater efficiency than ever before. It is now the worthy rival of the victorious cavalry of Virginia, whose deeds of daring and valor it has successfully imitated. The people owes to it a debt of gratitude, for the protection it has given Middle Georgia against the marauding raiders of the enemy. Their gratitude and applause are unstinted. The praises of the gallant and glorious cavalry of the army of Georgia, are on every tongue.

"New leaders have appeared on the field among whom the gallant Iverson, Roddey, Jackson, and Williams are conspicuous. . . ."[251] But not a word for Wheeler.

Our force of about forty-five hundred men had the following organization:

Martin's Division

Allen's Brigade	Iverson's Brigade
1st Alabama, Lt.-Col. David T. Blakey	1st Georgia, Col. Samuel W. Davitte

250. *ORR*, I, 38, pt. 5, pp. 950-951.

251. Augusta *Chronicle*, August 13, 1864, quoted in Richmond *Enquirer*, August 19, 1864.

Allen's Brigade (cont'd)

3rd Alabama, Col James Hagan
4th Alabama, Col. Alfred A. Russell
7th Alabama, Capt. George Mason
51st Alabama, Col. Milton L. Kirk-
  patrick
12th Alabama Battalion, Col. Warren S. Reese

Iverson's Brigade (cont'd)

2nd Georgia, Col. Charles C. Crews
3rd Georgia, Col. Robert Thompson
4th Georgia, Col. Isaac W. Avery
6th Georgia, Col. John R. Hart

Humes' Division

Ashby's Brigade

1st Tennessee, Col. James T.
  Wheeler
2nd Tennessee, Capt. William M.
  Smith
5th Tennessee, Col. George W.
  McKenzie
9th Tennessee Battalion, Maj. James
  H. Akin

Harrison's Brigade

3rd Arkansas, Col. Anson W. Hobson
4th Tennessee, Lt.-Col. Paul F.
  Anderson
8th Texas, Lt.-Col. Gustave Cook
11th Texas, Col. George R. Reeve

Kelley's Division

Robertson's Brigade

3rd Confederate, Lt.-Col. John Mc-
  Caskill
8th Confederate, Lt.-Col. John S.
  Prather
10th Confederate, Capt. W. J. Vason
12th Confederate, Capt. Charles H.
  Conner
5th Georgia, Col. Edward Bird

Dibrell's Brigade

4th Tennessee, Col. William S. Mc-
  Lemore
8th Tennessee, Capt. Jefferson
  Leftwich
9th Tennessee, Capt. James M.
  Reynolds
10th Tennessee, Maj. John Minor
11th Tennessee, Col. Daniel W.
  Holman

Hannon's Brigade

53rd Alabama, Lt.-Col. John F.
  Gaines

Williams' Brigade

1st Kentucky, Col. J. R. Butler
2nd Kentucky, Maj. Thomas W.
  Lewis

Hannon's Brigade (cont'd)

Williams' Brigade (cont'd)

24th Alabama Battalion, Maj. Robert B. Snodgrass

9th Kentucky, Col. William C. P. Breckinridge
2nd Kentucky Battalion, Capt. John B. Dortch
Allison's (Tennessee) Squadron and Hamilton's (Tennessee) Squadron, Maj. Joseph Shaw

Artillery

Freeman-Huggins Battery[252]

Although the boys didn't have any confidence in Wheeler, they felt pretty good about the division and brigade commanders. The oldest division commander was Will T. Martin, a Major-General.[253] At that time Martin was forty-one, old enough to have had a career before the war; he was a successful lawyer in Natchez. He served first in the Army of Northern Virginia, and received his Brigadier's rank when he was ordered to the Western army. It was pretty commonly known that he shared Forrest's view of Wheeler. Folks said that he blamed Wheeler for the defeat that he had suffered in June, 1863, in Tennessee, and that when he requested a court of inquiry to clear himself, Bragg told him that no blame attached to him.[254] His men liked him, but didn't care much for his brigade commanders, Iverson and Allen. Brigadier-General Alfred Iverson, aged thirty-two, also came west from the Virginia army, but the rumor was that

252. *ORR*, I, 38, pt. 3, p. 673.

253. Ezra J. Warner, *Generals in Gray* (Baton Rouge: Louisiana State University Press, 1959), p. 214.

254. Letter, General William T. Martin to Miss Ellen Martin, July 19, 1863.

his transfer was because of Lee's dissatisfaction with his behavior at Chancellorsville and Gettysburg.[255] Brigadier-
General William Wirt Allen, aged twenty-nine, seemed a good
enough leader, for his men performed[256] well at Sunshine
Church. But they didn't seem to care for him, particularly.

The second division commander was Brigadier-General
William Y. C. Humes, thirty-four, of Tennessee. Before the
war he was a lawyer in Memphis. He was always in artillery
and was Wheeler's chief of artillery before he became a division commander. His boys felt that Humes was a little too
excitable and dependent on Wheeler, but beyond that he
seemed acceptable enough.[257] One of his brigade commanders was Colonel Thomas Harrison, "Iron Sides" to his men,
a forty-three year old Texan, who had one of the best
known outfits in the cavalry service, with such regiments
as the Third Arkansas, Fourth Tennesse ("Paul's People"),
and Eighth Texas ("Terry's Texas Rangers"). The other
brigade, a Tennessee bunch, was commanded by Colonel
Henry M. Ashby. Although only twenty-four years old at
the time, Colonel Ashby was completely trusted by his men,
who were fiercely loyal to him. He had had his right heel
shot off in a skirmish up in Kentucky a couple of years
before, so that he had to favor it and had some difficulty
in walking. But it didn't bother his riding, and he was known
as one of the best horsemen in the Army of Tennessee.[258]

The other division commander was Brigadier-General John

255. Warner, pp. 378-379.

256. Letter, Isaac Barton Ulmer to his mother, September 10,
1864. Isaac Barton Ulmer Papers, Southern Historical Collection,
University of North Carolina.

257. John Coffee Williamson, "The Civil War Diary of John
Coffee Williamson," *Tennessee Historical Quarterly*, XV (March, 1956),
61; see also *ORR*, I, 38, pt. 5, p. 971.

258. Coffin, 121.

H. Kelly,[259] of Alabama. He became the youngest general officer in the army when he was appointed, in November, 1863. Now he was an old man of twenty-four, universally admired by his men as a gallant leader. He may not have been that well liked by Wheeler, though, for he had signed Pat Cleburne's petition for the enlistment of blacks, and Wheeler certainly was opposed to that policy.[260]

Kelly's brigade commanders were a mixed lot. The oldest was Brigadier-General John Stuart Williams, aged forty-six, who loved to be called "Cerro Gordo" in honor of his exploits at that battle in the Mexican War, but who was affectionately called "Old Pap" by his men. He was a huge man, tipping in at better than three hundred pounds, who cussed fiercely and drank with rare enthusiasm.[261] The saying was that he had been half of the first fight of the war: back in 1860 he had gotten into a fist fight with Richard J. Oglesby, on election night, up in Illinois.[262] Oglesby became a Yank general, but the two men had not had an opportunity to resume their fight.

Although Williams had been a brigadier since early '62, he had not had much of a career.[263]. He got drunk during a battle in the fall of '63, at Blue Springs, Tennessee, and had to be superseded by a Colonel Giltner.[264] Williams asked to be relieved and came to Georgia, where he was given a new command. Adjutant Will Allen, of the Fifth Tennessee, told us about his commander, Colonel George McKenzie, getting

259. Warner, p. 168.

260. DuBose, p.. 258.

261. Dyer, p. 258.

262. Shelby Moore Cullom, *Fifty Years of Public Service* (Chicago: A. C. McClung and Company, 1911), p. 198.

263. Warner, p. 338.

264. George D. Ewing, "The Battle of Blue Springs, Tennessee," *Confederate Veteran*, XXX (February, 1922), 46-48.

into a quarrel with Williams during the campaign between Dalton and Atlanta. Williams' command was ordered to relieve McKenzie's men, who had been without food for more than twenty-four hours, but Williams, who was drunk, told McKenzie that he would feed his own men first. McKenzie protested and the two got into such a fierce argument that they didn't see the Yanks ride up to within three hundred yards of them and plant a battery. The two men just stood there cussing each other and when Allen told them of the battery, each started telling the other what a mess the cannons would make of him. It took two or three rounds dropping around them to convince each that he might get hurt.[265]

There was talk that "Old Pap" had been too drunk to be in the fight at Sunshine Church, but other talk that he had had the bloody flux. If so, he may have taken the whiskey as medicine.

Old Colonel McKenzie wasn't the kind of man to be faced down by "Old Pap" Williams, for he, too, had been in the Mexican War.[266] And he had a fine regiment that he was proud of; no less a man than General Forrest had said that the Fifth Tennessee had the best staying qualities on a skirmish line of any regiment under Wheeler's command. Other regiments in the corps said, though, that the Fifth's success at slowness was not because of McKenzie's training, but rather because those boys in the Fifth had been hog drovers before the war and had gotten slow-motioned in that line of work.

Another older brigade commander was George G. Dibrell,

265. William Gibbs Allen, "Breastworks Attacted [sic] — A Fight Near Oostanaula River Between Resacca and Rome," newspaper clipping in William Gibbs Allen Papers, State of Tennessee Archives.

266. Valentine C. Allen, *Rhea and Meigs Counties in the Confederate War* (Dayton, Tennessee: no publisher, 1908), pp. 92-93.

of Tennessee. A Union man to the state convention in '61, he nevertheless went along with his state when it seceded, enlisting as a private. In '62 he went behind the lines to raise the Eighth Tennessee Cavalry, which fought with Forrest's command. In July of 1863 he took over Forrest's "old brigade," after Starnes was killed.[267] The brigade was transferred from Forrest's command to Wheeler's at Dalton, but many of the men still thought of themselves as Forrest's. In early August, '64, camp talk was that Colonel Dibrell had been nominated as a Brigadier on July 26, but he still signed his papers "Colonel." You can see what was happening to the Army of Tennessee by using the Eighth Tennessee as an example: Colonel Dibrell said it mustered in, in September, 1862, at nine hundred twenty-one men; in August, 1864, it boasted one hundred forty mounted and ready for duty.[268]

A full generation younger was Felix H. Roberston, the son of old "Polly" Robertson, a Brigadier in the Virginia army. Young Robertson, known as "Comanche"[269] because of his looks and actions, was to have graduated from West Point in '61, when he was twenty-two, but resigned and came south. He was commissioned in the Regular Army as a Second Lieutenant, but he seems always to have been ready to oblige Bragg and Wheeler, hence his rise was rapid. He took over Wheeler's artillery in January, 1864, and was nominated a Brigadier the following July. As we began our expedition he replaced R. H. Anderson, who was disabled by the wound he had received at Newnan.

Milton L. Hannon had that little brigade of Alabamians, but I didn't and don't to this day know anything about him.

267. Mark Mayo Boatner, *The Civil War Dictionary* (New York: D. McKay Company, 1959), p. 239.
268. Lindsley, p. 669.

IV

Cherokee Georgia: "tearing up a railroad"

(August 10-17, 1864)

𝒯 hose of us that had been camped around Covington moved up through Lawrenceville, while Williams' Kentucky Brigade headed north from Athens, towards Gainesville. The weather was as hot as you'd expect for August in Cherokee Georiga, with just enough rain to keep the air close and smothery all the time. We kept looking for cits, forage, and crops, but didn't find any; we later discovered that the cits had been driven four miles away from the State road on each side.[272] Since we had been de-

272. Hoehling, p. 351.

pending on green corn for forage, our horses began to suffer
by the end of the first day out. And we couldn't stray off
the road, to find forage, for our whole plan had to be to
move fast, wherever we might be going.

BROWN'S BRIDGE
AUGUST 11

By Thursday night, August 11th, the front units got to
Brown's Bridge, on the Chattahoochee. The main body got
there by noon the next day, and brigade orders were issued
that sent Hannon off toward Marietta and the other commands by different roads to Frogtown, on the Hightowa
River.[273] Commissary Sergeant John Coffee Williamson,
of Company E, Fifth Tennessee, recorded the events of
that day like this: "We started very early and did not march
so fast as yesterday. We got to Brown's Bridge about 12
o'clock — here Kit gave out and I swapt for Rosenantee
from an old citizen that had come to mill. I gave Jake Milburn a call and found him badly pestered — the boys had
taken two horses from him and left two rips in their place.
Milburn looks well and his family all look promising. Milburn and his wife and children came to the road to see the
cavalry and the boys made remarks about his size. Here we
struck one of the Federal roads and came on to Frog Town
and camped. I got a good nap but nothing [for] [Rosenant]
to eat."[274]

273. *ORR,* I, 38, pt. 5, pp. 958-959.
274. Williamson, 62.

FROG TOWN
AUGUST 13

On Saturday, August 13th, it rained most of the day — a dreary day for dreary business. The cits complained to Kelly's Division, which was in the lead, about being pestered by bushwhackers and deserters. So every time a hard character was spotted, he'd be caught or shot if he ran. Those that were caught were hanged and left hanging. A good many of the boys would agree with O. P. Hargis, coming up behind in Martin's Division and spotting the swaying bodies: "It was a bad looking sight."[275] But John Coffee Williamson had something else to think about: "We started at about an hour by sun and crossed the Etowah at a private ford and came on into the Coosawatee Mountains and our scouts caught two deserters and killed one and hanged the other. During the day 7 were killed. It rained most of the day. The road was rough and my horse fell with me in Talking Rock Creek and I lost my saddle bags. I got very wet."[276] During the day Martin's Division was detached, to take a short route, then hit the railroad at Tilton.

DALTON
AUGUST 14

Kelly's Division, still in the lead, got up on August 14th to a hot and rainy morning and decided to break the Sab-

275. O. P. Hargis, "We Kept Fighting and Falling Back," *CWT Illustrated*, VII (December, 1968), 37.

276. Williamson, 62.

277. Garrett and Lightfoot, p. 31.

278. Diary Entry for August 14, 1864, William Sloan Diary, State of Tennessee Archives, typescript, p. 74.

bath, so they mounted up at 7:00 a.m., to ride the twenty
miles, to attack Dalton.[277]. Humes' Division was back at
Carter's Quarters, where there were enough watermelons
for everybody, so they lazed a little.[278] Some of the boys
in the Fifth Tennessee had relations in the neighborhood,
so they went visiting for a spell. John Coffee Williamson
was such a one: "I started from camp very early and took
breakfast at Abe Johnson's. I stopped at old Cape's and saw
George Grady's wife. I came on into Murray County and
found many people very glad to see us coming. The bushwhackers are having everything their own way, and are taking
any kind of property that they want and dividing it among
themselves. I visited father's and found all well. The Yanks
had not mistreated him. Passed through Spring Place and
found things in a very dilapidated condition. Came on to
Conasauga River and fed Rosenant. He turns out to be a
better horse than I had thought for."[279]

Both of Kelly's brigades, Dibrell's and Robertson's, went
into Dalton by the Spring Place road and hit the Yank pickets about 4:00 p.m. Kelly's boys could see lots of running
about as they rode in; there seemed to be a half a dozen
trains headed one way or the other, and by then the firemen
could be seen just slinging the chunks of wood into the
fire boxes, while Yanks with guns were jumping out of the
trains and running toward the depot and Yanks without
guns, that maybe had got off to stretch and get something
from a sutler, were mostly limping and crutching to get
back on the cars. But, instead of fanning out and blocking
the up and down tracks, Kelley's boys were ordered to
dismount and form a skirmish line, with each fourth as

279. Williamson, 62.

Route, August 10-15

Brig.-Gen. William Y. C. Humes

Maj.-Gen. William T. Martin

horse-holder.[280] Those trains just got up steam and pulled out, just like there wasn't a Reb within a generation of them.

The telegraph wires hadn't even been cut yet, and you can just bet that they were being used to tell some Yank two-star up there in Chattanooga about our little surprise party.[281] But Dibrell's and Robertson's boys just stood facing off against the Yank skirmishers a couple of hundred yards away. Then Wheeler sent in a message under a flag of truce:

> HEADQUARTERS CAVALRY CORPS
> ARMY OF TENNESSEE
> "Around Dalton, August 14, 1864
>
> "OFFICER COMMANDING U.S. FORCES,
> "Dalton:
> "To prevent the unnecessary effusion of blood, I have the honor to demand the immediate and unconditional surrender of the forces under your command at this garrison.
> "Respectfully, yours, &c.
> "Jos. Wheeler
> "Major-General, Commanding"

There now; that's a proper calling card, polite and high-toned.

The reply was pure Yank talk:

> "OFFICER COMMANDING CONFEDERATE FORCES IN FRONT OF DALTON:
> "I have been placed here to defend this post, but not to surrender.
> "B. Laiboldt
> "Colonel Second Missouri Volunteers
> "Commanding Post"[282]

280.   "Q.P.F.," New York *Times,* August 26, 1864.
281.   "Dr. Adonis," "Facts and Fancies from the Sunny South," Louisville *Journal,* August 23, 1864.
282.   *ORR,* I, 38, pt. 1, p. 323. Laiboldt's Report.
283.   Nashville *Daily Press and Times,* August 23, 1864.

The word that came back with the flag was that the Second Missouri wasn't about to surrender — its time was too nearly out.[283]

General Wheeler sent his flag back in again to request a personal meeting with Laiboldt, whom he knew from previous engagements in Tennessee, or, failing that, to inform Laiboldt that he had sixty second to surrender. Either Laiboldt didn't have a watch or he didn't care to be sociable, for the minute came and went.[284] So a skirmish line was left, while Dibrell's men were sent around below town and Robertson's Brigade was stretched across the railroad going north.[285]

By then Humes' Division was coming into town, and Chaplain Bunting was aware of how much had changed since the winter before, when Dalton was Confederate: "Approaching that place we see rows of deserted cabins, all surrounded by high weeds. They were the winter-quarters of the Army of Tennessee. Once they were full of bustle and life, but now quiet reigns in the cabin-village. It is late in the evening, and an enchanting scene is around us. In the front is Taylor's ridge, which lies beyond Dalton. Here, in full view, is 'Dug Gap,' where Granbury's Texas Brigade ambuscaded the advancing foe, and inflicted such dreadful chastisement upon him. Just over it the sun was quietly going down to rest in his chariot of gold, shedding such a radiant glory from his glowing wheels that the western horizon was lit up in the most gorgeous colors, until the view was magnificently glorious beyond description. Then far away to the eastward, as we gazed back, the green hills were bathed in a dark silvery shade, the mingled reflection

284.   ORR, I, 38, pt. 1, p. 324. Laiboldt's Report.
285.   "Osceola," "Wheeler's Raid — Letter from Osceola," Atlanta Intelligencer, October 21, 1864.

of the departing light and the approaching night. It was beautiful exceedingly! Looking upon such a panorama of blended loveliness and glory in nature, we almost forgot that we're engaged in scenes of war and death. Soon the sharp crack of the Minnie broke the pleasant reverie, and we are in front of Dalton."[286]

The Yanks had put out a few horsemen as skirmishers, coming toward our two dismounted brigades, and when Humes' Division came up, it was sent forward to attend to the Yanks. Those old boys, it turned out to be a part of the Tory Seventh Kentucky, fought like sore-headed bears. One fellow wouldn't surrender, instead emptied his pistols, and then clubbed one of Humes' boys up the side of the head. Four of the Reb's buddies then lost their patience and stuck their pistols right into the Yank's gut and pulled out, yelling, "God damn you, we'll make you surrender.!"[287] The rest of the Yanks had skeetered back across that field like it was a greased skillet, by then. It turned out that that feisty fellow was named Joe Morelock and that he had been a Reb back in the early days of the war; he must have decided that if he was taken in, he was bound to be recognized by somebody and shot then, so he might as well chance it then and there.

The artillery still hadn't come up, but we were quickly running out of daylight.[288] Dibrell was ordered to send his skirmishers forward, to put a little more pressure on the Yank skirmishers. But when he gave the order to the skirmishers the whole Tennessee Brigade thought it was for them, so they up and charged, with old Elbert Peacock, the brigade

286. Bunting.
287. Nashville *Daily Press and Times,* August 23, 1864.
288. Osceola.

color-bearer, out in front.[289] Dibrell, joined by General Kelly, rode ahead and tried to stop the charge. But the Tennesseans must have decided that this was the only way that they'd get to prowl that town, so they just kept right on going. General Kelly must have seen that they *meant* to go, for he finally stood up in his stirrups and swung his sword and shouted at the top of his voice, "Forward, my brave Tennesseans!"[290] He might have added "hungry" and still been truthful.

Over on the Tennesseans' left the Confederate Brigade found their behavior catching, so it charged, too, right past Colonel McCaskill, commanding the Third Confederate, who doubled up and dropped, as he took a ball in the entrails. We pushed them right out of town to a place where they had breastworks, and inside there were two houses, a large brick one used by General Hood as headquarters a few months before and a large white frame one used by General Bates. We would have chased them right up the chimneys of those houses — if we hadn't been recalled. We started withdrawing, and the Yanks, having heard the order to pull back, really poured it to us.[291] The Tennesseans, thinking it was General Kelly's order, really started yelling and wanting to know what in hell was going on. But the order came from General Wheeler, who said that he had accomplished his objective, to take the town and then break the road, and that if he could trade one man for the entire Yank garrison he wouldn't trade, for he couldn't keep the Yanks anyhow.[292] Later there was talk that he was angry

289. C. L. Nolen, "Dibrell's Old Flag was not Surrendered," *Confederate Veteran*, XIV (November, 1906), 510.
290. "Osceola."
291. Lindsley, p. 669.
292. "Osceola."

that the attack had occured in the first place; we wouldn't
have been surprised, for he was angry at General Martin for
not coming up with his command from Tilton, as he was
supposed to.[293]

Right about that time the artillery finally came up. Wheeler sent a flag of truce in to tell Laiboldt that he'd better
surrender before those guns could get planted.[294] But Laiboldt fired on the flag, as he had said that he would. So
the artillery blammed away.

By then the boys didn't care:

> "Theirs not to reason how,
> Theirs but to fight and prowl."

And prowl they did. We went through that town like a
plauge, even though the Yank grape and cannister was
dropping on the iron roof of the depot like a hail storm.[295]
We got into the commissary and sutler stores and found
something for everybody. There was a ration of oats for the
horses, which had been living mostly on grass, and soft corn
if it could be found.[296] There was milk in cans;[297] will you
feature that, those Yanks had learned how to take milk
out of skin and put it in tin. That was the future! But many
of the boys were much more interested in the present, so,
as Stephen Jordan, of the Ninth Tennessee, noted, "Boys
got on a bender, . . ."[298] General Robertson was much more

293. *ORR*, I, 38, pt. 5, p. 489; *ORR*, I, 38, pt. 3, pp. 957-958.
Wheeler's Report.

294. *ORR*, I, 38, pt. 1, p. 325.

295. William Gibbs Allen, "Incidents of Wheeler's Raid," *Confederate Veteran*, XIX (June, 1911), 288.

296. Ben W. Darsey, *A War Story* (Statesboro, Georgia: News
Print [1901?]), unpaginated but containing twenty-three pages of text.

297. DuBose, p. 384.

298. Garrett and Lightfoot, p. 31.

discreet: ". . . the town furnished whiskey sufficient to create confusion. . . ."[299]

The artillery continued just enough to disturb the Yanks'
sleep; it didn't seem to be having any other effect. The
Yanks, for their part, kept trying to pick off the boys when
they would step into the light of a burning building. Pretty
quickly the quartermaster and sutler stocks were parcelled
out, so that the different commands were willing to leave
the town. The Texas Rangers went on picket up toward
Dug Gap,[300] and many units went to work ripping up the
railroad. The usual method was to prize up the rails, drape
them over a pile of ties, and then fire the ties; the heat would
bend the rails and their own weight would twist them out of
shape. Even so, it was not a job that you'd clamor for; as
Ben Darsey, of the Fifth Georgia observed, "Tearing up
a railroad is no easy job for a fellow inexperienced in the
business."[301]

MILL CREEK GAP
AUGUST 15

Nobody got much sleep that night, though we knew that
we ought to, for the next day would be busy. Those trains
that ran wild up to Chattanooga would be returning — with
more people, of which there seems to be no end, as the
Preacher says in *Ecclesiastes*. When morning came, this would
be Monday, August 15th, we had a most interesting breakfast. Having stuffed our haversacks with bacon, crackers,
coffee, and sugar, we ate what we couldn't carry away —

299. Letter, Felix H. Robertson to Braxton Bragg, October 6,
1864, in Bragg Papers, Houghton Library, Harvard University.
300. Bunting.
301. Darsey.

preserved fruits, pickels, even oysters.[302] The fare didn't seem to go together too well, but there were no complaints that we heard of.

Before we could even brush off our mustaches and start sucking our teeth, the sound of pop and skirmish could be heard up near Mill Creek Gap, where the Eighth Texas and Fifth Tennessee were on picket.[303] Pretty soon the word came back: it looked like about four regiments of Yank infantry, one fanned out as skirmishers, and three bunched up behind them, and, by God, the one on our right was black![304] If that didn't take the cake! We had never faced smoked Yanks before, because Sherman wouldn't have them in his army. But we had heard that Banks was using them up in Virginia, and we all knew that Forrest had killed off a bunch of negro troops at Fort Pillow, out on the Mississippi above Memphis.

Well, we had no time to think about it then. That number of Yank infantry was too much for us to handle; they had come down during the night on the cars, and there was no telling how many more might be flanking us right now. The order came for our wagon train to get moving, and it didn't have to be repeated for the hard of hearing. Those wagoners started whipping their teams like they were possessed.[305]

The thing was, now, to give the wagon train a little start, so our skirmishers were kept out. For William Sloan, of the Fifth Tennessee, that day would always be remembered with a shudder: "A large body of yankee infantry came out from Chattanooga and drove in our pickets at Buzzard Roost,

302. Bunting.
303. Williamson, 62.
304. *ORR*, I, 38, pt. 1, pp. 619-620. Sirwell's Report.
305. Lindsley, p. 803.

and our regiment was ordered out on foot to hold them in check until our wagon train could get away. We fought them some time, but at length they charged us with a heavy line and drove us back. We were in a most unfavorable position for a retreat, it being a long slope in our rear, for more than a mile, and the enemy had us in complete range, with artillery and infantry, for that distance. It was raining at the time and the ground was so muddy that it was a task to pull our feet out of the mud, for which reason some of our men surrendered, and part of them were barbarously murdered by some negro troops, after they had surrendered. I came very near surrendering myself, and had I done so it is more than probable that I would have been murdered. I was so exhausted that I could scarcely drag one foot after the other, and I got so far behind my comrades that the enemy fired a number of artillery shells at myself alone, as I was all the time in plain view of his battery. At last I dragged myself over the top of a small hill out of the enemy's view, and found our regiment in line of battle on horseback, and I scarcely had strength left to mount my horse."[306]

It was a sight, the way those negroes acted. From prisoners we learned that they were the Fourteenth Colored and had been stationed up in Chattanooga, pulling fatigue duty for some months.[307] They had become real smart with their drill, you know, just like a minstrel show, with all that natural ease, and held parade for everybody from General Thomas to the Irish washerwoman every afternoon. But nobody much had expected them to fight. When they faced off against the Eighth Texas and Fifth Tennessee, though, they acted like veterans. They took fire without flinching

306. Sloan, p. 74.

307. Henry Romeyn, "With Colored Troops in the Army of the Cumberland," MOLLUS – DC, *War Papers,* Number 51, p. 13.

and obeyed the order not to fire. Once in a while, one could be heard saying, "Kernel, mayn't I shoot? I think I can fetch one."[308] But they didn't fire, or even move, until ordered. The boys said it was *close,* down there in the hog weeds, between those old huts, in the rain. At the start of their advance, the negroes had seemed a little unsure of what to do. The first prisoner they took, they didn't know what to do with him, and they asked a white officer. The answer was, "Kill him." After that they shot or bayonetted every Reb that slipped in the mud, all the while yelling, "Remember Fort Pillow!"[309]

That hour was a bad time, and the boys didn't soon forget the blacks. All in all, our little stop at Dalton for crackers and cheese cost us about ninety killed and wounded[310] left behind with Surgeon William A. Mulkey, who no doubt got to spend the winter at Camp Chase.[311] Our outlook, though, was just like the weather; a mile or so outside of Dalton, back on the Spring Place road, it hadn't rained at all, and the boys brightened up, happy and relieved to be mounted and moving again. They began pulling some of their treats out of their haversacks and snacking on them. Up in the column, in the Confederate Brigade, General Robertson and the others were laughing at Colonel McCaskill, who had only been hit by a spent ball the day before that had just made a big black bruise on his belly. He had prowled a fancy

308. New York *Tribune,* August 25, 1864.

309. "A Soldier Who Knows," Monroe [Michigan] *Commercial,* September 1, 1864; William R. Hartpence, *History of the Fifty-First Veteran Volunteer Infantry* (Cincinnati: The Robert Clark Company, 1894), pp. 218-220.

310. "Q.P.F.;" Edwin W. High, *History of the Sixty-Eighth Regiment Indiana Volunteer Infantry* (Metamora, Indiana: no publisher, 1902), p. 180.

311. Richmond *Enquirer,* October 19, 1864.

dressing gown in town, probably from some Yank officer's billet, and was wearing it gaped open, with nothing else on, to show off his bruise.[312] In that get-up, he looked just like a madam along Smokey Row, up in Nashville, welcoming some new boys to her establishment.

It was almost like a lark. One old boy from Doane's Mill, Alabama, by the name of Grove, said, "My, my. A body does get around. Here we ain't been coming from Georgia but a week, and now it's already Tennessee." Everybody just had to laugh at such a good-natured fellow. If he lives he'll no doubt pass on his fondness for traveling to his descendants. He just rode along, sucking sourdeen juice off his fingers, hoping to see the elephant.

BENTON
AUGUST 16

We rode back to Spring Place. Humes' Division took the lead and traveled forty-two miles before going into camp at dawn, on August 16th, near Benton.[313] Since Kelly's Division had gotten the rough end of the stuck at Dalton, it stayed with Wheeler, who set up his headquarters at Spring Place.[314] Williams' Kentucky Brigade had come up by now, and it was sent up the Spring Place road to hit Red Clay and Graysville.[315] Wheeler also selected six detachments of thirty men each to stay behind and continue disrupting the Yank railroad.[316] These units were taken from Martin's Division,

312. Felix H. Robertson, "On Wheeler's Last Raid in Middle Tennessee," *Confederate Veteran*, XXX (September, 1922), 335.
313. Bunting.
314. Darsey.
315. Black, p. 23.
316. Dodson, pp. 250-251.

which had rejoined the column.[317] The talk was that Wheeler and Martin were building toward a real blow-out: Martin didn't trust Wheeler's judgment, and Wheeler didn't think that he got full support from Martin.

The rest of the command left Spring Place on the morning of the 16th. Before leaving, Wheeler sent back a slightly stretchy report to General Shoup, who was Hood's newly appointed Chief of Staff:

"General: Colonel Thompson destroyed railroad near Big Shanty for one mile on Friday night. Colonel Hannon, commanding brigade, destroyed the railroad near Calhoun on Saturday night, capturing 1,020 beef-cattle and a few wagons. Allen's brigade and Humes' and Kelly's divisions destroyed the railroad for several miles between Resaca and Tunnel Hill, and Kelly's and parts of Humes' commands captured Dalton Sunday evening with a considerable amount of stores, 3 trains of cars, and 200 fine mules. The train and part of the stores were destroyed and the remainder appropriated.

"Prisoners report-re-enforcements at Chattanooga, said to be part of A. J. Smith's troops. On Monday morning we were attacked by General Steedman with about 4,000 infantry, and obliged to leave Dalton. Our entire loss up to this time about 30, most of them still with the command.

"The most violent rains have embarrassed me very much, and made some of the roads very bad. The large force sent from Chattanooga prevented our working at the tunnel. I have several parties still working at the railroad.

"Respectfully, your obedient servant,"[318]

On ahead, Humes' Division had gotten up in the neighborhood that many of Ashby's Tennesseans came from, and a

317. Hargis, "We Kept Fighting and Falling Back," 38.
318. ORR, I, 38, pt. 5, p. 967.

good many of them sought out friends and relations. There were reasons to be shocked, as John Coffee Williamson found out: "Daylight found us near Benton, Tenn., feeding Cal Hood's corn. I took breakfast with Sol Summey. Everybody has taken the oath and all seem to avoid the Rebels — very different from three years ago. At 10 o'clock we took up the line of march for the Savannah old farm. On the way I met General Gamble and he seemed glad to see me. The boys had prowled some horses from him and he thought that they were Yankees and had come out to get pay for them. I called on P. B. Mayfield but got poor comfort from him. He has taken the oath, and that accursed oath defiles all good society. A good woman gave me a pair of socks but told me not to tell it to anyone so as the Yanks would find it out. We came on to the Savannah and camped and had plenty of feed. All of the home guards have run off to the mountains and to Cleveland."[319]

Probably most of the guards hightailed it for the mountains, for that section was one of the trashiest places in all creation, and that's just where a bunch of homemade Yanks would come from. Benton is the county seat of Polk County, which was a part of the Cherokee Purchase; but the meaty part of the County, away from Benton, is over the mountains — Starr's Mountain, Little Frog, and Big Frog — and beyond, Greasy Creek, where lie Duck Town and Turkle Town.

Before the big copper boom at Duck Town, that whole section was a hotbed of unemployment and lawlessness, for the high sheriff couldn't very well get in and they sure weren't coming out. But then a law was passed that a witness at a trial got seventy-five cents a day and four cents a mile; that changed things by building up an admirable community

319. Williamson, 62.

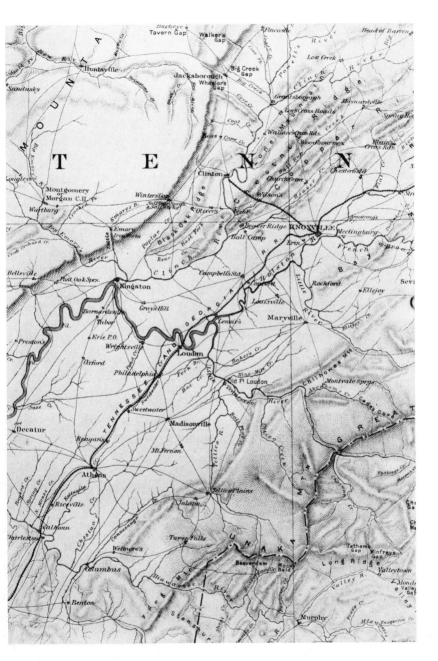

Route, August 16-26

Bridge at Strawberry Plains

spirit: on a certain day, some of the boys would be delegated to be the "fighters" and the rest would be lined up around them to be "witnesses." Then off they'd all go across the mountains to Benton, some to be charged and the others to get their Witness Tickets.

This kind of law-abiding would soon enough have put old Polk County in the red. Fortunately, there was a brave and far-seeing judge, whose eloquent plea to a wise grand jury motivated it to rescind the Witness Ticket law: "Gentlemen, before closing, I must impress upon your minds the threatening bankruptcy of our county. If there is not an immediate stop — a crushing extinguisher — put to these Duck Town rows and theatricals, they will bankrupt your county. It is with them a most profitable speculation. They are making more money by these rows than they ever did by their industry — they are growing fat at the business. They are, gentlemen, a singular people, and no wonder, for they live in an eccentric region. And right here, gentlemen, a myth in regard to Duck Town and its environs comes up to my mind with great distinctness, which I will relate before I suggest to you what course to pursue. I cannot tell you whether the myth is Egyptian, Assyrian, Persian, Grecian, Roman, Scandinavian or Indian, but here is what it relates, you can have it for what it is worth: 'The Gods finished the job of creation in the regions of Duck Town, and having some surplus mud on their fingers, in a fit of good humor at being through with their labors, at a given signal, they threw the mud off their fingers and shouted, BE THOU DUCK TOWN! and it stood forth as you now behold it.' I now charge you, gentlemen, to let these people fight on, if they choose, and pay no attention to them, unless some one is killed."[320]

320. "Skitt," "Duck Town," *Southern Literary Messenger,* XXI (November, 1860), 340-341.

William Sloan was another local fellow, who found it painful to be so close and yet so far: "At home once more. I arrived at home this morning at two oclock and found the family well, which consists of our Dear Pa and Ma and two little brothers, Wisner and Nevins. They are having a lonely time here with the enemy around them, and have a hard time to live, as they are robbed by the vandals every time they are known to have any thing on hand to eat. I only remained with them a few minutes, and then continued with my company on a scout through the mountains. We crossed Ocoee River at Haskins' Ford, and moved down the north side of the river to the Helderbrand Ford on the old Federal Road, and encamped. Thirty men of the Ninth Tenn. Battalion are here on picket duty. This is only three miles from my home, yet I dare not go home to stop over night for fear of the prowling enemy hid about the neighborhood. All of our men who can do so in safety are visiting their home."[321]

SAVANNAH

AUGUST 17

All day long on August 17th, Humes' Division stayed in camp at Savannah old farm, where the old Indian town used to be, on the Hiwassee River. Harrison's Brigade of Texans and Arkansans spent the day washing their clothes and cooking rations for the time when orders came to be moving on.[322] The commissaries were sent out to the neighborhood mills, to get flour for those rations. Many of Ashby's men were trying to get home for just a while; Colonel George

321. Sloan, p. 75.
322. Bunting.

McKenzie, of the Fifth Tennessee, took three companies on a "scout" to Meigs County,[323] but what do you want to bet that they somehow wound up at home?

Wheeler brought the boys in Kelly's Division on up directly toward Cleveland. He sent the Ninth Tennessee, of Dibrell's Brigade, ahead, and those boys rode all night and took Athens without any resistance.[324] They burned the depot and tore up the track to keep any down trains from coming to the support of Cleveland when Wheeler attacked it. Then they robbed the town. Sam Brown, a local boy, was with Captain Reynold's boys, and he guided them from door to door, taking up a collection of greenbacks and other valuables.[325] The boys called the collection a "burnt offering," for if they didn't get an offering, that particular house might get burnt. They also hung a couple of deserters that they flushed out.

Meanwhile Wheeler was bringing the rest of the division up to Cleveland. About noon they drove in the pickets and pretty soon after that began to draw artillery fire in return. Wheeler then tried the old bluff game, for he sent in a message by flag of truce:

"HEADQUARTERS CAVALRY CORPS
August 17, 1864

"OFFICER COMMANDING U.S. FORCES,
"Cleveland, Tenn.
"I desire to know if you intend compelling me to shell the town?
"Respectfully, your obedient servant,

"Jos. Wheeler
"Major-General, C. S. Army"

323. Williamson, 63.
324. Garrett and Lightfoot, p. 31.
325. Cincinnati *Daily Commercial*, August 31, 1864.

After a while, the flag of truce came back with a message from the crusty old regular army officer who was commanding:

"HEADQUARTERS U. S. FORCES
"Cleveland, Tenn., August 17, 1864

"Maj. Gen JOSEPH WHEELER,
"C. S. Army:
"GENERAL: In reply to your note just received, I have to say that I have no objection to your shelling the town.
    Very respectfully, your obedient servant,

"H. G. GIBSON
"Capt. Third U. S. Artillery and
"Col. Second Ohio Heavy Artillery"[326]

The good colonel turned out to be a wily old geezer. We tried all afternoon to work around behind him, but he seemed to have just enough cavalry, the Tory Sixteenth Kentucky it turned out, to foil us. Then, just as soon as it was dusky dark, and before the full moon was up, he pulled back into a fort, which had artillery that commanded the whole town. All we could do was to tear up the tracks at either end of town and move on.[327]

The talk was that Wheeler was testy all day, and not just about being euchred by the Yank commander at Cleveland. Maybe the "War Baby" had the colic? Or the traveler's lament, for we had been on the road a week now, with a good deal of green corn to eat. We suspected that he was getting ready to cross the Tennessee River and that he wanted the command to tighten up. But Martin's Division was still back down toward Spring Place, serving as rear guard. And Wheeler must have thought that Humes was too

326. *ORR,* I, 38, pt. 2, pp. 743-745.
327. Diary Entry for August 17, 1864, Myra Inman Diary, Southern Historical Collection, University of North Carolina.

far off to the east and had therefore fired off a hot note
to him, for he got this reply on Wednesday night:

"Headquarters Humes' Cavalry Division
"Savannah Farm, 9.15

"Maj. W. E. Wailes, Assistant Adjutant General

"Major: I regret very much that by my march to this place, which
was made in obedience to orders, I have incurred the displeasure of
the major-general commanding. I regret also that neither your dispatch nor the courier who bore it gives me any information of the
whereabouts of General Wheeler. A scout from Athens reports thirty-
seven men at that place. Citizens report a small force at Charleston,
and a concentration of forces from Knoxville and Chattanooga at
Cleveland. I would be glad to be informed how long I am to wait
here for General Wheeler, and if driven from here where I may be
able probably to join him. I have been most anxious to join him.

"Very respectfully, &c.,"[328]

The boys knew that Humes had been worried, for John
Coffee Williamson noted in his diary: "Humes has been very
uneasy about Wheeler. He has not had any communication
with him since near Cleveland. He fears that Wheeler has
been entirely cut off, but Wheeler came up all right having
marched slowly from Dalton the way Humes ought to have
done. Humes is too easily excited *and marches too far.*"[329]
But that was Humes' problem; the boys just took the chance
to rest themselves and their animals. William Sloan recorded
this happy event: "I went home and spent several hours with
family. Took dinner with them, . . ."[330] And Chaplain
Bunting worked his own vineyard: "At night the bugle
sounds the Church call, and a large congregation meet and
listen with deep earnestness to the gospel message. About a
dozen bow at the close for prayer. It was a solemn scene;

328. *ORR,* I, 38, pt. 5, p. 971.
329. Williamson, 63.
330. Sloan, p. 75.

near us was the beautiful river rolling by; around us the grand old mountains, where the tory bushwhackers had their dens, perhaps then listening to our songs of praise; above us the full orbed moon, hanging out from the sky like a silver globe, now and then shaded by the passing cloud, emblematical of the chequered scenes of the soldier's life. Such events will be green spots in our memory for long years to come. 'Tis on such occasions that souls are born into the kingdom of God."[331]

331. Bunting.

V

East Tennessee: "a regular bilt frolick"

(August 18-27, 1864)

heeler sent word back to Humes to move out the next day, August 18th, and to cross the railroad at Riceville. All commands were to move toward Decatur, so that the Tennessee could be crossed at Cotton Port Ferry.[332] Preparations were accordingly made: scouts

332. *ORR,* I, 38, pt. 5, p. 592; *ORR,* I, 38, pt. 3, p. 958. Wheeler's Report.

were sent ahead to check out the condition of the river after all the recent rains; and the following circular was sent around to the various commands:

> "Division and brigade commanders with their entire staff will stand on the banks of the river and not permit a man to attempt to cross until they are satisfied his cartridge and cap boxes and ammunition are so arranged as not to get wet in crossing the river.
> "By order of Major-General Wheeler.
>
> "Wm. E. Wailes
"AAG[333]

As we rode along that day, we couldn't help getting a little excited. From the van, with the Kentucky Brigade,[334] on back, the news swept the column that Sherman was reported to be retreating from Atlanta back into the Kennesaw Mountains, so we felt that we were accomplishing something, after all. Then, too, we were getting ready to cross the river and go across Walden's Ridge into Middle Tennessee, which was home for lots of the boys and which had fond associations for the rest of the command that didn't live there. Many a boy was heard to say that he didn't plan ever to leave Middle Tennessee again. And that was the case for a good many of them. We wanted to get on, so we hardly made a pass at Charleston, even though the garrison there started firing some God-awful big guns at us that must have carried two miles.[335] We just ripped up a little track and moved on. Toward sundown, the clouds began to gather and after a while a storm broke loose that was the worst anybody in the command had ever experienced.[336] Not even the Texans claimed they had ever seen or heard tell of such a

---

333. *ORR*, I, 38, pt. 5, p. 975.
334. Black, p. 24.
335. Cincinnati *Daily Gazette*, August 27, 1864.
336. Bunting; Williamson, 63.

storm. It was like the river had been emptied out of its banks and then dumped back on us. And there was no place to get; we had to lie down and sleep in wet clothes about 10 p.m.

ATHENS
AUGUST 19

And that wasn't the worst of our tribulations with water — not since General Pharaoh and the Egyptians has any army had worse luck with it. The next morning, August 19th, we arose considerably wrinkled, clothes and skin, but still not grouchy enough to do anything rash. Then the word came down the lines where we were saddling that the Tennessee had risen ten feet and couldn't be forded anywhere below Kingston.[337] That meant several days more of living on green apples and corn. The Eighth Tennessee was in a hurry to get on home, and their scout, Captain McReynolds, said that the river could be crossed, as planned, so Colonel Dibrell requested permission, but Wheeler would not grant the request.[338]

It was "a gloomy, foggy morning," Jim Black, up in the Kentucky Brigade, noted;[339] but the day went along well with our feelings. We packed up and rode back into Athens, where the cits were right surprised to see us again. There weren't any men, save old gray beards and boys; the others were in one army or the other or were lying out in the woods to avoid conscription. The women turned out, though, and Ben Darsey, of the Fifth Georgia, Confederate Brigade, observed their behavior: "In Athens as in many places, some

337. *ORR*, I, 38, pt. 3, pp. 958-959. Wheeler's Report.
338. Lindsley, p. 669.
339. Black, p. 24.

of the ladies demonstrated their loyalty to the Confederate cause by waving their handkerchiefs, and their private Confederate flags. I could but say in my heart, God bless the women of the South! But here and there the union flag was waving as if in proud defiance."[340]

Humes' Brigade had come over from Savannah by now and pulled in behind the other commands by noon and started burning track. Colonel McKenzie came back from his little scout, in the afternoon. John Coffee Williamson got a little disgusted with its commander: "The Yanks have caught 16 of his men and the Col. narrowly escaped. They acted very imprudently — all scattered and went home. The Yanks had nothing to do but go around and catch them. Companies B, C, and I are scattered and cut off."[341] That Fifth Tennessee sure was disorganized by homecoming; William Sloan had to hustle to catch up: "A courier reported about noon that the entire corps under Wheeler moved off in the direction of Riceville yesterday. By some mistake they failed to call in the 9th Battalion pickets, and we were therefore left behind. We all started together, and crossed Hiwassee at Columbus a little before sunset; went down the river to Knox's Ferry, and took the road to Athens."[342]

In Athens that night, after the organized commands had passed on through, the rowdies that always hang around the wagon train looted the stores and homes. The merchants had tried to hide their stock by taking it home from their stores, and that only made things worse. For the rowdies only used that move as justification for entering private homes. Then the robbers rode the streets with torches, saying that the town would have to be punished for its niggardness of

340. Darsey.
341. Williamson, 63.
342. Sloan, p. 75.

spirit and hardness of heart. But wouldn't you know it, another of those cloudbursts came up and dampened the rowdies' spirits, and their riot fizzled out. The cits claimed that the storm was "providential interposition,"[343] so the local churches must have been somewhat fuller the next Sunday. By midnight Colonel McKenzie had rounded up what he could of his command, about eighty men and had borrowed about the same number from the First Tennessee.[344] Although most of the horses were broken down, the Colonel took off, to go get those boys captured by the Yanks in Meigs County, including the Colonel's son, who, like the Prodigal, had gone home a-hungering.

SWEETWATER

AUGUST 20

The rest of the column slept the slumber that comes from honest toil and a clean conscience, arising on August 20th to view a bright, clear day. The line of march was up the tracks toward Sweetwater, from which a train of Yanks had run down to skirmish with us the day before.[345] We might just gobble up some Yanks today, the boys felt. Going along, the troopers seemed lost in their private thoughts. Stephen Jordan remembered that it was his bridal day nineteen years before.[346] Jim Black was still wondering what was going on: "As yet our operations have not developed the intention of the comdg Genl."[347] Back in Athens, John Coffee Williamson, trailing the command, observed, "Our

343. Louisville *Journal*, September 3, 1864.
344. Lindsley, p. 891.
345. *ORR*, I, 38, pt. 2, pp. 736-737.
346. Garrett and Lightfoot, p. 31.
347. Black, p. 25.

boys have robbed Athens and robbed some good Southern people."[348] William Sloan caught up with the body that Williamson was with and learned what had happened to his mates: "We arrived at Athens before day-light. Our regiment is gone down on Tennessee River to Meigs County. I learn that a good many of them were captured by some yankees who were stationed on the river cutting timber, and Col. McKenzie has gone in pursuit. The men who were captured had gone home, and had appointed a place to meet before returning to the regiment. The yankees (who were mostly niggers) found out their place of meeting, and waylaid and captured them as they arrived."[349]

Chaplain Bunting lingered behind in Athens for a while, too, for he intended to get off an account of the raid to the Houston *Daily Telegraph*: "I regret not being able to write more fully by the bearer, Major S. P. Christian of the Rangers, who goes home on a short furlough. We regret to lose his valuable services to the regiment for any length of time, yet we are willing that he should have the privilege of returning to Texas for a visit. Coming out as a private in Company K, Major Christian has gained his present position by true merit. He has ever been most faithful and conscientious in the discharge of duty, and has won the confidence of officers and men by his prudence, judgment and gallantry, as displayed on numerous occasions. Amidst his duties as a soldier, he has had time to seek the salvation of his soul, and having found the pearl of great price, he returns home as a soldier of the cross. We shall await patiently his return, with the prayer that the good providence of God shall watch over and preserve him from all the perils of the

348. Williamson, 64.
349. Sloan, p. 75.

way."[350] The good Padre failed to fess up that Pat was really going to Texas to gather up deserters, as William Nicholson had written his aunt.

Like many of the others in the column, Chaplain Bunting had been picking up copies of Parson Brownlow's *Knoxville Whig and Rebel Ventilator,* which was read in East Tennessee like the Bible itself. Bunting noted for his Houston audience, "Let all our people take courage, and soon we will be free. I find that the prevailing Union element in this country utterly repudiate Lincoln and Johnson, and will vote for any man who is the Democratic Peace candidate. Brownlow, etc., represent the radicals and the minority. His vile sheet is more bloody and fiendish than ever." That day, Ben Darsey, of the Fifth Georgia, also observed the influence of that "vile sheet": "One day, while on advance guard, with instructions to have some bread cooked at Sweet Water, a small village on the Knoxville road, one of the ladies to whom we applied, readily agreed and went at it with a vim, but soon gave us to understand that she was no friend to us. It fell to my lot to do the talking, and I discovered that she, like most of the common class of East Tennesseans in talking used the adjunct 'uns' to pronouns. So our talk ran into the following:

"She said, "Weuns whipped some of youuns the other day down in Georgia.'

"'No mam,' said I, 'Weuns always whip youuns only when youuns [f]lank us by over balance in numbers.' I asked her to what point she referred.

"'At Decatur weuns whipped youuns bad.'

"I assured her that she was mistaken, for there had been no fight there except a small raiding party of yanks entered the place and my command got after them, and the yanks

350. Bunting.

ran, so we couldn't get a fight. She fully believed they had whipped us for it was in the papers, she said. I asked her for the paper containing the news. She gave it to me and I found that it was 'in the papers' sure enough. I proved to her by my companions that we were actually in the engagement referred to and that the statement in the paper was false."[351]

Just ahead of the commissaries like Ben Darsey was Martin's Division, which was the only outfit to engage the Yanks that day. Those Georgians and Alabamians had moved out early, working up the railroad toward Philadelphia, burning bridges and tracks. The Yanks came down on a train from Loudon about dawn and skirmished for about three hours.[352] Then the Yank commander, knowing that Martin might cut the track behind him and leave him with a train that had nowhere to go, put his boys on his toot-toot and took them back north.[353]

Sometime during that day Martin's Division had a little excitement of a different sort. Orders were sent to General Martin relieving him of command and placing him in arrest for disobedience of orders and disrespect to a superior officer. Various reasons floated around through the smoke of the burning tracks — some said it was because Martin's Division didn't come up promptly at Dalton, while others said that Martin had been ordered to blow up the tunnel at Tunnel Hill and failed without excuse,[354] and others said it was just bad blood between Martin and Wheeler. Most felt that the argument had been bound to come, from the time Wheeler was given Forrest's command. And, too, Martin had been somebody of note back in the Virginia army: such

351. Darsey.
352. *ORR*, I, 38, pt. 5, p.. 658.
353. *ORR*, I, 38, pt. 2, pp. 737-738.
354. *Daily Chattanooga Rebel,* September 8, 1864.

folks often didn't get a good reception out in the western army. Isaac Ulmer, of Martin's Escort, spoke for most of the Division when he said that the men preferred Martin to Wheeler. But orders were orders, so a half dozen of the Third Alabama and a half dozen from the Twelfth Alabama Battalion were detailed as escort, and General Martin went back to Atlanta.[355] General William W. Allen was appointed to take Martin's command, and he got a pretty disgusted bunch of boys, all in all.

Later that day Sweetwater really got dusted up. It should have been named Strongwater, for two barrels of whiskey were captured, and after a while the town was pretty well smashed,[356] even though it was mostly a Southern town. Madam Rumor didn't say whose command it was that did the smash job, but you've got a pretty good idea, don't you?

That night the column swung off the railroad at Philadelphia. We were getting too close to Loudon, which was too heavily fortified to attack, indeed too heavily cannoned to even ride by. So we turned east and crossed the Little Tennessee at Davis' Ford. It was a wet crossing, already flooded so deep that the smaller horses had to swim.[357] But that didn't matter, for it was raining, as usual. We rode all that night, getting tireder, wetter, muddier; Wheeler must have figured that we were already as miserable as we could get, so that we wouldn't notice that we hadn't camped.[358]

355. Letter, Isaac Barton Ulmer to his mother, September 10, 1864, Isaac Barton Ulmer Papers, Southern Historical Collection, University of North Carolina.

356. Louisville *Journal,* September 3, 1864.

357. Bunting.

358. Garrett and Lightfoot, p. 31.

FRIENDSVILLE

AUGUST 21

The rain kept up most of the next day, which was Sunday,
August 21st. We were moving up through Blount County,
through Unitia, Friendsville, Louisville. The name "Friendsville" will clue you to what kind of people lived in this
area, and John Coffee Williamson formed a very good opinion of the neighborhood: "The people of this neighborhood
are very kind to the soldiers, moreso than at any place we
have been. I attribute the kindness shown us to the influence
of those good Quakers, whose policy it is to treat both
Union and Confederate kindly. The Quakers . . . did not
get to go to church, first Sunday that they have missed
since the settlement was founded. Our Cavalry Column was
passing between them and their church house."[359] We had
to abuse their hospitality, though, and take everything we
could get from them, for our horses were broken down,
totally. The Quakers were strong in their faith, though, and
took it well; one cit, a Riley Lee, spoke for all of them:
". . . Wheeler's raid . . . took us all by a general surprise, we
heard he was coming about two hours before the advance
column got into town, it was on first day morning, what
little time we had was spent in hiding our horses and other
property, and some of the boys hid themselves, but it was
no use hiding horses; I sent my best mare out to the back
field, it was not an hour after they came to town that I
saw a Reb leading her in. Frank Hackney, George Hackney,
Hart, Boring and several others lost all they had. Grandfather saved one; Wayne Lee took two he had and Ephraim
two and got over into Welch's Hollow; but that evening
while some of the rebels were taking oats at grandfather's,

359. Williamson, 64.

Ephraim noticed that one of them was on one of his horses,
it had broken away and they picked it up in the woods.
I had left one old mare in the stable, she had a young colt,
and was so poor in flesh that I had not worked her for
some time, but that made no difference to them, some fellow took her out and left a sore-sided mule to take care
of the colt. The next that suffered was oats; our crop was
the best we had had for ten years, so they had good picking;
they took it clean. Dave Poland said 'it was the first time
he got out of oats at the same time he got out of horses,
and got out of horses just as he got out of oats. Even and
even.'"[360]

Williams' Brigade had taken up the advance. Just north
of Friendsville the Second Kentucky came upon about
twenty-five Yanks. They chased those Yanks into Maryville
and right into the courthouse, which was barricaded and
pierced with port holes.[361]

The Rebs demanded a surrender.[362] The reply was that
they might be Yanks, but that they were Tennessee Yanks,
and that they weren't about to come moping out of there
just because of a little musket fire. So General Williams
stomped and swore and waited all day for the artillery
to come up. When the Rebs finally got a battery planted,
about two hundred yards off, the battery officer told Williams that they couldn't get a clean shot because of a shed
that was in the way. So Williams ordered the shed burned —
at which time the wind shifted and burned down all of
the business section of town *except* the courthouse. And
every living one of those buildings was owned by a Reb

360. Letter, Riley Lee to his uncle, Jeptha W. Morgan, in Iowa,
printed in the Maryville *Enterprise,* March 3, 1932.
361. Black, p. 25.
362. Riley Lee Letter.

partisan, except old Parson Dowell's house.[363] And if he's like all the other Yank preachers we had heard of, he probably appreciated that kind of chastisement and mortification as a test of his faith. But the whole town burning like that makes you wonder if that was some more of that "providential interposition" that the cits down in Athens had bragged about.

At least the artillery then had their clear shot.[364] They fired two rounds into the second story, where the Yanks had been laughing and catcalling as the town burned. Then they fired two rounds into the ground story, and the Yanks sent word that they had been overwhelmed. So all twenty-three of them marched out and surrendered to Williams' whole brigade, which by then was pretty well down in the mouth with the whole thing, knowing that they'd be the laughing stock of the column as soon as the story got around. And, sure enough, by the time it got back to the draggle-tailed body of the Fifth Tennessee that was present, it had become a scandal. William Sloan, who had relatives in Maryville, exploded and wrote in his diary: "Whoever is responsible for this amazing piece of cowardice and vandalism, be he Gen. Wheeler or a Kentucky Colonel, ought to be court-martialed and dismissed from the service."[365]

MARYVILLE
AUGUST 22

The next day, August 22nd, was a Monday — wash day in the country that we were passing through, but since we

363. *Knoxville Whig and Rebel Ventilator,* August 31, 1864.
364. Riley Lee Letter.
365. Sloan, p. 76.

didn't have much to get wet, we just stayed in camp trying to get dry. The commissaries scoured the country, for the only food that we had had for several days had been roasting ears and fresh fruit, and there was beginning to be quite a bit of flux among the men. When they weren't heading for the bushes, the boys were engaged in some of the other activities of camp life.

Colonel McKenzie rejoined the column with the members of his command that he had freed.[366] Those boys said that their homecoming wasn't what they'd expected; Tom Smith told how it was with him: ". . . with Pleas Hunter and Mike Ingle, I made my way through the woods west of Decatur, to a point near John Hunter's house. By this time it was daybreak, and the roads were full of negroes with axes, saws and log wagons going to their work of cutting logs. . . . I managed to slip, undiscovered, up to the back porch at Hunter's. . . . Just as I stepped on the porch, [John] Hunter stepped out with a pan of water in his hands . . . he told me to leave; that he had taken the 'oath' and would have to report [us] . . . even if one was his son." Confident of a different reception at his own home, Smith carefully made his way through the woods in that direction: "When I got close enough to see the house, I discovered seven yankee soldiers sitting around the front door, one of them [holding] my little daughter about two years old."[367] Indeed, the Yanks covered that section like the dew, and by the end of the day had picked up eighteen of the Fifth who'd come calling.

But Colonel McKenzie, with part of the First and the Fifth Tennessee, had ridden all night Friday, and hit the Yanks at Stewart's Landing at dawn on Saturday morn-

366. Cincinnati *Daily Commercial*, August 27, 1864.
367. Stewart Lilliard, *Meigs County, Tennessee* (Sewanee: The University of the South, 1975), p. 120.

ing.[368] The Yanks, civilian lumbermen and their army guards, were bossed by "a corpulent old gentleman who was known by the euphonious title of 'Old Dad'."[369] The Yank camp was right on the Tennessee River, for the lumbermen were cutting the nearby pines and rafting them down river to Chattanooga. McKenzie and his boys hit them right at breakfast time and went whooping through the camps past the big steaming camp kettles of coffee and the sizzling slabs of bacon that were draped over sticks across the fires. McKenzie found his captured boys in an old corn crib, and they helped to gather up the captured Yank soldiers. The negroes who escaped had to jump into the river and swim for it; the others were led into the woods and "lost." One of the freed Rebs "lost" three wounded negroes by cutting their throats with his bowie knife. But one old darky was saved, who recognized a Reb and asked him to help. All in all, it was a close call, for the steamboat that was to pick up the captured Rebs came into sight while the skirmish was going on.

Adjutant William Allen had been trying to catch up with Colonel McKenzie, but he got just close enough to be over-run by the Yanks fleeing for their lives. They fired wildly at Allen, like he was a copperhead in the path, and kept right on going. One of their shots killed Allen's horse, and he tumbled off, right concerned, not knowing what had happened and being stranded so deep in enemy country. He went down to the river, to look across longingly, for his home was over there. He knew that he could get a horse and food — and maybe see his wife — but he had no boat. As he sat there, a girl named Jane Luske, coming to the spring for her Ma, told him about a hog trough that was

368. Sloan, p. 76; Lindsley, p. 891.
369. Valentine C. Allen, pp. 109-111.

hidden in the willows. So he crossed over that way, to find only more green apples, a horse so broken down that his only gait was hobble, and no wife. So he took passage back across in his trough and was lucky enough to find McKenzie and the others.[370]

Parson Brownlow was still provoking the boys with his paper. In the Iverson Brigade camp, the boys got hold of a copy where the old devil was doting on his son, Colonel Jim, of the First Tennessee Tory Cavalry, that we had whipped just three weeks before down at Newnan. Col. John R. Hart, commanding the Sixth Georgia, decided to put a cork in that old barrel of blather, so he wrote the following letter to Colonel Jim:

> "Camp Sixth Georgia Cavalry
> "Near Louisville, East Tennessee
> "August 22, 1864
>
> "Colonel — In perusing the columns of the 'Weekly Knoxville Whig' of the 20th ult., I find the following paragraph of a letter written by yourself, to a friend, at which I take exception:
>
> 'I can whip twice my number anywhere. This may look a little like boasting, but I am willing to take the contract.'
>
> I challenge you to prove the assertion; but will not require you to bring into the field a greater number than that of my regiment, and I will not select the men, but fight the whole regiment and in its present organization.
>
> You may choose the ground upon which your assertion is to be proven, so that it be free from timber and other shelter, and between or on either flank of the two armies. We will fight dismounted, with Enfield rifles, bayonets fixed, and two army or navy pistols to the man.
>
> Having fought you several times, I consider you, Colonel, a foeman worthy of my steel; otherwise this challenge would not have been written.
>
> I am, Colonel, your most obedient servant."[371]

370. William Gibbs Allen, "Incidents of Wheeler's Raid," 288.

371. Dayton [Ohio] *Journal*, September 15, 1864.

Although the boys were not nearly so taken with that kind of Cavalier style as they once had been, they thought that this time it was justified by Brownlow's bumptiousness. They looked forward to Brownlow's printing the challenge and Junior's response to it.

The Eighth Texas was also aware of being within the web of that spiteful old fanatic, Brownlow. As Chaplain Bunting remembered that time, "An incident occurred in the camp [this] evening which shows the dreadful condition of society in these parts. A middle aged citizen came to Col. Cook, saying that his only horse had been pressed by a soldier and requesting his aid in procuring it. For, when we leave it will be necessary for him to go with us, with his family for a place of safety. The tories had already sworn vengeance, and now would be the time to carry out their threats. That horse was his only chance for escape. In speaking of the infamous Brownlow and his pernicious teachings, he says that many of the wealthy Methodists of East Tennessee do not concur in his doctrines of negro equality, &c., but, says he, in great earnestness, 'I tell you, sir, he is stirring up hell among the Methodists.'"[372]

The Eighth Texas and the rest of Harrison's Brigade were not pleased with the way things were going at all. The boys in the brigade were either from Tennessee or had good feelings for Tennessee, so that they had been very put out at the treatment Southern sympathizers had received in Athens and Maryville and Sweetwater. They called a brigade meeting in camp that morning, and several speeches were made demanding stern discipline for the entire column and more protection for Southern people, many of whom had sons in the Reb army. But before any action could be taken, the brigade was ordered to move out.

372. Bunting.

KNOX COUNTY
AUGUST 23

All the commands broke camp on the morning of August 23rd, a fair and pleasantly warm day,[373] to march with quiet watchfulness through the rugged country between Little River and the French Broad. The route lay along Bays Mountain, a neck of the woods that that Knoxville fellow George Washington Harris used to write about, in William T. Porter's newspaper, *The Spirit of the Times,* which was one of the greatest casualties of the cussed, misfortunate differences that led to the war. In such a tale as "The Knob Dance," Harris could really talk about life on Bays Mountain: "You may talk of your bar hunts, Mister Porter, and your deer hunts, and knottin tigers' tails through the bung-holes of barrels, an cock fitin, and all that but if a regular bilt frolick in the Nobs of 'Old Knox,' don't beat 'em all blind for fun, then I'm no judge of fun, that's all! I said *fun,* and I say it agin, from a *kiss* that cracks like a wagin-whip up to a *fite* that rouses up all outdoors — and as to laffin, why they *invented* laffin, and the *last* laff will be hearn at a Nob dance about three in the morning! I'm jest gettin so I can ride arter the motions I made at one at Jo Spraggins's a few days ago."[374]

There was no fun in the knobs that day we went through, though. The only woman we saw was the one who tried to put out the fire we set in her cabin, after we were fired at by a bushwhacker.[375] We were happy to get out of that dreary

---

373. Garrett and Lightfoot, p. 32.

374. George Washington Harris, "The Knob Dance," in *Native American Humor,* ed. Walter Blair (San Francisco: Chandler Publishing Company, 1960), p. 368.

375. Williamson, 64.

country into the valley along the French Broad, where there were huge fields of corn, and sheep and hogs to butcher. At that point General Humes allowed Captains Mims and Mullendore to take their companies of the Fifth Tennessee and go on a scout home to Greene, Cocke, Grainger, and Hawkins County.[376] Their departure raised the image of home in the minds of the Kentuckians; as Jim Black of the Kentucky Brigade put it: "Our destination yet wrapped in mystery. Every pulse beats faster & heart throbs warmer at the idea of going to KY."[377]

STRAWBERRY PLAINS
AUGUST 24

A good night's rest and a good meal helped everybody, so that by the next morning, August 24th, fair again and pleasant, we had perked up enough to worry. Our scouts were telling us that Yanks were all around; Gillem had a force up at Bull's Gap and there was no telling how many Yanks there might be congregating at Knoxville. We had broken the railroad from Chattanooga, but their cavalry from Chattanooga could travel the same roads that we had. And too they had the river: The *Missionary* could pass up as far as Kingston, from there the *Holston,* which drew less water, could come on up to Knoxville, especially with the river up because of all the rain.[378] We had been safe as long as we didn't have to contend with Yank cavalry, but now we couldn't be sure that we wouldn't be chased, and with us

---

376. "Report of Detached Officers and Men Absent on Duty from the Fifth Tennessee Cavalry," January 10, 1865, Container 30, Folder 7, Regimental Collection, Western Reserve Historical Society.

377. Black, p. 26.

378. Chattanooga *Gazette,* August 26, 1864.

on horses and mules that couldn't fall down without some help.

We wanted to get across the French Broad and then the Holston, finally to get across the water that had driven us so far out of our way, for it turned out that Wheeler had intended all the while to head for Middle Tennessee. At daylight we crossed the French Broad at Seven Island Ford, where the water was deep and swift. There was no opposition, though, so we moved along swiftly, through the water and then through the grove of dappled sycamores that lay by the river.

When the advance got to McMillan's Ford on the Holston, it immediately drew fire from the other side. The woods came right down to the water, so that the advance had no idea of the strength of the opposition. It waited, then, for Wheeler to come up, while the column began to stack up, unable to cross. The Third Arkansas, of Harrison's Brigade, was dismounted and ordered to advance down to the bank, to see if it could get any information.[379] As those boys spread out and slipped down through the ferns and rocks, General Williams rode up to Wheeler, to request that he be allowed to take his own brigade and one other, and half the artillery, go up the east bank of the Holston, and capture the garrison and destroy the railroad bridge at Strawberry Plains. He said that he knew the area well because he had served there before and that the destruction of the bridge would obstruct the supplying of the Yank forces in upper East Tennessee. Wheeler refused, saying that the whole column had to move through the Knoxville area as quickly as possible.[380] But Williams persisted, saying that, if permitted, he would reduce Strawberry Plains as quickly as the

---

379. Bunting.
380. *ORR*, I, 38, pt. 3, p. 959. Wheeler's Report.

main column could get across the Holston and that he could march by moonlight to catch up. Wheeler then gave in, and Williams took Robertson's Confederate Brigade with him. You know, it might have been that Williams thought that this way was an opportunity for himself and his command to redeem themselves for that poor showing down at Maryville a day or so before.

Williams pulled off to the right, sending Willie Breckinridge and his Ninth Kentucky up to Newport to picket against Gillem's command of Yanks at Bull's Gap. At the same time, Wheeler set his plan for crossing the ford.[381] The Third Arkansas was to remain in place and provide a covering fire for a mounted charge. General Wheeler called for volunteers, and so many of the Eighth Texas stepped up that he had to select from among them.[382] He allowed Companies C (Lt. Smith), G (Lt. Stormfeltz), and K (Capt. Hunter) to have the honor, and although utterly ignorant of the footing of the ford or of the number of enemy that they were facing, they formed by fours and charged right down into that dark water. The fire was heavy until they got within ten yards of the other bank, then the Yanks, seeing that the charge was going to be successful, broke and ran. They had been brave, but they couldn't hit the side of a barn door. Only one horse was hit, and the only injury, a sprained back, was suffered by Albert Kibbe, Company C, whose saddle turned on him just as he reached the far bank.

We rounded up seven Yanks, one of them badly wounded. As soon as General Wheeler came across, he talked with the

381. Bunting.
382. Leonidas Blanton Giles, *Terry's Texas Rangers* (Austin: Von Boeckmann-Jones Company, 1911), pp. 86-87.

the prisoners, who were from the Tenth Michigan Cavalry.[283] Since there had been no Reb casualties, we were not particularly angry at those boys, who were just doing their job. Wheeler rode up to the wounded boy, who said his name was Alexander Griggs, and asked, "Well, my man, how many men had you at this ford?"

Griggs looked up from the ground and said, "Seven, sir."

Wheeler wasn't convinced; he thought that Griggs said that, since seven was all that we had captured. "My poor fellow, don't you know that you are badly wounded? You might as well tell me the truth; you may not live long."

Griggs got huffy. "I am telling you the truth, sir. We only had seven men." We thought for a minute that he was going to hold up seven fingers.

Wheeler laughed, and so did his staff. "Well, what did you expect to do?"

Griggs said, "To keep you from crossing, sir."

Wheeler got a good laugh out of this. "Well, why didn't you do it?"

Griggs was an earnest sort of a fellow, and he said, "Why you see we did until you hit me, and that weakened our forces so much that you were too much for us."

Wheeler just sparkled at Grigg's spunk and told another prisoner to take care of him, that he was too brave a fellow to be allowed to die. Then he turned to another prisoner, John Dunn, and asked if all the Tenth Michigan was as brave. Dunn shook his head and said, ". . . we are the poorest of the lot. We are mostly horse farriers and blacksmiths and special duty men, and not much accustomed to fightin." Maybe that explains why their aim was so poor. Wheeler

383. Michigan, Adjutant General's Office, *Record of Service of the Michigan Volunteers*, Volume XL (Kalamazoo: Ihling Brothers and Everard, 190), pp. 8-9.

was really impressed, now, for he ended the interview by saying, "Well, if I had 300 such men as you, I could march through hell."

That may be, but hell's a lot easier than Tennessee ever was.

Since it was noon before the entire command could be crossed, the word was passed along that the column would rest until all units had come over. The Eleventh Texas, of Harrison's Brigade, was sent forward, to scout towards Flat Creek Bridge, which was on the way to Blain's Cross Roads, our destination for the night. After a while, the Eleventh sniffed out some Yank horsemen; then the Texans spread out across the road to confront the Yanks. But damned if the Yanks didn't ride right over them! Most unusual! Colonel Reeve had a dozen or so of his boys get gobbled, and the others were chased back down the road through the woods.[384]

Right behind them, the Yanks reached out with their sabres, just like they were trying to lift the hats off those boys, and came right on, just yelling and whooping. They thundered across Flat Creek Bridge — to run smack into Hume's whole division stretched across both their flanks and with three cannon pointed right at their buttons. That pulled the Yanks up short and quietened them down, you may be sure, to have all those Rebs just silently sitting their horses there, about three hundred yards off.

Since the Eleventh Texas was a part of Harrison's Brigade, old "Iron Sides'" other regiments were particularly figgity to get back at the Yanks. Leonidas Giles, of the Eighth Texas, thought that the command would never be given: "Our regiment was formed in an open field. Colonel Harrison took position in front. We went forward in a walk at

384. *ORR,* I, 38, pt. 2, pp. 740-741.

first, and then in a trot. The men were impatient. Officers
kept saying:

'Steady, men! Keep back there!'

Then we heard the popping of pistols, and all eyes were
turned on Harrison. The routed Confederates came into view.
Next the enemy in close pursuit. The men could hardly be
restrained. Finally Harrison shouted,

'Well, go then! damn you, go!' "[385]

And go they did, with Ashby's Brigade by their side,
banners flying in the afternoon sun.[386] The entire division
ran the Yanks for five miles and recaptured all the Eleventh
Texas who had just been taken, as well as about forty of
the Yanks. Then the command was given to cease the pursuit,
for by then it was determined that the Yanks presented no
danger. Some of the Rangers needed new outfits, though,
so they chased individual Yanks, like the fattest chicken
in the barnyard, until they surrendered.[387] These they
stripped right down to their drawers; then the Yanks were
advised to get back to Knoxville, about twenty-five miles
down the road, before they took a chill.[388]

Humes' Division halted, while the prisoners were paroled
and their various liberated articles were discussed. Since the
telegraph wire from Strawberry Plains was still up, Colonel
Cook sent his lightning man up the pole, to see if he could
sucker the Knoxville operator into giving any information.
But that old Yank was too cagy, so our man sent a little
salutation to Parson Brownlow, and then we cut the wire.[389]

General Williams hadn't been having as much luck as the
main column. He got his command formed into a fair skir-

385. Giles, pp. 86-87.
386. Williamson, 64.
387. Bunting.
388. Michigan, Adjutant General's Office, p. 9.
389. Bunting; *ORR*, I, 39, pt 2, p. 294.

mish line by 2:30 p.m. or so, and ordered it up the hill and into the village of Strawberry Plains, on the south side of Holston.[390] From there, behind buildings and trees, the boys could sharpshoot into the fort across the river.[391]

Some of the local cits told Williams that there were no troops in the fort to speak of, that they had all gone up the country with Gillem. But the Yank sentries were still walking their posts around the fort, so that Williams smelled a rat: "Oh, you can't fool me. Those Yanks are full of tricks. Those men wouldn't be walking about there so unconcerned if they hadn't plenty of men to back them."[392]

All the while, the Yank artillery was blasting away at any congregation on the southern bank, so that Williams was completely stymied: he couldn't take the place, but he couldn't bear to give it up. At 4:00 p.m. he sent Wheeler a plea:

"We have driven the enemy across the river, and have possession of the fortification on College Hill, which commands the bridge, but with the guns we have I do not think we could inflict such serious damage to the bridge as would warrant the expenditure of ammunition. There are 216 tents visible on the opposite side of the river, which I think accommodate two regiments. I cannot advance farther without crossing the foot bridge, which is completely enfiladed by the enemy's works, and is within rifle range of the redoubt and pits in which all his forces seem to have assembled. I desire to know whether you design attacking on the opposite side, so that I may govern myself accordingly."[393]

390. Darsey.
391. *ORR*, I, 38, pt. 2, pp. 741-743.
392. Michigan, Adjutant General's Office, p. 9.
393. *ORR*, I, 38, pt. 5, p. 987.

Wheeler sent word back to Williams to give it up and re-join the main column as soon as possible.[394] By the time Williams got Wheeler's reply, things were going from bad to worse, for the Yank artillery had blown up one of his pieces, and he had begun to take pretty severe casualties.[395] It seemed to be a repeat of Maryville for Williams; fairly or not, stubborn defenses had a way of making Williams appear to be a poor general. His artillery seemed to reflect his frustration, for it began to fire at the Yanks' unmounted horses, for want of a better target.

Williams didn't withdraw his command, apparently hop-ing that after dark the boys could slip in to burn the bridge.[396] It still couldn't be done, though, and the only consequence of the night was the increased misery of a body of men, as Ben Darsey, of the Fifth Georgia, could testify: "We lay in line of battle all night suffering intense hunger — not for yankee blood particularly, but for some-thing that would satisfy the inner man, as we had had noth-ing to eat for nearly two days except green apples."[397] The next morning, the boys buried the twenty or so Rebs who had fallen to the artillery or to the sharpshooters, and, weak with hunger, rode out to catch the main column.[398]

BLAIN'S CROSS ROADS

AUGUST 25

That morning, August 25th, the main column struck the Emory road at Blain's Cross Road, to go west down a valley

394. *ORR*, I, 38, pt. 5, p. 959.
395. *ORR*, I, 38, pt. 2, pp. 741-743.
396. *ORR*, I, 38, pt. 2, pp. 739-740.
397. Darsey.
398. *ORR*, I, 338, pt. 2, p. 740.

that ran some ten or twelve miles north of Knoxville. The Eighth Tennessee, leading the way, had no one who knew the country, so a boy named Ward, from the Fifth Tennessee, was detailed to serve as guide.[399] The day was pretty much uneventful, and the boys felt easy, for they figured that they had met what Yank cavalry there was in the area the day before. According to John Coffee Williamson, even though the afternoon was rainy, it was pleasant enough: "A scout of Texans went to Clinton and prowled the town of boots and hats. The citizens all ran away. . . . I have felt unwell today. I notice some of the boys have whiskey. The upper East Tennessee companies in the 2nd and the 8th have all gone home on a scout. I notice some pretty girls today. We came down Beaverdam Creek and crossed Bull Run." The Clinch River was forded at Lee's Ferry, ten miles south of Clinton, and camp was made on Cross's farm.[400]

Cerro Gordo Williams' two unlucky brigades trailed along behind the main command by half a day. Having spent the night on the skirmish line, the boys were worn out and grouchy. Someone wisely ordered early camp, and, like the others, Ben Darsey got busy: "That day we halted a little before night and struck camp for the night in order to secure food for men and horses. I was one that foraged for horse feed while others butchered some mutton and obtained flour from a mill near by. My squad had some difficulty in finding forage, but finally we found a lot of wheat shocked in a field about two miles from camp. Without asking permission of any one we loaded our horses. No one but a cavalryman knows how much he can tie to his saddle.

399. "Report of Detached Officers and Men Absent on Duty from the Fifth Tennessee Cavalry."
400. Williamson, 64.

It is no job to carry seventy or eighty pound of wheat or oats in the straw. It was after dark when we reached the camp; it being dark and the locality strange to us, it was with some difficulty that we found our immediate commands.

"But we reached our regimental line all right, and my organs of smell told me that supper was being cooked, and on nearing the fire, I found that our company's cook had roasted a lot of mutton and baked a pile of 'slap jacks' about a knee high. My hunger rose to its highest pitch as I had eaten nothing but green apples for the last three days and insisted that our cook make haste for I was hungry, tired and sleepy. His reply to me was not satisfactory which elicited from me some uncomplimentary words. It was dropped however, and in a few moments he announced "all ready,' and right then and there we ate one of the best meals of our lives; or at least I enjoyed it best."[401]

ROBERTSVILLE
AUGUST 26

The main column had found food too, and had enough left over for breakfast, for John Coffee Williamson noted of August 26th: "We were on the march as soon as brigade headquarters got breakfast. I am told that Col. James Wheeler eat like he thought that it was the last meal he would get this side of middle Tennessee."[402] The men, so many of them from Middle Tennessee, were anxious to see home, so they rode eagerly, passing Robertsville, still on the Emory road, hoping to catch a glimpse of the Cumberland Mountains before nightfall. At first the country was hilly, as

401. Darsey.
402. Williamson, 65.

Chaplain Bunting observed: ". . . we pass some very rough country until the afternoon, when the valleys are rich, yet greatly desolated. The Big Emory is before us, and swollen from the heavy rains, and with a rough ford disagreeable crossing after dark. . . . Safely across the stream we are overtaken by the most violent and terrific storm which we have yet experienced, and in the midst of it we are ordered to camp, with no rations but roasting ears and occasionally a little meat; such traveling by night and day is anything but agreeable."[403] That storm was something else: Major John Minor, commanding the Tenth Tennessee, Dibrell's Brigade, described it as ". . . one of the hard rains as ever fell. . . ,"[404] and Stephen Jordan noted in his diary, "Cloudy & very heavy rain, wind, thunder & lightning at night, traveled until very late, crossed Emory River, Roane Cty, crossing very rough & dangerous, traveled about 25 or 30 miles."[405]

Efforts had been made to have provisions ready for the men, but without success, as Commissary Sergeant John Coffee Williamson discovered: "I was sent ahead with a detail to get some rations but I failed completely. However I stopped on the bank of the Emory where Nancy Losehubit lived and got her to fix me up something to eat, and bake some bread. The brigade crossed the river after night. Our teams are much worn and our boys had a hard time getting their wagons out of the river. About 12 o'clock at night rained a very hard rain, with much thunder. I crossed after the rain and slept in an old schoolhouse by the road."[406]

403. Bunting.
404. Diary of Major John Minor, State of Tennessee Archives.
405. Garrett and Lightfoot, p. 32.
406. Williamson, 65.

Williams' command had planned to march over night, in order to catch up with the main column. It crossed the Clinch River early in the day, then marched to Robertsville, where orders had been left by Wheeler. General Williams was to take the Kentucky Brigade north, up to Wartburg, thence to Sparta. Jim Black, Ninth Kentucky, summed up the day in his diary: "Crossed Clinch river. At night the most terrific thunder storm I was ever exposed to. Camped about 18 ms from Watsburg on the Jimtown road."[407] General Robertson was ordered to continue on the trail of the main column, in order to rejoin Kelly's Division.[408] He pushed on some seven or eight miles before the thunder storm struck; it was so overwhelming that he had to stop: "we bivouacked for the night, a thoroughly drenched crowd."[409]

407. Black, p. 27.
408. Letter, Felix H. Robertson to Braxton Bragg, October 6, 1864, Bragg Papers, Houghton Library, Harvard University.
409. Felix H. Robertson, "On Wheeler's Last Raid," 334-335.

VI

Middle Tennessee: "a thrill of joy"

(August 27-31, 1864)

POST OAK SPRING
AUGUST 27

*J*t was clear and bright the next morning, August 27th, a welcome relief to that horrible storm of the night before. "Osceola," the correspondent for the Memphis *Moving Appeal,* from his vantage point in Dibrell's Brigade, waxed poetic as he dwelt upon the prospect: ". . . the radiant orb of light appeared at the usual hour above the horizon, and as he mounted the blue vault of heaven in undiminished splendor, three long columns of cavalry wound their snake-like way toward the summit of the pile of dirt and limestone which divides East from Middle Tennessee."[410] It almost sounds as if "Osceola" had been taking lessons in rhetoric from Brother Bunting, of the Texas Rangers, doesn't it?

All wasn't quite so placid in the Fifth Tennessee camp. When John Coffee Williamson left his snug schoolhouse and caught up with his regiment, he discovered that one of the things worse than camp lice had struck: "Col. Montgomery was prowled of one pocket of his saddle bags and a sack of good apples, that I had got up yesterday while prowling."[111] William Sloan was even more exercised about the incident: "A terrible rain fell during the night. Lieut. Col. Montgomery had one end of his saddle bags stolen. He slept with his head on his saddle bags, and the thief could not get it all without the risk of waking the Colonel up, so he cut one end off with a knife and took it, leaving the other half. It never rains too hard for a sneak-thief to prowl among camps and steal from honest men."[412]

But there was no evidence, not even an apple core or a worm, and no accused, so the Fifth Tennessee moved out along with the other commands. John Coffee Williamson resumed his independent ways: "We marched on soon and I went ahead to forage. Stopped at Bill Buchannan's and Bill Brown gave me a clean shirt. Came on to Wheeler's headquarters and learned that our division would take the Crab Orchard road. We will go different roads over the mountain all to meet at Sparta. It is a tight time about rations. We are living on roasting ears. We passed up the mountain and on to Crab Orchard where we fed and then

410. "Osceola."
411. Williamson, 65.
412. Sloan, p. 77.

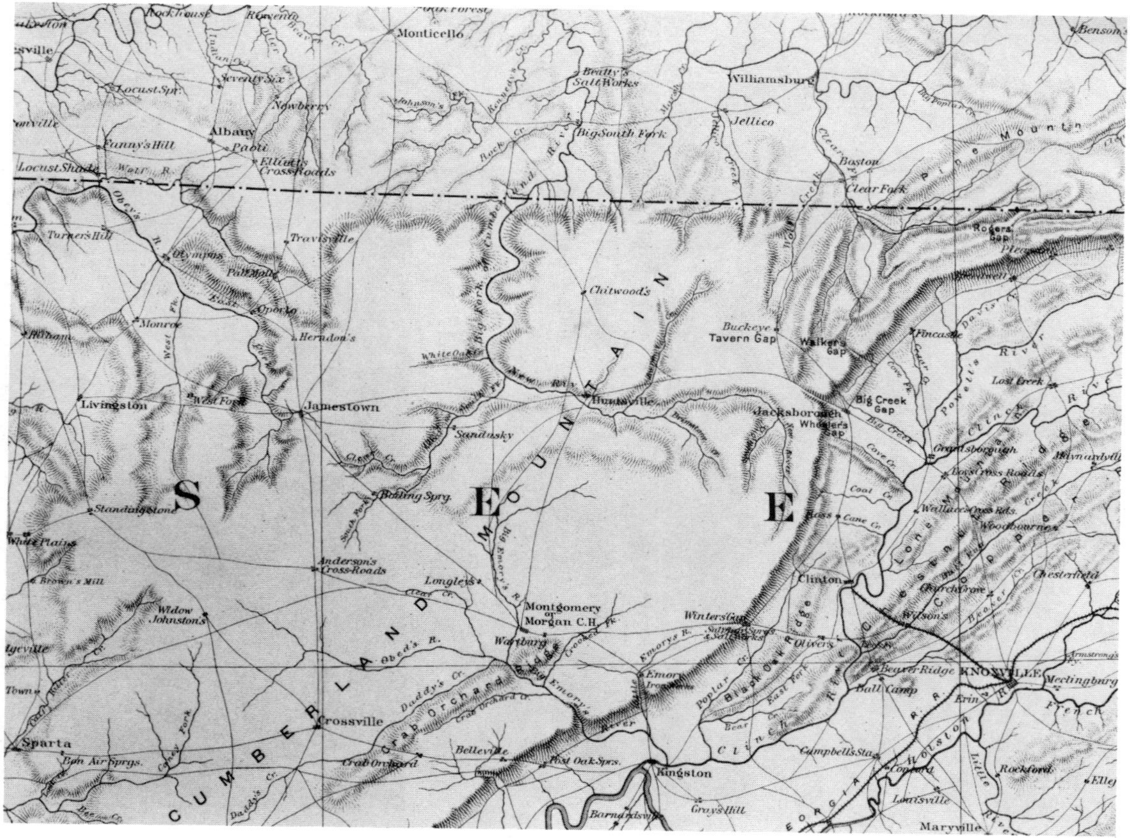

Route, August 27-31

Col. George G. Dibrell

Col. D. W. Holman

marched 2½ miles further and then encamped for the night. I saw Mary Walker at Crab Orchard. I have been very unwell all day. Very cool tonight."[413]

At Post Oak Springs, Colonel Dibrell's Eighth Tennessee was allowed to move out in advance of the other columns, so as to gain a day to spend at home. That day, that regiment rode the fifty-five miles to Sparta, where many of its members lived.[414] Osceola accompanied the men and reported on their homecoming: "Language is inadequate to describe the joyous welcome of the ladies — the long oppressed daughters of freedom. Their houses were opened up and their tables spread, and every demonstration of hospitality possible was made. Most of the men have taken the oath. The extent to which the oppressor has carried his infamous policy can be faintly imagined from some of the orders issued. Col. W. B. Stokes, commanding the post at Granville, Jackson county, issued an order prohibiting the ladies of the surrounding country from wearing their home-spun dresses of the color of the Southern uniform. The ladies, however, continued to show their devotion to our cause by wearing the 'Southern gray,' though Stokes threatened to send some of them to prison. When he heard that Dibrell was at Sparta, though forty miles, distant, he fled across the Cumberland, leaving commissary stores, guns, ammunition, and several horses."[415]

Before the remainder of the column moved out from Post Oak Spring, General Wheeler ordered Paul Anderson's Fourth Tennessee, from Harrison's Brigade, and the Ninth Tennessee Battalion, from Ashby's Brigade, to detach themselves, go down the Sequatchie Valley, then attack an un-

413. Williamson, 65.
414. Lindsley, 669.
415. "Osceola."

finished fort at Tracy City and the railroad tunnel at Cowan.[416] Then the main command proceeded slowly toward Middle Tennessee. The mountainous country was mostly unsettled, and Chaplain Bunting marveled that even the settled portion seemed deserted.[417] Food was extremely scarce, and most of the boys lay down hungry in their camps around Crossville. It was cold up there on the Cumberland Plateau, even in August; Major John Minor remembered, "I suffered with cold during the night though raped up in a blanket."[418]

General Williams traveled the Jimtown road that day, right through Unionist country. Jim Black indicated that it was a watchful day: "Struck the mountains, 11 ms from Watsburg. Stopped to feed about 1 ½ o clock. A man of 2nd Ky Batt wounded by Bushwhackers. Passed through Watsburg capturing 5 or 6 Yankees. Several times during the day the command was fired on. Travelled late at night."[419]

Still in all, the Kentuckians had an easier day of it than Robertson's Brigade. When it reached the Emory River early in the morning, eighteen hours behind the main column, the ford was twelve feet deep, after the storm, and rising at the rate of six inches an hour. Robertson said that it was not a pleasant position for a brand-new brigadier to be in: ". . . with the Cumberland Mt. in my sight . . . the military post at Kingston within seven miles of my left flank and an impassible mount. torrent in my front . . . I could either take the chances of attack and wait for the flood to subside, could turn back 16 miles and follow Gen. Williams or I could follow directly up the torrent by a road

416. George B. Guild, *A Brief Narrative of the Fourth Tennessee Cavalry Regiment* (Nashville: 1913), p. 73; Lindsley, p. 752.
417. Bunting.
418. Minor.
419. Black, p. 27.

reported practicable and find myself after losing the toilsome labor at Montgomery as far away from Sparta . . . as
when I stood on the banks of Emory. I decided to follow
up the Emory after being told by one of my men that he
had traveled up the road repeatedly. I reached Montgomery
after a toilsome march of 15 miles — over the worst of
mountain paths — after evacuating the only Ambulance
allowed. . . ."[420]

Such a brief comment does not adequately convey the
hardships of that trip, though. For one thing, the men were
worried about their horses, as cavalrymen always are. Ben
Darsey remembered the day in such a light: ". . . many of
our horses began to show signs of lameness from having lost
one or more shoes. In this rocky country a horse soon
becomes lame if he travels much without shoes. My horse
lost one off his hind foot before we left Georgia, but having a hard hoof he traveled all right so far. This caused
much uneasiness as we were in the territory of the enemy.
But our officers gave us permission to exchange with any
citizen if we so desired. Good horses were scarce in that
section at that time as the yankees had already pressed the
best of them. We reached the foot of Cumberland mountain
just below the Gap and ascended that afternoon and camped
on the mountain, and next morning we resumed our
march."[421]

The area was strongly Unionist to begin with, and there
would have been some bushwhacking because of that fact.
But when you add the fact that the boys had to steal every
horse they could find, you can imagine just how fierce the
reception for those two little brigades was. Captain Knox

420. Letter, Felix H. Robertson to Braxton Bragg, October 6,
1864.
421. Darsey.

Miller, of the Eighth Confederate, recalled that aspect of
the day, that and the hunger: "While in East Tenn we were
bushwhacked by the East Tenn loyalists at almost every opportunity & often had to keep out flankers for miles. Some
of our men — especially those of the 5th Georgia Regt were
killed or captured. Much of the country was sterile and it
was almost a fight among the men at times over a patch of
roasting ears. I remember on one occasion securing about
15 'nubbins' for self & horse — first gave him ten and took
five for my own empty stomach — then took two of his
ten for myself and tried to even up the corn and my conscience by the more or less plausible reasoning that 'he got
8 ears and the shucks of all 15.' "[422]

CROSSVILLE
AUGUST 28

The main column didn't linger around Crossville on the
morning of the 28th of August, for there was precious
little to eat and even less hospitality from the cits.[423] Champ
Ferguson, the Reb guerrilla, had been operating in that
section, and Yank patrols had occasionally come to smoke
him out. Ferguson gave as good as he got; the year before,
when the Reb army was still in those parts, he told some
of the boys: "I ain't killed nigh as many as men say I have;
folks has lied about me powerful. I ain't killed but thirty-
two men since this war commenced."[424] Although the

422. George Knox Miller, "Notes on 8th Confederate Regt.
Cavalry," Manuscript in George Knox Miller Papers, Southern Historical Collection, University of North Carolina.
    423. Williamson, 65.
    424. Quoted from *The Reminiscences of General Basil W. Duke*,
in Richard M. Weaver, *The Southern Tradition at Bay* (New Rochelle,
New York: Arlington House, 1968), p. 208.

Yanks hadn't had much luck with him, they had burned out most of the cits, who were suspected of cooperating with him. Reb or Union, the cits just wanted us out of there, so the column rode on, with more horses going lame and more men getting sick. Even that indefatigable scrounger, John Coffee Williamson, though he managed to turn up a little bread and milk to enrich his diet, nevertheless got sick. Many of the sick stopped at Bon Air Spring, to drink of the waters, as Stephen Jordan did, but you suspect that the effect was more spiritual than medicinal: "Rested half hour, drank of the Calybeate Spring, got some apples, took a look over the country from the summit; it sent a thrill of joy through my heart to look into Middle Tenn. one more time."[425]

SPARTA
AUGUST 29

The brigades camped around Sparta, which was occupied by the early arriving Eighth Tennessee. Humes took his division to Officer's Farm, from which at 5.45 p.m. he sent the following report to Wheeler: "My command has just arrived here. I shall camp here to-night and move between daylight and sunrise for the ford designated in your order. No instructions were sent for the artillery, and I do not know what road it has taken, whether to Sparta or this place."[426] His men killed three beeves and a hog, thus had plenty of meat — but no bread to put it on. The talk was that Sherman had fallen back from Atlanta, that Sheridan had been defeated in the Shenandoah Valley, and that

425. Garrett and Lightfoot, p. 32.
426. *ORR,* I, 38, pt. 5, p. 998.

Mobile still held out. But neither the news nor the meat helped John Coffee Williamson, so he took a dose of pills, kind unidentified and probably unknown, and was very sick all night long.

If anything the day had been rougher for General Williams' two brigades, which were struggling along well north of the main column. Jim Black had little to say to his diary that night, and little strength to say that little with: "Ate but one meal. Travelled all day, 14 or 20 ms without seeing an inhabited house. Portions of the road very rough. Travelled till 11 o clock & 12 ms from foot of the mountain. Forage scarce."[427]

The next morning, August 29th, a fair day, General Wheeler took the main command on through Sparta, leaving Colonel Dibrell to remain for two days more, recruiting and remounting, saying that if he had to fall back from Nashville, he would rely on Dibrell.[428] Kelly's Division, operating now without Robertson's Confederate Brigade or the Eighth Tennessee of Dibrell's Brigade, was in the advance. During the day Kelly passed through Smithville, crossed Caney Fork, and camped near Liberty, having ridden thirty-three miles by midnight, according to a sore Stephen Jordan.[429] Humes' Division, less Anderson's Fourth Tennessee and the Ninth Tennessee Battalion, which were still operating on the railroad off to the south, followed Kelly. The ailing John Coffee Williamson provided a sketch of the day with Humes' command: "We left camp at the Blue Springs and marched over on the Calf-Killer which is a little mountain stream, and on to Sparta. The women were very glad to see us. Most of them cheered us in the true

427. Black, p. 47.
428. Lindsley, p. 669.
429. Garrett and Lightfoot, p. 32; Minor.

lady style. Most of Sparta has been burned by the Yanks. From Sparta we took the Smithville Road and crossed the Caney Fork of Cumberland River. We got to Smithville just at night and then marched 2 miles on the Lebanon Road and we got no corn to feed. I have been very sick all day, and at night I was perfectly worn out. We got up no rations. I took a dose of morphine and slept soundly. The Chicago Convention meets today. This is to be a great day in this war's history."[430] William Sloan may have taken Williamson's place on detail, but he didn't seem to be the prowler that Williamson was: "I am on a detail to day to hunt rations. We passed through Sparta and Smithville and found no rations. We are moving toward Murfresboro."[431]

Many of the men were mindful of the calendar, for they realized that one of the objectives of their raid was poltical. If the Democartic Party, meeting in convention in Chicago, would nominate a candidate for the November presidential election who would accept Southern independence, and if a Northern population, tired of the terrible casualties which it was suffering, would elect that candidate, then the war could be ended to the South's satisfaction, in just a few months. It was necessary, then, to demonstrate to the Democratic Convention that Southern armies could range at will in the upper South and could jeopardize the Yank army hammering away at Atlanta, by cutting its communication and supplies, so that the candidate nominated would be sufficiently committed to peace that he would accept Southern independence.

The political significance of the date was not lost upon the men in Williams' force, either, for Jim Black made the following entry in his little black diary: "To day the Dem.

430. Williamson, 65.
431. Sloan, p. 77.

Convention meets in Chicago. The times pregnant with momentous issues. Camped down the mountain 1 mile to the left of White Plains & 18 or 20 ms from Sparta. Camped till morning of a spot made historic by Morgan."[432]

LIBERTY
AUGUST 29

The only action on August 29th was at Liberty, west of Sparta, and at McMinnville, some miles south of the same place. The advance hit the unfinished fort at Liberty late in the afternoon, and some fifteen of Stoke's and Garrett's tory Tennesseans were captured. One of Garrett's boys, the sixteen-year-old Jim Fite, later described the arrival of the Rebs, who had only to walk in, without even taking their hats off, since the Yanks had just come back exhausted from a mistaken scout to Lebanon, the wrong direction: "As it happened, I was not in the skirmish. On the expedition to Lebanon, my horse had broken down, and I rode an animal belonging to one of Stokes's troops until I reached my home, a mile west of Liberty, on the Lebanon and Sparta turnpike. Mother gave me a splendid supper. I recall particularly a peach cobbler. When I got up from the table, a comrade, Thomas G. Bratten, rode up to the gate with the information, 'They are fighting at Liberty,' and suggested that I mount my horse, and we would go and take part in it. When informed that I was then an infantryman, he rode on toward the villlage. Presently he came galloping back pausing just long enough to tell me that the Confederates were approaching. I kept a lookout for the advance guard. Directly four of the enemy came in sight.

432. Black, p. 28.

Though very young, I refrained from firing on them, believing they might burn our home if I shot from the house.
(I was under the impression that the raiders were Champe
Ferguson's men.) So I retreated in fairly good order to a
dense plum thicket in the rear.

"The four men rode inside the yard, bade my brother
hold their horses, and finished what was left on the table,
which had been set on the front porch. One who finished
eating first walked to the back door from which I had just
made my exit. Mother afterwards said she expected every
moment I would shoot him; but I told her it had never been
in my heart to shoot a man from the bushes, and I am glad
to this day that I made no effort to kill him, believing that
he had a mother somewhere waiting for him.

"About sunset quite a bunch of Confederates stopped
at our gate. Their officer proved a relative. He asked mother
for a pillow for a wounded soldier. They had him in a buggy
taken from one of our neighbors. She carried the pillow
to the gate and asked who was in command. She was told
that General Wheeler was, that the force numbered ten
thousand men and would be a week in passing. When this
news came to me, I was greatly relieved. With Wheeler I
would be safe if captured; but I was certain that Ferguson
would put me out of existence if I fell into his hands."[433]

Like the other Yank citizens of Liberty, Jim Fite had
good reason to fear Champ Ferguson, for he had been hound-
ed by Stokes, Blackburn, Hathaway, and Garrison, who all
called Liberty home. And when he came through, in the
rear of Wheeler's column, he seemed to be in character.
For no reason that we could learn, he burned James Lam-
berson's barn and thresher. Then, passing on through, he

433. Will T. Hale, "General Wheeler's Last Raid," *Confederate
Veteran*, XXIII (January, 1915), 30.

met a party of local cits, who had been to bury a local
lady, Mrs. John Bratten. Their fear of Ferguson must have
made their tongues run free, for one of them added that
they had also just buried an unknown Confederate soldier,
who had been killed by two local Yanks. The guerrillas
said that score would have to be evened at once and asked,
please, was there a Union man in the crowd? William Ford
must have feared that if nobody spoke up, the Rebs would
kill them all, so he fessed up that he was a Lincolnite. It
certainly looked bad for him, all right, but the other cits,
although loyal Southerners, spoke up for him so feelingly
that the guerrillas spared him.[434]

The action at McMinnville was a picnic. Colonel Dibrell,
having rested all the previous day, took some of the Eighth
Tennessee and the new recruits and absentees who were
armed, and rode down to dispose of Major Waters and his
homemade Yanks, who were something of a nuisance to
the neighborhood. It was no strain; the Yanks just about
let themselves get surrounded, then had to throw down
everything and hightail it for Tullahoma, leaving behind
all their camp truck, ten wagons, and an ambulance.[435]

At about the same time, Robertson and his Confederate
Brigade were serving Blackburn in like manner. When they
had gotten to Liberty, they had received orders to rejoin
General Williams once again. But since General Robertson
had left part of his command in Sparta to get shod, he got
permission to wait for those boys to rejoin him. That wait
wasn't spent in idleness, he later said: ". . . I improved the
time by driving the woods for Blackburn the bushwhacker
I got 125 horses from his clan — this mounted all my dis-

434. Will T. Hale, *History of DeKalb County* (McMinnville, Tennessee: P. Hunter, 1969), pp. 235-236.
435. *ORR,* I, 38, pt. 2, p. 490.

mounted men — I also pressed him so closely as to cause the release of some 70 prisoners he had taken. . . ."[436]

TOWARD NASHVILLE
AUGUST 30

On the 30th day of August, another fair, sunny day, Wheeler's main column hit the turnpikes to continue its drive toward the railroads that threaded out from Nashville. At Liberty, the divisions split up; Kelly's small command turned south and passed through Milton, while Humes' and Allen's boys moved on north toward Lebanon.[437] Everywhere it was a kind of homecoming, as the reclining John Coffee Williamson noted: "I got in the ambulance soon. We have traveled turnpikes all day. Some of them are in bad repair. We passed some small towns. I saw 15 home guards that had been captured at Liberty. The ladies were remarkably glad to see us. They were collected along the roads in crowds, all anxious to hear from their friends. We camped about 30 miles from Nashville on the Lebanon Road. I am yet very unwell."[438]

The success in recruiting and the warmth of the civilian population prompted General Wheeler to distribute a proclamation:

"TENNESSEANS: Confederate troops again press the soil of your noble State. The opportunity for which you have so long asked is now given you. The brave men, who, in this hour of your country's peril, still cling to your country's standard, appeal to you for aid.

436. Letter, Felix H. Robertson to Braxton Bragg, October 6, 1864.
437. Garrett and Lightfoot, p. 32.
438. Williamson, 65.

Shall they call in vain? Georgia has called her last available citizens between the ages of seventeen and fifty years. They are fighting beside your chivalrous sons before Atlanta. Other States are also throwing their entire male population into the field.

"Citizens of Tennessee. You who have always been ready to respond to our country's call, every one must rise to duty. If all you who should come will now join us, we pledge the honor of those States whose sons compose the Western army of the Confederacy that Tennessee shall be redeemed.

"J. Wheeler
Major-General"[439]

Typical of the boys who responded to Wheeler's appeal were ten classmates at Mount Vernon Academy, in Lebanon, including Alex Denton, Tom Harris, Ed Winters, Richard Stroud, Alexis Cook, John Guthrie, Henry Rogers, and his sixteen-year-old brother Ben. They had been figgeting as they watched the war go on without them, way down in Georgia. So when Captain Lindsay brought Company B of the Fourth Tennessee in town on a scout, those boys took their own horses and pistols and instantly became Reb cavalrymen.[440]

Meanwhile, Williams and Robertson finally, on the 30th, returned to the route taken by the other commands. Those whose horses were in good shape moved on through Sparta to camp on Caney Fork, about a mile and a half from Sligo, on the road west. But many of the boys stayed in Sparta to get their horses shod. Ben Darsey, of the Fifth Georgia, was one of them: "The road was plain and showed much travel. The water spouts which issued from those perpendicular walls of rock along the road side were perfectly magnificent and refreshing to a weary and thirsty soldier.

439. *ORR,* I, 38, pt. 5, p. 1004.

440. Civil War Questionnaires for Benjamin Duggan Rogers and Henry Jordan Rogers, State of Tennessee Archives.

The weather was excessively hot, men and horses were jaded. About the middle of the afternoon we reached the foot of the mountain, which put us in what is called Middle Tenn. Here we struck a thickly settled community of people of culture and refinement, and some of the richest lands I ever saw. Those people showed many acts of kindness to us, manifesting true loyalty to the Confederate cause."[441] About a hundred men of the force, under the command of Captain Brailsford, were left to go to the neighborhood smithies the next day.

TOWARD NASHVILLE
AUGUST 31

Business began to pick up for Wheeler's three divisions on August 31st, as they concentrated upon the Nashville and Chattanooga Railroad. For Kelly's Division the day's work began in the darkness of night; as Major John Minor, commanding the Tenth Tennessee, remembered it: "We march at 3 o'clock . . . avoiding Murfresboro and striking the RR at Smyrna, burning some rolling stock or boxcars loaded with forage and several miles of track[.] [W]e then marched on up the road toward Nashville burning as we went."[442] The other two divisions went south, hitting Smyrna from the north and sending portions of both Humes' and Allen's divisions on down to block any attack from Murfreesborough. William Sloan, of Humes' Division, was a part of the blocking force: "Our squadron (Capt. Rheagan's) was ordered to move on to Murfresboro and drive in the yankee pickets, but when we arrived we found no pickets

441. Darsey.
442. Minor.

outside the fortifications. We could see the sentinels on the breastworks, walking their beats. We remained about two hours on picket duty, within a few hundred yards of the works, and then we discovered a body of the enemy's cavalry attempting to get in our rear and cut us off. We fell back and avoided a collision. During this time our command was moving on to Smyrna to destroy the railroad."[443]

Colonel D. T. Blakey, commanding the First Alabama Cavalry, remained on picket for a longer period of time, so long that he thought fit to report to General Allen:

"MAJOR: I have sent you three couriers to-day before this one, and none of them have returned, so that I am ignorant as to whether they have reached you; therefore I give you a summary of my operations to-day:

"I moved up toward Murfreesborough this morning, passing a stockade at Smyrna, and one at the railroad bridge over Overall's Creek, both garrisoned, and struck the railroad just three miles from Murfreesborough. I spent about one hour in destroying the road and think that I thoroughly destroyed about 200 yards. I had sent a scout down the pike toward Murfreesborough; they ran upon a regiment of mounted infantry about one mile and a half from Murfreesborough, got very close to it before they were discovered, and had the opportunity of examining closely and determining exactly what the force was. This command fired on my scout and drove them back; they then advanced and drove in my picket. As I had accomplished all that was ordered in the way of destroying the road, and was in a very difficult position, having Stone's River on one side and Overall's Creek in my rear, with a force in a stockade that commanded the crossing, I decided to leave the positions and move to the north side of Overall's Creek, which I did by

443. Sloan, p. 77.

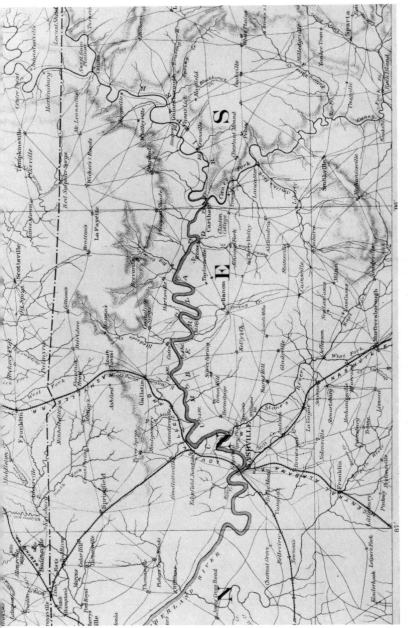

Route, September 1-3

Fortified bridge in Tennessee

crossing the river, moving down on the east side below the mouth of the creek, and recrossing the river. I then posted my command on the railroad six miles from Murfreesborough, and picketed the railroad in sight of the stockade, also the pike at the bridge across Overall's Creek. I am still in that position; I am one mile and a half in front of any working party."[444]

The greatest amount of attention was paid to the track between Murfreesborough and LaVergne. Since there was no Yank cavalry found about that stretch, it was a fairly simple matter to destroy the track — except where there were blockhouses. The Yanks had devised a system of placing blockhouses on the road at the points where it crossed a long trestle or bridge, the burning of which would cause a lengthy disruption and rile old Sherman. Such a blockhouse could protect not only a bridge, but also the track back up the road that fell within its field of fire. Naturally the boys were a little skittish when they were working near a blockhouse, for they never quite knew what kind of range those blockhouses might have. As W. A. Fletcher, of the Eighth Texas, admitted: "Our worst resistance was what were called 'block houses,' and we generally found them at the streams or openings where bridging or trestling, if destroyed, would cause much delay in traffic. Block houses were built of small logs notched down, with holes in the wall to shoot through, and were stationed at a point to best protect the structure, if attempted destruction. The country was fairly well supplied with worm rail fencing near one or both sides of the railroad track. We were moved in column of regiments near the side of the road and when the desired point had been reached, we were halted, generally fronting toward the road, dismounted — every fourth man holding the horses,

444. *ORR*, I, 38, pt. 3, p. 962.

and the balance put to carrying fence rails and placing
them on each side of the rail on each side of the track. Six
or eight rails all well connected would make sufficient heat
when fired, to bend the rails by expansion, and ruin the ties.
When a regiment had completed its front, it would move
to front of column and repeat the same performance, and as
there was a large body of us, by this method we destroyed
during twenty-four hours a good mileage of track; but at
all times, as far as I knew, we kept clear of the block house
sharp shooters."[445]

Not that we didn't try to take the damned things. The
blockhouse at Smyrna was approached early in the morning, and our boys demanded its unconditional surrender.
The Yank lieutenant commanding the defenders yelled
back that he did not know the meaning of the term;[446]
then, lest there be misunderstanding, he yelled, "No surrender." So, having been polite, we then backed off and
began to shell the place. We had four pieces, three 3-inch
rifled Parrotts and one 12-pounder smooth-bore, and in
about three hours we threw sixty-four shells at the building, all the while the cavalry cat-calling at the wild shots
and cheering the fair ones. Although several shells appeared
to penetrate the walls, there appeared to be no effect on
the defenders, for they continued to fire at anything that
moved within a thousand yards. John Coffee Williamson,
still sick and traveling by ambulance, observed the bom-
bardment and was not too impressed at the artillery's effort: "We struck the RR today at Smyrna station and the
road burns finely. The Yanks have run into their little forts
which proved after trial to be bomb proof. Many shots were
fired with no effect only to draw a reply of the small arms

445. Fletcher, pp. 112-113.
446. *ORR*, I, 38, pt. 2, pp. 506-508.

which shot wild. The Yanks shot too high. One artillery-man was wounded in the thigh. The boys burned a Negro's house. The darkeys were glad to be allowed to go home. Tom came up and got me a quart of good whiskey and I got so drunk that I went to sleep and knew nothing of that night's travel."[447]

The boys who went to the blockhouse at Stewart's Creek had better luck. They planted their artillery about twelve noon, blasted the building six times, and ceased when a white flag began to wave out of one of the loopholes. The boys yelled to come on out, and out marched thirty men of the 115th Ohio Infantry, commanded by a Sergeant Flohr, who said that the fort couldn't be defended in its present condition.[448] The boys certainly agreed with him, and burned both the fort and the bridge it hadn't protected.

Even on such a busy day, some of the boys got to pay social calls. Isaac Ulmer, of the Third Alabama, took his negro Elijah and went visiting: "Near Smyrna I called to see Miss Hadly that I had met before in Tenn. Dr. Davis received me kindly and cordially inviting me to dine. . . . They say they are watched and informed on by the tories and the few remaining negroes at every chance. Sometimes the men would ride up to a house and ask for something to eat. They would tell you that they could not give it, and aside would tell you to go in and *order* the servants to prepare it. They would say, we have *plenty* and you are more than welcome. We cant openly give, but you are *welcome*; go in and what ever you see, just *order* the servants to get for you. In that way they gratified the wants of the Southern soldier and kept themselves from Yankee wrath. All or nearly all have taken the *oath*; but can quickly see that it

447. Williamson, 66.
448. *ORR*, I, 38, pt. 2, pp. 505-508.

is from *the lips* and only to protect themselves."[449] Ah well, as the Scriptures have it, "The lips of the righteous feed many. . . ."

By sundown the road around Smyrna was thoroughly smashed, and the boys were driving through LaVergne toward Antioch. It was a beautiful, starry night, and, because of the lack of resistance during the day, some of the boys must even have thought that they would eat dinner at home in Nashville the next day. Some of the officers even got fired up to go calling. One of them put it to the "War Baby": "To be candid with you, General, . . . the press of the South has so vituperated and abused you that everybody has lost confidence in you except your own command and those of the army who have had an opportunity of knowing what you have done. Your own reputation and that of your command demand that you take Nashville."[450] Fortunately for a good many Reb cavalrymen, who were about ridden out, to begin with, Wheeler had enough sense to confront Southern newspapers rather than entrenched Yank infantry. He made a little speech, in which he said he would sacrifice his reputation to the cause, any time. About 11:00 p.m., Yank cavalry was encountered near the Lunatic Asylum[450a] — if we hadn't been in a hurry, we could have dropped off some officer candidates.

There were, of course, commands and stragglers all the

449. Letter, Isaac Barton Ulmer to his mother, September 10, 1864, Isaac Barton Ulmer Papers, Southern Historical Collection, University of North Carolina.

450. John Percy Dyer, *From Shiloh to San Juan* (Baton Rouge: Louisiana State University Press, 1961), p.. 151.

450a. W. B. Carter, *History of the First Regiment of Tennessee Volunteer Cavalry* (Knoxville: Gaut-Ogden Company, 1902), pp. 188-189.

way back to Sparta, where Dibrell's regiment was still assembling. His men were desperate to get horses, so that they could catch up with the main column; otherwise they would eventually be hunted down by Tennessee Yanks under Stokes and Blackburn and killed or captured — and if they were captured, they would probably be labeled outlaws and hanged on the spot. They ranged, then, all over the Cumberlands for horses, as one Union woman, Mary Catherine Sproul, a thirty-one-year-old school teacher could testify. Her father had gone to Kentucky to fetch her home to Livingston, and as they approached home, rumors of the Rebs were heard: "As soon as day light appeared we mounted our horses and made for home. About ten O clock in the Morning we reached Mount Zion Church where we met a gentleman, we asked him how many rebels there were in the Country he said Diberal and Wheeler had 17 Begads and that 1000 Texas Rangers had just passed on to Monroe. We traveled on though we could see no tracks of horses and when we reached Monroe they told us there, no Soldiers had been there, . . . We came on rapidly and in 4 or 5 miles of home we met three rebels Soldiers, they cast their vicious [looks] at us as though they intended to dismount us. Some of Diberals men lived in Overton and they had come home to see there friends, and to commit all depredations upon Union citizens. We are at home. My Mother comes to meet me with joy Mingled with pain. My Brother was glad to see me, but distressed for fear he would again be driven from home. After our arrival awhile and we listened to the performances of the rebels during Fathers absence. Mother Said the night before our arrival three men rode up to the gate and called. She Spoke to My Brother and told him to Step out at the back door, for they might abuse him, as Soon as My Brother had made his exit, My Mother went to the door and these rebels asked where my Father was. She told them he had gone to Ky, after his daughter, they then asked where my Brother was Mother told them he had gone to a neighbors house, they then asked for our horse Mother told them My Father had rode him to Ky, then they asked for a halter. Mother told them we had no halter that She knew of they Swore we had and dismounted and came in pretendiary to look everywhere; they then demanded Something to eat, Mother prepared them Supper as quick as She could, and while She was getting something they were plundering the house. Among the many things they purloined that night was My Mothers Bonnet and Combs. I speak of this because these devils robbed My Mother while She was cooking for them and to Show you what little things a rebel will Stoop to. After eating and cursing the Union men to their hearts content, they left Screaming and cursing. As the grey eyed morning began to peep over the eastern hills, My Brother emerged from his dewy bed and with a sinking heart went to the house and with eager ear listened to Mothers doleful story of her Nights trouble.

"I desired to leave here, but Saw there was no chance, we had but one horse and that a very indifferent one, and the rebels were after him daily. We had to keep that horse concealed, for they had threatened to take him. The whole country was alive with rebel Soldiers."[451]

Williams' command, having passed a pleasant night on Caney Fork, spent that last day of the month riding to catch up with the three divisions that were with Wheeler. A relaxed Jim Black outlined the day in his diary: "The bugle's blast aroused us early. Was very much refreshed by a bathe. After a spare breakfast on rarely cooked beef & a

451. Albert W. Shroeder, Jr. (ed.), "Writings of a Tennessee Unionist," *Tennessee Historical Quarterly*, IX (December, 1950), 358.

ear of corn, we started on the march. Passed through Smithville & Liberty & camped at Alexandria. Things look as
familiar as the scenes of our childhood. Capt. Blackburn
annoyed us some."[452]

452. Black.

VII

Franklin, Tennessee:
"Well, boys, I reckon we will have to try it"

(September 1-7, 1864)

NASHVILLE
SEPTEMBER 1

*T*he next morning, the first day of September, reveille for the Rebs with Wheeler was sounded by the steam whistles of the Nashville factories, for they were that close to the city, as John Coffee Williamson learned when he awakened at 5:00 a.m.[453] The Yanks started the festivities for what promised to be a busy day; they charged the pickets of the Eleventh Texas. The Texans were driven into a heavy grove of cedars, but what the Yanks didn't realize was that that grove masked the camp of Harrison's Brigade, which came charging out to join the party. For a while there was a general mix-up with revolvers and sabres. Then the Yanks, who turned out to be Jim Brownlow's First Tory Tennessee, that had somehow recovered from Newnan and gotten up to Middle Tennessee, decided to seek after valor elsewhere. They left five dead on the field, including one color sergeant who went down with his guidon staff shot right in two. Then the Texans and Arkansans rode down twenty prisoners,[454] who maybe stood too much on ceremony.

By then the sun had grown very hot, and that, together with the early morning action, should have set the tone for the day, but strangely there was very little noise to speak of after that. Not even Humes' other brigade, Ashby's, was ordered out of camp.[455] The other divisions began sliding off to the west, heading toward the Nashville and Decatur Railroad at Franklin. Chaplain Bunting noted that the country was very familiar: "We are now in the region of our earlier soldier duties . . . But oh! how changed from three years ago. Then this beautiful country was in the highest state of cultivation, but now desolation and destruction mark it everywhere."[456] Meanwhile, back down the road, Williams' command stayed in Alexandria all day and then started for LaVergne on rested horses about sundown.

453. Williamson, 66.
454. Carter, pp. 190-192.
455. Sloan, p. 77.
456. Bunting.

Colonel Willie Breckinridge must have spent part of that day writing a letter to his wife in Canada, for he got a friendly citizen, "J. H.," to post it for him in the U. S. mails in Smyrna the next day — such a direct routing would take weeks or even months less than the Confederate mail service and the flag of truce exchange boat.[457]

THOMPSON'S STATION
SEPTEMBER 2

By daylight on September 2nd Wheeler's Rebs were furiously tearing up track at Thompson's Station, three miles south of Franklin. The boys turned to with a right good vigor, for they wanted to get the job done and get going, since folks weren't being very hospitable. Sometimes their hurry cost heavily: Major August Ingram, leading a working party of the Twelfth Alabama, had one of his legs mangled by a cross-tie that was being flung down by his men and had to be left in agony at a farm house.[458] Then his men rode on, for it seemed like half the force was scattered across Middle Tennessee, and those who were dismounted and working on the rails felt that they weren't getting enough protection.

Some of the boys were taking it easy that morning. Bill Watson and Jim Richardson, McLemore's Fourth Tennessee, had spent the night as advance guards and had been relieved when the column struck the Columbia and Franklin turnpike. Their company commander, Captain James T. Pierce, lived in the neighborhood, and since he was going home for

457. Letter envelope postmarked September 2, in Volume 236, Breckinridge Collection, Library of Congress.
458. "12th Alabama Cavalry Regiment," manuscript in Military Records Department, State of Alabama Archives.

breakfast he invited his two good soldiers along. They rode north up the pike, over Winstead Hill, but before they got to their turning-off place they ran into Yanks. They had met some blacks along the way who told them that "Mister Rebels" still held Franklin, but the blacks were either lying or didn't know Rebs from Yanks. The three Rebs were on tired horses, so they were afraid to turn tail and run; they just eased about, sauntered along at a jog until they reached the top of Winstead Hill, then lit out to warn the wrecking parties.[459]

But the Yanks got to the top of the hill before the three Rebs got all the way to the Reb pickets. J. H. Fussell, of Colonel Wheeler's First Tennessee, had about one hundred fifty men deployed as protection, and they watched as the Yanks came over the brow of the hill. First the sharpshooters "scrambling down the south side, taking advantage of trees, rocks, bushes, &c."[460] Then the Yanks busied about and set up their batteries there on the road and pretty soon they were sending the grape and cannister toward the Rebs working on the tracks. There was a hill on either side of the road, and General Wheeler saw that if he could take one of the hills he could either flank the Yank artillery or capture it.[461] So he sent word to General Kelly to go forward to charge the Yank right flank on their hill. General Kelly took a good long look at that hill, then gave the courier his response: "Go back and tell General Wheeler that we can't take that position."[462]

459. Frank N. Smith, *History of Maury County, Tennessee* [typescript] (n.p.:1969), p. 67.

460. Smith, p. 118.

461. Carter, pp. 192-194.

462. J. G. Witherspoon, "Confederate Cavalry Leaders," *Confederate Veteran*, XXVII(November, 1919), 414-417.

In a few minutes the courier came trotting back to repeat the same order. General Kelly never looked more like the young man that he was than at that moment; he didn't say anything that betrayed what might be on his mind, he just looked around at his few worn-out troopers and hesitated. But he was a soldier, so he said, "Well, boys, I reckon we will have to try it."

He had only the Ninth, Tenth, and Eleventh Tennessee with him, not very many more folks than the mourners at a banker's funeral. But the men were formed by platoons on the turnpike and ordered forward at the double quick. At first the column advanced in an orderly fashion, like it was just out for a routine scout, but when it got within seventy-five yards of that gap that the road went through, the Yanks opened up with musketry and artillery, and it was fierce. The column could take only so much, then began to panic. Rushing to the head of the column, General Kelly ordered his men to dismount and form along a fence of field stones that bordered the road. Still mounted, he waved his sword toward the hill, ordering an advance to another fence farther up the hillside.

Lieutenant Fussell knew that Kelly was getting within range of the Yank sharpshooters, so he sent a runner to warn him as he rode up to a brick house that was shaded by a row of locust trees. But "Kelly did not seem to mind it, but with his two friends remained on horseback at the yard gate at the locust tree."[463] A few of Kelly's men had actually gone forward, maybe thinking that the Yanks would be more apt to overshoot them if they were behind the nearer fence. Although the hill was beginning to get smokey from the firing, the Rebs could see that it was their old friends, Brownlow's First Tennessee, there on the ridge

463. Smith, pp. 118-119.

line defending the Yank artillery. There was a cheer at that moment, as Colonel Brownlow was seen to go down. More Rebs started forward, including General Kelly, now with his revolver in his hand. There were perhaps twenty or thirty Rebs taking shelter behind the wall, and Kelly was trying to get them moving. At that moment a Yank sharpshooter, who had crept closer than his comrades, fired off three shots, one of which passed through Kelly's chest.

Bill Watson had ridden up to Kelly just at that moment and saw the young general reeling in his saddle. He caught Kelly's bridle, as the wounded man fell out of his saddle and into an officer's arms. Major John Minor, still mounted, jumped down and saw at once that the wound was fatal, In that instant Minor's horse had been killed and had fallen down almost without threshing, so Minor got the blanket from under his saddle, placed Kelly on it, and tried to minister to him.[464] John Brown, General Kelly's courier, watched helplessly, as several officers bent over the general there in a ditch. As one of them tried to take his coat off, Kelly had strength enough to moan, "Damn it, cut off the coat."[465] He seemed to be dying even then, but he was "very game," Bill Watson thought. Lieutenant Fussell, back farther than Kelly's command, had seen the whole affair and sent for an ambulance, which came "at a rush." The dying man was taken back to a brick house about a half a mile down the road, so that he wouldn't have to die in enemy hands. He was left there with a nurse, but the others had to go back and fight for two hours, until the entire wagon train got onto the turnpike and headed south.

Sergeant J. G. Witherspoon, Company F, Ninth Tennessee Cavalry, was one of the boys who had gone forward

464. Minor.
465. Smith, p. 119.

Brig.-Gen. John H. Kelly

Brig.-Gen. John S. "Cerro Gordo" Williams

to the second fence, but he soon had reason to think about his position in life: "I looked around and found that I was alone, within less than two hundred yards of the enemy's lines, with the command in full retreat in considerable disorder. If the enemy had not overshot them, the loss would have been terrible. I soon saw that it was either capture or run for me, and I decided to run. I noticed a small thicket about a hundred yards up the fence that would give me some protection, and to that I crawled. I had to 'stoop low,' for every time my back got a little too high a bullet would whiz over me. With the slight protection the thick corn gave me, I 'lit a shuck,' as the boys say, down a corn row and literally outran the bullets, for they continued to fire on me till I was out of range.

"When I reached the fence on the south side of the field, I happened to run right into my company. An uncle of mine, J. F. Pitts, brought my horse to me as I was climbing the fence. He told me that General Kelly had been killed; that Captain Johnson had caught him in his arms as he fell and had carried him to a brick house about half a mile away, which he pointed out to me. He said that everything was demoralized and for me to get on my horse and try to form the company and get things in some shape. After getting my breath a little, I got on my horse, rallied my company, and we covered the retreat. Fortunately for us and for the whole command, the Federals did not follow us. I have often wondered why General Wheeler ordered that charge and what he expected to gain by it. I know that General Forrest would not have done it."[466]

The skirmishing continued through the day, as Wheeler worked his way down the railroad. There was very little work now being done on the tracks, for the boys just wanted

466. Witherspoon.

to escape with their wagons and their skins. But the Yanks were as feisty as a pack of dogs and kept yapping at the heels of the column. On one occasion Harrison's Brigade was sent back to caution them, but it ran upon them hidden behind a stone fence and got the worst end of it. Colonel Hobson and a good many more of the Third Arkansas were wounded, as the Yanks rose up a mere twenty feet in front of them.[467] Fortunately the Yanks had been punished as severely as the Rebs, for they did not again press the issue. At dark Wheeler left the road a few miles south of Spring Hill and headed west to Columbia.[468]

The boys in the Kentucky Brigade spent the day getting even more anxious about rejoining the main column. They had been separated by then since August 24th, and they wanted to find out what was going on. When they got to LaVergne, only a day behind Wheeler, they found a Yank force between themselves and Wheeler's new stomping grounds, over on the Nashville and Decatur road. To their amazement, they spent the entire night at LaVergne, instead of trying to find a way to get around the Yanks.[469] The amazement turned to disgust later, when they found out that the Yank force was infantry and could not have hampered their movement much.[470] There they were, all cavalry, without as much information as a Methodist circuit-rider on a jake-legged mule could pick up going to the spring and back.

Back in Sparta, Colonel Dibrell moved his command out toward Lebanon. His force had grown from about one hundred thirty men to about eight hundred, with the addi-

467. Bunting.
468. Sloan, p. 77.
469. Black.
470. ORR, I, 38, pt. 2, p. 911.

tion of new recruits, absentees, the part of Robertson's
command that had remained in Sparta to get shoes for
their horses, and the guerrillas who were being forced to
leave the area because the Yanks had in recent months
begun to make it too hot for them.[471]

Despite the Union bushwhackers and the organized Union
forces, the boys in Dibrell's column, though most of them
were unarmed, got pretty well scattered and were in a high-
spirited mood. Ben Darsey, of the Fifth Georgia, recalled
the day with some pleasure: "While on our way to Lebanon
to meet Col. Dibril and his men, we were permitted to
march at leisure, and at times we were considerably scattered. There were no federal soldiers in that immediate
section and we felt comparatively secure though we were
few in number. While riding along I noticed a road
leading off to a plantation a few hundred yards from the turn
pike which we were traveling. Just then I conceived an idea
that by going to that place I could obtain a fresh horse; so
without telling the boys my object, I took the road and in
a few minutes was at the gate. A middle aged lady and
her little daughter come out to the gate and spoke to me.
She recognized me as a confederate by my dress. I at once
told her to what command I belonged and my business or
motive in coming by. She told me that her husband was
in the Confederate army, and the yankees had taken every
horse from her, and robbed her of many other things. She
expressed her regret at not being able to furnish me with
a fresh horse. She talked so kindly and interestingly that
I delayed some time. As I was about to take my leave, she
asked me if I would have something to eat. I thanked her

471. Will T. Hale and Dixon L. Merritt, *A History of Tennessee
and Tennesseans* (Chicago: Lewis Publishing Company, 1913), Volume
III, pp. 644-645.

and answered her in the affirmative. She hastily brought me a dish of cold chicken pie, a plate of biscuits and a pitcher of milk; telling me at the same time that she could not invite me into her house as the yanks had forbidden her entertaining the Rebs, and she wanted a clear conscience in telling them she had not. I commended her for this, and at the same time I seated myself upon a large rock which lay near the gate. I hastily ate my unexpected meal, and while eating I heard her tell her daughter to go in the house and look in a certain place and get a pair of socks and bring them to her. The girl obeyed her mother and in a few moments the good lady gave them to me — a pair of home knit wool socks; and at the same time told me to take the remainder of the biscuits for further use, which I did. Putting the bread and socks in my haversack, I asked her name and she told me her name was Smith. I then expressed to her my gratitude, assuring her that Providence would reward her some day."[472]

COLUMBIA

SEPTEMBER 3

By the morning of September 3rd, the raid had lost any organization that it ever had. There was no communication between the separated commands, and each was being pretty easily hassled every time it stopped to water the flowers. Wheeler's column marched cross country around Columbia all day, going through the farms of Generals Polk and Pillow, among other places. It was a scorching day; in one of the jolting ambulances John Coffee Williamson

472. Darsey.

dozed, and in dozing dreamed of good fortune.[473] Other men were also dreaming even though they were awake; they were getting closer and closer to home and wondering if they would get to see their families. Wheeler made an attempt to see that some Rebs lived to see their families, for he sent the following message to Major-General Rousseau, the Yank commander of the Nashville area:

"I am informed that the following named Confederate soldiers are to be executed in Nashville on the 9th inst.:

"John Young, Jesse Broadway, Milam, Mosley, Elliott, Lieutenant B. Bridges.

"I cannot conceive that such can be the case. Have the kindness to inform me if it is so, and stay any action until you can hear from me.

"All Federal soldiers who have thus far been captured behind our lines, no matter how far in the rear, have been treated with all the courtesy due prisoners of war."[474]

Over at LaVergne, Williams' Brigade turned southwest and finally camped at Salem, four miles southwest of Murfreesborough.[475] Early that morning it had been joined by the detachment of the Ninth Tennessee Battalion and the Fourth Tennessee commanded by Lieutenant-Colonel Paul Anderson. Those boys had had an exhausting, but not very profitable excursion. Going down Sequatchie Valley, after they had left the main column, they had passed Pikesville on the morning of the 29th of August.[476] On the 30th those boys had hit the fort at Tracy City; George Guild was there

473. Williamson, 66.

474. Dodson, p. 256.

475. Homer Peyton Pittard, *Legends and Stories of Civil War Rutherford County,* Unpublished MA Thesis, George Peabody College for Teachers, 1940, p. 113.

476. New York *Herald,* September 6, 1864.

and witnessed the confusion: "Upon reaching the place,
Lieut. Col. Paul Anderson made his disposition for capture
by detailing Lieut. W. H. Phillips, of Company F, with ten
men to charge down the road leading to the fort in order
to attract their attention, when Colonel Anderson would
come up from the rear, where the fort was said to be unfinished and open and capture it. Before reaching his position, Colonel Anderson discovered that the opening had
been closed and that there were as many of the enemy on
the inside of the log structure as he had on the outside. He
at once dispatched a message to Lieutenant Phillips counter-
manding the order; but before it was delivered Phillips,
growing impatient, charged as directed. The courier reached
there in time to see Phillips upon the ground in front of the
fort shooting at the portholes, and saw him scramble to his
feet and stagger across the road into the timber where his
comrades sought protection. He had been terribly wounded
in the breast and shoulder, showing evidence of paralysis
from the wounds. A conveyance was impressed with a
view to taking him and others who had been wounded with
us; but after traveling a mile or two, Phillips was suffering so that he asked to be left at a house to die."[477]

The command had to go on, for its only weapon was
surprise. On the 31st, it scouted Jasper, then in the evening
tried to attack the railroad tunnel south of Cowan.[478] But
the tunnel was made of solid stone and could not be dam-
aged, so they had to settle for burning a little track and
cutting the telegraph wires. Totally exhausted, they rode
on toward Winchester, near which they pursued a Yank
wagon train, as Adjutant Allen remembered: "In their
efforts to get away boxes of crackers were broken open and

477. Guild, pp. 73-74.
478. ORR, I, 38, pt. 5, p. 740.

wagon beds rolled down the mountain, till the whole place
was strewn with provisions of every sort. At Winchester we
came again to the railroad, which we tore up, and destroyed
all the enemy's provisions that we could find. Riding from
this place, I was with Dr. [Dulaney] at the rear of the column. It was very dark; and when those in front of us halted,
we waited also, until I became impatient and went forward
to see what was the matter. I found some of the men asleep
on their horses, quietly awaiting orders to move on. They
were the most surprised men imaginable when we awakened
them; but the command was gone, and we had to follow as
best we could. Dr. Dulaney and I rode around in the dark
until we came to what we thought was Colonel Anderson's
camp. We went to it and asked for Colonel Anderson before
we found that it was a Yankee picket post. Then we got out
in a hurry, followed by several shots."[479]

They rode, or maybe it would be more truthful to say
"staggered," on, as they followed the railroad tracks,
throughout September 1st. About 3:00 a.m., on the morning of the 2nd, the two little regiments tried their hand at
attacking a train. This was within six miles of Murfreesborough; they piled wood on the track and planned to fire
on the train when it stopped. But there turned out to be
two trains, and the Yanks began to hop off and fire, re-
sponding to shouted commands that revealed that the trains
were loaded with troops.[480] The Rebs were forced to flee,
and Adjutant Allen had to take drastic evasive action: ". . .
the whole load of Yankee soldiers jumped out and swarmed
all over the place to see what had stopped them. I knew
they would get me, so I hid in the river, with only my head

479. William Gibbs Allen, "Incidents of Wheeler's Raid," 288.
480. *ORR*, I, 38, pt. 2, pp. 491-492.

sticking out."[481]

Some how, Adjutant Allen got out of the river: "When I awoke I was in a cedar thicket. I had lost my horse. I listened for sounds. I heard horses feet on the Pike. I moved up close so I could see who was passing. I made my self known. I found it was Gen. Williams Ky Brigade. I asked to be sent to his quarters. I found him drunk, as usual, he received me and told me to stay at his quarters." During the day Williams' boys mounted two charges upon Murfreesborough that failed. And when they were joined by Robertson's command, General Robertson himself led yet a third charge. After it failed, the enlarged force cut southwest of the town that they couldn't take and went into camp.[482]

LEBANON
SEPTEMBER 3

The same day, September 3rd, Dibrell's column got to Lebanon, learned of the death of its division commander, General Kelly, at Franklin, and of the retreat of Wheeler toward Columbia. Dibrell decided to strike south by way of Murfreesborough in an effort to join Wheeler.

PULASKI
SEPTEMBER 4

On September 4th the main column continued its way down the railroad below Columbia. Colonel James Wheeler's

481. William Gibbs Allen, "Incidents of Wheeler's Raid," 288.
482. William Gibbs Allen, "War Reminiscence."

First Tennessee, of Ashby's Brigade, attempted to take a Yank fort, but, as before, it withstood the Reb artillery.[483] During the day, as the column moved toward Pulaski, the companies of the Tenth Tennessee that had been raised in the neighborhood were released to go home for a short time.[484] Every time the column would stop to feed, the Yanks would come up and drive in the pickets. The Rebs dared them to come to scratch, but they just hung back and pestered, not giving the Rebs a minute's peace, as bad as a drove of fleas on a nursing dog. Wheeler ordered an all night ride, hoping that such action might evade the ceaseless pursuit.

That same day Dibrell's column was moving toward Murfreesborough, sending out scouts to little effect. By now his best source of information was the Nashville newspapers that he could liberate.[485] The boys didn't care much for the war news in the *Daily Times and True Union* for September 1st, but they did enjoy the contribution by Petroleum V. Nasby:

"Church uv the Noo Dispensashen
Gooly 30, 1864

"Our class meetins hev ben sumwhat neglectid uv lait. Sumhow it is in our church ez it is in the hetrodox — we air hot and cold alternitly. Last Sunday we hed a preshus seezn.

"Bro. Siples spoak. He confest he was a week mortel. He hed his ups and downs, bad. It wuz full on him. Wenever Grant and Sherman hed a success his faith faled him and sumtimes he hed difficulty in cuming in time even wen Lee whipt Grant. But he hed recently paid $2 per gallon for whisky and that stird him. With wun hand upon his 2 often

483. Williamson, 66.
484. Minor.
485. *ORR*, I, 39, pt 1, pp. 495-497.

empty jug and tother pointed to heaven he had sworn eternal hostility tu them ez hed razed these prices, which is ablishnists. If convenyent he askt the betrhring to pray fer him.

"Bro. Hopp riz. He hed his ups and downs also rayther more downs than ups. His sole was full wen Forrist killed the niggers, but alas woe wuz on him wen Sherman flaxt em at Atlanta. Now the skizes is brite. Lee holds out bully, and tother day 4,000 niggers wuz killed at Petersburg.

"At this pint I interrupted bro Hopp. The killin uv niggers is no coz uv rejoisin. Wat a distruction of property! 4,000 niggers at 1,500 a nigger is $6,000,000! This sum uv munny, even at the present ablishn prices, wood predooze 50,000,000 nips! Wood, o wood, that I wuz condemn to consoom em all! Ef them niggers had been white men I woodent hev keered. Wy? Bekoz, white sojers is all ablishnists. Don't shake yer hed, bro. Gramp, it's so. Yoor own son, even backslid. He it wuz who rit hum a sayin that if he had kum back and found that old hipocrit Nasby a ceting chickens about yoor hooze, he'd plump a ounce ball into him. Hipocrit! Chickins! Sich baseniss confirms me in my beleef in the doctrin uv totle depravity. I am an onobtroosive gest at the table uv my flock. Troo I ete, but wood eny uv em say that chickings wus a equivalent for my improvin conversashin? Ez fer the paltry munny I borror, I allez giv my noat, wich settles them transactions.

"2 resoom. Every nigger killed inflaims our brethren powerful. Imagin my brethrin, a suthrin artilrist a bringin uv his peace to bare upon the advansin enemy. He sees their air niggers, and his hart sinks. Neerer and neerer they cum. Seezing a glass, he vews em and horror! in the front rank, 'clothed in soots uv blu,' he beholes his indivijile niggers! Neerer! neerer! Fain would he spare em, for them very niggers may be the uncles uv a dozen his children (wich is patriarkle) to say nuthin uv the mony he has inweasted in em. But no! The order is given! 'Fire.' He pulls the fatle string and ez he beholds his own property a bleedin on the plane, he swoons away. My jentil freinds I maik no doubt that haff the cases reported in the Suthrin papers ez sun stroke wuz from that doz.

"Uther brethrin giv their experience in. The feelin is improvin sence the draft, and I hev faith that if our groseries kin hold up till Sept 5, under the credit sistem, and too menny dont run 2 Kanady, we will abe able to whole enny Provo Marshel's fose they kin send again us.

"Petroleum V. Nasby
Paster uv sed Church in charge"[486]

It was Williams' command that had the greatest difficulty with their Yank pursuit on that Sunday. They got an early start, planning to head north, then west to Triune dirt road; by eight o'clock some of them had reached the home of Willie King, a young country boy with Southern loyalties: "To our surprise a squad of men rode into our front yard, where our horses were grazing; catching our horses, unsaddling their poor broken-down horses, and when I saw them, I thought at first they were Yankees, and I was mad. But they said they were Confederates, belonging to General Williams' brigade. I was soon convinced and told them to take the horses and leave their poor ones. I walked on keeping up with them to the Franklin Road, talking to them and looking at the soldiers as they were passing on, and at General Williams. He was a big, fat man, about five feet and seven inches in height, and weighing about two hundred and twenty-five pounds or more. About

---

486. Nashville *Daily Times and True Union*, September 1, 1864.

the time we reached the Franklin Road, I heard a cannon boom. I said, 'What's that?' and instantly, I said, 'I must go,' and went home as fast as I could. Sampson who was holding a horse while a soldier was tacking on shoes, said, calling out to me, 'Mars Willie, where you going?' I replied, 'I'm going home,' but I did not stop. As I passed on, I heard Sampson saying to the soldier, 'Massy, massy, let me go with my young Master.' Just as I reached the house, Yankees were coming through the back way into the yard. Mother, seeing Sampson and Dilly . . . coming up the avenue, called to them to come in quickly. The Yankees heard her calling and were very much enraged. They said she was calling the negroes to come to catch them."[487]

The Rebs were exhausted, fearful that they would be out-numbered, and certain that they would be out-gunned, for they were just about out of ammunition. So General Williams made what were probably the only preparations for the encounter: he ordered his men to dismount long enough to take down every other panel of that rail fence along the road, so that the column could melt away if it was over-run. The artillery was set up in advance, in hope that it would be so effective that the Yanks could be kept at a distance.

The pressure was so intense, though, that the artillery was forced immediately to retreat to a slight rise in the road. When it stopped again, Captain Pue fired off the shot that Willie King heard, fired it off as quickly as possible, without running up the elevating screw. The aim was far wild, of course, but by luck, the shell hit a huge limb of a tree which hung over the road. It dropped just in front of a Yank troop that had appeared at that moment and was charging down a side road, which joined the Reb road right

487. Pittard, pp. 114-115.

in the middle of the column.[488]

Quickly General "Comanche" Robertson, commanding the rear brigade of the column, seized the opportunity that the lucky shot had provided. Yelling to some fifty men of the Fifth Georgia under Major Davant, he charged the Yanks, who were milling about, stunned and bunched up, fighting the branches of that limb. Someone that he talked with later described the ensuing action: "Robertson and his men galloped ahead at once. The Wacoan rode a 'bidable and kindly disposed little mule' that he had exchanged with his bugler for a fine gray horse which had crippled itself with a stone cut in the foot. The mule, however, flew into battle with all the spirit of a charger and Robertson's first bullet took effect in the chin and neck of a Federal soldier standing in a fence corner as he rode by. The second shot from his unerring pistol mortally wounded the Yankee commanding officer. The latter, however, remained seated in his saddle until Major Davant rode up and thrust him in the shoulder with a saber.

"Shot three was wasted, but just at that instant a Yankee attempted to evade Robertson's fire by bending low on the other side of his horse and galloping by Robertson laid his pistol over the man's saddle pommel and fired. The fellow hit the ground with a thud. Shots five and six found shelter in Yankee soldiers under similar circumstances. The melee, hot and short, was soon ended with the Federals fleeing and the little Confederate force victorious.

"All of a sudden, though, somebody shouted that the enemy was wearing gray uniforms and gray belonged distinctly to the Confederates! Whether there had been some mistake — or whether the enemy had attempted to gain an

488. Felix H. Robertson, "On Wheeler's Last Raid in Middle Tennessee," 335.

advantage by wearing the gray — Robertson rode back to
find out among the dead and injured. He discovered that
the peculiar brown dust of the road, settling in the Union
blue, had created the illusion, and that the defeated force
were after all wearing their own uniforms. He drew the
dead commander out of a fence corner to investigate his
wound.

"It had gone in about where the suspenders crossed in
the back, and unbuttoning the dead man's clothes Robertson saw the two balls with which the pistol barrel had been
loaded within two inches of each other in the Yankee's
abdomen."[489]

The dead Yank commander turned out to be Lieutenant
Colonel Eifort, of the Second Union Kentucky, who had
his regiment and part of the tory Fifth Tennessee. It was
said that the plan had been for the tory Tenth Tennessee
to attack in flank, but they didn't do it, so Eifort had been
left out there in front high and dry.[490] The Rebs gathered
up all the prowledge, especially the cast-off weapons and
the cartridge boxes from the bodies of the dead Yank troopers,[491] and then hustled back to join the column, for, as
Sergeant Jim Lambright, Fifth Georgia, recalled, the Yanks
quickly counter-charged: "The enemy soon rallied and continued the advance in full force, our command retiring slowly toward Triune. The enemy having concentrated their
forces decided to make another rush, and advanced their
cavalry in a charge upon our line, which was retiring. General Williams, commanding the Kentucky Brigade, anti-
cipating this movement, had dismounted his men and formed

489. James H. Cogin, ed., "The Life Story of Brig. Gen. Felix
Robertson," *Texana*, VIII (Spring, 1970), 176-177.

490. *ORR*, I, 38, pt. 2, pp. 493-494.

491. DuBose, p. 388.

them into a line facing the approach, hidden from view. After our Regiment passed this line the enemy, advancing rapidly, the Kentucky boys opened a destructive fire upon their advancing line, which utterly demoralized them to such an extent as to cause a hasty retreat on their part, leaving their dead and wounded on the field where they fell."[492]

Throughout the day, Robertson's rear guard would turn and snarl at the pursuing Yanks. At Triune, about 5:00 p.m., pursuit ceased, and the Rebs turned south on the pike and traveled all night to within five or six miles of Farmington.[493]

As soon as the column under Williams and Robertson had moved on from the place of the skirmish, Willie King and some of the men of the neighborhood rushed to the lane where the two forces had met. There Willie saw a dead Confederate: "The soldier's pockets were turned wrong side out with nothing in them, or papers to identify him. I don't recollect where he was shot, except it was not in the head or face.

"Near where the soldier was lying was a beautiful chestnut sorrel mare, lying dead, killed in the fight, and probably it was his horse, and in the pursuit and charge of the Yankees this horse was killed, dashing its rider with force, killed the rider, the soldier. . . .

"Mr. Alex Smith, who ran a contraband farm, that is, negroes working for cotton, had a dozen or more negroes working for him. He took three or four negro men with hoes and shovels, and we went down where the dead soldier was lying and brought him up to the northeast corner

492. James T. Lambright, *History of Liberty Independent Company* (Brunswick, Georgia: Press of Glover Bros., 1910), unpaginated.

of our field. Mr. Sutton, who lived near Bellbuckle, Mr. Hicks' son-in-law was present, also, Mr. Hicks. I proposed that we go to our mill and get some planks and make a coffin to put the soldier in for burial. I was but a boy and this was not considered. The negroes dug a hole about three and one half feet deep; the soldier was wrapped in his blanket and was put in the hole in the corner of the fence. The grave was on the north side of the road in the southwest corner of my father's farm.

"Before he was buried, a Confederate soldier, well armed, came riding leisurely by, on the Road going west. He rode up to the soldier's feet, and while he was looking at the dead soldier, I asked him if he knew him. He said he did not know him, but thought he belonged to the Ninth Kentucky Cavalry. This is as near his identity as I know. I requested him to inquire of the regiment about the missing and let it be known of his death."[494]

TO THE TENNESSEE
SEPTEMBER 5

The situation on the morning of September 5, then, was that Wheeler's force was so fragmented that his main column could only flee toward the Tennessee River and safety; that Wheeler knew that Williams was trying to reach him, but seemed unable to accomplish that feat; that Wheeler had no knowledge of the whereabouts of Dibrell or of the command under Paul Anderson that had been detached a week since to attack Tracy City. So Wheeler could only struggle on, with the initiative completely taken away from

493. *ORR*, I, 38, pt. 2, pp. 492-493; Black.
494. Pittard, pp. 115-116.

him. John Coffee Williamson detailed the state to which the main column was reduced: "Daylight found us in the saddle. When we stopped to feed the Yanks run in our pickets. Wheeler pushed on to Campbellton where he found the Yanks in force. We marched through the town at a double quick. One shell struck at the head of our division and several burst over us. Our boys marched steady. A brisk skirmish was going on. Some ladies run out of the fight at double-quick and hollowed something about the Yanks. It was a very interesting scene. I saw one Yankee line of battle. It was Cavalry. I saw one of our men pass his wife and daughters amidst the skirmish and shelling. He waved his hat and his wife and daughters wrung their hands and shouted. He passed on but I think he went back. We came over into the woods and dismounted but Wheeler got his wagons around the town and he then withdrew his forces. We are evidently on our way from here to the Tennessee River. We got to Lawrenceville (or Lawrenceburg) after dark awhile, and encamped for the night without food for either man or horse. Rosseau is said to be after us with 4000 cavalry. Wheeler is watching Rosecran with great care. Roddy is at the Tennessee River and has possession of the ford."[495]

The "brisk skirmish" that Williamson observed was between the Alabama Brigade, which was the head of the column, and a Yankee cavalry force. As a boy in the Twelfth Alabama observed it, "As the command was passing through the village, Genl Rosseau attacked the Ala Brigade with a mounted Brigade of Cavalry armed with Spencers seven shooting rifles & Colts pistols. Their position was a splendid one being almost perfectly protected by a stone fence. A half mile in the rear he had 3000 Infy and a Battery of

495. Williamson, 66-67.

Artillery strongly posted on a hill — which commanded the
Country for a mile around — The Cavalry attack was so
vigerous and quick that for a few moments a little confusion
prevailed in the entire Brigade — The brave and intrepid
Allen soon had everything in order and at the head of the
Ala Brigade (save the 12th which was held in reserve) charged
with Sabres and pistols. The position was such that the
enemy could not be moved on horseback. Col Reese (Comdg
12th) was ordered to dismount his men and move at a
double quick through a field of growing corn and strike
them on the flank. The order was promptly obeyed by
Col Reese's charging the enemy's right flank, who it will
be remembered were mounted and numbered about Eleven
Hundred. The Regiment was upon them before they knew
it. Their first warning of its approach was Reeses Buglers
sounding the *"charge,"* the yelling of his men & the whist-
ling of their bullets. The surprise was so great that they
commenced flying panic stricken. The officers did their best
to stop the stampede. The 12th was armed with short Enfield Rifles & Navy pistols. The enemy were crowded up
in a field and could not get their horses to jump the fences.
This added to the confusion. They at last made their escape but not until 2 captains, 5 lieutenants, and 60 privates
were killed & wounded. On the part of the regiment Lieut.
McKinney, a daring officer, was killed and seventeen men
killed and wounded. The Col. and Buglers all had their
horses badly shot. General Allen complimented the Regt.
on the field and said that 'it was the best fight he ever saw
made under the circumstances.'"[496]

During that same day Williams' two brigades marched
without opposition. As they passed through Farmington,

496. "12th Alabama Cavalry Regiment," manuscript in Military
Records Department, State of Alabama Archives.

then Lewisburg, then Cornersville, the boys kept hoping
that they would hear from the scouts that they could reach
Wheeler. But then the scouts reported that there was too
large a force of Yanks between them and Wheeler, and
would continue to divide the two. Adjutant Allen said
that Williams and Robertson disagreed about what to do:[497]
Robertson wanted to continue trying to reach Wheeler,
while Williams decided to turn back and try to get out of
Tennessee "on his own hook," as General Robertson put
it.[498] Better that plan, Williams must have felt, than to get
trapped or even to get to the Tennessee after Wheeler had
already crossed and then get caught by the combined Yank
forces, which wouldn't be at the riverside just to baptize
them. The entire command bivouacked at Cornersville, "a
beautiful place," as Jim Black noted,[499] and that night
General Williams, still drunk, pressed Adjutant Allen as
his guide back to East Tennessee, even though Allen protested that he did not know the country.[500]

Dibrell had, on September 5th, continued his way towards the southeast, hoping to catch up with Wheeler.[501]
By late afternoon he was on the Las Cassas Road, and when
he got to Blackshop, he learned from a local cit that the
Yank cavalry was active around Murfreesborough.[502] This
news caused him to call the regimental commanders together for a conference.

While Dibrell and the other regimental commanders met
to decide upon their next move, Ben Darsey and some of

497. Williams Gibbs Allen, "War Reminiscence."
498. Letter, Felix H. Robertson to Braxton Bragg, October 6,
1864.
499. Black.
500. William Gibbs Allen, "War Reminiscence."
501. *ORR*, I, 38, pt. 2, p. 504.
502. Guild, pp. 97-98.

the other boys engaged in some other activities: "Just before night we halted, fed horses and butchered a beef; but as we had no time then to cook, each fellow took a piece of raw beef and put it in his haversack. As I was specially fond of beef liver, I put a piece in my haversack, hoping soon to have time to broil it and have one more good meal of beef liver with the remainder of biscuit which I still had in my haversack."[503] The column mounted up and moved out, Dibrell having decided to move toward Tullahoma, by way of Readyville, there either to cross the railroad and fight to join Wheeler or to go out of Tennessee through the mountains to the southeast, if it could be determined that Wheeler had retreated below the Tennessee River.[504]

The march continued until midnight, when Dibrell halted the column at McBroom's farm, just south of Readyville.[505] Although Ben Darsey had that piece of luscious raw liver in his haversack, he didn't even think of it, so tired was he: "There being a field of corn near by we hastily fed our horses. But about the time I got my horse fed, and was in the act of lying down upon the ground to rest, I was detailed to go out on picket post with Robert and Taylor Walthour of my regiment and Abbot of the 8th Alabama. We were posted near by a large residence situated on a big road about four or five hundred yards west of our camp. Abbot and I took the first watch while the Walthours slept. Abbot watched in one direction while I watched the other, which led in the direction of the residence. I soon dismounted, tied my horse and walked cautiously up in front of the house to see if I could see or hear any one about the premises. While there I saw a dim light in a negro house a short

503. Darsey.
504. *ORR*, I, 39, pt. 1, pp. 495-497.
505. Lindsley, p. 670.

distance up the lane. I cautiously approached the house and gently knocked at the door. The occupants seemed asleep but soon awoke, and I soon found that some women and children occupied the house. I asked if they had seen any rebels about there recently, feigning myself to be a federal soldier. To this they replied negatively, but they had heard that some of them had been around Murfreesboro and had played havoc with the railroad and were fighting the yankees in the direction of Nashville.

"I then went back, mounted my horse and remained on post until our time expired when the Walthour boys relieved us. I dismounted, and being so anxious to sleep, I took no time to take my rubber and blanket from my saddle, but lay down upon the ground, holding my bridle reins in my hand, and in almost no time was sound asleep.

"In a seemingly short time I was suddenly awakened by a rumbling noise as if a mighty raging storm or an earthquake like unto that which destroyed ancient Lisbon. I sprang to my feet and saw it was day dawn and Bob Walthour cried out, "yankees, boys!" I looked and through an open wood, southward I saw a column of yankee cavalry charging our camp at full speed, yelling as soldiers always do on like occasions. Abbot and I instantly sprang into our saddles and went at full speed for our camp. The Walthour boys being already mounted on post had the advantage of us in getting the start and succeeded in reaching camp before the charging yankees did."[506]

The attack had been well planned, and the surprise was complete. The Rebs were just getting up, and few horses were saddled. At that moment the camp was hit by a charging column of Yanks with sabres drawn. There was no possibility of making a stand, so the Rebs tried to saddle,

506. Darsey.

fire, and back away individually before the horsemen. Then they ran right into a perfect storm of fire, for the Yank commander had dismounted part of his force and slipped them around to the Reb left rear.[507]

It was a general mix-up. A couple of Rebs laughed at the Yank major who was in charge of the horsemen, saying, "Look at the old _____," but the major, humorless old wretch that he was, shot them dead.[508] The Yanks headed straight for McBroom's house, figuring that the Reb commander would be quartered there. They thus wasted some valuable moments, for Colonel Dibrell had slept under a sugar tree among his men. But that slight delay gave Dibrell's captains a brief chance to form up a slight line, Bilbrey and Gore on the hillside, and some others on the other side.[509]

This small group provided enough of a shield to protect most of the eight hundred recruits, most of whom were unarmed. The whole mess stampeded down the pike toward Woodbury, but few Yanks followed. Some of those who did were met by Captain George Carter and some of his men, who quickly paid the Yanks for their eagerness. Most of the Yanks were content to stay in the camp and round up the hundred or two recruits who had been unable to get saddled or find a hole to crawl into. Some of the captured Rebs were pretty well cut up; one boy who later rejoined the column said that he watched from the bushes as one recruit was led away. He was a fat old boy, whose scalp had been opened up from behind, so that the hide was hanging down over his eyes; as they led him along, he was fuming and crying, "They promised to make a quar-

507. "Ninth Pennsylvania Cavalry," Philadelphia *Inquirer*, September 22, 1864; *ORR*, I, 39, pt. 1, p. 495.

508. James Cooper Miller, "We Scattered the Rebels," *CWT Illustrated*, VIII (August, 1969), 43.

509. Lindsley, p. 670.

termaster of me. Now look at me."[510] No doubt a Yank surgeon made that shingle lie down; he will just have to stay out of high wind the rest of his life.

The wonder was that the Yanks didn't pursue in force. Dibrell had only three hundred armed men, with some of them wounded. One fellow, G. K. Grimsley, got a funny wound — he was one of those fighting in a cedar thicket, and a Yank ball barked a tree so close to his eye that splinters exploded into his left eye and put it out.[511] They asked him afterwards if he was going home, and one old boy said, hell, he's got it all over us, for he won't have to squint when he fires from now on.

Outside of Woodbury, Dibrell halted his gang of fugitives and began to get them organized; that old silver-haired farmer could boss his men. He ordered them east to a camp below Rock Island, across Caney Fork, where he planned to await all the stragglers.[512] It would be hard to do much for them, even to get them prayed over, for Brother William Whitsitt, chaplain of the Fourth Tennessee, had been gobbled up.[513]

BLUEWATER

SEPTEMBER 6

The other two columns were in just about the same predicament that day, September 6. For Wheeler's column

510. Miller, 43.

511. G. K. Grimsley, Soldier's Application for Pension, Number 2028, State of Tennessee Archives.

512. Lindsley, p. 670.

513. Nashville *Dispatch,* September 4, 1864.

it was simply a hot, rainy day, without much food.[514]
There was constant pursuit, but the command was able to
travel about thirty miles, passing Lexington, Alabama, about
noon and going into camp at Bluewater, about five miles
from Waynesboro. The recovering John Coffee Williamson
was in a jaunty mood when he recorded the events of the
day: "We mounted at daylight and marched. The Yanks
attacked our rear under Col. Hearst. They broke his line
twice but he charged them and put them back and they
were no more trouble during the day although they were in
our rear and on our flanks all day. We marched through a
very poor country. We came through the town of Lexington and struck the old military road and encamped two
miles from the Tennessee River on the Blue Creek. We
will cross the river where Jackson crossed his army in the
time of the Indian wars. All the boys are wearing out. All
is now safe. We have done much mischief to the Yanks and
are now all safe, the most successful raid that I ever knew.
I saw two men that had been wounded by bushwhackers.
These woods are said to be full of deserters and robbers."[515]

SHELBYVILLE
SEPTEMBER 6

For Williams' column the day was only slightly different.
Those two brigades started from Cornersville, then attacked
Shelbyville, which was defended only by a home guard.[516]
But since the Rebs had only a round or so of ammunition

514. Sloan, p.. 77; Garrett and Lightfoot, p. 32; Bunting.
515. Williamson, 67. Williamson's "Col. Hearst" is probably
Col. John R. Hart, Sixth Georgia Cavalry, Iverson's Brigade.
516. *ORR*, I, 38, pt. 2, p. 493.

to the man, they could not attack with any force, so that the home guard was able to remove all government supplies across the Elk River bridge and then defend it.[517] That left only "private plunder," as Jim Black put it, for the Rebs.[518] There, as at Dalton, Jim Lambright recalled, they shared their loot with the local Reb sympathizers.[519] They had to leave so quickly, though, that they destroyed neither the railroad nor the telegraph, moving on to camp twelve miles beyond Shelbyville, toward McMinnville.[520]

BLUEWATER

SEPTEMBER 7

September 7th was a rare day in Wheeler's camp — the men stayed put long enough to wash their clothes. Cleanliness being next to godliness, Chaplain Bunting was delighted to see the Eighth Texas assume the domestic: "There being no word from the Yankees, we breathe easier, and devote the . . . day to washing our only suit — for although we came out full handed and rich last fall, this time we were poorer than when we started, and certainly much dirtier, for we had no change in all our trip — gathering up rations, &c. It was amusing to see with what earnestness the Rangers go about their washing. Some are in the creek, and others are along the bank. Some have soap, and others have none. whilst the most have their only clothing in the water. This work over the drying process begins, and they rest in the bushes until their garments are ready

517. *ORR*, I, 38, pt. 5, p. 842.
518. Black.
519. Lambright.
520. *ORR*, I, 38, pt. 5, pp. 841-845.

for wear. Some, however, are less fortunate than their fellows, for the Yankees are advancing and we are ordered to the front. Wet or dry, we must go at once. Capt. Kyle, Co. D. goes forward as a picket, whilst the Brigade stands in line of battle. The enemy advances, and engaging them, Walter Caldwell, Co. D, is severely wounded in the thigh. This is our first casualty of the kind during the raid. He is with difficulty brought out and sent over the river where the train is already gone. He suffers much, but is doing well. He is one of our best and most gallant soldiers, and it is regretted that he should be wounded when we are so near the end. The enemy do not press us, and moving down toward Florence, we hunt forage until midnight and camp."[521]

Still on the mend, John Coffee Williamson apparently did not feel the domestic impulse that motivated the Texans: "I got up and helped to cook and I eat a hearty meal and then I lay down under a big oak tree and slept till 12 o' clock when the alarm was raised that the Yanks were coming to attack us. All hands saddled up and away we went until we crossed Shoal Creek and then away in the night we got over to Huffs and camped. A flag of truce came in today. It was in answer to a flag that Wheeler had sent into Nashville threatening to retaliate if certain men were hung that were under sentence. The Yanks said that they were not soldiers but robbers and bushwhackers. The Yanks also said by the flag of truce that Atlanta surrendered on the 4th of September, 1864."[522] Since that was true, it meant that our raid had not accomplished its main purpose, which had been to lift the seige of that city. Oh yes, the Yanks had also wanted to know if we had any prisoners to trade

521. Bunting.
522. Williamson, 67.

for those boys they had — those people have business on the brain.[523]

The other two commands stayed on the run on September 7th. Williams and Robertson brought their scared and worn-out boys through Wartrace and Beech Grove, to within four miles of McMinnville. Dibrell remained at Rock Island, on Caney Fork, as his stragglers found his camp, their tails between their legs.[524]

523. Marshall P. Thatcher, *A Hundred Battles in the West — The Second Michigan Cavalry* (Detroit: published by the author, 1884), pp. 184-187.

524. Black; *ORR,* I, 38, pt. 5, p. 835.

VIII

Back Across the Tennessee:
"in all respects victorious"

(September 8-20, 1864)

ROCK ISLAND
SEPTEMBER 8

*T*he next day, September 8th, Dibrell made his decision. He ordered his men to cook five days' rations and to be ready to march the next morning. They would, Dibrell planned, move across the mountains and attempt a crossing of the Tennessee River at Cotton

Port, which was where he had wanted to cross on the way up to Tennessee. Late in the evening, though, Dibrell received a dispatch from General Williams that his column was marching to Sparta and that Dibrell should join him there.[525] Williams had not yet completely given up the idea of reaching Wheeler, for at the same time he sent a hundred of Anderson's Fourth Tennessee that had joined his command back to contact Wheeler, tell him that if attacked he and Robertson would have to surrender, and ask him to move over and create a diversion in their favor "south of the Tennessee River above Chattanooga."[526]

Wheeler never got Williams' message, for the scout was attacked at Woodbury and driven off toward Lebanon. Even if he had, Wheeler could have done nothing about it, for he was still being pursued himself. His food situation was also getting desperate. John Coffee Williamson took William Sloan and some other boys on a detail to Cowpen Mills, but could only get one day's ration of flour, for the Yanks had burned the mills out.[527]

SPARTA
SEPTEMBER 9

Williams and Robertson rode into Sparta to meet Dibrell on September 9th, and the three of them had several discussions about what course to take.[528] If there was any chance to join Wheeler, they wanted to take it, rather than

525. *ORR*, I, 39, pt. 1, pp. 495-497; Lindsley, p. 670.
526. *ORR*, I, 39, pt. 1, pp. 501-502; *ORR*, I, 38, pt. 5, pp. 844-845.
527. Williamson, 67; Sloan, p. 78.
528. *ORR*, I, 39, pt. 1, pp. 495-497.

risk being placed in arrest for disobedience to orders when they got back — they must have remembered the fate of General Will Martin, back at Dalton. Finally it was agreed to follow General Robertson's strategy, which was to go back out of Middle Tennessee the way that he and Williams had brought their brigades in.[529] Perhaps the other two acquiesced to their younger colleague because of their knowledge of Wheeler's fondness for him. At any rate they selected Major J. F. Foard as their guide and made preparations to leave the next morning.[530]

Not all of Dibrell's men had gathered together, for up at Livingston Mary Catherine Sproul was still trying to fend off the demands made by some of them: "It was as beautiful a night as I ever witnessed. Not a Cloud could be seen the Sky clear blue and serene, the Stars twinkled and the Moon shed a beauteous Silver light and as the night birds Sang a farewell to Summer, the tramping of horses awoke me from my painful Slumbers, for my heart ached all the time. A low voice, Father Mother awake and get away from here the rebels are at the gate Hello! they cry at the gate My Mother responds, they ask for Father Mother told he was not at home; they asked for the horse Mother told them we had disposed of the horse, they then Cursed Mother telling her it was a D-nd lie and upon hearing my poor old Mother called a liar I sprang to the door and told them the horse was where they nor no other horse theives would ever get him, they then Swore they would Come in and take the worth of the horse. I told them to come on, at the same time going toward them near the gate. Only one of the villains Said something unbecoming. I told them

529. "The Last General Officer," 366.

530. J. F. Foard, "Vivid Prison Experience," *Confederate Veteran*, XXI (November, 1913), 529.

Morgans rogues had taken all our horses Save the one they were after and that they had had no right to our property they Swore we were Lincolnites and enemies to our Country and that they had orders to take every Union mans property. I told them plainly they would never get our horse for we had sent him away, he then said We will be here tomorrow and if that horse is not here We will shoot your Fathers head full of holes a D-nd old Lincolnite. I told them My Father had never harmed them and if they killed him I would tear this country up before one week, they Cursed me but rode away — I have since learned that gentlemans name who officiated most conspicuously it was Charles Coleman a Man Whom I shall remember long and treasure his name upon the Scroll of theives and Midnight Assassins. These rebels had gone to meet Diberal and on the way they heard of a little reverse he had met with at Woodbury Tenn. and they were to meet him next day somewhere. After the departure of these theives Father and Brother came to the house, we could hear them traveling all times of the night. The next day My poor Father with tottering Steps and quivering limbs Said it was uncertain how long these men would Stay in here and that he could not keep the horse. So Father and Brother Concluded to leave the Country. We were looking every moment for these desperadoes to return as they had promised the night previous I looked around at the care worn form of My Father, his face was wrinkled and pale and the big tear Stood in his eye and he burst forth in tones which I shall never forget. Said he I must leave you Notwithstanding I have never harmed a man on earth; My Son alike must go, and leave you alone It is too much to bear, I do not know what you will do — Mother & I told them to go, and to be in haste, for I was looking every moment for a band of rebels to come & kill them. With a Short preparation they left us. Oh! What a Sad family; they had been gone but a Short time when here came the rebels again making the same interrogations as before — Mother told them they need not come any more on Such errands that Father and Brother were gone to Ky. and had taken the horse they wished to get — I told them we had a fine mare at the Stable if they would go down they could take in welcome. I had an old Mare 25 years old and very thin, they knew what I meant and did not take her. I told them She was the best I had to offer them, they knew it was a burlesque and went off cursing me and muttering to themselves."[531]

SINKING CREEK
SEPTEMBER 10

Not all the cits were so hostile to the Rebs, though, as Captain Knox Miller discovered the evening of September 10th. The combined command had moved eight or ten miles north from Sparta that day, to Sinking Cane, and the men were tired from a rugged march, as Jim Black noted in his diary.[532] Captain Miller had just gotten his horse unsaddled and eaten his roasting ears, when he and the other members of the Eighth Confederate Regiment were ordered to saddle up and mount. General "Commanche" Robertson rode up, then, and led them off into the darkness.[533]

It was unusual for a general to lead a scout, so the men were indeed curious about their mission. They rode for several hours, to find themselves eleven miles west of Sparta,

531. Schroeder, 358-361.
532. Black.
533. "Notes on 8th Confederate Regt. Cavalry."

at the Old Taylor Homestead. Pickets were thrown out all around, and the men were ordered to dismount and stand to horse. The house was not large, not a Georgia planter's house at all; it was just a two-story frame house with a porch stretching across the front. But it was lighted up inside and conveyed a feeling of peacefulness that Captain Miller and his men had not experienced for a lifetime, it seemed. After a long while, word was sent out that General Robertson had just gotten married, to a beautiful red-haired girl, Miss Sallie Davis, whom he had met in Shelby-ville back in 1862, when the war was a great deal younger. They must have gotten in touch with one another during the raid, somehow, and decided that there wasn't much pos-sibility that he would be coming back to Tennessee any time soon, so they'd best be getting married, if they were going to.[534]

The general remained with his lady until dawn, then came out and mounted his mule, and led his sleepy honor guard back to the command. He was quiet, but proud, that dawn — certainly deserving of his name *Felix,* the happy one. He must have thought, though, of what his life would have been if it hadn't been for the war: by then he would have been a West Point graduate, a young officer virtually assured of a brilliant career. On the way back, Isaac, General Robert-son's negro, told him that he would be leaving and going back to Georgia. Now that the general was married, he wouldn't be needing Isaac to take care of him, and Isaac meant to get married himself. Robertson laughingly a-greed.[535] The men got back in time to join the march toward

534. Letter, Felix H. Robertson to George Knox Miller, June 10, 1895, in George Knox Miller Papers, Southern Historical Col-lection, University of North Carolina.

535. Colgin, 173.

Brig.-Gen. Felix H. "Comanche" Robertson

Old Taylor Homestead

Champ Ferguson

White Plains on the Lexington Road, heading off to East Tennessee, half-starved, half-armed, and half-dead. Isaac watched them move out, then turned south.

FLORENCE
SEPTEMBER 9

Back on the north side of the Tennessee River, Wheeler was still waiting to hear from Williams, vowing that he would not cross over until he had heard from his two lost brigades.[536] So, on September 9th, his men went about their regular camp duties. Sergeant John W. Hill, of the Eighth Texas, was taking an inventory of his very successful trip: "I got a good pr. boots a Hat two Six Shooters three horses and saddles the horse I gave to the Company I sold the Saddles for fifty (50) dollars a piece got a silver Watch for which I took fifty-five ds in green back. . . . I also got three pocket knives. I shot one fellow in the back not more than five feet from him and he fell from his horse but I did not stop to see whether he died or not But run on till I had Shot out every load and then got three prisnors. . ." His only concern, in fact, was that his Brother Tom had taken off on a "french furlow," to visit relations in Aberdeen, Mississippi.[537]

In the same camp nearby, William Nicholson took advantage of the opportunity to write his first letter home since leaving Covington:

"Rangers Camp near Florence Ala. Sept 9th '64
"Dear Aunt:
"Capt Kyle will leave us to day enroute for Texas and we are all busily engaged in writing home and consequently

536. *ORR,* I, 38, pt. 2, p. 501.
537. Letter, John W. Hill to his sister, September 15, 1864.

he will have a great many letters to carry. I have told him
to call and see you if he gets there safely. Maj. Christian
goes with him, also two commissioned officers from the
11th Texas and two from the 3rd Arkansas . . . Capt Kyle
will go to see Walter Caldwell, who suffered a good deal
as he had to be brought some distance to be secure from
the Yankees   We all hope he will soon recover   he is one
of our best and bravest soldiers. — You have doubtless
heard before this of Wheelers great raid   we started from
Covington Geo. on the 11th Aug. striking the railroad at
Dalton where we destroyed the track for several miles   we
then followed up the Ga & E.T. R.R. destroying as we went
passing around the places too strongly guarded . . . at Strawberry Plains, above Knoxville we had some fighting to do
the 10th Michigan Cavalry hearing of us as only a small
raiding party came in great haste up to the plains driving in
and capturing a scout from the 11 Tex our regiment charged
them when they came in sight and drove them back to
within 3 miles of Knoxville. we recaptured the prisoners
and captured and killed about 40 of the enemy we lost
none in the regt either killed or wounded Walter Caldwell
is our only loss since we started the regiment has been very
fortunate on the trip We crossed the Cumberland Mts at
Crossville & Sparta we then went to the R. R. following
it to within 8 miles of Nashville we then went across to
the Nashville and Columbia R. R. The Command had considerable fighting to do near Franklin. Brig. Gen. Kelley,
comdg. one of our divisions was mortally wounded. Col.
Hobson, 3rd Ark. lost an arm, the 11th Texas lost several
killed and wounded our regiment was only under artillery
fire, which is not very fatal. — We destroyed the R. R. to
near Pulaski, Giles Co., — when we retired The People in
Md Tenn. are much oppressed the Federal authorities have

compelled them all to take the oath of allegiance they
were rejoiced to see us, and every thing they had was at
our disposal. — We found several Rangers in Mid. Tenn.
who had been separated from us for some time, John Rector
is one he has been staying near Nolinsville, Co. H & Shipp
was killed near Sparta some time ago — We have traveled
night and day, not stopping long enough to rest and sleep
sufficient We get to read plenty of Northern papers I
have Frank Leslie of Sept 3rd would send it to you if I
could. My last letter from home was May 7th I wrote home
from Covington on the 10th. W. N."[538]

Not everyone could stay in camp, for food had to be
scrounged up. Sergeant Williamson, of the Fifth Tennessee,
took his detail back to the mill that morning. But before
they could get all of the flour that they wanted, some of
the boys began to say that they could hear the boom of
cannon way off in the distance. Pretty soon a courier came
to get them, yelling that the Yanks in force had driven in
the rear pickets near Florence and that the column was
moving to the ford at Colbert Shoals.[539] Wheeler had had
his decision forced upon him.

Ashby's Brigade was in the forward part of the column,[540]
so the Tennesseans forded the river in the daylight and had
an easy time of it. But by the time Chaplain Bunting and
the Texas Rangers got to cross, it was ten o'clock at night
and very dangerous: "There is no time to delay — a wide
rough river is before us and the enemy behind us. It is by no
means an hour of pleasant thoughts. The advance takes
the water, but it only requires a short time to lose the ford,
and then the winding columns become more crooked as
each successive regiment passes over. It is swift, rocky and in

538. Letter, Will Nicholson to his aunt, September 9, 1864.
539. Williamson, 67.
540. Sloan, p. 78.

places swimming. Woe the luckless man whose horse fails amid that washing current! Onward we creep along our winding way, and after awhile the land is reached. We are relieved, and if ever men were grateful to God for his protecting care it was at this juncture. But soon the conjecture becomes reality. We are on an island and there is yet another deep water to cross. Its a bitter thought, but we cannot tarry. The scene is reenacted again, although deeper and swifter. The majority come through safely, although some have lost all, whilst a few are left lodged here and there against a rock or tree in the swift current, calling for help, whilst others laying hold of horse or mule tails, have floated safely to shore. A few alas! sent down under the whirling waves, and when morning came they were sleeping beneath the deep waters of the Tennessee. Thank God our little band are all safe once more."[541]

William Sloan didn't say how he felt about divine providence, but he was very happy about his four-footed assistance: "When I returned our cavalry had all gone in the direction of the Tennessee River. I followed on and overtook the Georgia Brigade near the river, and we all crossed in the night at Colbert's Shoals. The river was several miles wide at that place, being interspersed with many small islands, and some places the water was almost swimming deep to the horses, and many of them fell down in the swift current. It was reported that a few men were washed away and drowned, but nothing serious happened in that part of the column in which I was traveling. I was riding a tall mule which proved to be splendid in deep water, as he braced himself with great firmness against the current, and never stumbled, and he brought me and my sack of flour safe and dry across the river."

541. Bunting.

"I left my favorite little horse, Sparrowhawk, at Covington Ga. to be rested and fed, and I rode a mule on this raid, but the first one was not very satisfactory, and I changed him off for a larger and better one after reaching Middle Tennessee. He makes a splendid cavalry animal." [542]

John Coffee Williamson was also with Iverson's Georgians, but his experience at the river left him a good deal more subdued than his regimental comrade, William Sloan: "I marched with Red Floyd of the 4th Ga. We got to the river about midnight and marched across. I swam 4 times. Some of the boys went too low and could not get back, They cried very piteously for help. I was got out but the Lord only knows what became of the others. I got out all wet and could not find the road out. I tied up and dried. It was dark as I came over. The moon had gone down and it was very dark, the water swift and deep as my mule swam past the shoal. The poor fellows that had been swept over by the current and could not get back uttered the most piteous cries for help. Others were praying. I thought, taking everything into consideration, that it was the most solemn moment that I ever saw. I had a stout mule and I went through the swift water most nobly. It is said that 6 Georgians got drowned. We missed the ford. We had no guides. There was a good ford near the place but we did not find it. The fault must have been with Gen. Wheeler. He had made arrangements at the River."[543]

Then the rear guard went over. Lieutenant-Colonel James H. Lewis, First Tennessee, Colonel Wheeler, tells how it was with them:

"On the evening of day Wheeler's command crossed over. Our regiment brought up the rear, in the meantime

542. Sloan, p. 78.
543. Williamson, 67-68.

skirmishing with the enemy. The regiment was small — not more than two hundred, men and officers. We were ordered to hold the enemy in check at all hazards until dark, then ford the river and join the brigade. A guide, with a small detail of men commanded by a Lieutenant, was to wait for us at the bank of the river. The guide knew the ford well, his home being in the immediate neighborhood. At dark we were within a mile of the river, and could distinctly hear the water rushing over the rocks on the shoals. The head of the regiment reached the bank of the river about one hour after dark, but no guide was to be found. There was starlight, but no moon. The stream at this place was about a mile wide, including a small island near the center. It was difficult and dangerous to cross, but one of two things had to be done — either to attempt to ford the river, or be killed or captured the next morning. The enemy was behind us thousands in number. We determined to cross the river. This was done by placing two men, good swimmers, on strong horses a few yards to the right and left of the column. When they found the water deepening in one place they turned to the right or left, as was necessary, the head of the troops marching midway between in column of twos. The ford was very tortuous and rough. The water rushed along, seething and foaming around us, making it very difficult for our horses to move forward. We reached the opposite bank just at daylight, having been in the water all night. The men were wet to the skin. In crossing, a few of the horses fell down; others got into swimming-water. Some of the men lost their guns. At this stage of the war the men were inured to hardships and dangers, but not a few of them swore they would rather take their chances in battle than cross the river again under such circumstances. It turned out that the guide and men with him became alarmed for their safety, and followed in the rear of the

brigade, leaving us to our fate. The next day they could not
be found."[544]

BELOW THE TENNESSEE
SEPTEMBER 10

So the great raid was over — it had been hell and high
water the whole way. A few days later, on September 20th,
Wheeler met with Forrest, the man with whom he always
suffered comparison, who was now to take *his* troopers north
of the Tennessee. General Allen was with Wheeler when
they joined Forrest for dinner, and Allen said that Wheeler
was really in the dumps as he talked with Forrest. The whole
expedition had been dogged by bad luck — rain, high water,
lost commands, and those damned block houses. Forrest
perked up at the last difficulty cited and allowed: "Wheeler,
when I go over there, I'll take them."

General Wheeler didn't at all need to be confronted by
this kind of kill-devil confidence, but he held onto his
temper, and just quietly said: "General, you may do so, but
I don't see how you are going to do it."

Forrest just grinned like the old clever Tennessean that
he was and said: "Well, I'll tell you how. When I come to
one of those block houses, I'll draw my men up around it,
and we'll charge it and thrust our six-shooters into the
port-holes and then they'll be our holes."[545] And he'd
do it — to tell the truth, we wouldn't have been surprised
if he had said that he was going to give his troopers cow-

544. Lindsley, pp. 891-892.
545. Isaac Barton Ulmer, "Reminiscences of the Third Alabama
Cavalry," typescript, pp. 15-16, State of Alabama Archives.

bells, as General Joshua gave the Israelites trumpets at Jericho, so that they could march around the block houses seven times.

After the dinner, Forrest wrote a letter to Lieut. Gen. Richard Taylor, his commanding officer, about Wheeler's humiliation: "His command is in a demoralized condition. He claims to have about 2,000 men with him; his adjutant-general says, however, that he will not be able to raise and carry back with him exceeding 1,000, and in all probability not over 500. One of his brigades left him and he does not know whether they are captured or have returned, or are still in Middle Tennessee. He sent General Martin back in arrest, and his whole command is demoralized to such an extent that he expresses himself as disheartened, and that, having lost influence with the troops, and being unable to secure the aid and co-operation of his officers, he believes it to the best interest of the service that he should be relieved from command. . . . General Wheeler has turned over to me what he has of my old brigade, numbering sixty men. When I left it with him last November it then numbered over 2,300 for duty. . . ."[546]

Time heals all wounds, though, so they say. By the time he turned in his official report, on October 9th, General Wheeler had begun to see the whole affair in a much different light. The War Baby summarized the results in this fashion:

"First. Causing the enemy to send to their rear to re-enforce their garrisons, troops several times as strong as my force.

"Second. The destruction of the enemy's line of communication for a longer period than any cavalry expedition, however large, has done.

546. *ORR*, I, 39, pt. 2, p. 859.

"Third. The capture, destruction, or appropriation of stores.

"Fourth. Breaking up depots and fortified posts in Tennessee and Georgia.

"Fifth. Capture of 1,000 horses and mules, 200 wagons, 600 prisoners, and 1,700 head of beef-cattle.

"Sixth. Capture and destruction of over 20 trains of cars loaded with supplies.

"Seventh. Bringing into the service of the Confederate States over 3,000 recruits.

"All this was accomplished behind the enemy's line with a loss of but 150 men killed, wounded, and missing. In every engagement with the enemy's cavalry we were in all respects victorious, capturing prisoners, colors, and arms. . . ."[547]

547. *ORR*, I, 38, pt. 3, pp. 960-961.

IX

On the Holston:
"incide of our own lines"

(September 11-27, 1864)

DRY VALLEY
SEPTEMBER 11

So Wheeler and his command were back in Dixie, while the men under Williams, Robertson, and Dibrell were still wandering around in the wilds of Tennessee. General Robertson and his sleepy escort rejoined the command on September 11th, as it continued

its way north from Sparta. The column had passed through
the valley of Calf Killer Creek during a dull, leaden day and
camped in Dry Valley. The newness of the war hadn't worn
off for the sixteen-year-old Ben Rogers, for he remembered
having "the pleasure and curiosity of riding with Major
Ferguson up a beautiful Tennessee valley for several hours."
Ben found Champ Ferguson "an affable, well-informed
gentleman."[548]

Dry Valley was very familiar ground for Ferguson and
the other guerrillas who had joined the command, for they
had fought a force of stokes' homemade Yanks there in
the previous February.[549] Many of the leading guerrillas,
hearing that the Yanks were coming, had gathered among
the boulders that lay along Dug Hill Road, which climbed
out of Dry Valley into the mountains. Among those present
were Ferguson, George Carter, who was a captain in Colonel
Dibrell's Eighth Tennessee, John M. Hughes, who had been
colonel of the Twenty-fifth Tennessee Infantry, W. S. Bled-
soe, and John Gatewood.

When the Yanks had come along, in the afternoon, two
of the Rebs had pretended to be scared pickets, who fired
one time, then had ridden off up the mountain road. The
Yanks had chased them — right into the trap. Then the Rebs
had fired from behind the boulders and the laurel, occasionally darting forward to jerk a Yank off his horse. John
Gatewood called upon five Yanks to surrender, and they
did, thinking that there must be more men with him. But
when they discovered that Gatewood was alone, two of
the Yanks tried to run away. Gatewood started to fire
at them, for he had a pistol in each hand, when George
Carter ran up.

548. Dixon Merritt, *The History of Wilson County* (Lebanon,
Tennessee: History Associates, 1961), p. 345; Black.

549. *ORR*, I, 39, pt. 2, p. 391.

"Hold on, John!" he called. "Don't waste your ammunition, as we have to fight for all we get!" The slope was covered with rocks, and he bent to pick up several fist-sized ones as he came up to Gatewood.

The next day, when other Yanks came out to recover the bodies, they found forty-one, thirty-eight shot in the head and three with heads crushed by rocks. . . .[550]

IN THE CUMBERLAND MOUNTAINS
SEPTEMBER 12

The next day, September 12th, Williams' command continued east toward the range of mountains that separates Middle from East Tennessee, following the guide from Dibrell's Brigade, Major Foard.[551] The route was a mere path, which became so rough that the last rolling stock, a light battery and an ambulance, had to be abandoned. In their desire to be out of that area, which was also infested by Union bushwhackers, the men traveled almost all night.

ON THE JIMTOWN ROAD
SEPTEMBER 13

On September 13th, the column traveled until midnight, past Wartburg, five miles down the mountain. In that little town of Swiss immigrants the Rebs had learned of the fall of Atlanta and the death of John H. Morgan, on September 4th,[552] at Greenville, toward which they were heading.

550. Hale and Merritt, 652-653.
551. Foard, 529; "The Last General Officer," 366.
552. Black

The latter news was especially distressing to some of the men in Williams' Brigade, for they had originally served under Morgan, back when the war was much younger. Very likely they read the news in Parson Brownlow's *Knoxville Whig and Rebel Ventilator,* for the issue of September 7th had contained the following obituary:

"John Morgan is no more! And when he died a THIEF and coward expired! He was killed in Mrs. Williams' back yard, or cabbage patch, skulking from danger. He was shot through the heart by Andrew Campbell of Company G, 13th Tennessee Cavalry, while trying to escape. — There should be a salute fired *in front of every horse stable in the land* in honor of his death! — And all fine *horses* and *mules* should be notified that they may now *repose* in quiet at night, and *graze* in peace in the day time.

"Morgan leaves a large amount of gold and greenbacks, cotton and real estate, the proceeds of his thieving exploits, resulting from untold murders and robberies, through a space of three years. Who his legal heir is will be difficult to settle. His first wife was the sister of Col. Bruce, of Ky. She died in Lexington from the neglect and bad treatment of her debased, gambling, and thieving husband. His second wife was a *negro wench* he had with him during his residence in this city. She is in Kentucky. His *third wife* is the daughter of Chas. Ready, of Murfreesboro', and she is at Abingdon, in Va. — Our own opinion is, that the *negro wench* has the oldest claim upon his estate, but we leave this grave question of law to be settled in the Confedearte Courts, or by special act of their Congress.

"Gen. Gillam is in our town, and brought with him 86 of Morgan's men, on Monday evening, who we saw turned over to the jail we were once an inmate of. Some of them were barefooted, and bare-headed and bare-backed. All looked dirty and mean, as though they were fit subjects to be commanded by a *common horse-thief.*"[553]

HARRIMAN

SEPTEMBER 13

By now the command was beginning to straggle, for there weren't as many bushwhackers. On the afternoon of the 13th the command came down the valley of the Big Emory River that General Robertson had climbed about two weeks before. Adjutant Allen, still impressed as a guide, gleefully reported what happened that afternoon: "At Harriman, Williams stoped to feed and rest. Some one stole his pants, he was a wysky bloat, and had to stay in his room till he could get a pairt of pants made that would go arround his bloated corpulaceny." Allen said that Williams had two boys from the Second Tennessee Cavalry who happened to be along arrested and hanged — it was never clear whether they were hanged for stealing Williams' pants or for some less serious crime.[554]

IN DUTCH VALLEY

SEPTEMBER 14

On the 14th the advance entered Dutch Valley, north of Knoxville, stopping to feed at the house of James Ross, six miles north of Clinton, at 9:00 at night. The main party was well disciplined and compact; it did not venture the

553. *Knoxville Whig and Rebel Ventilator,* September 7, 1864.
554. William Gibbs Allen, "War Reminiscence."

six miles off the course into Clinton, which had been prowled about two weeks before, on the trip down country, by the Texas Rangers. Nor did the main party linger long; having eaten, it moved to Moore's Ferry, on the Clinch River, two miles east of Clinton, crossing, as Jim Black noted, at midnight, and capturing a Yank forage train of thirty wagons at 5:00 a.m.[555]

IN DUTCH VALLEY
SEPTEMBER 15

But when the stragglers came through Dutch Valley the next day, their behavior was atrocious. Their first victim was the Reverend George Baker, whose offense seemed to be that he was Unionist and had a son in the Tory Third Tennessee Infantry. He was shot to pieces in his own yard, and then his house was stripped of anything of value.[556] The Dail homestead was one of the next to be pillaged, and when the guerrillas left it, they came upon Captain James Wilson and Mr. Carr Davis in the road, and shot Wilson dead and wounded Davis before he was able to jump from his horse, run into the woods, and hide. Captain Wilson had just received his discharge from the Union Eleventh Tennessee Cavalry and was on his way home to Morgan County when he was murdered. Maybe the guerrillas justified his death as a payment for Morgan's death — maybe his death was just for the hell of it. Mr. Davis hid under a log with his little dog, which licked the blood off his wound, as two

555. *ORR,* I, 39, pt. 2, p. 384; Black.
556. "The Conduct of Fiends," *Knoxville Whig and Rebel Ventilator,* September 28, 1864.

guerrillas stood on top of the log under which he lay.[557]

The next cit to feel the wrath of the raiders was old Nathan Farmer. When the guerrillas came upon him, he was carrying a shovel, and they must have thought that he had been out burying his valuables. They told him to lead them to his burial place or they would kill him. His response was to unbutton his shirt, and pull it open to make them a good target, saying, "I am an old man and poor. The only thing you can rob me of is a few days."[558]

Since those days weren't worth anything to them, he was spared. But they camped on his farm, going from there to raid the Lienart's, the Brummit's, and old James Ross' place. Ross was shot in one of his eyes as he struggled to get out of bed to answer their assault on his door.

By that time the women of the community had prepared the bodies of George Baker and James Wilson for burial. Somehow they got the bodies down to the graveyard near Uncle Billy McKamey's house, but the ground was late-summer baked, so hard and rocky that they could not get the graves dug. There they stood, profiled in the late evening sun, crying as their mattock blows simply bounced off the earth. The raider camp was within sight, and the local men were hiding in the woods, afraid to come out to help the women. So the women struggled on in futility, until one of the Dail men risked his life to come help them. No Reb came about, though, and the man dug a little trench and then left the women to pile up dirt and then rocks from the fence row, to keep the animals from digging up the bodies. The war was through with Dutch Valley.[559]

557. As related to the author by Fletcher Dail, Dutch Valley, August 15, 1973.

558. As related to the author by Wayne Farmer, Nathan's great-grandson, August 15, 1973.

559. Fletcher Dail.

ON THE MULBERRY GAP ROAD
SEPTEMBER 15

That same day, September 15th, the main column continued its rapid march to the northeast. Because of their shortage of ammunition, the Rebs feared any pursuit from Knoxville. Following the Mulberry Gap Road, they camped at Big Springs that evening.[560] For Jim Black the day possessed this significance: "Recrossed the Clinch. Received intelligence that rendered the report of the death of Genl Morgan & evacuation of Atlanta fully reliable."[561]

BIG SPRINGS
SEPTEMBER 16

The next day, General Williams must have concluded that any pursuit had been evaded, for he did not order the column to march too far.

Jim Black noted, thankfully, that the command "at night went regularly into camp." Behind them, the stragglers came on, each one leading as many as three horses, with the squawking chickens of Dutch Valley tied to their backs.[562]

SNEEDSVILLE
SEPTEMBER 17

On September 17th, the main command passed through

560. Message, Lt. Reed to Brig.-Gen. Jacob Ammen, September 16, 1864, Ammen Manuscripts, Illinois State Historical Society.
561. Black.
562. Black; "Wheeler's Thieves Returning," *Knoxville Whig and Rebel Ventilator,* September 21, 1864.

Sneedsville, in the area where those strange Meluneons live. Nobody knew much about those dark-eyed, dark-haired people who bury their dead above the ground. Some said that they were the descendants of the Lost Colonists of Roanoke Island; others said that they were derived from Modoc and his Welsh or Portuguese sailors who shipwrecked off Carolina. But whoever they were, they were tough and secretive, so the command marched until nightfall, not to stop until the Clinch River was again crossed. That meant that the day following, the tired troopers could pass through War Gap into Carter's Valley. There the guide, Major Foard, took General Williams to Long Meadow, the home of his father-in-law, John Young. General Williams was invited to use the house as his headquarters for a few days, and the men spread themselves out to recruit their horses, get shoeing done, and gather the fruit now in season, in order to relieve their diet of roasting ears.[563] Looking for just such a chance, Adjutant Allen solved his Williams problem: "Here I ran away from him and went to Genl. J. C. Vaughn, who was camped at Limestone 6 mi below Jonesboro. I told Gen Vaughn that I had ran a way from Williams and if Williams made requests for me, that I did not [want] to be turned over to him, I had three brothers in Vaughns old 3rd Tenn. bro T. A Maj George W and V. C. Allen. Vaughn said go, visit your Brothers and the Rhea County boys. I will take care of you."[564]

563. Black; Foard, 529; Edward Owings Guerrant Diary, typescript, p. 1142, in Guerrant Papers, Southern Historical Collection, University of North Carolina.

564. William Gibbs Allen, "War Reminiscence."

ROGERSVILLE

SEPTEMBER 19

Nothing much happened on September 19th, at least anything that Jim Black thought worthy of being written down in his diary. There was some activity in the Fifth Georgia camp, as a casualty report was put together. Captain Isaac Marsh, Company C, was going up to enter the hospital at Emory, Virginia, and he promised to write up the report and send copies to southern Georgia newspapers through the Confederate mail system. Since the boys knew that they'd be turning back toward North Carolina within a few days, they said goodbye to Captain Marsh, probably for the war.[565] The other commands mostly just rested in the area around Rogersville, and, if the stragglers hadn't caught up before, they came in that day, and camp talk about Dutch Valley began to spread.

ROGERSVILLE

SEPTEMBER 20

The next day some of the command had rested enough to take up pen and paper. Colonel William Campbell Preston Breckinridge, commanding the Ninth Kentucky, thought of his wife, Issa, who, like many other Kentucky Confederate officers' wives, had fled to Canada, after hearing that the Yanks intended to send the group down the Mississippi on a transport and dump them in Dixie.[566] He knew how

565. "From the Fifth Georgia Cavalry," Savannah *Republican,* October 4, 1864.

566. Mary Elizabeth Massey, *Bonnet Brigades* (New York: Alfred A. Knopf, 1966), p. 297.

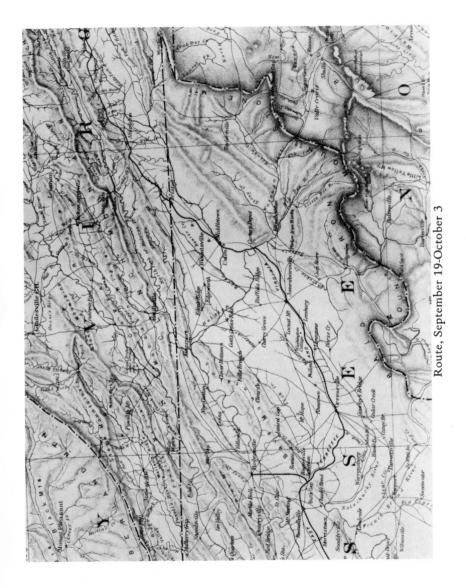

Route, September 19-October 3

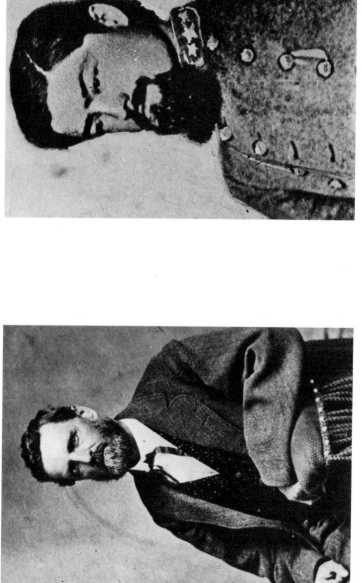

Brig.-Gen. Basil Duke

Brig.-Gen. John C. Vaughn

worried she must be, so he attempted to write as reassuring a letter as possible:

"Camp on Holston River

"September 20th 1864

____ing wife will be glad to hear that I have ____ this far from the raid safe & well. I have ____ every day since we left Athens, Georgia. All your acquaintances & friends with me are well — George Dryden, Pres West, Strother Hawkins, Lewises, Gaines Holleys, Craig — Sonny Payne — are well. I wrote to you several times on the road & several ladies promised me to write to you for me. I know how anxious you have been about me & hope that you have received some of these letters. I have heard nothing from you since your note of June 29^t (by Joseph) & I fear that in the evacuation of Atlanta our letters were destroyed. I cannot tell you how anxious I am to hear from you & Ella — very anxious my darling. Would to God I had you with me. It will be some days before we reach our lines — that is where mail facilities are & several weeks before we are back in Georgia. Until then I do not expect to hear from you — long anxious weeks. Yesterday was the anniversary of our marriage — one two years passing away from each other — oh! how sadly. My own darling knows by her own loving heart how I loved her on yesterday — how full my heart was of her & our precious child; I love you & our child with an unutterable love. Give my kindest love to your Father & Mother & Molly — remember me to the servants kindly. Let Capt Frazer's wife know he is well. With infinite love. . ."[567]

Then Colonel Breckinridge wrote his father, the Reverend

567. Volume 237, Breckinridge Papers, Library of Congress; ____indicates burned portions of the letter.

Robert J. Breckinridge, the most noted Lincolnite in Kentucky and the chief adviser of the hated Steve Burbridge, the Union commander of Kentucky.[568] Although the family was split into opposite camps by the war, the love of each member for the other was only deepened, not diminished. The son wanted, therefore, to ease his father's heart a bit, if possible, by restoring, through an exchange, his brother Joseph, a Union Lieutenant, whom he had captured the month before at Jug Tavern, Georgia. The son wanted to tell his father, too, that he had not heard of Major Theophilus Steele, who was his brother-in-law, also a Confederate officer. He wrote:

"My Dear Pa,

"I propose to make an effort to effect a special exchange between Joseph & Harry Clay. If you & his friends in the N. States will use your influence with the Federal government, I believe it can be effected. I am anxious to have this exchange made before Winter. I have been in the saddle beyond mail facilities since I wrote to you of Joseph's capture & of course have heard nothing from him. It will be some days yet before we reach our lines — I take advantage of a courier to send this to Bristol. I am very well indeed — have never been in better health in my life. I have not seen or heard from Major Steele since he was exchanged — indeed I have had no opportunity to hear. Give my kindest love to all of the family with you & _____ with profound love. . ."[569]

Willie didn't tell his father how Harry Clay came to be captured, which was at Greeneville when Morgan was surprised and killed. Clay was the grandson of Henry Clay and the brother of Willie's first wife, Lucretia, who died in

568. William H. Townsend, *Lincoln and the Bluegrass* (Lexington: University of Kentucky Press, 1955), p. 328.

569. Volume 237, Breckinridge Papers

1860. Harry was a member of Morgan's staff and a rather dudish fellow, as staff officers often were. He had recently married a young widow from Rogersville named Nannie Bynum, whose first husband, a daring and gallant man, had died in action on the street there. When Morgan was attacked, Clay and another staff officer took cover in a garden in a pit that was being prepared for winter potatoes. There they were rousted out by a Tennessee Yank soldier, who yelled to his partner, "Gawd! just think of Nanny Bynum's fust husband being drug out of a tater hole."[570]

ROGERSVILLE

SEPTEMBER 21

On September 21st, word swept through the camps that some men of the Tennessee Brigade had been arrested.[571] It was said that they had engaged in atrocities in Dutch Valley. A defense was offered that the accused parties had been maddened by the treatment that John Morgan had received, being killed after surrendering and then, as a corpse, being subjected to gross indignities. But the charges against the men were found to be true by a court-martial. The court found a lieutenant and three privates guilty and reported the verdict to General Williams, who ordered the extreme punishment, to be executed the next morning. At the announcement of the sentence, all but one member of the court petitioned General Williams to commute his punishment, but he replied with the reason that always strikes

570. H. H. Thomas, "Personal Reminiscences of the East Tennessee Campaign," in *Military Essays and Recollections*, MOLLUS — Illinois, Volume IV (Chicago: Dial Press, 1907), p. 299.

571. Guild, pp. 99-100.

terror in the heart of a person who gets caught up in the absurd — that it is necessary to provide an example that will deter others. Thus, having become "examples," in a sense strangers to their comrades who had somehow so far escaped such a fate, the Tennesseans were duly hanged the next morning.

GREENEVILLE
SEPTEMBER 22

Then the command broke camp and headed toward Greeneville. The boys learned that General John C. Vaughn, who was in command in East Tennessee, had asked for General Williams' cooperation in driving the Yanks from their fort at Bull's Gap, but they were not taken with that idea, for one of them remembered the way Sut Lovingood had immortalized that community:

"I haint never gin you the account ove my travels in the regin ove Bull's Gap, last winter. I hev kep hit back, case I were feard while I wer mad I mout do the cussed branch of hell injestis. But now I've got over hit, an am prepared, bad as hit is, to gin hit far play. Ef ever a yearthquake cums round en dus the same, you'd never see Bull's Gap agin, that's all.

"I means to tell jist what I seed, hearn and felt, an don't speck enybody what haint been thar'll believe a word ove hit; but I don't keer a durn, for I aint spected to act ur talk like human, no how.

"Well, Bull's Gap am a bottomless mud hole, twenty odd miles long, mixed with rocks, logs, brush, creeks, broken stages, dead hosses, mean whisky, cold vittils, and cross dogs. . . ."[572]

The boys doubted that the addition of Yanks would have had much of a salutary effect upon the locale, so they were pleased when General Williams decided to go directly to Greeneville, to seek ammunition and arms, knowing that his command was in no shape to fight any unit larger than a corporal's guard. They stayed in Greeneville on the 23rd. There they learned from Morgan's men, now commanded by Basil Duke, what a distressing shape that East Tennessee was in. Morgan's last raid to Kentucky had been disastrous: about a fourth of the various commands made it back, and many of them without weapons; back for over two months, many of them still roamed the countryside because of indifferent supervision; those who did come back were split into factions by charges and counter-charges about bank robberies in Kentucky; Morgan's entrapment itself was the result of negligence and carelessness; commands were operating with such independence that there had been pitched battle between two commands on occasion.[573]

There would be little reason for Wheeler's boys to linger long in that quarter of Dixie, where things, if possible, were

572. George Washington Harris, "Sut Lovingood at Bull's Gap," in Sut Lovingood's Yarns, ed. M. Thomas Inge (New Haven: College and University Press, 1966), p. 230.

573. Letter, John Echols to John C. Breckinridge, September 18, 1864, in John C. Breckinridge Papers, Chicago Historical Society.

worse than in Georgia. No doubt they would cross the mountains through the Carolinas and rejoin the War Baby in short order. Some of Williams' men did receive a pleasant surprise that day — Jim Black, for example, got a letter from Stamping Ground, Kentucky: "Received a letter from Pap dated 11th inst. brought through by private conveyance."[574] And many others met fellow Kentuckians who had recently come out.

IRON FURNACE
SEPTEMBER 24

The next day the column moved on up the valley, to camp at Iron Furnace, on the Nolichucky River, near Davy Crockett's birthplace, resting and getting horses shod for the trip ahead.[575] John W. Cotton, of the Tenth Confederate Regiment, Robertson's Brigade, apparently got enough rest that night, for the next day he undertook a chore more demanding than fighting:

"East tennessee Camp 4 miles from Jonesborough 100 miles north east of noxville September 24th 64 My dear beloved wife it is with uncertainty that i rite you a few lines you may get this and you may not but I hope you will these lines leave me well this is the 45 day we have been on this rade and I have been well all the time dont bee uneasy about me we hant had but little fiting to do but I have been in it all and hant been hurt yet I think we are out of danger now we are incide of our own lines we have had three men captured on this trip Burten Shaw and William Deason and a

574. Black.
575. Letter, Felix H. Robertson to George Knox Miller, June 10, 1895.

man by the name of Broice and one wounded Porter and Brown is well and all of the company is well how come us here we act behind general wheeler and got cut off from him there is a 2 briggagdes of us and a part of another our men were uneasy while we were in the yankey lines for fear we could bee captured but we got out safe we whiped the yankeys where ever we came in contact with them we have tore up a great deal of railroad on our rout but I am afraid it hant done much good we here that the yankeys has got atlanta but I here that our men has taken it back it ant worth while to say how bad I want to see you I hant here a word from you since I left home and this is only the three letter I have rote to you if I could see you I could tell you a heap I will rite more as soon as I get the chance nothing mor I remain your true lover til death"[576]

After forty-five days on the road, Cotton and the others welcomed a rest, a little peace and quite. And they got a few such days, for as the Bristol *Gazette* of September 22nd acknowledged, "The past week has been one of comparative quiet in our front." Indeed, the *Gazette* went on to proclaim that the only serious breach of peace in the area recently had been a slight matter: "We learn that Gen. Vaughn sent a detachment of Osborne's scouts into a disaffected portion of Scott county, Va., on Friday last to look after a company of deserters and Yankees. They were discovered about the 'Minny Sink' country, pitched into by our boys and some six or eight killed and several wounded. The fight took place on Saturday last."[577]

General Vaughn, the new commander of Confederate forces in East Tennessee, was making a determined effort to develop morale. To that end he was concentrating his

576. Griffith, p. 118.
577. As quoted in Lynchburg *Virginian*, September 24, 1864.

few available troops for an attack upon the Yanks in their forward position at Bull's Gap, while at the same issuing such orders as would reduce the number of military distractions:

"Head Quarters Cavl Force

East Tenn

"Carters Depot

"16th Sept 1864

"Special Orders

"I Information having been received by the Genl Comdg the forces of E Tenn that citizens and Soldiers are continually bargaining and selling, exchanging and buying *Greenbacks* and thus depreciating the Confederate currency it is therefore ordered that any person guilty of selling for or buying with *Greenbacks* that the full penalty of the law made by act of Congress of fine and imprisonment in the state penitentiary shall be enforced all officers of the CSA now under my command are to report any breach of this order upon the part of any citizen.

"II Brigade Commanders are hereby ordered to pull down and destroy all distillerys in the vicinity of their camps now distilling or one which is frequented by either citizens or soldiers in any part of this command, without they have permission from Department HdQuts."[578]

Conditions in general were so good (if not so sober as General Vaughn might have preferred) that the *Gazette* was tempted to editorialize (not that it took any great effort to get an editor to editorialize): "Taking into consideration the great change that has apparently come over the troops in this Department, for the better, there is some hope that the enemy's domination will be somewhat limited

578. Special Orders, September 15, 1864, in E. O. Guerrant Papers, University of Kentucky.

in the next few days. — We are gratified to know that 1500 well mounted recruits from Middle Tennessee together with 1000 regulars under a gallant leader have come to our lines the present week which speaks much for the devotion of the people inside the enemy's lines for our cause. We dare say that, if our armies could occupy Tennessee and Ky. that 50,000 men would flock to our standard. Even the reoccupation of East Tennessee would be but an opening for recruits from Middle Tenn., Kentucky and Indiana. We flatter ourselves that some step will soon be taken to redeem this country if for no other purpose than above alluded to."[579]

But Miss Bellona was as fickle in East Tennessee as elsewhere, for the very day that John Cotton was writing home that all was quiet, the rumor began to be passed that a Yank invasion from Eastern Kentucky could be expected. General Williams, who had gone to Abingdon, Virginia, to see about arms and ammunition for his men before they departed for Georgia, was told of the impending raid on the salt works at Saltville by General John Echols, commanding the Department of Southwest Virginia. Williams immediately agreed to commit his command to the defense of the department, if approval was secured from the Secretary of War.[580]

To help in securing Secretary Seddon's approval, two Congressmen visiting in Wytheville added their voices. Landon C. Haynes (Tennessee) and Theodore L. Burnett (Kentucky) wrote: "This department is in much peril. Troops are much needed. General John S. Williams in it with 2,500 men. He is under orders to go to Georgia. If he leaves, it is

579. Lynchburg *Virginian*, September 24, 1864.
580. "Gen. John S. Williams — The Hero of Saltville," Augusta *Chronicle and Sentinel*, November 1, 1864.

equivalent to our abandonment of this department. We do not think it can be defended without him; if he stays till the crisis passes it can be defended. We earnestly urge that he be ordered to report for duty temporarily to the commanding general of this department."[581]

IRON FURNACE
SEPTEMBER 25

On Sunday, September 25th, the men at the camps near Jonesborough were awakened well before dawn by a courier from General Vaughn, at Greeneville, beseeching their help in repelling an impending Yankee raid. General Robertson, who commanded in the absence of General Williams, ordered the men to saddle up and move out. Down the road they galloped through Rheatown, through Tusculum College, raising the dust and giving the roadside trumpet vines yet another coating. Every so often, they stopped to listen for cannon fire, but the only sounds were cow bells and church bells. They reasoned, though, that the church bells might be a warning to the nearby cits to beware the Yanks. Late in the morning, the command charged into Greeneville, Andy Johnson's digs before he became hooked up with such lunatics as Parson Brownlow. Well, come to find out, the war chief, John Vaughn, was at church with a number of ladies, when General Robertson located him.[582] And, come to find a second out, it was all a misunderstanding; there were no Yanks east of Bull's Gap. So back to camp General Robertson took the tired, thoroughly dis-

581. *ORR*, I, 39, pt. 2, p. 878.
582. Letter, Felix H. Robertson to George Knox Miller, June 10, 1895.

Jonesborough

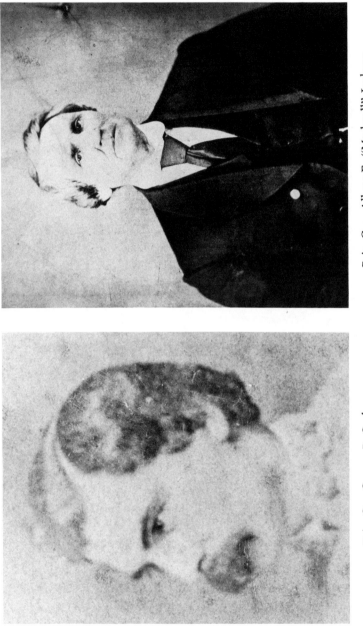

Brig.-Gen. Albert E. "Mudwall" Jackson

Brig.-Gen George B. Cosby

gusted troopers, himself expressing the opinion that Vaughn was playing general and merely wanted to move pins around on a map and increase his command. One of Vaughn's staff dogs said that he was like that, that earlier in the week he had tried to relieve Colonel Henry Giltner of a regiment to increase his own command. First he begged Giltner to remain with him, rather than transfer to Southwest Virginia, saying that he had more confidence in Giltner's Brigade than any other in his department. When Giltner refused, Vaughn then made his try for one regiment of the brigade; his request was refused by a staff officer, Ed Guerrant, who said privately, "It is not a judicious request. Detach one *regt.* from a small Brigade — to go alone with 2500 men to whip 1500 Yankees — Genl. Vaughn has *too much* confidence in us."[583]

BRISTOL

SEPTEMBER 27

For a day or so, though, the Wheeler boys did get to rest, while the rumors grew stronger that a two-pronged Yank attack was expected. General Gillem was to move out from Bull's Gap, up the East Tennessee and Virginia Railroad toward Bristol, while Steve Burbridge was to come through Pound Gap and attack Saltville; then as a joint expedition they might head toward Wytheville and even Lynchburg. Finally, the refreshed Rebel troops received orders to move northeast, and they reached Bristol on the 27th, where "Osceola," correspondent for Dibrell's Brigade, mailed the Memphis *Moving Appeal* an account of the last forty-five days. "Osceola" closed his exuberant narrative with an

583. Guerrant Diary, p. 1145.

effort to strengthen the resolve of those areas of the South
yet unfamiliar with the Yank capacity for playing with
matches; speaking of his comrades and of the Tennessee
cits they had met, he concluded:

"Having a very small supply of ammunition, they considered it impractical to attempt to get to Gen. Wheeler,
so they returned by way of McMinnville to Sparta — formed
a junction with Gen. Dibrell, and came across the mountains
via Montgomery, in Morgan county, Tenn. Passing near
Cumberland gap, we arrived at this place yesterday, without
encountering any opposition with the exception of a few
bushwhackers, who were summarily disposed of by Champ
Ferguson, the famous rebel guerrilla, so much talked of by
the Yankees. Champ has come out, announcing his intention of going with the regular army — Capt. George Carter,
also of guerrilla fame, came out with us. The recruits are
all in fine spirits, and will, no doubt, do their duty, when
the time comes for their metal to be tried. I feel no hesitancy in asserting that the re-occupation of Middle Tennessee
for one month would increase our army twenty-five thousand men.

"They have felt the oppressors heel, and though most of
the citizens have been forced to take the oath of allegiance
to the Lincoln Government, Middle Tennessee is today more
loyal to the South than some more favored sections farther
South. Nearly every family circle has been broken, having
lost some bright jewel since the inauguration of this un-
natural war — many hearthstones and door sills have been
stained with blood, citizens having been murdered for daring even to think their sentiments — and yet, the messages
sent by old gray haired men and venerable matrons — by
blooming maidens and doting wives — to their sons, grand-
sons, sweethearts and husbands in the army, are to 'fight

Bristol

Maj.-Gen. John C. Breckinridge

Brig.-Gen. John Echols

on' as long as a Yankee footstep pollutes the soil of their native South. The ladies of Middle Tennessee say that if the men cannot win our independence, when they are all killed, they (the women) will then take up arms and fight eternally our dastardly foes.

"Timid ones in the far South, take courage. Such a people never was and, with the helping of God, never will be conquered. In conclusion, I will mention, for the benefit of young officers and soldiers in our army, and the fair daughters of Dixie, who are spoiling for matrimony, an incident of the raid. A few evenings previous to our starting to recross the mountain, the gallant and dashing young Brig. Gen. Felix H. Robertson was married to a Miss Davis, near Sparta. A few short hours of connubial felicity and the general parted from his fair young bride, leaving her, however, among kind friends, and returned to the post where duty called. We have marching orders. It is said that we go to Saltville, Virginia, to meet a Yankee raid on the salt-works."[584]

It did seem a bit jarring to read of Felix H. Robertson and Champ Ferguson in the same account. It's like when Prince Hamlet shows the portraits of the two brothers, Hamlet the Elder and Claudius, to his mother:

Look here, upon this picture, and on this,
The counterfeit presentment of two brothers.
See, what a grace was seated on his brow:
Hyperion's curls, the front of Jove himself,
An eye like Mars, to threaten or command,
A station like the herald Mercury
New-lighted on a heaven-kissing hill,
A combination and a form indeed,

584. "Osceola."

Where every god did seem to set his seal
To give the world assurance of a man.
This was your husband. Look you now what follows:
Here is your husband, like a mildwe'd ear,
Blasting his wholesome brother. Have you eyes?
Could you on this fair mountain leave to feed,
And batten on this moor?
Ah, well, they say war makes strange bed-fellows — that
truth seems to extend to printer's beds, as well.

X

To Saltville, Virginia:
"there is no fiting going on yet"

(September 28-October 1, 1864)

CASTLEWOODS, VIRGINIA
SEPTEMBER 28

On September 28th, most of Williams' command left Bristol, ordered to Castlewoods, there to block the Yanks who were reported to be entering Virginia by the Pound Gap road. Four hundred recruits were sent on to Abingdon, for they were still without weapons and would be useless in a battle.[585] And Robertson's Brigade was left in position, probably because it was Sunday coming up again, and General Vaughn might need somebody to go to church with him in Greeneville.[586] The Yankee raid was now a virtual certainty, and the *Gazette* published that day wanted to reassure its readers that all was in preparation:

"We are excited here at the expected raid of General Burbridge from Kentucky, through Pound Gap, some eighty miles from this place. We were excited some days since, fearing that we had not force sufficient to meet him. His force is reported to General Echols at 8,000. We have now ready for any emergency in this Department sufficient to whip him, and to hold in check any raid that may be sent in this direction from Knoxville.

"General Echols is alive as to the interest of this Department. Generals Vaughn, Williams, Duke, Cosby, and Robinson have seen too much of this war to be daunted by such a force as Burbridge would sweep this country with. When last heard from he was reported to be at the mouth of Beaver, destined for Pound Gap. We say let him come on and welcome."

In addition to uttering a challenge in that issue of his paper, the editor also offered a clarification of a report offered in the previous issue. Williams' boys must have gotten a good laugh out of the kind of warfare practiced in East Tennessee and Southwest Virginia:

"FALSE ALARM

"The account we published last week of a fight in Scott

585. Guerrant Diary, p. 1145.

586. John S. Wise, *The End of an Era* (Boston: Houghton, Mifflin, 1899), p. 379.

county, Va., between deserters and bushwhackers and our forces, turns out to be a general row among our own men. It seems that the company sent there by Gen. Vaughn to look after deserters, &c, instead of fighting the enemy, got into a fight among themselves. The following particulars of the affair ware furnished us by Messrs Henry L. Wood, James C. Larky, Sr., and Fred. Saunders, three responsbile citizens of the county, one of whom Mr. Saunders, saw the fight himself.

"They state that the company referred to came into the county on Sunday, and, after dividing into three squads, commanded by a captain and two lieutenants, encircled the 'Minny Sink' neighborhood, and, after robbing and ambushing nearly every family they passed, including widows and soldiers families, met about the centre of the Sink country, when each squad being drunk, (a few excepted), commenced firing upon each other, swearing they had found the enemy, when many of them were wounded, several severely. After this they became somewhat sobered and determined to return and report their victory, in doing so they continued their depredations upon the best friends of our cause in the county, taking every horse they could find.

"As they passed up Robert's Creek they were fired upon by a gang of fifteen or twenty deserters, who say they done it in defence of their families. The whole affair is represented as a most disgraceful thing and calls loudly upon General Echols to have it investigated."[587]

587. Bristol *Gazette,* reprinted in Richmond *Enquirer,* October 4, 1864.

The next day, September 29th, Williams arrived at Castlewoods with the Kentucky Brigade and such of Dibrell's boys as were armed. At that point he was on the road between Pound Gap and Saltville, equidistant between them, and from that point he sent out scouts both northwest and northeast. Then his boys hunkered down to wait. That close to home, many boys in the Kentucky Brigade wrote letters that would be carried into that state and slipped into the Yank postal system. Sam Leavy, Ninth Kentucky, wrote his father about their raid through Tennessee and about the heroics of his colonel, Billy Breckinridge, back down at Jug Tavern. He also wrote that his buddy, Strother Hawkins, was in good health and that Mr. Hawkins ought to be so informed.[588]

CASTLEWOODS

SEPTEMBER 30

Back in Abingdon, although he was relieved that Williams' force had arrived, General Echols was still apprehensive. During the day, on September 30th, he telegraphed Judge Theodore Burnett, the Congressman, who was awaiting Breckinridge's arrival in Wytheville: "Say to General Breckinridge that I have just received information of the advance of the enemy on Saltville. Their advance reached Richland last night, thirty miles west of Saltville. I hope that the general will reach here to-night. Vaughn was fighting on the Watauga this morning when I last heard."[589] The general

588. Letter, father Leavy to father Hawkins, October 14, 1864, Volume 237, Breckinridge Papers.
589. *ORR,* I, 39, pt. 1, p. 559.

and the congressman did not arrive in Abingdon until the morning of October 1st, though.

By that afternoon, out at Castlewoods, General Williams had developed and proposed an offensive movement to Colonel Henry Giltner, who was commanding the cavalry before Saltville on the Richlands road. The Yanks appeared to have divided their force, with a part of them entering Virginia through Pound Gap, northwest of Williams, while the remainder were coming up the Louisa Fork and the state salt road toward Richlands. Williams thought that he and Giltner could combine their commands to hit the Yanks approaching by the Richlands route and that he could then swing back into position to attend to the force approaching from Pound Gap.

When he learned that General John C. Breckinridge had arrived to take command of the overall operation, he sent Breckinridge the following message, even as his column moved north to make its move toward Richlands:

"4:30, Hendricks, on south side of
Clinch Mountain

"GENERAL: I have just learned of your arrival in the department through a note from Captain Hargis, at Hyter's Gap, who also informs me that Generals Duke, Cosby, and Vaughn, with their commands, would be in Abingdon tonight. I inclose a letter which I had written and sent to Colonel Giltner just before the reception of this intelligence. The movement proposed therein is, of course, subject to your approval. My command is very much weakened by the sending off of Robertson. My fighting force, exclusive of him, does not exceed 1,000 men. My unarmed men left at Abingdon have not yet joined me. I have written several letters to know whether arms have arrived and where Duke and Cosby's brigades are, but have received no communication whatever on the subject from General Echols. If you think well of the movement and could send me Duke and Cosby, with their commands, it would render success certain, I think. Write me at once, and please order a fresh horse for my courier that he may return before day.

"I am, general, respectfully, yours. . ."[590]

Later that afternoon, on the road, Williams sent another message back to Abingdon to Breckinridge's headquarters. Both his objectives in sending the report seem to be all too common to the generaling business: one, to accumulate as large a command as possible, and, two, to paint as rosy a picture of a proposed operation as the canvas will bear:

"General: I send you inclosed a note from Henry Stonestreet, a very reliable scout, whom I sent this morning to look after the enemy in the direction of Wheeler's Ford. This force is about forty miles from the force at General Bowen's, and I am midway between them, with my back to Hyter's Gap. Unless I have a stronger force than I now have with me my movement upon the enemy at Bowen's may become perilous, for the force at Wheeler's by following me up would cut me off from all means of crossing to the south side of Clinch Mountain. This information was received after I wrote to Giltner and you this evening.

"Respectfully,

J.S.W.

"Since writing the within a scout sent out by Colonel Giltner has just returned from Louisa Fork, and reports to me that the force of the enemy that came into Tazewell by the Louisa Gap road does not exceed 2,000 men, a large portion of them negroes.

J.S.W.

590. *ORR*, I, 39, pt. 1, p. 562.

"Have you received my dispatch, written at 4 p.m. today, containing copy of my letter to Colonel Giltner, &c.?"[591]

Williams was wrong on several counts.[592] The Yanks had
camped on General Bowen's large farm at Richlands the
previous night, but had moved out by 9:00 a.m., had pushed
Giltner's men out of the way several times, and, by the
time of his second report, had cleared Laurel Gap, only
five miles from Saltville. The Yank force totaled at least
six thousand men, only about six hundred of whom were
black (and therefore presumably raw and undependable).
Saltville was ripe for the picking, and when, after dark, the
order came for Williams to move there immediately, his
men must have known that it would be impossible for
them to reach that place in time. A steady, severe rain had
begun to fall, making the night so dark that troopers with
torches had to be stationed along the road that took them
south across the Clinch Mountain.[593] Even if they were only
fifteen minutes late, it would be too late, for the Yanks
would need only that short time in order to swing their
sledge hammers against the evaporation pots and pans and
drop cannon balls down the wells. Such simple actions
would stop the salt manufactory for months.

At that moment Saltville was poorly defended, indeed.
By far the largest body of defenders consisted of about
seven hundred Virginia reserves. Then, too, Dibrell's three
hundred recruits, newly armed, had arrived, even though
they refused to take orders from Malish officers.[594] And
there was Giltner's Brigade of less than seven hundred, which
had been shadowing the advancing Yanks for over a week.

591. ORR, I, 39, pt. 1, p. 561.
592. Guerrant Diary, pp. 1164-1168.
593. "Gen. John S. Williams, — The Hero of Saltville."
594. ORR, I, 39, pt. 1, p. 560.

The best picture of the home guards was sketched by a young man who had just joined them. The picture may be a bit severe, though, for the young man was John S. Wise, son of General Henry A. Wise, and he was accustomed to his father's brigade of regulars on the Petersburg line. At times John Wise and his father must have thought it strange that they wound up fighting against the Stars and Stripes, when Henry made such a to-do about that flag the day that John was born. Henry was United States Minister at Rio de Janeiro during President Tyler's administration, and when his son was born in the Consular Mansion the proud father ordered a dozen different American flags flown there. He wanted it to be known by all that his son had been born under the American flag, even if not on American soil.[595]

In 1864 Henry thought that he had his son safely tucked away out at Lexington, Virginia, as a student at the Virginia Military Institute. But then when the boy had served in the Corps of Cadets in the Battle of New Market, in May, and had gotten himself slightly wounded, his father had attempted to remove him even farther from the war. He got his son commissioned a second-lieutenant, to serve as a drill master for Colonel Robert T. Preston's command of reserves from the Dublin Rendezvous. Young Wise caught up with Preston at Glade Spring Junction, where the reserves were catching a train of flat cars that would take them the eight or ten miles to Saltville:

"The day I joined him, he had a veritable Falstaffian army: his regiment of eight companies presented every stage of manhood, from immature boyhood to decrepit old age. One of his companies drawn up in line looked

595. Frances Carpenter, *Carp's Washington* (New York: Mc-Graw-Hill Company, 1960), p. 170.

as irregular as a pile of barrel-hoops. There was no pretense of uniform; they wore everything, from straw hats to coonskin caps. A vision of Colonel Bob's regiment must have presented itself to the mind of General Grant when he informed the country that the Confederacy was, like Micawber, 'robbing the cradle and the grave.'

"One thing uniform they had, — every man had a Belgian rifle, and a cartridge-box filled with pretty fair ammunition. . . .

"Nobody realized the ludicrous appearance of his soldiers, or enjoyed it more thoroughly, than did Colonel Bob. He would have had a laugh at his own funeral, if opportunity had occurred. 'Look at that!' said he, stroking his beard and chuckling a comfortable, inside-shaking laugh; 'look at that! Your cadets could n't beat it.. He was pointing to his command, scrambling pell-mell, helter-skelter, upon the dirty flats which had been backed up. Two strapping young fellows were tugging at an old one, who looked as if he would come to pieces, pulling him up on the car, while a third was pushing him from behind."[596]

Despite their appearance, the reserves would fight, the Colonel felt. When the train arrived in Saltville, Preston, accompanied by Lieutenant Wise, reported to General Albert E. "Mudwall" Jackson, the local commander, for orders:

"Old 'Mudwall' was a common-looking man, with a drawl in his voice, and appeared to be taking things very easy. Still, he showed courage and intelligence in his dispositions. He told us he was expecting to be reinforced by Robertson's cavalry, which was coming up from east Tennessee. He hoped they would arrive before morning, but

496. Wise, pp. 374-375.

intended to fight whether they reached him in time or not.

"'Kernel,' said he, 'my men tell me the Yanks have got a lot of nigger soldiers along. Do you think your reserves will fight niggers?'

"'Fight 'em?' said the old colonel, bristling up; 'by _____, sir, they'll eat 'em up! No! not eat 'em up! That's too much! By _____, sir, we'll cut 'em up!'"[597]

"Mudwall" ordered Preston's reserves to go forward a mile or so, to McCreedy's Gap, there to camp and make what preparations for battle they could. There the reserves wistfully awaited the arrival of the Confederate regulars that were promised, Williams' force from the northwest and Robertson's from Tennessee. The ones which did arrive didn't provide that much comfort for Colonel Preston, as his report to General Jackson on the afternoon of October 1st indicates: "No doubt is now entertained of a purpose to attack this place. The enemy variously estimated from 4,000 to 8,000, the main force in front of Giltner, but it is reported 2,000 are dismounted and are moving upon us by the Russell road. Nothing yet heard from General Williams. The 300 men ordered here last night have come in, but in a state of perfect insubordination. I have finally succeeded in getting them off to a gap five miles west of this place (the Tumbling Creek Gap). Without further reenforcements we can make but a feeble defense, but will do the best we can. Our men all armed, but ammunition insufficient, particularly caliber .69. We hope additional troops will arrive before the enemy."[598]

597. Wise, p. 379.
598. *ORR*, I, 39, pt. 1, p. 560.

SALTVILLE

OCTOBER 1

The reserves had only Giltner's Brigade between the Yanks and themselves, and by the afternoon of October 1st, that seemed to be a feeble defense. Trimble's Tenth Kentucky Cavalry had skirmished with the Yanks at Cedar Bluffs, on the afternoon of September 30th, but was easily flanked. Then, the next morning the brigade ambushed the Yanks on the side of Clinch Mountain; after thirty minutes Giltner ordered a retreat, though some of his men questioned his decision. His adjutant, Ed Guerrant, in particular, thought that the opposition being offered was not strenuous enough:

"Fought sharply some half an hour — when Col. G ordered us to fall back. — Thought the enemy were flanking us. Was very much opposed to it. Thought we should detain them longer here.

Cut a few trees in the road & moved off to the top of the next mountain. —

"Thought the whole way should be blockaded — & fight them over it all — Col. went along back — heedlessly — I thought. Lost my temper, & said so.

"We had heard nothing from *Echols* or anybody since 28^{h} ulto. — Knew there was nobody at the Saltworks but a few raw militia led by that old imbecile, "Mudfence Jackson". — Despaired of the Saltworks — & abused the stupidity, & carelessness of commanding officers, to permit such a column of men to march unopposed to the very heart of Va. & the Salvator of the S. C.

"Col. concluded to go along free & easy, & let things take their course. I was in favor of fighting and cutting &

blockading as if our efforts could save all."[599]

Colonel Giltner had his men prepare another ambush at the peak of Flat Top Mountain, and by 2:00 in the afternoon, the watchful, but confident Yanks showed up. Only the Sixty-fourth Virginia and the Tenth Kentucky could be spared for the trap, for the Fourth Kentucky and the Tenth Kentucky Mounted Rifles had to guard another road. The Yanks, consequently, had little trouble dismounting and then flanking their opponents, thus forcing the Rebs once more to retreat.[600]

That left only one more defensive position between the Yanks and Saltville — Laurel Gap. When Giltner got back to that point, he found Colonel Bob Smith's Thirteenth Battalion of Virginia Reserves, about two hundred fifty old men and young boys, guarding the place. Giltner must have felt either awfully confident about his own brigade or awfully dubious about the malish, for he sent them on back toward Saltville. They didn't look back, either, so they escaped the fate of Lot's wife, which was just as well, considering that they would have been a drug on the local market. Then Giltner set the order of battle for his boys; the Fourth Kentucky and the Tenth Kentucky Mounted Rifles were sent to the cliff that provided the left side of the gap, and the Sixty-fourth Virginia was ordered to the hill on the right. Then he took his staff to a belated meal at the home of Mrs. Sexton, who, restrained by her patriotism, charged them only $3.00 a piece.

By 5:00 in the afternoon the Yanks had come up and attacked in force. They must have known who to pick on — the Sixty-fourth Virginia had lost half its force by cap-

599. Guerrant Diary, pp. 1165-1166.
600. Guerrant Diary, pp. 1166-1167.

ture the year before, had its colonel cashiered, had been
unbrigaded so long that it would just as soon fight Reb as
Yank, when it would fight at all.[601] Captain Ed Guerrant
noted the outcome with disgust: "the enemy appeared in
heavy force, dismounted. — attacked us promptly in the
Gap — scaled the mountain on the right & came down
upon the 64th which lost no time in changing it's position."[602]

Since Laurel Gap was the last defensible position before
Saltville, both Giltner's boys and the Yanks knew that
that place was, as Ed Gurrant put it, "gone up." The Yanks
were so confident of taking it the next day that they didn't
even try to rush on to it that night. And by now the Rebs
knew that the Yanks had no reason to fear or to be in a
hurry. From escaped prisoners and scouts Giltner knew
that he faced six to eight thousand men, divided into three
brigades under good men whom the Rebs had faced before
— Hanson, Hobson, and Ratliff. Ratliff's brigade was especially respected; it contained the veteran Eleventh Michigan Cavalry and the Twelfth Ohio Cavalry, as well as the
raw black troops that were so grandly called the Fifth United
States Colored Cavalry.

Colonel Giltner withdrew his boys with that easy, un-
fazed way that he always had and moved them back to
Broad Ford.[604] There he saw to it that the bridge was destroyed behind them, and then, although the Yanks were

601. For the condition of the Sixty-Fourth Virginia, see *ORR,*
I, 43, pt. 2, pp. 868-871; Lee A Wallace, *A Guide to Virginia Military
Organizations, 1861-1865* (Richmond: Civil War Commission, 1964),
pp. 194-195; James D. Fox, *A True History of the Reign of Terror*
(Aurora, Illinois: J. D. Fox, 1884), p. 21.
  602. Guerrant Diary, p.. 1167.
  604. Guerrant Diary, pp. 1168-1169.

only a mile or so away, he got his brigade fed. Since from that point there were two roads back to Saltville, the river road and the Poor Valley Road, Giltner divided his force, in order to picket both routes. Ed Guerrant was with the Fourth and Tenth Kentucky, which stayed on the river road, the probable route of the invasion. These regiments camped in Pierson's Bottom, along side of some of the jumpy malish. The only news was bad news; an annoyed Guerrant recorded a mocking response to a timid message from "Mudwall" Jackson: "Rec^d. a communication from Gen. Jackson this evening, announcing that he expected reinforcements at Saltworks, but none had arrived. Great Goodness!" "Mudwall's" apprehension was even stronger in the communique he sent back to General Echols, in Abingdon: "Colonel Giltner has been compelled to evacuate Laurel Creek Gap this evening, and is falling back on this place. Doubtless an attack will be made on this place early to-morrow. If reenforcements are not sent to-night it will probably be too late."[605] About this time Jackson must have decided to save what he could, for all the ammunition for the six-pound guns and much of the small arms ammunition were sent down the tracks to Glade Spring Junction, nine miles away.[606] Most of the civilians of the town found such behavior affecting, for they took up what they could and skedaddled. As one cit, J. M. Gibson, wrote to Zeb Vance, the governor of North Carolina: "I left home on the 2d with the *funds* of our bank and thought it probable that I would pay you a visit. . . ."[607]

605. *ORR,* I, 39, pt. 1, p. 560.

606. T. L. Burnett, "The Battle of Saltville," *The Southern Bivouac,* II (September, 1838), 20-22. (First appearance, Richmond *Enquirer,* October 18, 1864).

607. Letter, J. M. Gibson to Z. B. Vance, October 12, 1864, in Z. B. Vance Papers, Volume V, State of North Carolina Archives.

Saltville

Salt Valley, with Chestnut Ridge at the Right

Lower Salt Works

The sense of helplessness was general in the little town, for when General Robertson brought his exhausted troopers in, late that Saturday night, he found "the reserves and all authorities scared to death."[608] The Confederate Brigade had ridden up from below Bristol, where it had been left, apparently to be applied as reinforcements, either in East Tennessee or Southwest Virginia, depending upon the need. The men enjoyed the rest; since they were back in Dixie, many, such as John Cotton, made an effort to inform their families of their wellbeing:

". . . Mariah I will rite a few more lines as I have not had the chance to send off my letter yet I am still well and hope these lines may find you all well and doing well I hope ann is well by this time I saw oald anchy meneal about two weeks ago and he said he was at the still and he never herd any complaint that is all that I have herd from home since the 18 of august and I recken you no that I want to her from home by this time we have had a powerful rain it rained a day and two nites but it is the first rain we have had since I got back from home except one little shour we have had the dustyest time that I ever saw I have seen the dust so thick that I could not see no more than I could the darkest kind of a nite it looked like it would stifle men and horses on a march I hant seen asa in some time but I think I well see him today I am going to the post office and they say it is 7 miles from here every thing is still here yet there is no fiting going on yet but I am looking for it every day Meneal told me that the cavalry that were hunting up deserters killed oald stephen thomas I was sorry to here of it I dont no what else to rite nothing

608. Letter, Felix H. Robertson to Braxton Bragg, October 6, 1864.

more I will rite again before long. . . ."[609]

Like the rest of Wheeler's Lost Tribe, the Confederate
Brigade, having been in the saddle amost two months, was
nearly naked and therefore chilled that rainy, cold night it
reached Saltville. Back on August 10th, the boys had been
permitted by Wheeler to take only "saddle blankets one suit
of clothes and oil cloths." Thus, General Robertson said of
his boys: "there is not half a shirt in my brigade to ten men
I myself am ragged — having obeyed the order to the letter
— numbers barefooted — and all infested with vermin on
acct of not having a change." "Not a blanket to a man — in
short their condition demands prompt attention," he concluded. Then he vowed: "I shall do all in my power I never
saw more uncomplaining men."[610]

609. Griffith, p. 118.
610. Letter, Felix H. Robertson to Braxton Bragg, October 6,
1864.

XI

Saltville: *"a very pretty affair"*

(October 2, 1864)

The Confederate Brigade nevertheless looked good to Giltner's small force, which was being chased around like a pretty girl at a church social, as the Yank advance began early the next morning, Sunday, October 2nd. To one of them, Adjutant Guerrant's clerk, George D. Mosgrove, General Robertson was very impressive: "I was charmed with the appearance of General Robertson. He was the youngest looking general I had seen in the army, apparently not more than twenty-four years of age and wearing good clothes, *en neglige,* gallant and handsome."[611] Nor was Mosgrove alone in his opinion; Basil Duke, who saw Robertson the next day, thought him "a young and very dashing officer."[612] Giltner's boys had contested the Yanks on both roads, but as the Yanks got their whole column into motion, the Rebs were getting more pressure than they could bear. Consequently they were delighted to discover that help had arrived, however small the dose might be.

In time Giltner's brigade united on top of the large hill that separated the two roads. His boys had succeeded in warning all the local cits that the raid was for real and that those who were going to Saltville had better be about it. Eight year old Fannie Roberts saw the war come to her door. Her mother had just used the last flour in the house to make enough dough for a loaf of bread for Sunday dinner. Just as she put it in the oven, a Reb trotted by to tell them to get. The father was away, hiding the horses, so the mother took Fannie, her brother Edward, and the other children out of the house at once. As they ran down the path amid the sound of firing along the ridge tops, a Yankee soldier came rolling down the steep hillside, right to their feet. The children ran to him, to help him up, but it was plain that he was dead, so they left him there among the ferns, staring at the sky.[613]

Giltner's boys made a stand sufficient to cause the Yanks to dismount and come forward as infantry. Giltner requested

611. George Dallas Mosgrove, *Kentucky Cavaliers in Dixie* (Jackson, Tennessee: McCowat-Mercer Press, 1957), p. 200.

612. Basil W. Duke, *A History of Morgan's Cavalry* (Bloomington: Indiana University Press, 1960), p. 544.

613. William B. Kent, *A History of Saltville* (Radford, Virginia: Commonwealth Press, 1955), p. 36.

that the reserves come up to join the line, when he saw that the Yanks had been slowed down. But the malish seemed to be reserved.[614] Congregated around the Sanders house and barn and in its orchard, back down the hill toward Saltville, the local forces had been placed under the command of Colonel Jack Prather, Eighth Confederate, by General Robertson, whose own men held the right rear, on the much higher Chestnut Ridge. Prather would not advance the malish without Robertson's permission, so they stayed put and Giltner had to abandon his line, to retreat himself to Chestnut Ridge.[615]

When the Kentuckians took their place to the left of Robertson's line, they noticed that more troops had arrived and taken position on Robertson's right. They were Dibrell's Tennesseans, and it was said that all of the yelling that Giltner's boys had heard shortly before was from Dibrell's recruits, who had been waiting for the arrival of their comrades.[616] Now Prather's reserves, still standing pat, were in front of the main line, instead of behind it.

By then it was almost 11:00 o'clock. The remainder of Williams' men arrived, and when "Old Pap" himself appeared in his huge corporeal substance on Church Hill, he, as ranking brigadier, assumed command of all Confederate troops on the field. "Mudwall" Jackson retired to a battery which was placed on top of a hill and from that commanding position he watched the day's festivities through his spy glass. George Mosgrove was near the church on the hill to record Williams' arrival: "I was standing in the main road at the base of the left end of Chestnut Ridge, when General Cerro Gordo Williams rode up at the head of

614. Guerrant Diary, p. 1170.
615. DuBose, pp. 388-389; "The Last General Officer." 366.
616. Lindlsey, pp. 671-672.

his command, early in the morning. He looked much the same as when I had seen him last in Tennessee; massive, tall and commanding, the picture of robust health. With the voice of a stentor he ordered his men up the ridge. Standing there in the middle of the road, he stormed and swore while hurrying the men, and continued to storm until the last man was in position."[617] Such bustle had its effect; as Ed Guerrant noted, "Genl. Williams appeared on the field about this time, & greatly inspired our troops."[618] Many of the officers were privately not that reassured by "Old Pap's" presence, though, for they knew too much about him from the year before, when he had been commander of the brigade now so efficiently led by Colonel Giltner.[619] They remembered one time when Giltner had had to relieve Williams, who had been too drunk to direct his troops.[620]

Saltville is surrounded by a circle of hills. To the east is the higher elevation, Chestnut Ridge. Extending from its left, or western, end is Church Hill, which becomes, in turn, a row of bluffs facing a hundred yards of meadow and corn field bordering the Holston River. With the lay of land in mind, Williams made his disposition of forces.[621] He just left the reserves where they were. He did shift Giltner's Brigade off Chestnut Ridge and onto Church Hill and the bluffs facing the river. The Tenth Kentucky faced the ford that led up the hollow between Church Hill and Chestnut

617. Mosgrove, p. 200.
618. Guerrant Diary, p. 1171.
619. *ORR*, I, 43, pt. 2, 868-871.
620. Ewing.
621. Lewis Preston Summers, *History of Southwestern Virginia, 1746-1786, Washington County, 1777-1870* (Baltimore, Genealogical Publishing Company, 1966), pp. 538-539.

Ridge, with its back to the graveyard. Then the Tenth Kentucky Mounted Rifles and the Sixty-fourth Virginia, and, at the lower crossing of the river, the Fourth Kentucky. In front of the Fourth Kentucky, down in the corn field, lay Colonel James T. Preston's malish, while his cousin, Colonel Bob Preston, had his old men and boys in reserve along the road behind the Tenth Kentucky. On the extreme left Williams held his own Kentucky Brigade, temporarily commanded by Billy Breckinridge, mounted and in reserve.[622]

Robertson's and Dibrell's boys were hidden by the tangled briers and brush on Chestnut Ridge, high enough up so that they could look down upon the Yanks forming their lines in the open fields just east of the Sanders house. As they waited, they piled up rocks, logs, fence rails, to make sure that they were not stampeded when the reserves fled back to the main line. For they were convinced that as soon as the Yanks started down the hill toward the house, the malish would run like rabbits.[623]

At 12:15 p.m. it was still occasionally quiet enough for the crying of the Sanders children, barricaded in a giant fireplace and surrounded by feather ticks, to be heard.[624] Then Dibrell's videttes heard the beginnings of a speech by a Yank officer, saying that the destruction of the saltworks was worth more than the capture of Richmond and a lot more such stuff and ended up by appealing especially to his black troops to give a good fight.[625]

At 12:30 the three regiments of Yanks charged down the

622. Guerrant Diary, p.. 1171; Summers, pp. 537-538.
623. Lindsley, pp. 671-672.
624. Kent, p. 31.
625. Lindlsey, pp. 271-672.

open hill toward the Sanders house.[626] The Yanks had not expected much opposition, for they knew that they were facing reserves. But the four hundred old men and boys held their ground, fighting stubbornly, even after the Yanks had surrounded the house. Then the malish fought hand-to-hand, losing twenty to thirty killed, about fifty wounded, and perhaps the same number captured. It was a magnificent stand, and the regulars up on Chestnut Ridge cheered the bravery of the reserves.[627] But at the same time, it was heart-breaking, for as General Robertson recalled: "They had never been under fire, their clothing was clean, shirts were white. It was a sad sight to see those tender troops cut all to pieces, old fathers crying over their baby boys, and children weeping over old sires with bald heads and often with long white beards. . . ."[628] What made it even sadder was that it was all so unnecessary. Watching the scene from Church Hill, Ed Guerrant observed, "They fought with more courage than prudence."[629]

Only when they were run over did the malish fall back, threading their way down the hill, through the honeysuckle thicket in the ravine, and up through the blackberry briers and vines on the side of Chestnut Ridge. The brush was so thick that neither side could form a line; it was single Reb against single Yank, firing at a noise, a shadow, a shaking bush half a dozen steps away. Often, from their works, the Reb regulars could see those lonely fights, even though they frequently dared not interfere, for fear of hitting the wrong one. They watched as a Reb tried to grab a stand

626. "Our Army Correspondence," Detroit *Advertiser and Tribune,* October 20, 1864.
627. Guerrant Diary, p. 1172; Mosgrove, p. 199.
628. "The Last General Officer," 366.
629. Guerrant Diary, p. 1172.

of colors from a Union sergeant, for example, only to get run through with the spear head that topped the staff.[630] About 1:30 in the afternoon the last malish had broken across the clearing below the works, toppled into the rifle pits, and lay gasping. In time the Yanks gathered at the edge of the briers, about fifty yards from our lines. Then a Yank colonel yelled, "Remember Fort Pillow and take no prisoners," and gave the order to charge, and here came those three regiments struggling up toward us, slipping, sliding, and tugging at any hand-hold. Most of our attention was captured by the novelty of those blacks, who "marched in perfect order," said J. P. Austin, of the Ninth Kentucky, "as if on dress parade."[631] Well, maybe they took two steps like that, but after that it was crouch and crawl. Still that left them "conspicuously exposed," George Mosgrove noted, so that the blacks "fell in heaps before the rifles of the enraged Tenneseeans."[632] Many of the boys seemed to realize for the first time that Burbridge was actually daring to use negro troops against white men, as the black regiment appeared on the Yank left. They were so shocked that they went crazy. Colonel Dibrell remembered that moment on the Eighth Tennessee part of the line: "As the enemy began to emerge from the brier-thicket, some of the Eighth became exasperated when they saw it was negroes in front. Lieut. John Webb, of Company F, leaped over his log breast-works, with pistol in hand, and was shot down. His brother, Lieut. Thomas C. Webb, Alex. A. Reagan, and several others were badly wounded. The gallant Capt. George Carter

630. Frank H. Mason, *The Twelfth Ohio Cavalry* (Cleveland: Nevins Steam Pub. House, 1871), p. 65.

631. J. P. Austin, *The Blue and the Gray* (Atlanta: Franklin Printing and Publishing Company, 1899), p. 100.

632. Mosgrove, p. 200.

was killed, and the soldier who shot him was riddled with balls."[633]

Company C got it as bad as any. Lieutenant A. A. Reagan was maybe the luckiest man on the field — he was shot through the jaw, the ball coming out behind his ear at the base of the brain. That close to his spinal column, the wound caused only a fractured jaw bone and permanent paralysis of the right side of the face.[634] Dr. Luke Ridley, working on him on the field, must have been amazed that he lived. In the same company one-eyed G. K. Grimsley got a ball in his left foot that shattered the bone into dozens of splinters and crippled him for life. We said that that ought to get him home, but one old boy said, what the hell, he's in the cavalry, ain't he — he can still *ride* to war. And, sure enough, after a stay at Emory, he rejoined his regiment.[635]

Still the Yanks came on, as the Rebs ran out of ammunition for their carbines and were mostly depending on their pistols by then. That meant that they began to suffer more casualties, as the range shortened. Among them was young Ben Rogers, Company B, Fourth Tennessee, who was tumbled by a ball in the right knee, a wound that surely meant amputation and probably death from shock or, later, gangrene.[636] The first two charges against the Reb rifle pits failed, but the third one carried. To the shock of the Rebs, it was led by the black troopers.[637] That kind of behavior

633. Lindlsey, pp. 671-672.

634. Soldier's Application for Pension, Number 10008, State of Tennessee.

635. Soldier's Application for Pension, Number 2028, State of Tennessee.

636. Confederate Questionnaire, State of Tennessee; Merritt, p. 345.

637. *ORR*, I, 39, pt. 3, p. 200.

wasn't at all what our boys allowed themselves to think blacks could perform, so that some of them swore that the Yanks had gotten the blacks drunk.[638]

Robertson's boys were also under intense pressure. Sergeant Lambright, Fifth Georgia, said it was "as fierce a fight as I ever witnessed or took part in." Then, regarding that moment, he laconically added: "Here we came in contact for the first time with mixed troops, white and negroes. No quarter was asked, or given."[639] It was hand-to-hand, as the Yanks captured a cannon which our boys were trying to drag farther up the hill. Then the Rebs counter-charged and recaptured the piece.[640] The Confederate Brigade was in danger of being overrun; General Robertson remembered that hour thus: ". . . the struggle occurred in a briar patch and was a hand to hand fight — several were knocked on the head by the Negro troops with muskets whilst fighting with revolvers after the ammn had been exhausted for Rifles."[641] Finally the right flank of Robertson's line broke, and his boys started scrambling farther back up the ridge.

Such a movement left Dibrell's left rear exposed and forced his boys to retreat.[642] The blacks were in upon Dibrell's men, fighting savagely, for the Tennesseans weren't taking any prisoners, either. Some Yanks caught Lieutenant W. P. Chapin, after his mortally wounded horse had fallen on him, and as they led him off, Captain Andrew Dale and his company caught them and killed most of them before

638. W. M. Henderson, Recollection, State of Georgia Archives.
639. Lambright.
640. Mason, p. 65.
641. Letter, Felix H. Robertson to Braxton Bragg, October 6, 1864.
642. *ORR*, I, 39, pt. 1, p. 497; Lindsley, pp. 671-672.

getting Chapin back. In such a mixup, the Tennessee Brigade had to pull back, scrambling up the hill to McClung's Battery. From that new line they fired with their revolvers and tried to depress the cannon enough to keep from overshooting the Yanks, who now occupied the line of rifle pits. The firing slacked off to almost nothing, for the Yanks were also yelling back for ammunition.[643] The Yanks didn't attack any more, and the Rebs had retired in reasonably good order — but the fact remained that the Yanks, including negroes, had charged a nearly straight-up-and-down hill, through briars, against regular troops, for over two hours, and even at that moment still occupied the Reb line.

While all of this was going on, other Yank units were hitting Giltner's boys at both fords.[644] Maybe that explains why Williams didn't send any reinforcements up to Chestnut Ridge. But he didn't order any help to Giltner's boys, either; in fact, he didn't do any generaling at all, just stood in the road on Church Hill and cussed the Yankees, all day long.[645]

New to the whole business, Lieutenant John Wise was intensely interested in the whole show, and as soon as his battalion of reserves reached its assigned position over the hill behind the Tenth Kentucky he was free to watch: "The hill in our front, on which our advance line was posted, concealed us completely from the enemy. Behind us, another hill of unusual height, cleared on its summit, gave a battery planted there the range of the ford and of the ground beyond. Our front lines had not completed their formations

643. Mason, p. 65; "From the Eleventh Cavalry," Detroit Free Press, October 20, 1864; "Our Army Correspondence."
644. ORR, I, 39, pt. 1, p. 557.
645. Guerrant Diary, p. 1178.

on the river bluffs when we heard first a volley, and afterwards a dropping fire of musketry. Our pickets beyond the river were engaged, and falling back before the advancing enemy. Climbing the hill behind us, the view was excellent.

"Soon our videttes were all safely across the ford and within our lines, and the next move in the game was to be made by the enemy. Out he came in due time, in battle array, — infantry, cavalry, and artillery, — showing himself along the edge of the woods which crowned the slopes of pasture land beyond the ford.

"'Bang!' went the guns of the battery on the hill behind us, and a flock of little six-pound shells flew singing over our heads towards some cavalry debouching from the woods a mile away. The artillery of the enemy promptly took position and delivered a return fire, but was unable to secure an elevation sufficient to reach our battery.

"Out of sight, fully protected, our regiment lay there between those dueling batteries. It was very noisy, for the shells of the enemy exploded in the woods on the hillside in our rear. Curious to know how our raw recruits would behave under fire, I returned to where they were, and was much gratified at the spirit of the men, especially the youngsters. It was with difficulty that the colonel kept them from scrambling up to the top of the hill in our front to watch the fight. The men were conducting themselves like veterans. Many of the boys were sighting their guns, and showing how they would 'shoot a nigger,' if they had a chance.

"'Where are your field officers, colonel?' said I, observing that he was the only one upon the ground.'The lieutenant-colonel is on furlough, and the major cut his foot with an axe last week, and is in the hospital at Dublin,' said he, apparently unconscious that their absence made any difference, or should be supplied. 'Say, young 'un, you'll have to give orders to the left side. I'll attend to the right.' By the left side he meant the left flank of the regiment. He proposed that he should act as colonel and lieutenant-colonel, and was unconsciously promoting me to be major.

"'But, colonel,' I protested, 'will not your senior captains take offense that you do not assign them to the positions to which their rank entitles them?'

"'Shut up!' said he fiercely; 'I'm running this regiment. They don't know, and don't care a _____ _____ about that! I know what I want. If you put such notions in their heads, there'll be no end of trouble here. You go and do what I tell you! Do you hear?' So off I went, and perched myself opposite the left battalion. I did not know a man in the regiment, or half a dozen officers. It would not have surprised me to hear them tell me to to to the devil when I undertook to give them commands. It seems, however, that they considered me as a *member of the colonel's staff,* and nobody raised any question of precedence."[646]

The Yanks hit the upper ford first, came at it in three columns under Hobson, one off Sanders Hill, one down the river, and one — a cavalry charge — across the big bottom to the left.[647] The cavalry charge, of about seventy-five men, cleared enough ground so that the Yanks could bring two little mountain howitzers forward and set them up.[648] But they sounded like pop-guns, against the Reb batteries, and they couldn't reach the Reb batteries, anyway. So that once the boys working the Reb pieces discovered that they didn't have to fear their opposite numbers, they wheeled

646. Wise, pp. 381-383.
647. Guerrant Diary, p. 1173.
648. Frank Moore, *The Rebellion Record,* Volume XI (New York: D. Van Nostrand, 1868), pp. 423-425.

their pieces out into the open and, as one Yank later said, "practiced upon the Federal line as though enjoying a day's target drill."[649] Ed Guerrant noted the effect of one cannon planted near his post of duty: "One rifled piece near the church did good service on the column which fought Trimble at the Ford — One shot killed a major and a Capt. Qr. Mr. —— on the point." But much of the remainder of the artillery fire was, he thought, rather useless:

"During all this time, our artillery was terrible in *sound*, if not *effect* — Its reverberations among the gorges of the mountains were grand beyond description. One report sounded like a hundred cannon; & no doubt this had a salutary effect on our enemy. One long, unsophisticated soldier called this reverberation — "The Echo a-comin' out. —

"Some of the pieces on the tip of the high hill — made some very poor shots — a great majority of their shells exploded in mid heavens, halfway to the enemy."[650]

The Yank charge was more than enough to threaten the destruction of the Tenth Kentucky, so Giltner moved the Sixty-fourth Virginia, Colonel Auburn Pridemore, and the Tenth Kentucky Mounted Rifles over to their right to support Ed Trimble's boys.[651] George T. Atkins, of Giltner's staff, took the order to Pridemore: "I did not ride up & down the lines — was stationed on a close neighboring hill watching the fight between Trimble & Pridemore's 64th & the Yankees close by.

"Col Giltner sent Lieut. Crit Ireland to tell Pridemore to withdraw part of his command to the hill that I was on — covering their retreat with the other half — Crit brought me the order — I dashed over there & found Adjutant Hyams on

649. Mason, P. 67.
650. Guerrant Diary, pp. 1176-1177.
651. Guerrant Diary, p. 1173.

the line & I tell you those fellows we had laughed at were fighting — standing out in the open field — Yanks not 60 feet away — they were loading & firing — not a single shirk — by Jove those boys fought — 'Where is Pridemore?' 'Down at the other end of the line.' replied Hyams — I gave him Giltner's order & withdrew — when I got to the gully between hills — I noticed the bullets falling around me — looked back & found the whole line behind me on a run & Yankees pouring it in — I spurred to the top of the next hill — I'd picked up a lot of stragglers & had them laying down behind the crest of the hill — 'Up boys now fire into them' 'Are those the Yanks' 'Yes damn them fire'

"It saved Pridemore's boys & drew their whole fire — I got one ball through the top of my hat — another through my horses neck — but I got the boys off safe."[652] Captain Atkins, George Mosgrove felt, was acting as if he was determined to get killed.[653] Ed Guerrant was another member of Giltner's staff who was responsible for transmitting orders. Consequently he, too, had an opportunity to observe the movements of the different regiments:

"Col. Giltner & staff had taken post on the ridge near the graveyard — between 10^h & 4^h Ky. Lt. Ireland's horse was wounded & the cross fire became so hot it was deemed advisable to change locality — The Col galloped to the Reserves — posted in trenches at the church & prevailed on them to lead a battn to the support of Trimble, who was struggling to hold his position against large bodies of the enemy — fighting in the open field at 50 yds distance —.

"I remained on the ridge nearby to rally the stragglers who were leaving by dozens — the fight was so desperate — The

652. Letter, George T. Atkins to E. O. Guerrant, 1892, pp. 52-54, in Guerrant Papers, University of Kentucky.
653. Mosgrove, p. 116.

Reserves charged down the road, & up by the graveyard to where Trimble was fighting — delivered a terrible volley into the enemy but never formed, — & fell back, creating greater confusion —. At this critical juncture the brave young Col Trimble fell dead, pierced thro' the head by a ball — which struck him just beneath the star — * — he wore on his hat. At nearly the same time Maj Cox — was shot from his horse at the corner of the graveyard, & was carried from the field, — dangerously wounded — Capt. Ja's. Honaker of the same Regiment was wounded — and Lt James Crutchfield of 10^h Ky M. Rifles, was killed. . ."[654]

It was Wise's battalion of reserves that Colonel Giltner had called upon, and the young lieutenant had not lost his delight in the military spectacle:

"The battle of Saltville was a very pretty affair. The enemy advanced with great spirit to the attack, but our troops on our first line had little difficulty in repulsing him. Only once were we brought under fire. Near mid-day, some colored troops of the enemy found a rather open place on the left of our line, near where the streamlet, coursing through the depression we occupied, entered the river, at a point where it was shallow and rocky. They pushed up dangerously near to this possible crossing, and their bullets began to search our valley. The officer commanding the line in our front ran down to where we were asking

654. Guerrant Diary, p. 1173. B. F. Day ("Service with Col. George R. Diamond," *Confederate Veteran,* XXVIII (March, 1920), 86) is the only witness from the Tenth Kentucky who claims that it was confronted by the black troops: "At Saltville we fought a brigade of negroes under Burbridge with our revolvers at close quarters; the officers were all down save Colonel Diamond, we did not let up while we could see a negro." He is supported by Wise, however. It may have been, therefore, despite Mosgrove's statement to the contrary, that there were Kentuckians among the murderers the next day.

for reinforcements. Colonel Bob, without a moment's hesitation, moved our left battlion down the valley and up the hill.

"There the men laid down on the bluffs, and were hotly engaged for fifteen minutes, driving the enemy back with a loss of but one or two of our men. Then we were ordered to withdraw and resume our place in reserve, and took no further part in the action.

"The Confederate losses were quite heavy, especially upon the hill in our immediate front. There Colonel Trimble, in command, was killed in sight of, and but a hundred yards in front of our men. His death was remarkable. He was standing still, directing the firing of his troops. Of a sudden he sprang high in the air, with arms and legs extended at full length. He leaped at least five feet, and fell to the ground collapsed and stone-dead. We afterwards learned that he was shot through the heart, and were told that this spasmodic action is not at all unusual in such instances."[655]

Ed Guerant was not quite so filled with scientific curiosity about Colonel Trimble's fall:

"In this part of the fight our little Brigade sustained it's heaviest loss — a braver man never fell than E. Trimble, Col of 10[h]. K'y Cav. A true patriot, an accomplished scholar, a devoted friend, & a good soldier. A Kentuckian by birth, a Texan by adoption, he enlisted at the very beginning of the war as a private, & served under Floyd during the N. W. V[a]. campaign. Was afterwards a Lieut. in the old 5[h] Ky. Reg't. & gradually rose to the honorable position of Col. of May[s] 10[h] Ky. Cav. He was distinguished for his soft, quiet, modest manners in company: & his great coolness & gallantry on the field of battle.

655. Wise, pp. 383-384.

"He was a noble, brave man, & his death will not go unavenged! It *did* not go unavenged — for many a vandal
bit the dust where he fought & fell so gloriously in the
ranks of freedom. —

"(It is said he was somewhat despondent for a day or
two previous to the battle. I did not observe it, tho' with
him all morning. It is natural for such things to be
said —)"[656]

It would have been easy for Ed Trimble to have been
depressed, for there had been a pattern to his life lately
that he must have seen. On September 2nd, he had applied
for a sixty-day furlough for himself and his Tenth Kentucky
Cavalry, since many of them had not been home to Kentucky
for three years. On September 7th, his brigade commander,
Colonel Giltner approved his request, but limited the length
of the furlough to forty days. On September 9th, his departmental commander, General Echols, disapproved of the application because of the pending emergency. But, seemingly,
as a reward Ed Trimble was promoted to Colonel, September
12th, upon the resignation of Andrew Jackson May. On
October 2nd, Ed Trimble became a dead colonel.[657]

At about that time there was an outbreak of firing in
the rear of the Yanks, and bunches of blue coats could be
seen running back to the area where the horses and pack
train must have been. We didn't know who it might be,
whether it was Bart Jenkins and his boys, who had been
cut off the day before, or maybe Whitcher coming down
from the Kanawah, or maybe Billy Breckinridge's brigade,
which is who it should have been, if Williams had been
doing any generaling at all. Whoever it was, was welcome,
for the attack distracted the Yank forward movement for

656. Guerrant Diary, pp. 1174-1175.
657. Guerrant Papers, University of Kentucky.

a good long time. It turned out to be Bart Jenkins and company.[658]

After his horse had been wounded, George Atkins dismounted, hoping that the lack of exertion would enable the wound to stop bleeding. But the flow continued, so Atkins got Colonel Giltner's permission to go to the rear, to exchange horses. He went behind the bluffs, toward town, past Billy Breckinridge and his courier, Jim Black, and then past the remainder of Williams' Brigade, still mounted and still unused.[659] Those boys were anxious to get into the fight, for most of them had personal scores to settle. As one of them, Milford Overley, recalled: "Our men knew they were to fight Burbridge, the red-handed monster who had, in obedience to Sherman's cruel orders and to satiate his own hellish thirst for the blood of Kentucky Confederates, some of whom were his own near relatives, murdered so many of their comrades; and had he been taken, no power nor authority at Saltville could have saved his life."[660]

George Atkins reached the lines of the Fourth Kentucky just as the Yank right, under Hanson, charged the lower ford: "Down in the cornfield — bordering the river — lay the Home Guards and militia — right in the open field — nothing but a few fence rails with corn stalks thrown over them — they fought — above them ensconced around the hill hidden in the bush was the 4th Ky — commanding the ford — around the bluff comes Hanson in platoon double-quick column to rush the ford — they never got it — the concentrated fire of the 4ths Enfields swept the head of the column away."[661]

658. Guerrant Diary, p. 1177.
659. Letter, George T. Atkins to E. O. Guerrant, pp. 54-55.
660. Milford Overley, "Williams Kentucky Brigade, C.S.A.," *Confederate Veteran*, XIII (October, 1905), 461.
661. Letter, George T. Atkins to E. O. Guerrant, pp. 55-56.

George Mosgrove was with the Fourth Kentucky, so that he noted how the third desperate battle of the day occurred: "For more than an hour an interminable column of horsemen and footmen had been disappearing on the side of the mountain and eventually appearing in front of the Fourth Kentucky and Preston's reserves. This Federal column was commanded by Colonel Charles Hanson, a gallant officer. The Fourth Kentucky boys bore the brunt of the hot engagement that then ensued and drove the enemy back with heavy loss, there being only slight casualties in their own ranks. Captain Jim Willis was knocked down by a ball, but retained his place at the head of his company. With their long-range Enfield rifles the Fourth Kentucky made many a Federal bite the dust, and they guyed and tantalized the wavering, dispirited boys in blue unmercifully. They would fire a volley and then yell, 'Come right up and draw your salt!' Silas Sims, a dead-shot, would draw a bead on a blue-coat, blaze away and then hail the 'Yank' with the interrrogatory, 'How's that; am I shooting too high or too low?'"[662]

Although the Yanks couldn't get anywhere near the Reb lines, they kept on trying. The river was too deep to wade all along, so they had to bunch up, in order to cross at the ford. And even if they made it across the river, they still had to climb a nearly perpendicular hill of about one hundred fifty feet. Still they kept coming, until their leader, Colonel Hanson, was seen to go down, wounded or killed. Only then did they melt back into the underbrush on their side of the river.

In a while a new Yank colonel came forward, Colonel True, it was allowed by some of the boys from Kentucky.

662. Mosgrove, p.. 200.

He tried to get the Yank line moving again, with company captains and color sergeants backing him up. But by that time the fresh Reb brigades belonging to Cosby and Duke had arrived; they marched up to the bluffs and fired off one great volley that made any further Yank attack unthinkable.[663] So the few Yanks that had followed their leaders out toward the river disappeared again. After a while, there was a great yelling along the Yank line, and we thought for a few minutes that they would come charging out again, after all. But they didn't and we later learned that the shouting had been from satisfaction, when the Yanks learned that Burbridge had turned command of the entire force over to Hobson.[664] Those boys had good reason to distrust Burbridge; he had ordered three separate, uncoordinated attacks on different Reb positions each time, without ever apparently considering the hostility of the terrain or the fact that the reserves had been heavily reinforced. Perhaps his poor tactics resulted from the fact that he had stayed too far to the rear, as his men later charged.

It had been cloudy most of the day, but just before dark, the sky cleared, and there was a beautiful sunset. The men on Church Hill had a clear view of the Yanks across the river, as they scurried about searching for the wounded among the blue-coated bodies and taking them back to the surgeons. There was still time to push the Yanks back and try to get a Reb victory, so Scott Barrett and others of Giltner's Brigade gathered about him and "begged to be allowed to charge them," as George Atkins observed. "Giltner replied 'he was not in command — Genl Williams was.' They plead so hard that Giltner finally told me 'to ride to

663. Mason, p. 66.
664. Moore, pp. 423-424.

the top of the peak behind our lines where Williams was — to say the enemy were whipped & retiring — that he would like to advance with his regiment.'

"I spurred up the peak & from its top everything could be seen — sun nearly setting — Yankees running back & I delivered Giltner's message. 'Tell Col. Giltner "No" — I know the Yankees are whipped — but I don't care to risk any men.'

"I then plead 'Let us go General we are all wild to charge them. I'll lead the charge myself' 'Mr. Atkins — I wish I had a squadron to give you — but you can't go —'

"That ended it."[665]

As darkness fell, the Yanks built big campfires, eighteen of them, in a line that stretched across our front.[666] They seemed to be in good shape: although some units had lacked ammunition late in the day, they could be replenished from that huge pack train, which had not been disturbed by anything more serious than a swarm of flies all day, and although some units had suffered moderate casualties, no unit had been hit so hard as to be disorganized. We, on the other hand, were still far outnumbered, even with the arrival of the fresh brigades. Nor could the reserves be expected to be effective in any kind of action involving movement or extended firing. We had every expectation, therefore, that the Yanks would resume the battle the next day.

For that reason, there was no jubilation in Saltville that night, and life on our side of the Holston was quiet and purposeful. Sentinels were put out all along the line. There were a few shifts made: the Fourth Kentucky came up from the lower ford to replace the Tenth Kentucky Cavalry and

665. Letter, George T. Akins to E. O. Guerrant, pp. 55-57.
666. Guerrant Diary, p. 1179.

the Tenth Kentucky Mounted Rifles, both of which had lost their leading officers, and Dibrell's and Robertson's boys, who had been manhandled, came off Chestnut Ridge and camped in Palmer's meadow. When Ed Guerrant went up to Palmer's for supper he saw General Robertson, who "said he had killed nearly all the negroes." Those two brigades must have been a little tender about getting pushed back by the raw black troops. General Robertson continued to be impressive; although he had met Ed Guerrant for the first time that morning, under very distracting conditions, he nevertheless recognized the lower-ranking adjutant in the dark and addressed him by name. How's that for military behavior?

In the camp of Preston's reserves all was not quite happy. Lieutenant Wise reported: "'Not much of a fight for us,' said Colonel Bob contemptuously. . . . He seemed graveled at the better luck of his cousin Tom." The other Preston's reserves had met the Yanks at the river, in front of the Fourth Kentucky, and had, as a result, Wise said, "acquired a great reputation for its gallantry in the action, and sustained severe losses." The only thing that soothed Colonel Bob's temper was the fact that his night's sleep was apt to be a good one: "'Well, the Yankees did n't kill papa's little bouncing ball after all,' said he contentedly, as we hugged up together under the blankets that night. 'I'm glad of it, for you're warm as a toast, and my back is better already.'"[667]

667. Wise, p. 384.

XII

After Saltville: *"horrible, most horrible"*

(October 3-7, 1864)

SALTVILLE
OCTOBER 3

*I*t was foggy at dawn, as Saltville often is, and Ed
Guerrant woke up wondering why he heard no
gunshots from across the Holston. There was
a visibility of about fifty yards, and that hour under such
circumstances would have been the most favorable time
for an attacking force. But there was only silence, which

soon tempted the venturesome to steal across the river to prowl the battlefield.

Soon enough Major-General John C. Breckinridge and Brigadier-Generals George Cosby and Williams called at Giltner's brigade headquarters, to inquire about the Yanks. When the first reports came back that the Yanks had skedaddled, General Breckinridge, the departmental commander and now the commander on the field, ordered a scout. Ed Guerrant picked Captain Dick Gathright, who promptly led his boys off up the river. Then General Breckinridge gave further orders: Giltner was to take his brigade in direct pursuit of the Yanks, while Williams was to take five brigades (his own, Robertson's, Dibrell's, and two fresh ones, Cosby's and Duke's), go around through Hayter's Gap, and set up an ambush at Richlands.[668]

General Breckinridge next accompanied General Williams to the camp of Robertson's and Dibrell's boys.[669] Most of them were still at breakfast, and they gathered around while Williams gave a short talk approving their behavior the day before. He then deferred to General Breckinridge, who spoke warmly in complimenting the boys. Jim Lambright, Fifth Georgia, Confederate Brigade, said that Breckinridge "delivered an address to our three brigades commending our boys for their fortitude and gallantry during the fierce and repeated assaults made by the enemy upon our lines in their effort to capture and destroy the salt works, and that our presence in that section was opportune, as the enemy outnumbered the available troops two to one, even with our added force."[670] Then General Breckinridge must have turned down the line to inspect other units,

668. Guerrant Diary, p. 1180.
669. Lindsley, p. 672.
670. Lambright.

probably Duke's and Cosby's. Both brigades had new commanders and needed their morale boosted. Especially was
Duke's Brigade, formerly that of John H. Morgan, in sad
shape after his disaster in Kentucky just a few months before and his death in Tennessee just a few weeks before.
Not all of Robertson's and Dibrell's boys heard the
speeches, for they had already moved out, to see if there
were any Yanks to pick up. Capture came as a shock to
the sluggard Yanks. One of those who was caught was Dan
Reynolds, a hospital orderly in the Eleventh Michigan. In
a little log cabin that had been taken over by the Yank
surgeons, he experienced that first befuddled moment:
"About daylight . . . I was suddenly aroused from my pleasant dreams by a kick. I raised up and looking around saw
the Graybacks collecting the guns. One says to me, 'Give me
that gun and take off that sabor!' I then began to realize
that I was a prisoner and that our troops had retreated
back during the night and left us all that were at the hospital to be taken prisoners."[671]
     Another Yank who got a rude awakening that foggy
morning was Harry Shocker, Twelfth Ohio: "My partner and
I were lying wounded on the field the morning after the
battle, when I saw [a man] coming across the field. I saw
him pointing his pistol down at prisoners lying on the
ground, and heard the reports of the pistol and the screams
of the men. While [he] was coming toward us, I crawled
away about forty feet and stretched myself out.
     "[The man] came up to my partner, Crawford Hazle-
wood, and asked him what he was doing there and why
he came up there to fight with the damned niggers. [He]

     671. Paul H. Giddens (ed.), "Memories of Libby Prison by
Daniel N. Reynolds," *Michigan Historical Magazine*, XXIII (Autumn,
1939), 391-392.

then took out a piece of paper and wrote something, after which he pulled out his revolver and asked my partner, 'Where will you have it, in the back or in the face?' My partner said, 'For God's sake, don't kill me, soldier,' and then I heard the report of a pistol and my partner fell over dead."[672]

Dressed in a butternut suit, with long hair and beard, [the man] walked past Harry Shocker, apparently fooled by Shocker's pretense. After fifteen minutes or so, two Rebs came by, and Shocker asked them to take him to the hospital. He was horrified to discover where it was: "They took me to the log cabin, the same one I saw [him] enter. There was a hollow between the battlefield and the cabin, and as we got to the side of the hollow next to the cabin, [he] was coming out with two negro soldiers towards us. The Rebel soldiers with me said, 'Wait, and see what he does with them.' We saw him take them into the hollow about one hundred yards away and shoot them. He fired ten shots with a revolver.

"I asked the Reb soldiers to hurry me to the hospital, as I was afraid he would overtake and shoot me, and they got me to the log cabin before [the man] got back. He took two more negroes when he returned and not long afterwards, I heard more pistol shots."

Another wounded member of the Twelfth Ohio, Captain Orange Sells, was nearby: "I was also at the log house near the field after the battle and saw a good many negroes killed

672. Thurman Sensing, *Champ Ferguson, Confederate Guerrilla* (Nashville: Vanderbilt University Press, 1985), pp. 185-186. Although Shocker uses Ferguson's name, he was making his identification nearly a year later, at Ferguson's trial; he would not have known Ferguson's identity at the time of the event, so I felt justified in editing the name references.

Prelude to Saltville?

Massacre at Fort Pillow, April 12, 1864

there. All of them were soldiers and all were wounded but one. I heard firing there all over the place; it was like a skirmish."⁶⁷³ The firing was so heavy that Ben Rogers, lying wounded behind the lines, "thought the battle had reopened." The sound drew a curious George Mosgrove to the front that morning: "I mounted my horse, and guided by an occasional pistol or rifle shot made my way through the fog until I had arrived at a point some distance to the front and right of the position from which I had started I soon became aware of the fact that I was in the front of Robertson's and Dibbrell's brigades, and the desultory firing was at once explained — the Tennesseans were killing negroes. Dead Federals, whites and negroes, were lying all about me. Of course many of the negroes had been killed in battle, but many of them had been killed after the battle, that morning. Hearing more firing in front, I cautiously rode forward and came upon a squad of Tennesseans, mad and excited to the highest degree. They were shooting every wounded negro they could find. Hearing firing on other parts of the field, I knew that the same awful work was going on all about me. It was horrible, most horrible. Robertson's and Dibbrell's brigades had lost many good men and officers, probably shot by these same negroes, and they were so exasperated that they could not be deterred from their murderous work. Very many of the negroes standing about in groups were only slightly wounded, but they soon went down before the unerring pistols and rifles of the enraged Tennesseans."⁶⁷⁴

Mosgrove rode on, to observe that Robertson's and Dibrell's men were sweeping up the valley toward Laurel Gap,

673. Sensing, p. 183.
674. Mosgrove, p. 206.

killing every black in sight: "Some of them were so slightly wounded that they could even run, but when they ran from the muzzle of one pistol it was only to be confronted by another. Entering a little log cabin, I paused at the threshold when I saw seven or eight slightly wounded negroes standing with their backs against the walls. I had scarcely been there a minute when a pistol-shot from the door caused me to turn and observe a boy, not more than sixteen years old, with a pistol in each hand. I stepped back, telling him to hold on until I could get out of the way . . . . the boy . . . shot every negro in the room. Every time he pulled a trigger a negro fell dead. Generally the negroes met their fate sullenly. It was bang, bang, bang, all over the field — negroes dropping everywhere."[675]

There were eight blacks in the cabin that George Mosgrove entered. William Gardner, a surgeon in the Yank Thirtieth Kentucky, who had stayed behind with the wounded, had charge of a cabin where five blacks were murdered, and there was talk of yet another field hospital where fifteen were killed. The Rebs engaged boasted that they had been land-office busy all morning long. If a person wanted to go around and do a census, a body-count, as you might say, he would find about one hundred fifty black ones, at least one hundred of whom died that morning.[676]

By then the Rebs had reached the huddle of Yank prisoners that included Dan Reynolds. Being white, he was spared, but the blacks with his group were doomed: "One poor fellow tried to escape and was ordered to halt with three or four shots. He gave himself up. An officer on horseback

675. Mosgrove, p. 207.
676. *ORR*, I, 39, pt. 1, p. 554; E. T. Peters, "Saltville," Philadelphia *Inquirer*, October 21, 1864.

took him by the collar and marched him down to the bank
of the creek and putting a bullet through the back of his
head, threw him over into the creek, there to wait Gabriel's
trumpet. That was done before our eyes!"[677]

Back where George Mosgrove was a helpless observer,
there were some new arrivals: "About this time General
Breckinridge, General Duke and other officers appeared
on the scene. General Breckinridge, with blazing eyes and
thunderous tones, ordered that the massacre should be
stopped. He rode away and — the shooting went on. The
men could not be restrained. I saw a youth approach a
bright-looking mulatto boy standing quietly in front of
a log cabin, who seemed to think he was in no danger. The
young soldier leveled his pistol, and then the little mulatto
jumped behind a sapling not larger than a man's arm, and
cried out that General Duke had ordered him to remain
there until he should return. It was of no use. In another
moment the little mulatto was a corpse. It was said, I know
not how truly, that General Duke had recognized the young
negro as one who had belonged to the family of Morgan,
or Duke, at Lexington, Ky."[678]

Up the valley, the group of prisoners that Dan Reynolds
was with got the word to fall in. Surrounded by guards,
the group stumbled down the road toward Saltville: "A
little farther on we met General Williams in command of
the Rebs. There we stopped and he made us a short speech,
that was to the effect that General Stoneman had ordered
some of their men to be shot as spies and that he, Gen. Williams, was going to retaliate by shooting us, if he could
get us turned over to him. We thought our doom was sealed.

677. Giddens, 392.
678. Mosgrove, pp. 207-208.

Then they commenced to rob us of what we had. I owned a fine pair of boots. 'Give me them boots, give me that jacket, give me that ring!' And in return they gave me an old pair of shoes that hurt my feet so I couldn't wear them. I had to go barefoot the rest of the way up to the Salt Works. . . ."[679]

One of the last Yanks to be rounded up was Lieutenant C. D. King, Thirty-fifth Kentucky Mounted Infantry. General Hobson had put him in charge of the detail to kindle the fires and keep them going all night, to give the Yank force time to retreat. As the lieutenant understood his orders, he was to hold his position until further orders. But when dawn came, and he saw the Rebs approaching through the fog, he decided that he had fulfilled his orders, so he and his sleepy troopers lit out. They were so far behind, though, that they couldn't catch up; with broken-down horses and without any rations, they scattered. But the Rebs overtook them, one by one. When Lieutenant King was captured, the Reb party made him step out of his uniform and then gave him a Reb suit that was crawling with "graybacks." Then the meanest looking Reb of the lot drew his knife and came towards him with it raised toward his throat — and cut off the lieutenant's mustache, now laughing as he commented that the Yank looked too damned savage.[680]

General Breckinridge had left specific orders for Giltner, so the boys were immediately set to work cooking two days' rations. But as the minutes swept by, Giltner knew that his task was becoming harder. So, finally, at 8:00 a.m., he ordered his brigade to move out without waiting for rations.

679. Giddens, 892.
680. Louisville *Journal,* November 20, 1864.

At the same time Generals Duke and Cosby knew that their chances of getting ahead of the enemy by another road were fading away like the fog, which was being burned away by the early morning sun. But General Williams, who was to lead the column, was still up the river. The observant George Mosgrove was nearby: "I observed that General Basil Duke, whose brigade formed the advance of Williams' division, was promptly in the saddle and at the head of his column, restlessly impatient, awaiting the pleasure of Breckinridge or of Williams for him to move forward. I have often thought of the brilliant young general's appearance on that morning. He was the impersonation of the ideal cavalier, a veritable Prince Rupert or Henry of Navarre. His agile, symmetrical form was in constant, nervous motion. Restlessly turning in his saddle, his dark eyes flashing, he impatiently awaited the order to advance. His was an attractive, martial figure. It must have been about 8 o'clock when the expected order came. Like a flash General Duke wheeled in his saddle, shouted 'Forward!' and was off like a shot. . . ."[681] Ed Guerrant, who was also on the scene, watched a friend, Henry Stone, ride off with Duke's brigade. Stone had been chatting with Colonel George Dibrell, so Guerrant had an opportunity to observe the commander of Williams' Tennessee Brigade: "Dibrell a very ordinary looking man. Remarkably soft, slow, & easy in his manner —. Silver haired."[682]

At the same time Giltner's boys moved forward, crossing over at the ford where Colonel Trimble had died the day before. The Kentucky boys were not in a very charitable mood, as they thought of their losses, so they didn't lose

681. Mosgrove, pp. 208-209.
682. Guerrant Diary, p. 1181.

any tears over the dead Yanks that lay about on the other side of the river. George Mosgrove was with the Fourth Kentucky, as the command began its march, and saw one of those boys, Silas Sims, say it for many of them. As they rode by the body of a Yank officer, whose head had been partly blown away by a cannon ball, Sims took a handful of salt from his pack, pitched it in the mangle of skull and brain, and said, "There you came for salt, now take some."[683] He might have added, according to the Scriptures: "Better *is* an handful *with* quietness, than both the hands full *with* travail and vexation of spirit."

The Giltner boys rode on up the river, about a mile. At the same time, the cits began to return to their cabins. Mrs. Roberts took Fannie, Edward, and the other children back home — the children went directly to stare at the dead Yank, who lay just as they had last seen him. Then they went into the house, to see that tables and cabinets had been pried open and feather ticks had been slit, as the Yanks prowled for things. Tired, sleepy, hungry, they just began to cry at the differentness of things, while their mother, by habit the homemaker, absently surveyed the kitchen. The stove had been left alone, and the fire was long since out, but when she opened the oven, there sat a perfect loaf of bread, whose savoriness the children would remember all their lives.[684]

All around the Giltner Brigade was the trash of war. They could see the mess that the Yanks had made of *things*: prowled outside of cabins, broken furniture, smashed just because it couldn't be stolen. Then they could see the Yanks who had become *things*: bodies lay about, some sprawled

683. Mosgrove, p. 203.
684. Kent, p. 37.

where they had dropped, some straight and composed where they had been carried. But all had been prowled — pockets pulled out, if the body had been left with its clothes on, all boots taken, scraps of paper lying about. When the road took them near the river, the boys occasionally saw the hump of a black body swept into the willow branches that trailed the river.

After a while the word swept back through the column that they had come across that Yank colonel, Hanson, who had been dropped at the lower ford the day before. Together with some wounded blacks who had been so far overlooked, he was in a little hovel, attended by a Yank surgeon, Dr. Hunt. The Yanks had tried to take him along with them and had even gotten a carriage to carry him in, but the surgeon had said it was useless and to let him die in peace. So the carriage, without its horse, sat empty, even of chickens, who had followed the Yanks. For some reason Hanson was still very much alive, and Colonel Giltner, Doctor Scott, Colonel Bob Stoner, and George Mosgrove went in to inquire after his condition. George Mosgrove told what they found: Hanson "was lying on a rude bed and swearing horribly. Several canteens of brandy hung at the head of the bed, and it was evident he had been drinking copiously of their contents. His surgeon, Doctor Hunt, an old acquaintance, whom we had captured at Mt. Sterling, was attending him. The colonel was familiarly well acquainted with Colonel Bob Stoner, calling him 'Bob,' and to him he addressed most of his conversation. He expressed his opinion of Burbridge in language more forceful than polite, and said that Burbridge had kept well to the rear, 'too damned cowardly to go where he had sent his men.' A minie ball having passed through his body the surgeons declared the wound was mortal, but although he thought himself in

the immediate presence of death he made no effort to make
his 'peace, calling and election sure,' but continued to 'cuss
a blue streak.'

"Colonel Hanson was a tall, well proportioned, exceedingly handsome man, quite drunk and seemingly very wicked.
We did not have time to remain with him long, and when we
left him he was still 'cussin'' and drinking brandy."[685]

At Laurel Gap Robertson's and Dibrell's boys stood
aside, to let Giltner's boys pass. Williams stressed his orders
to Giltner; as George Atkins summarized them: "Williams
ordered Giltner to follow the Yankees — throwing out a
strong advance guard & feeling the enemy — *not push
them* — as he wanted time to cross over to Genl Bowens &
get his whole command in ambush on the Louisa fork of
Sandy — when he attacked them — attack them in the
rear. . . ."[686] Then Giltner's boys headed out north, led
by Colonel Andrew Jackson May and Captain Bart Jenkins,
the two who had led the attack on Burbridge's pack train
the afternoon before.

As they rode along, they noted the effect of the invasion-
and-retreat on the local cits. At George Gillespie's house,
everything was taken. The black soldiers didn't respect
the personal belongings of even the local blacks; they took
two plugs of tobacco and her "*best* apples" from Aunt
Phebe. Furiously she demanded that Ed Guerrant go kill
a dozen of the "black varmints" for her. Then, up the road,
Guerrant asked a young barefoot girl standing in a cabin
doorway if her family had lost anything:

"Have the Yankees been here — Miss?"

"Yes, they have that."

---

686. Letter, George T. Atkins to E. O. Guerrant, p. 57; Felix H.
Robertson, "On Wheeler's Last Raid," 335.

"Did they rob you all?"

"Yes, they took a right smart."

"What did they take from you?"

"They tuck a *skillet,* a *tin bucket,* & a *hammer.*"[687]
And so on, up the mountain. Those who couldn't find anything to eat often straggled to get wild grapes and paw-
paws; the Sixty-fourth Virginia picked up eleven at one
time. Following on, from the top of the mountain the
Rebs could see the Yanks going into camp at General
Bowen's.

Just at dark, the boys in the advance hit the Yank rear
as it forded the Clinch River. The Yanks were fairly well
caught: they were trying to march prisoners, like old "Governor" Sanders, who had been captured when they overran
the militia at his house; they were trying to take all the
blacks from the area who wanted to go to Kentucky; and
they had a large number of riding wounded. Giltner allowed
his brigade to go into camp, knowing that the next morning
he could easily nudge the Yanks into Williams' ambush.

At the same time, the other column of Rebs, under Williams, was cutting cross-country, to come out at Richlands
ahead of the Yanks. The Yanks had to travel forty miles,
while Williams' force took a route that was only twelve
miles in length. But the shorter route was only a bridle
path. It was bad enough in daylight, with the boys having
to dismount and lead their horses. But when night came,
the path struck terror in both men and horses. George
Guild, of the Fourth Tennessee, described it thus: "The
night was very dark, and it was hard to discern the path.
Occasionally a horse would make a misstep and tumble
down the steep mountain side, when you could hear the

687. Guerrant Diary, pp. 1182-1183.

noise of falling stones for minutes afterwards as they rolled down and down the precipitate mountain side."[688] Finally the line of men and horses just stopped, to wait for day-light.

RICHLANDS
OCTOBER 4

With the coming of dawn, October 4th, Giltner's boys were back on the trail. Word came back once that the Yanks were preparing an ambush of their own, so the Sixty-fourth Virginia was put into position to receive it. But the information didn't pan out, so the boys continued slowly, just pressing enough so that the Yanks would be more inter-ested in what was behind them than what they might ex-pect in front.

Giltner's boys impatiently hung back, until it was 10 a.m. Their last word was that the Yanks were still in camp. So they kept waiting for the sound of firing, which would an-nounce that the Yanks had moved out — and into the am-bush. Finally, Giltner gave the order to move up.[689]

George Atkins was with the advance, as those boys ap-proached the point that had been designated as the place of ambush: ". . . at daybreak — I went to the advance guard — Col Jack May & myself rode at the head of it — When we came out where Williams ought to have been — we saw a man come out in the road — we took cover at the sides — in the woods advancing cautiously — the man came down the middle of the road to us — Jack May questioned him — 'Where are the Yankees'

688. Guild, pp. 101-102.
689. Guerrant Diary, pp. 1184-1185.

'Gone'
'Where is Genl Williams'
'Over there'
'Was he here when they passed'
'Yes'
May never asked another question. Said 'Shit Atkins I am
going home. I am done with the war' & he was."[690]
Actually, there had been a skirmish. Duke's and Cosby's
men got lost, but finally got up in time to hit the Yanks
on the flank and rear, rather than in the front. It was a
hot little skirmish in which the Eleventh Michigan, acting
as rear guard for the Yanks, lost a lieutenant-colonel, James
B. Mason. The boys tried pretty hard; they made eight
separate charges against the dismounted Yanks. But it
was no use, and the Yanks rode off Big Sandy Mountain
unmolested.[691]
Giltner's boys were furious. George Atkins summed up
their attitude: "I never was as disgusted in my life — so
were Giltner & all of us — we had them cooped — a wild-
erness in front — a bold steep mountain bluff at their back —
a regiment in their rear — a brigade across the river in easy
shot — they were completely at our mercy & yet they were
let go — not a shot fired — I do not know any reason for
it — I never heard any. But Genl Williams should have been
court martialed then & there — No matter how much I
liked him personally — such is my opinion."[692] Everyone
was suffering from "mortification and disappointment,"
as Ed Guerrant noted, but Colonel Giltner, ever the practical
commander, seeing that the day was "oppressively hot,"
and that the men were going to be unemployed, immediately

690. Letter, George T. Atkins to E. O. Guerrant, pp. 57-58.
691. "Our Army Correspondence."
692. Letter, George T. Atkins to E. O. Guerrant, p. 58-59.

ordered his brigade into camp on the only farm in the valley that hadn't been trashed by the Yanks.[693]

RICHLANDS

OCTOBER 7

Giltner kept his boys in that vicinity for several days. There, on October 7th, his AAG Ed Guerrant received the following note from his friend Henry T. Stanton, another AAG:

"Head Quarters Dept W^n Va & ET

"Abingdon, Va. Oct 5th 64

"My dear Col,

"I merely write you a note to say that Gen Echols goes to Dublin and I go with him temporarily. I will send you a copy of the order under which he will act.

"It gives me great pleasure to be able to say that your recent contact with the enemy has won for you golden opinions from those who can be of service to you and who are your friends. Gen B- - - - expressed himself with regard to you to me in a manner flattering beyond your expectations.

"Give my love to Ed & Barney and tell them to write when they get in camp in some quiet place."[694]

Williams' command didn't exactly camp — it just fell apart. Williams sent back a message to General Breckinridge explaining that his return to Saltville would be a slow proposition: "My command, with Giltner's brigade, encamped last night in the neighborhood of Liberty Hill, except Generals Cosby and Duke, whom I sent by the New

693. Guerrant Diary, p. 1185.
694. Guerrant Papers, University of Kentucky.

Garden and Elk Garden roads to Abingdon. My horses are entirely broken down. Unless I can rest them for a few days and place shoes on their feet they will be ruined. I have quite a number of men almost naked and barefooted. Could not some clothes be found in the department for immediate use? The enemy retreated with such rapidity that we were unable to intercept him."[695]

Those boys finally made it back, to camp around Saltville and prowl for what they could find, for they were desperate. A fortunate few had relatives in the neighborhood to visit. One such lucky man was Willie Breckinridge, Colonel of the Ninth Kentucky, who visited his Preston kinfolks in Montgomery County. He stayed at "Smithfield," the estate of Ballard, whose father, William Ballard Preston, had served in both the U. S. and then the Confederate Congress, before dying in 1862.[696] It was only half a mile to "Solitude," Colonel Bob Preston's estate, and Willie visited his cousin and Bob's beloved Alice several times. From "Smithfield," Willie wrote his wife to let her know that he was safe and well and that their freinds were thick in the vicinity: "I have seen Duke, Steele, Allen, the Morgans, Cabell Breckinridge, Jimmie Clay, Stoddard Johnston, George Hunt, Vorhies, Howard Smith. . . ."[697]

695. ORR, I, 39, pt. 1, p. 562.

696. Ezra J. Warner and W. Buck Yearns, Biographical Register of the Confederate Congress (Baton Rouge: Louisiana State University Press, 1975), pp. 196-197.

697. Letter, W. C. P. Breckinridge to his wife, October 11, 1864.

XIII

Back to Georgia:

"there is a good time coming"

(October 3-9, 1864)

SALTVILLE
OCTOBER 3

ack at Saltville, after the battle, there was a good
deal of activity. Like many others, John Wise,
of Preston's Reserves, wanted to write his family,
not only, like others, to let them know that he was safe,
but also to reveal that he had been in action. For he had

felt deep humiliation in being sent away from his father's brigade on the Petersburg line: "I felt as if I had been treated like a baby, tucked away in a place of safety, and was consenting to turn my back upon the enemy just when every man was most needed in Lee's army. And was I not a man? Of course I was. I was nearly eighteen!"[698]

Wise knew that his father had put him on the train "with the solacing reflection that I, at least, was out of harm's way." It was sheer delight, then, not merely to write his father that he had been in a battle, but to write, one military man to another, about the tactics of the battle:

"The topography of the country in the immediate vicinity of the battle field is mountainous. It is about one mile from the salt works, and a part of it can be distinctly seen from the works. Our reserves, who behaved like veterans, were stationed in a deep valley, and were charged by the Yankee cavalry from the eastern slope of the valley, over a clear field. In this charge we lost twenty-one, who were taken prisoners. The reserves then fell back and occupied the western slope of the valley, which is thickly covered with briars and undergrowth.

"Here the enemy attempted another charge, coming with sabres drawn, and yelling like wild Indians. Our reserves stood like a wall of adamant, with cheeks unblanched and hearts unmoved, awaiting the onset. When the Yankees arrived within full range, the sturdy sons of Southwestern Virginia, recollecting the gallantry of their forefathers, and the sacredness of their homes and firesides, poured volley after volley into the massive columns of the foe, causing him first to recoil and ultimately to fall back in great disorder. The dead bodies of the invaders thickly strewed the

698. Wise, pp. 372-373.

ground in all this vicinity, and the stench is intolerable.''
Williams' and Giltner's boys must have been astonished
to discover in the Petersburg *Express,* where a proud father
allowed his son's letter to be published, that they had
been rescued from those horrible Yanks by the reserves.[699]

SALTVILLE
OCTOBER 4

There were many sight-seers at the saltworks, especially
after Williams' command returned from its wild goose chase.
Many of those boys had never seen anything like the works.
Each state had its own furnace; altogether the furnaces
produced ten thousand bushels of salt a day. There was a
work force of two thousand men, and some of the boys
probably understood for the first time the real value of
negro slaves.[700] For they could do the hard, sweaty work in
such a manufactory that white men either couldn't do in
good health or just wouldn't do.

As they walked around the valley in which Saltville is
situated they could have used as a guide book a description

699. Petersburg *Express,* quoted in Richmond *Daily Dispatch,*
October 12, 1864. The author has no certain knowledge that the
writer of the letter was Lieutenant Wise. He has not been able to discover the existence of a copy of the Petersburg *Express* containing the
letter, in order to determine its signature. He bases his attribution on
these observations (1) Lieutenant Wise was the only participant among
the reserves who later focused his narration of the battle upon their
behavior, and (2) he was the only participant among the reserves who
would have had a pressing reason for writing such a detailed letter to
the Petersburg area.

700. Edward King, *The Great South* (Hartford: The American
Publishing Company, 1875), pp. 571-572.

which appeared in *Harper's New Monthly Magazine* a few
years before:

"The valley contains several hundred acres of rich meadow, producing corn and grass in abundance, and sustaining
numerous herds of the finest cattle. It is surrounded by a
chain of conical hills from five to eight hundred feet in
height, so regularly formed that, but for their extent, they
might be mistaken for artificial mounds.

"These hills are overlooked by lofty and rugged mountains, whose frowning precipices contrast strikingly with
the softer beauties of the valley.

"But these are only the superficial attractions of this
interesting region. At the distance of two hundred and
thirty feet below the surface is a bed of fossil salt of un-
ascertained extent and thickness, while gypsum, its invariable
geological associate, has been recently developed near the
surface by excavations on the line of the railroad. The
preparation and exportation of plaster, already commenced,
bids fair to be an important addition to the wealth of the
valley. The salt is procured by sinking wells to the depth
of the salt-bed, when the water rises within forty-six feet
of the surface, and is raised from thence by pumps into
large tanks or reservoirs elevated a convenient distance
above the surface.

"The brine thus procured is a saturated solution, and for
every hundred gallons yields twenty-two gallons of pure
salt.

"The process of manufacturing it is perfectly simple. An
arched furnace is constructed, probably a hundred and
fifty feet in length with the doors at one end and the chimney at the other. Two rows of heavy iron kettles, shaped
like shallow bowls, are built into the top of the furnace —
in the largest works from eighty to a hundred in number.

Large wooden pipes convey the brine from the tanks to these kettles, where the water is evaporated by boiling, while the salt crystallizes and is precipitated. During the operation a white saline vapor rises from the boilers, the inhalation of which is said to cure diseases of the lungs and throat.

"At regular intervals an attendant goes round, and with a mammoth ladle dips out the salt, chucking it into loosely woven split baskets, which are placed in pairs over the boilers. Here it drains and dries until the dipper has gone his round with the ladle. It is then thrown into the salt-sheds, immense magazines that occupy the whole length of the buildings on either side of the furnaces.

"This process continues day and night without intermission for about a week, when it becomes necessary to cool off to clean the boilers, which have become thickly coated with a sedimentary deposit which impedes the transmission of heat.

"This incrustation, sometimes called pan-stone, is principally composed of the sulphates of lime and soda, and its removal is the most troublesome and least entertaining part of the business.

"The salt thus manufactured is of the purest quality, white and beautiful as the driven snow. Indeed, on seeing the men at work in the magazines with pick and shovel, a novice would swear they were working in a snow-bank; while the pipes and reservoirs, which at every leak become coated over with snowy concretions, sparkling like hoar-frost and icicles in the sun, serve to confirm the wintry illusion."[701]

701. "A Winter in the South," *Harper's New Monthly Magazine,* LXXVIII (September, 1857), 444-448.

But while the sight-seers may have been aware of the beauty of the salt, they were more aware of its practical value, easily calculated by the number of slaves needed to load the sacks of salt onto the railroad cars. There simply was no other place in the South to obtain enough salt to supply more than a small surrounding area. Thus there could never be enough meat cured or bread baked to supply an army in the field. The boys better understood why the Yanks had come such a long way on their raid and why they had endured such heavy casualities; they accepted the way they had been forced to such efforts to arrive in time to defend the place. Just an hour's occupation would have provided the Yanks the opportunity to drop cannonballs down the wells to plug them and take sledge hammer to the iron boiling kettles.

There were other groups out looking over the countryside: the burial parties were picking up the corpses, or fishing them out of the river, in the case of the blacks. Not all of them were found, for the river was up, and bodies were spotted for some time afterward. Those that were collected were pitched into a sinkhole near Cedar Branch at the foot of Chestnut Ridge.[702] Most of the dead Rebs were taken to Emory and Henry College, a few miles away, and "decently buried," as Colonel Dibrell put it, in the military cemetery there.[703] It had been necessary for the bodies of the soldiers who had died in the army hospital on the campus. Some Rebs, like Colonel Trimble, were buried privately.

The ten or so Yanks who were all in one piece had been

702. B. L. Van Meter, "General Burbridge in Kentucky," *Confederate Veteran*, XX (November, 1914), 512.
703. Lindsley, p. 672.

penned up in an old fort.[704] There they lay on some straw, happy enough to rest, after two weeks of steady traveling, even though it had been chilly the night before. As Dan Reynolds recollected, the Yanks were of considerable local interest: ". . . they brought some flour and we got our rations of salt. That was our bill of fare at the hotel and we cooked it ourselves in any style we chose. Salt with flour and flour with salt! After partaking of our frugal repast we were then allowed to receive our company which consisted of old ladies and young ladies that wanted to see what a yank was like. One of the boys said, 'Did you think we had horns?' She replied, 'If you did, you have shed them.' One lady to entertain us sang 'The Bonny Blue Flag that Carries a Single Star.'"[705]

The slightly wounded Rebs either stayed with their commands or, if they were malish, went home to recover. But about seventy-five Rebs had wounds serious enough to put them in the hospital at Emory.[706] And about a hundred Yanks, including, somehow, a few blacks, were confined to the third and fourth floors of the main hospital building.

EMORY

OCTOBER 5

The Yanks had their own surgeons, who had been paroled the morning after the battle, and the Reb authorities did

704. Richmond *Sentinel*, October 10, 1864.
705. Giddens, 392.
706. Richmond *Whig*, October 7, 1864, *ORR*, I, 39, pt. 1, p. 567; Emory Register, in United Daughters of the Confederacy Museum, Richmond; Lynchburg *Virginian*, October 8, 1864.

what they could to assist, so the wounded Yanks settled in
to recover as best they could. On the morning of October
5th, though, they discovered that the hospital was no haven.
For two men walked into the room where Harry Shocker
and some other wounded lay. One of them said, after the
country fashion, "How are you getting along, boys?"

The visitors took chairs, appearing to have in mind a
chat with the sick. The one who hadn't yet spoken now said
rather pleasantly to his partner, "There is that boy now,"
nodding to a wounded Yank from the Eleventh Michigan.
"I saved his life."

The first one replied by speaking to the wounded boy,
"If I had seen you lying among niggers, it would have been
all day with you."

The second one asked the boy if he had any money, and
when the boy said that he didn't, the man pulled out ten
dollars in Confed and gave the bill to him, saying that that
would keep him in tobacco.

The first one turned to Harry Shocker, to ask what command he belonged to. When Shocker answered, the man
looked at him with a smirk. "I suppose you have hearn
tell of me" — he paused for effect — "I am Champ Ferguson." And then Shocker knew the name of the man who
had killed his partner, Crawford Hazelwood, the morning
after the battle.[707]

Ferguson then said to Shocker, "Do you know Lieutenant
Smith?" This one of the tribe of Smith was Elza, of the
Thirteenth Kentucky Cavalry.

Shocker said that he didn't, but Champ furiously rejected
that answer: "Yes you do, you damned Yankee — you
know him well enough, but you don't want to know him

707. Sensing, pp. 186-187.

now." Shocker said that Champ persisted: "Well, do you know where he is then?"

Shocker said that he just stayed mum and that the two visitors got up to leave. When they got to the door, Champ turned to look very intently at every wounded man in the room. "I have a begrudge against Smith," he said in a low voice. "We'll find him."

EMORY

OCTOBER 7

That he meant what he said, Shocker had no doubt. So he was not surprised to learn, on October 7th, that Smith had been found by Champ's men.[708] Orange Sells, of the Twelfth Ohio, was a patient in the same room as Smith, who was very severely wounded. Sells said that a man came to talk with Smith, to tell him that he had been accused of killing a Colonel Hamilton. Smith protested weakly that he had not killed Hamilton. He said that he had been in command of a party taking Hamilton from Lexington to Camp Nelson. Along the way Hamilton attempted to escape and was shot to death by one of the guards. Smith said that he couldn't help the death, that Hamilton had forced the issue. He reasoned for a long time with the man, saying that he had only done his duty, but when the man left, it must have been pretty clear that Smith's argument wasn't going to wash away a Champ Ferguson grudge.

When he heard a rustling in the hall that night, Sells must have thought that the man was bringing Ferguson back

708. Sensing, p. 184.

to confront Smith.[709] But when the door opened, the three men who came in were strangers to him. One man carried a candle, which gave off enough light to show that the other two visitors carried revolvers. Silently the one with the candle held it above each wounded man's face. When all three Yanks had been studied, one of the intruders said, "There are none of them here." Then they went out, as swiftly as they had come in, leaving Sells to wonder who besides Smith was damned to be the object of Champ Ferguson's wrath.

Whoever it was was in the next room, for almost immediately six shots were fired in there. Then there was only the sound of footsteps receding down the hall. After a moment, a black soldier wrapped in a sheet ran into Sells' room, as hospital attendants ran up to discover two dead blacks in the adjoining room. The head of the third black had only been grazed by the two shots fired at him. The hospital authorities practically admitted that they were defenseless by taking the surviving black to the home of a neighboring cit and hiding him there. It was said that after he had finished killing the Yanks on the battlefield on the 3rd, Champ had said, "That makes ninety-seven Lincolnites I have killed, and I am going to the hospital at Saltsville to kill three more to make up the hundred."[710] Maybe that writing that Harry Shocker saw Champ doing just before he killed Crawford Hazelwood was just another mark on his tally sheet?

709. Sensing, pp. 182-183.
710. "The Charges against Champ Ferguson," Nashville *Dispatch*, July 6, 1865.

About 4:00 p.m. the next day, October 8th, Champ made another addition to his total. A Reb major, W. W. Stringfield, of the Sixty-ninth North Carolina Infantry, on furlough visiting his refugee mother and sisters, was talking with Miss Maggie Wiley, on the lawn at the bottom of the slope that led to the hospital. As they stood there that bleak, unseasonably cold afternoon, the two of them were nearly jostled by a party of about fifteen men heading up to the hospital. Stringfield recognized the leader as Champ Ferguson, having met him at General Kirby Smith's Knoxville headquarters two years before. But Stringfield probably did not attach any significance to the body of men, for he had just arrived from his regiment in the Shenandoah Valley and probably hadn't been told of the post-battle violence.[711]

The wounded Ben Rogers must have been leery, though, as he saw the body of men ride up: "I observed from my third story window a score of Ferguson's men, who were easily recognized by their picturesque garb."[712] Champ had his men counted off in pairs, and he left a pair at each stairway between the floors. When he led his men up to the stairs that led to the third floor, he was confronted by a single sentry, apparently put there to guard against escape

---

711. W. W. Stringfield left three versions of his encounter with Champ Ferguson: (1) a very brief diary, in William W. Stringfield Papers, State of North Carolina Archives; (2) "The Champ Ferguson Affair," *The Emory and Henry Era*, XVII (May, 1914), 300-302; in Richard N. Price, *Holston Methodism* (Nashville: Methodist Publishing House, 1913), Volume IV, pp. 396-399.

712. Merritt, pp. 345-346.

attempts. Champ must have expected no opposition from the guard, for he did not attempt to surprise him. But the guard proved contrary, and when Champ said that he and his men were going to pass up those stairs, the guard, an Irishman, leveled his musket to Champ's whiskers and said to him that he would part them if he came any closer. The Irishman stood his ground, so Champ and the others backed off, went to the other stairway, and this time surprised and overcame that guard.[713]

Lieutenant George W. Carter, Eleventh Michigan Cavalry, saw the body of men as they burst out of the stairway onto the third floor. He was struck by their leader, who had a full beard and long hair and was dressed like a cit — dark frock coat and black plug hat. Then he studied the followers, who were also dressed pretty much like cits, but who were armed. Carter must have shuddered, knowing what had happened the night before when there were such visitors.

The intruders went to the room occupied by Lieutenant Smith. From his bed near the door, Orange Sells watched, when Champ and one other man came in. While the other man stood by Sells' bed, Champ walked to the middle of the room, asking calmly, "How are you, Smith?"

The wounded prisoner responded, "How are you, Captain?" It was as if he was so weak and dazed that his response was just a civil reflex.

Ferguson jerked the musket up in his left hand and smacked the breech with his right. "Look here, Smith," he said, as if to regain the attention of a distracted person. "Do you see this?"

Smith raised his head as much as he could, then pleaded, "For God's sake, Captain, don't shoot me."

713. Sensing, pp.. 178-179; Peters.

But Ferguson presented the musket and pulled the trigger. And a second time. On the third attempt the musket fired, and Smith fell back, with the top of his head blown off.

In the sudden silence the other man said quietly, "Champ, be sure your work is well done."

Both men stepped up to inspect the body. "He is damned dead," one of them said. Then, quickly, as if moved by the release of tension, they returned to the hall. There were shouts that Smith was taken care of and that Dagenfield and Hanson were next. They didn't know that Captain Dagenfield, of the Twelfth Ohio, who had chased Champ just a few weeks before, was the third wounded man in Smith's room or that Colonel Hanson was in the room just across the hall.[714]

By that time there was a crowd of hospital people, both Yank and Reb, running down the hall. When Champ and his men had begun brushing their way past guards, an attendant had run down the slope calling for Dr. James B. Murfree, the surgeon in charge of the hospital. Dr. Murfree immediately ran up the slope, while Professor Edmund Longley, who had been speaking with the surgeon, called to Major Stringfield, "Come and help us; Confederate soldiers are in possession of the building and are murdering the wounded Federal prisoners."

As soon as they reached the building, the three encountered a pair of guards left by Ferguson. Major Stringfield had on his full uniform, though, and was able to cow that pair and several other pairs. On their way, Yank surgeons frantically shouted, "Your men are up here killing our men."

"I am doing my best," Stringfield called with exasperation. "I will stop this or die on these steps."

714. Sensing, pp. 181-182; Peters.

When they reached the second floor, they met a guard with a drawn revolver. Dr. Murfree ordered him to go down the stairs, but he replied: "Captain Ferguson has ordered me to let no one pass up the steps."

Major Stringfield distracted the attention of the guard. "Put up your pistol, sir," he commanded, using that "sir" Southerners use when speaking to an inferior. "Put it up!"

At the same time Dr. Murfree darted on up the stairway, to confront Ferguson, who appeared at the head of the stairs with a roar. "What in the hell does this mean?" he yelled at his guard. "I told you to let nobody upstairs."

As he followed Dr. Murfree, Stringfield called, "This *is* hellish business, Captain Ferguson."

The sight of a ranking officer seemed to discompose Ferguson, so much so that he was taken aback by Dr. Murfree's attack. "Gentlemen!" the surgeon shouted, totally unconscious of the terrible error of his address. "You must go down from here; this is a place for the sick and wounded, and you must not disturb them"

Champ looked at the doctor in disbelief. "I will shoot you," he threatened, but his voice seemed to convey total puzzlement.

Dr. Murfree stood his ground, actually placing his hand on Ferguson. "I am in charge of this hospital. You must stop this confusion. I arrest you, sir."

"Arrest hell!" yelled a mystified Ferguson. "Out of my way, or I'll blow your damned brains out."

Murfree glared back.

Ferguson raised his cocked pistol. "I don't care who you are, damn you," he muttered. "I will kill you."

Then Major Stringfield tried to intervene. "I shall not attempt to arrest you, Captain Ferguson," he said, half-soothingly, half-forcefully, "but I notify you that you shall

not molest anyone else here unless you do it over my dead
body. This is a dastardly proceeding. You know it as well as
I do."

One of Ferguson's men, a Lieutenant Philpot, must have
realized that his chief was in over his head, that they could
be overwhelmed by the growing crowd of men, even though
most were surgeons and attendants, therefore unarmed.
He stepped between Ferguson and Murfree and began to ease
Ferguson down the stairs, with Murfree right by his side.
Fishy-faced with rage, Champ struggled to put on a brave
front for his band. "Come on boys," he was finally able
to shout back over his shoulder. "We have killed some
of the damned scroundrels, and we will come back tonight
and kill the balance."

Ferguson regained his control by the time he and his
men got out of doors. For there were shouts, as they yelled
to those who had held the horses at the bottom of the
hill. "We have killed the man that killed Hamilton," as if
that were their only reason for coming to the hospital.[715]

The threat that Champ would return was addressed at
once. Dr. Murfree added to the small guard force available
to the hospital by going through the Reb wards and detailing the wounded who were capable of walking and carrying
a musket.[716]

Meanwhile, there was still chaos on the floor where Smith
had been killed. Many men had been attracted by the sound
of the shot and, like Reb quartermaster sergeant A. J. Watkins, seen its result: "I saw a Federal officer dead in his
bunk. He had a fresh wound. He was shot through the head,

715. Sensing, p. 179; W. W. Stringfield, "The Champ Ferguson
Affair," 301.
716. Peters.

the ball entering the left side of the forehead and then passing through, tearing off the top of the skull. His brains were oozing out on the pillow." Others were busy sneaking Colonel Hanson out of the building, over to the home of a cit, to be kept there until other arrangements could be made. At the same time, a courier was sent to General Breckinridge, in Abingdon, to inform him of what had happened.[717]

General Breckinridge quickly determined to remove as many of the prisoners as could stand a trip. He ordered "Mudwall" Jackson over from Saltville to Emory to supervise the transfer. Before he left Saltville, "Mudwall" startled the Yanks, such as Dan Reynolds, who were penned up there: "One cold night we were marched out to go to the cars which were some two miles distant. It snowed and I was barefoot that night, as I couldn't wear the shoes they had given me. They put us in cattle cars and we all like to have frozen to death. We worried it through somehow. . . ."[718] The prisoners from the hospital who could travel, including Colonel Hanson and Captain Dagenfield, were put on the cars at Emory. Then a relieved "Mudwall" could report to General Breckinridge: "I have just succeeded in getting off to Lynchburg the prisoners, 61 in number, including the surgeons and attendants at Emory Hospital. . . ."[719]

Major Stringfield had had a busy day, but he nevertheless took a few moments to attend to his diary: "'Home again' — came last night & found all well and glad to see me — I visited the Hospital to day. The noted *Champ Ferguson*

717. Sensing, p. 181; Peters; Price, *Holston Methodism,* p. 399.
718. Giddens, 383; Guerrant Diary, p. 1190; The Charleston *Daily Courier,* October 18, 1864, confirms that three inches of snow fell at Wytheville, Virginia, nearby, on such an early date as October 8.
719. *ORR.,* I, 39, pt. 1, p. 561.

entered the Hospital & killed a Yankee Lieut. who he says had killed his brother & a Col Harrison of our. . . ."[720] In the stress of the moment, he hadn't heard Ferguson clearly — but he could be forgiven his error, couldn't he? For he had probably thought clearly enough to save other lives. He must have felt particularly happy about his efforts when he went to hear preaching by Chaplain Cameron, of Morgan's command, the following morning.

Like "Mudwall," General Breckinridge must have been much relieved to have one less concern, for he still had a war to manage, the defense of East Tennessee by General Vaughn. Then, too, he had to try to locate and defeat the gangs of bushwhackers operating behind his lines. There was also the need to respond to the overtures of the loyal cits, such as James W. Sheffey, who wrote him on October 4th: "Allow me to congratulate you and the Country upon the victory achieved by our army in the battle of Saltville on Sunday the 2nd inst. . . ."[721] And he had problems with generals.

Those of us who had gone on the chase after Burbridge were stunned the day after we missed the ambush to learn that a courier had come from General Breckinridge with an order relieving General Williams.[722] We immediately jumped to the conclusion that he was sacked because he had mismanaged the pursuit, but we wondered how in the world Breckinridge could have known in advance that the ambush would be a fizzle. We wondered if Breckinridge might have been angry that Williams had not counterattacked just before dark, the day of the battle. We agreed that while

720. Stringfield Diary.
721. Letter, James W. Sheffey to John C. Breckinridge, October 4, 1864, in Breckinridge Papers, Huntington Library.
722. ORR, I, 45, pt. 2, p. 776.

hindsight revealed such a movement would have been totally successful, Williams' decision to remain on the defensive was justified at the time. In short, while he hadn't done any generaling that helped, neither had he done any that hurt, that we could see.

Then we heard from Giltner's headquarters that Williams had not only been relieved, but arrested as well.[723] Some of the boys suggested that it was because Williams had failed to stop the killing of the prisoners the day after the battle. Indeed Williams had been heard to say that he would have some of the prisoners shot, if he could get them turned over to him. And everybody knew that Breckinridge was an officer devoted to good order and discipline.[724] He could even charge Williams with direct disobedience of orders, since he had ordered a halt to the killings, only to discover later that they had been continued just as soon as he left the scene.

But then we heard that the order placing Williams in arrest had come from none other than General Braxton Bragg, up in Richmond. It seems that General Wheeler, down there in Georgia, brooding, had decided that Williams' negligence in catching up with him had been the cause of the failure of his great Tennessee raid. So he had charges placed against Williams, charges which reached him at the moment when he was enjoying the highest point of a rather disappointing career. No wonder that when George Atkins saw him boarding the cars in Bristol to return to Georgia for court martial he could liken himself to another disappointed general — a black one at that — and growl: "No more for me the pomp & circumstance of glorious war."[725]

723. Letter, George T. Atkins to E. O. Guerrant, p. 38.
724. *ORR*, I, 39, pt. 3, 819-820. Breckinridge to Vaughn.
725. Letter, George T. Atkins to E. O. Guerrant, p. 38.

So old "Cerro Gordo" found himself as Wheeler's scapegoat. It would have especially galled him, if he had found a copy of the October 4th Richmond *Inquirer* on his train seat, to read of the lies being circulated by "Cavalier," probably some officer on Wheeler's staff:

"FROM WHEELER'S COMMAND

"The Macon 'Telegraph' is permitted to make the annexed extracts from a private letter from Gen. Wheeler's command. It is dated Athens, Ala.:

"We are just returning from our grand raid on Sherman's line of communications.

"The expedition thus far is a most perfect success in every way. We have destroyed effectually some fifty miles of the railroad in Middle Tennessee, and some twenty-five in East Tennessee and Georgia. We have captured hundreds of prisoners and an immense amount of U. S. government property of every sort. In every fight we have made with the enemy we have been victorious. — We went in about two and a half miles of Nashville.

"Our trip throughout Tennessee was a continuous grand ovation, and has given us some 2,000 recruits of most excellent material for cavalry. The people of Tennessee are very cheerful, and have the finest crops known for years, which they are very anxious for the brave boys of our gallant army to come and consume. In the midst of our brilliant successes, a cloud of sadness covers the scene, in the case of Gen. Kelly, who was wounded on the 21 inst., near Franklin, while arranging his line of battle. His wound was so severe that we were compelled to leave him in the enemy's lines, but in the hands of kind friends. Dr. Galt, the surgeon of his division, thinks he may possibly recover. His gallantry and his ability as a soldier was of the first order, and we never lost a more useful officer.

"Do not suppose the good people of Tennessee — and they are a host — are subdued. By no means. Milk and honey, and every other good thing to tempt the appetite was lavished upon us everywhere — and the 'God bless the rebels' was on every tongue.

"I think the damage we have done the railroads will require at least thirty days to have it repaired. In the meantime, how is Sherman to subsist his army? From the best information we could obtain twenty day's rations was the utmost of his supply. I can but think Gen. Sherman's army must retreat — at least to Chattanooga, if not farther."[726]

Which was all a bunch of pipe dreams and a pack of lies. We had known the truth of Wheeler's raid ever since we got to this department. Old General Humphrey Marshall had come down to Abingdon in connection with that Morgan bank-robbing business, and while there leveled with the boys in Giltner's Brigade. After admitting that things looked black in Georgia and that Wheeler hadn't helped a bit, he got carried away and said that we had to fight on, a year or even longer, up to our ears in blood. At which point Barney Giltner said to hold on, that he had only contracted to go in "*knee*-deep."[727]

When General Williams was relieved, General Robertson assumed command of the three lost Wheeler brigades and brought them back to Saltville. There he immediately wrote a lengthy, familiar letter to his patron: "My Dear General / Your telegram placing Gen. Williams in arrest assured me that you was not in the field on the Weldon R.R. as I had infered from the Yankee papers." He gave Bragg a summary of the Tennessee raid, carefully stressing that he had not

726. Richmond *Enquirer*, October 4, 1864.
727. Guerrant Diary, p. 1152.

known of the understanding between Wheeler and Williams
at Strawberry Plains: "I was simply ordered to report to
Gen W and consequently know not what were his instructions." Then he sketched in the activities of the brigades
in the Saltville battle, adding a tidbit calculated to please:
"Gen Breckinridge was not on the field nor in miles of it
until after the fight was over." Bragg had been trying to
destroy Breckinridge's good name since the winter of 1862-3,
indeed had used Robertson in his schemes, and would delight in any information that could be twisted into a truss
rope, however Liliputian.

He continued by relying upon innuendo. By referring
to the "McLemoe's Cove business," when the Union forces
escaped a trap during the Chattanooga campaign, he hinted
that negligence allowed Burbridge to escape: "somebody
to blame not my self — more I cant say." Whether the
culprit was General Williams or General Breckinridge, he
didn't say. He also suggested that there was so much hostility toward himself, because he had been compelled in
honesty to support Bragg's version of the Tennessee campaign, that his command was suffering for lack of clothing
and equipment: "I fear we will be unable to get anything
in this Dept. all manifest shameful apathy to our wants. . . ."

Finally he concluded with a mixture of ingratiation and
flattery:

"I sincerely hope to get off soon for Georgia — will you
please have us relieved here so soon as consistent with the
good of the public service. The men can not be kept in
this department unless their necessities are at once attended
to.

"I was married to Miss Sallie Davis of White County
Tenn. on my last trip — I am sorry I could not invite you to
attend — no flash in the pan this time — She is still in the

Yankee lines — I may sometime trouble Maj Parker with letters to go by flag of truce.

"Please give my regards to Mrs. Bragg and all the members of your military family. I was much gratified to see many who used to be very bitter against yourself in Middle Tenn. disposed to do you justice.

> "There is a good time coming
> "With Respect and Kind regard your friend
> "F. H. Robertson Brig. Gen."[728]

Those of us who learned of that letter were just about dumbstruck. We just hadn't had any warning that Robertson was that kind of man. We looked back over the whole march up the country, and we couldn't remember anything that stood against him. We remembered how proud Parson Bunting had been to report back to Texas: "he is a young man of distinguished gallantry, and has won for himself much glory. . . ." We recalled the afternoon at Dalton when Dibrell's Tennesseans had charged and carried a courageous Robertson and the Confederate Brigade along with them. And the next morning when Robertson and his staff were convulsed over John McCaskill's liberated bath robe. And the morning when he stood on the banks of the Big Emory, wearing his command so earnestly, trying to decide his next move. And the afternoon at Triune, when he saved the rear of the column by charging the Yank Second Kentucky and personally killing Colonel Eifort, their leader. And the morning on Falling Water Creek, when he had proudly emerged from the Taylor house as a married man.

728. Robertson's letter is docketed in the Letters Received Book, War Department, Pickett Papers, Volume 110, Confederate States of America, Library of Congress; the letter, without Robertson's identity as sender, is in the Bragg Collection, Houghton Library, Harvard University.

Then we heard that General Breckinridge had written
General Lee on October 5th to inform him of the killing
of the prisoners and to charge Robertson with a part in the
whole business.[729] Somebody remembered that officer

729. To William C. Davis, "The Massacre at Saltville," *Civil War
Times Illustrated,* IX (February, 1971), 4-11, 43-48, belongs the credit
of charging Felix H. Robertson as a culprit in the murders at Saltville,
October 3, 1864. I confess that I do not think that I would ever have
made the discovery on my own. I suspect that Dr. Davis, the highly
regarded publisher of *CWT Illustrated,* was able to make what is to me
a brilliant piece of detection because he was able to work backward,
from the result to the cause: in the process of studying his research
for his biography of John C. Breckinridge, he came to a letter from
Charles Marshall, ADC to Robert E. Lee, to Breckinridge, dated October 21, 1864, in response to a letter from Breckinridge to Lee, dated
October 5, 1864, reporting the battle and subsequent events (*ORR,*
II, 7, p. 1020). Such a letter I would never have had an occasion to look
at, since I was terminating my study with the departure of Wheeler's
lost troops for Georgia.

Marshall indicates that he was directed to congratulate Breckinridge
upon the victory; then he writes a second paragraph, describing Lee's
response to another topic of Breckinridge's report:

> He is much pained to hear of the treatment the negro prisoners are re-
> ported to have received, and agrees with you in entirely condemning it. That a
> general officer should have been guilty of the crime you mention meets with his
> unqualified reprobation. He directs that if the officer is still in your department
> you prefer charges against him and bring him to trial. Should he have left your
> department you will forward the charges to be transmitted to the Department,
> in order that such action may be taken as the case calls for.

Breckinridge's letter to Lee, October 5, 1864, is not known to ex-
ist. Without it, Dr. Davis could use only the process of elimination
to identify the Confederate general to whom Lee was referring. I must
also confess that when I first read Dr. Davis' article, I was not completely convinced that the culprit could only have been Robertson. Now,
though, on the basis of further research by both Dr. Davis and myself,
I no longer have the slightest doubt about the identity of Robertson
as the guilty general.

the Yank Dan Reynolds had told about: "an officer on horseback took him by the collar and marched him down to the
bank of the creek. . . ." But none of us were there, so that we

In a generous response to my inquiries, Dr. Davis gave me information that he had discovered after his article appeared, a letter in Robertson's compiled service record, National Archives, dated February
22, 1865, written by John Echols, saying that the Secretary of War had
directed him to convene a court of inquiry for Robertson and requesting that Robertson be ordered to Wytheville on March 15. It should
be noted that by that time Braxton Bragg had lost his influence in
Richmond and that John C. Breckinridge had become Secretary of War.
Indeed, J. B. Jones (*A Rebel War Clerk's Diary*) notes on January 22,
1865, that the rumors are that Breckinridge wants Bragg sent away
from Jefferson Davis as his price for taking the office. Both Jones (January 28, 1865) and Robert Garlick Hill Kean (*Inside the Confederate
Government,* February 6, 1865) understood that one of the motives in
securing the appointment of Robert E. Lee as General-in-Chief, to
which Davis was opposed, was to undermine Braxton Bragg. As a fol-
low-up to Dr. Davis' discovery, I was able to discover that the order
requested by Echols was issued by the Adjutant and Inspector General,
March 7: "Second Lieutenant F. H. Robertson, C. S. Army, will report
without delay to Brigadier-General John Echols, Commanding, &c.,
Wytheville, VA., that he may attend the sittings of a court of inquiry
to be held at that place on the 15th day of March, 1865" (Confederate
States of America. War Department. *Special Orders of the Adjutant
and Inspector General's Office, Confederate States, 1865,* p. 170.
Library of Congress). Having never received confirmation for any of
his appointments in the provisional army, Robertson was by that time
regarded as having only his original appointment to the regular army,
thus his rank of Second Lieutenant.

I was able to add other pieces of evidence. The Daniel Reynolds
narrative, written only eight years after the event by a Yank prisoner,
was not known to Dr. Davis. It can be used to argue negatively that the
culprit was Robertson. No witness asserts that any generals but Williams and Robertson advanced up the valley on the morning of October
3. Reynolds identifies Williams as threatening to hang prisoners if
permitted and mentions Williams' reason, that Stoneman had similarly

couldn't ever say for sure exactly what Robertson did.
We decided, though, that he didn't have to pull a trigger
to be involved. He was an officer, a general officer. He was

dealt with his men; Stoneman's behavior must have occurred during the
August raid on Macon; Williams' threat is entirely consistent with his
character, for he seems to have been very fond of the enlisted Confederate soldier's welfare. Certainly Reynolds would have identified
Williams actually carrying out his threat, if he had seen it or even heard
of it; Reynolds does describe an unidentified officer murdering a
black — he may have indeed been watching Robertson without knowing
it. But, the point is, if Reynolds did not identify Williams as the culprit, then it must have been someone else, who had to be Robertson.
Second, Robertson's letter to Bragg offers two kinds of circumstan-
tial evidence. One, the letter itself is evidence of Robertson's continued sychophancy toward Bragg, the earlier history of which is
described in Thomas L. Connolly's *Autumn of Glory,* the definitive
study of the Army of Tennessee. In the letter Robertson takes care
to inform that "Genl Breckinridge was not on the field nor in miles
of it until after the fight was over," no doubt pleasing that old an-
tagonist of Breckinridge. Two, Robertson acknowledges that several
of his troops "were knocked on the head by the Negro troops with
muskets whilst fighting with revolvers after the ammn had been exhausted for Rifles." This statement, together with Robertson's statement to Guerrant after the battle that his men had killed just about all
the blacks, argues that he was sensitive to the fact that his men had
actually been bested by the blacks and that he would take revenge,
if possible, for what he might even have felt was a personal affront.
After all, as Dibrell noted in his report of the battle, Robertson's
line gave way. The relatively large number of wounded reported by
the "Confederate" regiments suggests they occupied the right wing
of Robertson's brigade.

Third, Robertson later allowed other prisoners to be murdered, as
I have described in his biography (pp. 402-407). If he behaved in
such a fashion toward white troops, there is no reason to doubt that
he had not acted with equal brutality toward black troops and white
troops who had fought alongside black troops. Yet, though I am convinced that Robertson did something at Saltville for which Breckin-

responsible not only for himself, but for those under his
command. It could have been that he didn't order his subordinates to kill a single prisoner. It could have been that

ridge and Lee thought he should be condemned, I do not know speci-
fically what it was. I chose, therefore, not to narrow the range of
speculation in my narrative.

I do not think, however, that the mystery results from a massive
conspiracy to cover up Robertson's behavior. Some of the men who
left accounts may consciously have refrained from singling Robertson
out for comment, certainly Wise, probably Guerrant, Mosgrove, Duke.
Wise, Mosgrove, and Duke all write decades after the war, when the
romanticizing of the strife was well advanced. Guerrant, as a very self-
conscious diarist, may simply have been disinclined to record what
he had not himself seen. Others apparently either did not know of it
or did not think it significant. Atkins seems not to have known of it,
for he mentions in his letter the action at Marion a few months later
when Witcher's Confederates used three Yanks virtually as target
practice, and, breezy as he was, he would have mentioned Robert-
sons' behavior if he had seen it. During the same battle at Marion,
incidentally, black troopers from the U.S Fifth and Sixth Colored
Cavalry were witnessed in clubbing captured Confederate wounded
(J. T. Goodwin, Niles [Michigan] *Republican,* February 4, 1865);
that is to say, the killing of prisoners seems to have been much more
common than our "last war of gentlemen" myth acknowledges. Such
killing may have been so ordinary that some memorists of Saltville
did not even regard it as noteworthy, perhaps Miller or Lambright.
It should be remembered that the troops at Saltville from Wheeler's
Corps had fought with blacks before, to go no further back than
Dalton, and may have regarded such activity as a natural part of "no
quarter" fighting, as Lambright phrased it. George Guild, based on
his recording of the subsequent murders in Georgia, would apparently
at least have alluded to it, if it had been widely discussed in the
Fourth Tennessee camp. As adjutant he probably had duties that
foggy morning which kept him back in Saltville; hence he did not
witness, nor could he have made the protest that he later made about
the Georgia affair, while withholding information about a similar
affair in Virginia, and thus lay himself open to a charge of hypocrisy

he just didn't stop them when he saw the killing going on. It could have been that some Rebs were threatening to kill some prisoners, when an officer appealed to Robertson to order the halt to their plans; it may be that he replied, "They know best what to do with them"[730] In a way that would be worse: a man who has seen his friends killed, maybe even after they'd surrendered, can be understood if he loses control and takes it out on prisoners; but a man who just coldly makes a decision that those prisoners don't matter enough to him to say the words that would keep them alive, he just don't make sense. In a way you've got this choice, either a sane world where you understand why men lose control and act cruelly or a crazy world where you don't understand why men *choose* to act that way. Which isn't much of a choice.

After we heard of Breckinridge's letter, we waited for something to come of it. For, you see, after all of our talk we hadn't come to any agreement about Robertson. Some said that they were only Yanks and mostly blacks at .that and deserved whatever happened to them. Some said it was

by some knowledgeable reader of his book, such as Thomas E. Matthews. Finally, as an indication that the affair was not widely known, it should be noted that neither Burbridge, in threatening retaliation (*ORR*, I, 49, pt. 1, p. 765) nor the Champ Ferguson trial mentions Robertson's complicity in the murders. Yet, despite the low visibility of the action, the fact remains that the processes of law had been set into motion, so that Robertson would have face formal accusation by Confederate authority. Why action was not undertaken against him by Union authority, as was the case with Champ Ferguson, is probably best explained by the nature of Champ Ferguson's career. His murders had been highly publicized since their beginning; charges brought against him referred to his several actions, not just his involvement at Saltville.

730. Guild, pp. 107-108.

unfortunate, but that was war. Some said Robertson should-
n't be blamed for doing what the whole South had talked
about. Others argued that he must have acted in the heat
of the moment, that it was a one-time affair, and that he
oughtn't have his life ruined because of it. Others admitted
that his act was on his head and that he ought to pay for
it, but they certainly didn't know what a fit punishment
would be.

We waited, then, for General Lee to respond to the letter.
We thought of him almost like God Almighty; we just knew
that he would make the right decision, a judgment that
we would see the wisdom of, however different from our
own puny opinion it might be. A couple of the boys even
hung around the depot in Saltville, listening to the telegraph
traffic for a while, but they said it was either local stuff
from Bristol or Dublin or it was just noise, like the operator
at the other end was just drumming his finger on the key
out of boredom.

SALTVILLE

OCTOBER 8

Came Saturday, October 8th, and we heard that Hood
had telegraphed orders for Williams' command to start for
Georgia immediately. Then there was a bustle in the camps!
That was when Champ Ferguson must have decided that
if he had any business at Emory Hospital he'd better be
attending to it. And there still wasn't any answer.

The next day, another Sunday, Dibrell's Tennesseeans
and the Confederate Brigade rode out, leaving us boys in
the Kentucky Brigade to come on a few days behind them.
Some of our boys were off at church, others were breaking

the Sabbath to the bent of their individual imaginations. But there were a good many of us standing there waving to friends in the departing regiments. There went George Miller and John Prather in the Eighth Confederate, Raymond Cay and Jim Lambright in the Fifth Georgia, George Guild in the Fourth Tennessee. Only there really wasn't that much organization any more — as our march had continued we had become more like just a collection of mobs that happened to be going in the same direction. The column was led, of course, by General Felix H. Robertson, looking just as gallant as ever, and the tail was brought up by Champ Ferguson. Those boys had a hard march ahead of them: down to Jonesboro, over the mountains, where it would be plenty cold, dressed as they were, to Asheville, North Carolina, thence to Greenville, South Carolina, and finally back to Athens, Georgia, once again into the war. At that moment, most of us dismissed Robertson and Ferguson from our minds — the message about them hadn't come up here where it was quiet and orderly, so they would go on to Georgia, where the war would punish them or not, as it wished.

We stood there watching, as a chilly wind came up to scatter the snow in the shadows, rustle the corn blades, and swirl the fallen leaves. It had been summertime hot when we left Georgia, happy as schoolboys, Wilbur Mims said, to be freed from those trenches. We had told ourselves that we would lift the siege of Atlanta and that we would affect the Chicago Convention. We might just as well have told ourselves that we would walk on water. Now it was fall, and we would be going back to a Dixie that, like an old man, seemed to be withering before our eyes.

Nobody in the column was looking back, having nothing to want to remember. You could see that most had already

slouched down in their saddles to doze. We began to break
up and go about our private concerns. As we did, we noticed
the Scholar doing what he mostly did with his spare time,
sitting on a stump, reading this book that he had carried
the whole way. Now several of us were school boys, like Jim
Black and Ben Rogers, but we didn't know that book. Just
what in the hell is that *Anabasis*? It's the march up country,
the Scholar said, it's a history book about a Greek army on
a long march. Well, if that's what you write books about,
one fellow laughed and paused to spit tobacco, then maybe
someday, maybe you'll write a book about us. I doubt it,
the Scholar smiled, looking at his book, this is not so much
about the trip, but about the meaning of the trip that the
author thought out. Who could find any sense in what we've
done? We all laughed and agreed, except old Grove, from
Doane's Mill, Alabama, who got a little angry: "Well, I liked
it all. I've never been to Virginia, before."

After the Little March —

Akin, James Houston
Major, Ninth Tennessee Cavalry Battalion

Surviving the war, Major Akin spent the remainder of his life as a farmer near Thompson's Station, Williamson County, Tennessee. His most notable civic achievement was service in the Tennessee General Assembly, 1891-1893, 1895-1897, and 1899-1901. He died on January 21, 1911, at the age of seventy-eight.

—Biographical Register of the General Assembly
of the State of Tennessee

Allen, William Gibbs
Adjutant, Fifth Tennessee Cavalry

Adjutant Allen managed to stay clear of General Williams by remaining with General Vaughn's command. He accompanied that body as it marched toward Saltville from East Tennessee. His brother, Major George W. Allen, had been to Richmond to get the payroll for Vaughn's men, and Vaughn ordered Allen to take the money, ride off with it until the issue at Saltville was settled, then return with the money. Adjutant Allen missed Vaughn's force when it returned to East Tennessee, so he stopped in Bristol: "I rode to Bristol. I knew John King he was owner of the Saltwork. I went to his house, Stayed all night. Brother Georges wife was there. She was Mr. Kings niece. She talked loud and when I got to bed it was late. Mr. King had a yellow Girl, to help in the House, and she had a yellow Bow. I got a late start. . . ." What caused the late start must remain a minor historical mystery.

Despite his own troubles, General Williams made another effort to have Allen turned over to him for punishment. But instead General Vaughn ordered transportation by rail for him back to General Wheeler's command, by then at Gadsden, Alabama. Allen then served through the Savannah and Carolina campaigns, to return to Washington, Rhea County, East Tennessee. There he lived as a leading businessman and citizen (and contributor of war-stories to the Dayton paper), until November 27, 1924, when he died in his eighty-ninth year.

—*Confederate Veteran*, XXXIII (January, 1925), 25.

Allen, William Wirt
Brigadier-General, Division of Cavalry

General Allen continued to command Martin's Division after the Tennessee raid was concluded and on to the end. When peace was restored, he returned to his plantation. But in later years he was active in railroading and in fulfilling appointive offices. He was for several years the adjutant general of the state of Alabama and then a United States marshal. He died shortly after his fifty-ninth birthday, on November 24, 1894.

—Ezra J. Warner, *Generals in Gray*
(Baton Rouge: Louisiana State University Press, 1959).

Anderson, Paul F.
Lieutenant-Colonel, Fourth Tennessee Cavalry

Colonel Anderson removed to Helena, Arkansas, after the war. There he became the proprietor of Planters' Livery Stable. Later he branched out his business interests, becoming General Shipping Agent for the Arkansas Central Railway and conducting his own receiving, forwarding, and commission business. He was also thought to be the leader of the Ku Klux Klan in Spring Creek township, Phillips County. He died on September 12, 1878, of hematuria, "contracted during the recent political canvass."

—Arkansas *Gazette*, September 14, 1878;
Personal communication, December 10, 1976,
from Mrs. C. M. T. Kirkman, Helena, Arkansas.

Ash, John H.
Sergeant, Company A, Fifth Georgia Cavalry

Sergeant Ash rejoined his regiment after it returned to Georgia and participated in the winter and spring campaigns, 1864-1865. During that last period he was commissioned a lieutenant, but his increased responsibilities did not keep him from filling his little diaries, twenty of which he had sent his mother by the end of the war. Afterwards, he became a minister in Oliver, Georgia, living a long and satisfying

life. He died in Savannah, January 3, 1918, at the age of seventy-
four.

—Widow's Pension Application
State of Georgia.

Ashby, Henry M.
Colonel, Tennessee Brigade of Cavalry

On into the Carolina campaign, in the spring of 1865, Colonel
Ashby continued to be one of Wheeler's most admired subordinates,
always with a concern for the men. H. W. Graber remembered a night
in South Carolina when, as a courier, he took a message to Colonel
Ashby's headquarters: "I found him lying on a pallet in front of a
fireplace, surrounded by his staff, all asleep. I showed him the order;
after reading it and noticing that I was wet, having ridden in the rain
part of the time, he made me step up to the fire, then after drying
my clothes, take his pallet and sleep. . . . This kind treatment of
Colonel Ashby's was much appreciated, but was not a surprise to me,
having known him as one of the most gallant officers and gentlemen
I ever got acquainted with." Despite being severely wounded near
the end, Colonel Ashby survived, only to be murdered, back in Knoxville, on July 10, 1868.

The Knoxville *Daily Press and Herald* of the following day carried
a full account of the affair:

"The difficulty between Col. H. M. Ashby and E. C. Camp terminated yesterday in the death of Col. Ashby. It appears that Col.
Ashby went into Camp's office on Main Street, at about 5 o'clock
yesterday afternoon, and after some conversation, Camp proposed
to go out in the street and settle the difficulty. Accordingly they
went out, and when at the corner of Crooked Street, Col. Ashby
turned to go down towards the river, but Camp refused to go. A scuffle
ensued, when Camp drew his pistol and shot Col. Ashby through the
head. Col. Ashby fell at once, and after he had fallen, Camp fired
two more shots, one taking effect in the breast, and the other in the
mouth. Camp then walked off, and was met by Sheriff Bearden. He
was taken before Esq. Joroulmon and examined. The testimony of
Mayor Bearden and Mr. Rule was taken in regard to the previous
difficulty, and he was discharged upon $5,000 bail, to appear at the

next term of the Circuit Court. His bondsmen are George Andrews, William Rule, M. L. Patterson, and M. J. Childress.

The Inquest

The body of Col Ashby remained where it fell, surrounded by quite a crowd, until about 6 o'clock, when Esquire Joroulmon, acting as coroner, summoned a jury of inquest.

The body was lying upon the pavement with the head upon the curb stone and the hands crossed upon the breast. The face was powder burned, as was also the breast. A Derringer pistol, loaded and uncocked lay by the feet of the corpse, and the cane of the deceased was by his side.

After examining the body the jury withdrew to Esquire Barry's house, and the body was cared for by Col. Ashby's friends.

The evidence at the inquest was as follows:

THOMAS CAIN stated that he saw the whole affair. He was walking with Ashby and as they passed Camp's office, Col. Ashby said, 'Here's a man I had a difficulty with yesterday and I propose to go in and settle the thing right now.' I told him he had better not, but he said he didn't want any enemies or friends without he knew who they were, or something to that effect. The two Camps and Clotworthy were playing some game. Ashby went in and I followed him. When I got in he had said something and Camp got up and met Ashby in the middle of the room. Says he, 'Ashby I dont want any fuss but if you want to fight this thing out, you and I can go out on the street and settle this matter.' I said gentlemen this sort of talk looks like somebody was going to get killed. Camp said I don't know you and Ashby introduced us. He introduced me as having been in the Federal army, which I never was. Then Clotworthy went off, I called him back and told him he ought to stop this. He said he would look for a policeman, and went off again. Then Camp said, 'Gentlemen, you stay here, and Col. Ashby and I will settle this difficulty.' They walked along making gestures at each other. Ashby turned towards the river but Camp kept on and Ashby came back. Ashby threw his hand against Camp. Camp took hold of Ashby's stick. A scuffle ensued and lasted two or three seconds. Camp drew his pistol and shot Ashby. Ashby fell at once. Young Camp and I were looking at it. After Ashby fell, he had his hands crossed and Camp went up and pulled his hands apart and fired again. I think he fired twice. I think he had got Ashby's pistol in the scuffle, and after he had fired the last time he threw the pistol at him, and pushed his own hat back on his head and walked off.

WESLEY STEWART — Was at Baxter's office. Baxter was busy and I had to wait. Some one said, 'Those men are fussing.' I went to the door. They were walking near the brick house. Ashby started towards the river. Camp walked forward, and then Ashby came forward, and they sort of locked shoulders. Ashby threw up his arm — he whirled around and stopped. Ashby threw his hand up in Camp's face. Camp threw it off. Camp had his back to me, and had his hand in his pocket. Ashby had his hand behind him. He drew it out and Camp held it, and then Camp threw up his hand and I heard the pistol, and Ashby fell. Camp fired twice after he fell and then threw the pistol back at him. I did not see Ashby make any demonstration by drawing a pistol. Camp shot him twice after he fell.

The jury then retired and in a few minutes brought the following

VERDICT;

STATE OF TENNESSEE, KNOX COUNTY

We being duly elected, empanelled and sworn and charged by R. D. Joroulmon, acting as Coroner of Knox county, as a jury of inquest to enquire how, when and in what matter H. M. Ashby came to his death, on our oaths do say that one E. C. Camp, on the 10th day of July, 1868, in the county of Knox, did shoot and kill the said H. M. Ashby, by firing at and shooting him three times with a pistol, against the peace and dignity of the State.

Given under our hands, this 10th day of July, 1868.

H. BARRY,
N. H. COLCLASURE,
H. L. W. MYNATT,
S. BISSINGER,
J. H. McMILLAN,
G. M. PARHAM,
I. JOSEPH

THE PARTIES

Col. Ashby, the deceased, was about thirty-two or thirty-three years of age. He belongs to the family that became illustrious, during the war, in the names of Dick and Turner Ashby, of Virginia. At the outbreak of the war he was in Knox county, temporarily residing here. Like other young men of that age, he sought the saddle and the sword.

He became Col. of the 2nd Tennessee Cavalry, and in that capacity, surrendered with his command to Gen. Sherman. We leave others to give a fuller notice.

His slayer, E. C. Camp, is a lawyer by profession, and for some three years has lived in Knoxville. He is a man of no character, and his standing among lawyers has for some time been such, that his recognition has always been questionable. He belongs to that low order of shysters that frequent the Police Courts of Chicago and New York. The wonder is that Col. Ashby would have risked his life in such a contest."

Knoxville *Daily Press and Herald,* July 11, 1868;
Jane Griffith Keys, "Virginia Heraldry," Baltimore *Sun,*
December 10, 1905, p. 12;
James P. Coffin, "Col. Henry M. Ashby," *Confederate Veteran,*
XIV (March, 1906), 121.

Atkins, George T.
Captain, Fourth Kentucky Cavalry

Probably the only New Yorker in the Fourth Kentucky, Captain Atkins resumed his life as a commercial traveler after the surrender, for a New York City wholesale drug company. He went to Texas for that firm in 1872 and in 1878 settled in Dallas, where he became a retail druggist. At one time he left his profession to act as receiver for the Texas Trunk Railroad, but he afterwards resumed his career. He died in Dallas, August 8, 1920, in his eighty-third year.

Dallas *Daily Times Herald,* August 9, 1920;
Dallas *Morning News,* August 9, 1920.

Avery, Isaac Wheeler
Colonel, Fourth Georgia Cavalry

Permanently dependent upon crutches, from the wound received at New Hope Church, Colonel Avery removed to Dalton, Georgia, after the war. There the penniless veteran began the practice of law and, in his spare hours, the writing of a *Digest of the Georgia Supreme Court Reports.* In 1868 he located in Atlanta, to assume the editorship of the Atlanta *Constitution.* Thereafter Colonel Avery's time was taken up more by writing and editing than by the law. Having an acute respect for language, he had a corresponding contempt for its misuse; accordingly he had four affairs of honor, while editor of the *Constitution,* to force the retraction of irresponsible charges. His campaign against vilification in Georgia politics was successful, "correcting the evil largely." Turning over the *Constitution* to Henry W. Grady, whom he had introduced into journalism, Colonel Avery devoted his last years to the writing of history and the establishment of direct trading between the South and Europe. He died in Atlanta, September 7, 1897.

—*National Cyclopedia of American Biography*
(New York: James T. White Company, 1898), XII, p. 238.

Barron, Samuel B.
Lieutenant, Company C, Third Texas Cavalry

In the next Yankee raid after the Stoneman-McCook fiasco, the Kilpatrick raid of August 19-21, 1864, Sam Barron was captured. Pretending to be fatally wounded, he fell down and played possum, so he was left — to rejoin his command and take part in the bitter end of the war, Hood's Tennessee blunder. Then he returned to Rusk, Texas, to clerk in a general store. In 1870 he began to practice law, and in time he joined others in the incorporation of a tram railway to join with the I. and G. N. through tracks. In 1880 he was appointed County Clerk and subsequently he became County Judge. In his old age he published *The Lone Star Defenders* (1908), the story of Cherokee County's cavalry company in the Civil War. He died in February, 1912, not quite seventy-eight years of age.

—Hattie Joplin Roach, *The Hills of Cherokee*
(n.p., n.d.)

Bird, Edward
Colonel, Fifth Georgia Cavalry

After the surrender, Colonel Bird returned to Effingham County, Georgia, to reenter the timber and turpentine business. Active in politics, he was a Representative in the Georgia Legislature for the session of 1880-1881. He died on April 15, 1893.

—Memoirs of Georgia, II
(Atlanta: The Southern Historical Association, 1895), p. 420.

Black, James Conquest Cross
Private, Ninth Kentucky Cavalry

As one of Wheeler's cavalrymen, Jim Black had spent so much time in Georgia that he elected to remain there after the war, rather than return home to Stamping Ground, Kentucky. Georgetown College finally relented and awarded his degree. As he put it, "After removal to Augusta and the heat of those days had cooled, a diploma was issued." His eloquence continued to serve him well, for, after he became a lawyer in 1866, he quickly impressed his fellow citizens. He served as city attorney, a member of the city council, a member of the Georgia House of Representatives (1873-1877), and a member of the United States House (1893-1897). He was welcomed to Washington by his old Colonel, W. C. P. Breckinridge, then a prominent Representative from Kentucky. Declining any other political office, Jim Black presided as the dean of the Augusta bar, until his death, October 1, 1928, in his eighty-sixth year.

—James L. Harrison, comp., *Biographical Directory of the American Congress* (Washington: U.S. Government Printing Office, 1950; *Memorial Exercises in Honor of J. C. C. Black.*

Blakey, David Taliaferro
Colonel, First Alabama Cavalry

Colonel Blakey had graduated from the University of Georgia and read law before the war, so that he had no difficulty in resuming a civilian life. He spent the remainder of his life as a prosperous attorney in Montgomery, dying in his sixty-eighth year, on June 27, 1902.

—Thomas M. Owen, *History of Alabama,* III; *Northern Alabama, Historical and Biographical* (Birmingham: Smith & Deland, 1888), pp. 604-605.

Breckinridge, John Cabell
Major-General

Unlike Jefferson Davis, John C. Breckinridge evaded capture by the Yankee troops, made his way to Florida, thence to Cuba. From there he went to England and afterwards to Canada. Only in 1869 did he return to Lexington, Kentucky, where he practiced law until his untimely death, May 17, 1875, at the age of fifty-four.

—*Generals in Gray; Biographical Directory of the American Congress*

Breckinridge, William Campbell Preston
Colonel, Ninth Kentucky Cavalry

Colonel Breckinridge brought his regiment back to Georgia, to enter into the harrying operations against Sherman. With the arrest of General Williams and the transfer of General Robertson, Colonel Breckinridge assumed command of the Kentucky Brigade and fought it to the end. That brigade accompanied Dibrell's Tennesseans as an escort for the fleeing Confederate government, until further flight was hopeless. When the men were told to surrender, Willie Breckinridge decided to ride into Augusta to apply for his parole there. Milford Overley described Breckinridge's farewell to his men: he "took each soldier by the hand and with tearful eyes bade him good-by. When he and Gen. Dibrell clasped hands that day to say the parting words, had an angel from heaven appeared and told them that their next meeting would be in the halls of the United States Congress as members of that body from their respective States, they could scarcely have believed it. . . ."

Returning to Lexington, Colonel Breckinridge became the editor of the Lexington *Observer and Reporter*. In 1867 he announced his candidacy for the office of commonwealth's attorney for his district, to be joined by two other candidates. Then a fourth candidate presented himself — General John S. "Cerro Gordo" Williams. The campaign for the office was fierce, and one particular row split the two former leaders of the Kentucky Brigade. An article appeared in the Lexington *Observer and Reporter* which attacked Williams, saying that since he had just located in the district he had not fulfilled residency requirements and, further, that his frequent boast of being the savior of Saltville was based upon a distortion of the truth. Williams, of course, thought that Breckinridge had written the article and was furious. Breckinridge immediately sent word to Williams that offensive material had been written by an assistant and without his knowledge. Williams refused to be mollified, though — Basil Duke thought that Williams recognized a good issue to pursue, as he characterizes Williams' behavior in the culmination of the affair:

"[Williams] accordingly gave formal notice that on a certain evening he would speak in Lexington and answer seriatim and fully the statements contained in the said article, all of which he pledged himself to prove conclusively to be false and injurious. He invited his competitors to be present, and requested the largest possible attendance of his fellow-citizens, especially those who were entitled to vote, in order that he might establish fairly and fully the justice of every claim he had ever asserted.

"Of course, when the appointed date arrived a large and interested crowd was in attendance, and public expectation was on the alert to hear speeches in which the personal equation would be largely represented.

"When the audience, composed not only of citizens of Lexington and the immediate vicinity but of many others from neighboring counties, was assembled, General Williams mounted the rostrum. The other candidates, except Breckinridge, were present. Breckinridge was compelled to attend a meeting at a neighboring town that afternoon, where he was booked to speak, but had notified his friends that he would return in time to hear and answer anything which the general might say about him.

"If there had been any previous doubt that General Williams was disposed to make matters warm and interesting, it was dispelled by the first sentences which he uttered.

"He announced with impressive solemnity that a double obligation was imposed upon him; that he felt it just and proper to make a statement due to his own reputation, and necessary, also, to vindicate the truth of history! It might become his painful duty, he said, in the course of his remarks, to comment severly upon the conduct of one of his opponents, but, however, unpleasant that duty might be, he would not shrink from its performance; no consideration should restrain him from dealing with fairly and candidly with the people whose suffrages he asked.

"Then, with a voice constantly increasing in volume and unmistakable symptoms of a rapidly rising temperature, he read the article from the *Observer and Reporter,* in which his right to be styled the 'hero of Saltville' was questioned, and fiercely and unequivocally charged Breckinridge with its responsibility. By way of establishing the claim, which skeptical and sarcastic criticism was now assailing, he gave the history, not only of the battle, but of the campaign immediately preceding it. He recited the conditions which rendered it absolutely necessary to repel the threatened Federal attack and to conserve to the Confederacy the department of South-western Virginia — more especially the salt works — and in glowing and picturesque language described the consternation with which the approach of the Yankees had stricken the inhabitants of that region, and the concern so dire a threat occasioned the authorities at Richmond. With a modesty equaled only by the candid and convincing way in which it was stated, he related the judicious dispositions which were made — under his operations, although not by his sole direction — to meet and roll back this formidable invasion; and having thus wrought his hearers up to the highest pitch of expectation, he entered upon a description of the combat itself.

"Seated near the stand was a well known and gallant ex-Confederate officer — Capt. Orville West — who had served on General Williams' staff at Saltville; and in the course of his speech, more particularly when narrating some peculiarly striking and interesting incident, the general would turn to the captain and say, 'Isn't that so, Captain West?' or, 'Do you not remember this, Captain West?' and the captain would bow and smile assent.

"But as the speech progressed in a fervid flow of mingled imagination and invective, when the torrent of ardent and angry eloquence broke over the boundaries not only of memory, but of a reasonable credulity, and threatened to scorch like a stream of lava any one rash enough to hint dissent, Captain West became restless and apprehensive. A pained and startled expression replaced the original smile upon his face, and he looked like a man who wished to plead a pressing engagement and leave. But when General Williams reached the climax of his recital Captain West utterly succumbed.

"'Finally,' said the general, 'the Yankees, anticipated in every movement which they attempted, and foiled in every onslaught they made, essayed as a last resort to break through the left of my position by a determined charge of cavalry. I had expected something of the kind and had prepared to receive and defeat any such effort. The few troops at my disposal had been imperatively needed at other points of my line, and I could not strengthen this point without endangering others; but I had stationed there a battery of four pieces of artillery under an excellent and thoroughly reliable young officer. I warned him that the Yankees at some time during the battle would charge him with cavalry, and directed him what to do. "When they come," I said "reserve your fire until they are right upon you. Double-shot your guns with grape, and when the forefeet of the hostile horses are clanging upon their muzzles, pull your lanyards." He implicitly obeyed my instruction. The Yankee cavalry charged gallantly. They rushed upon that battery with sabres whirling, and at such speed that the foam from the mouths of the horses shot back into the faces of the riders. Nothing, it seemed, would be able to withstand their onset. But just as the horses were rearing in front of the battery and about to plunge upon the cannon, the lanyards were pulled and the red and deadly glut rushed forth. Fellow-citizens, I shudder even now when I remember the effect of that terrible volley. That cavalry went down before it as the half-ripened wheat goes down before a storm of wind and hail. Those who were near enough could hear the bones crash in that ill-fated column, as, in the bleak December, you have heard the sleet dash against your windows.'

"The entire audience was immensely impressed by this vivid picture. The old farmers, especially, realized its horror. Their hair stood on end and their flesh crept, notwithstanding the victims were Yankees. Then General Williams turned and in a voice like thunder asked, 'Isn't that so, Captain West?'

"Captain West was a loyal staff officer; no one was ever moreso. He desired to do his full duty and stand by his chief; but there are limits to human endurance. He essayed to furnish the usual tokens of corroboration; but he was over taxed, his nerve was flanked and, after an ineffectual effort to bow and smile, he dropped from his chair in a limp and fainting condition.

"Some time before General Williams had concluded his speech, Breckinridge entered the house and heard the greater part of the criticism bestowed upon himself. Even had he not been inclined to answer it, his friends would have insisted that he should do so; and he needed little urging. As soon, therefore, as Williams sat down, Breckinridge began to speak.

"He had little difficulty in convincing the audience that he was guiltless of the most serious charge the general had preferred, that of having used his editorial position to aid his own canvass and injure that of an opponent, but, smarting under Williams's caustic censure, he unfortunately, although quite naturally, retorted in kind, and with a severity that in his cooler moments he regretted. He not only successfully defended his own military record but attacked that of General Williams, and thus the Confederates witnessed, to their scandal and sorrow, two of their favourite representatives assailing each other, and doing more serious detriment to the Confederate prestige than many score of civilian politicians could have accomplished.

"The most lamentable, not to say ludicrous, feature of the matter, was that neither was sincere in his attack upon the other, for each was on record — and honestly so — as having testified to the other's merit as a soldier. But here were two comrades, who had 'fought, bled,' and nearly 'died together,' denouncing each other like scullions in the effort to obtain an office that neither would have sought had he known in advance that such altercation would have resulted.

"Breckinridge, excited by frequent· interruption, finally became so warm in rejoinder that a personal encounter between the two was barely averted. The discussion was brought to a sudden termination by a declaration from Williams that he thought the time for words had passed and that for action had arrived, and as Breckinridge manifestly entertained the same opinion, a clash seemed inevitable. Their partisans, having become thoroughly heated, loudly announced a willingness to participate in this sort of debate, and for a while 'blood' was thick 'upon the face of the moon.'"

The ritual had gone far enough, though, so that yet another candidate, Edward Marshall, interposed himself and, with a speech of about an hour's length, calmed the two hotheads and their partisans. Colonel Breckinridge went ahead to win the election. He was employed, too, at about the same time as a professor of law at the University of Kentucky.

In politics he served as delegate to the Democratic National Conventions of 1876 and 1888 and as Representative to the United States House from 1885 to 1895. In the House he was noted for his rhetorical ability and his short temper, the combination of which sometimes disturbed the tranquillity of the chamber. On one occasion, a row erupted between Willie Breckinridge and another representative, John Heard, so that Breckinridge shouted to Heard, "You are a dirty pup!" and Heard replied. "You are a damned liar!" Breckinridge started down the aisle after Heard, while the Speaker of the House pounded his gavel with such force that the head flew off and hit a page in the stomach. The two men were restrained, but it appeared that a duel would be required for the satisfaction of honor, for neither was willing to apologize. Their friends met in the Speaker's room and developed a script for reconciliation — the Speaker would present a statement on the matter, then each aggrieved party would acknowledge his acceptance of the statement and beg the pardon of the House. And thus it happened, following which there was a motion to strike all reference to the episode from the *Congressional Record,* which was so ordered. Champ Clark observed the resumption of relations between the two lawmakers:

"Heard said, 'Billy when men's beard get as gray as yours and mine, they ought to have more sense than to quarrel like boys.'

"'Yes, John,' replied Breckinridge, 'but it sometimes seems to me that the grayer we get the less sense we have.'"

Colonel Breckinridge could surely have illustrated his observation from his own life. About that time he was sued for breach of promise by a young lady who alleged that she had been kept by the Colonel for some time. His Congressional career was terminated, for he lost his campaign for nomination in both 1894 and 1896. He then retired to Lexington, where he became the chief editorial writer for the Lexington *Morning Herald*. He died November 18, 1904, at the age of sixty-seven.

—*Biographical Directory of the American Congress;*
Overley; Duke; Clark.

Bunting, Robert Franklin
Chaplain, Eighth Texas Cavalry

At the surrender Chaplain Bunting went to Macon, where he met his wife, who had recently come through the lines from Ohio with only their infant daughter and an old black teamster for company. Then the reunited family started for Mrs. Bunting's family home in Ohio, to await the arrival of another baby. The Reverend Bunting stopped off in Nashville, always a second home for a Texas Ranger, and while there was offered the pulpit of the First Presbyterian Church, salary twenty-five dollars a month and bed in the basement. The Buntings remained in Nashville until 1868, with Chaplain Bunting having great success in building the strongest church in Southern Presbyterianism. Then he felt the call to return to mission work in Texas, to which he had devoted his ministry before the war. Although the relocation meant a sacrifice of sixty-percent of his salary, Chaplain Bunting began a thirteen year tenure in Galveston. Then again it was the lure of Tennessee, for he returned, to become associated with Southwestern Presbyterian University at Clarksville. After a four year labor there, he served two years as the pastor of the church in Gallatin. At that time he decided to accept a call from the church in Brunswick, Georgia, where he and his wife might spend their declining years. He had one last service to perform for Tennessee, to serve as Stated Clerk at the Presbytery which met at Spring Creek Church, in Wilson County. On the morning of September 19, 1891, he arose to catch the 5:40 train to Nashville and hurriedly walked the half mile to the Lebanon station. Entering a car, he died instantly, of a heart attack, in his sixty-third year. He was buried at Gallatin, his last ministry, and that grieving congregation installed a stained glass window in their church to commemorate him.

—Nashville *Banner*, April 27, 1944;

Nashville *Daily American*, September 20, 1891;

Nashville *Banner*, September 19, 20, 1891.

Caldwell, Walter H.
Private, Company D, Eighth Texas Cavalry

Walter Caldwell was highly regarded by his comrades, and his wounding was frequently mentioned in letters home. Will Nicholson wrote, "Day before yesterday Walter Caldwell was wounded in a picket fight his wound is in the thigh near the joint and the bone is fractured but not broken as was at first supposed the ball did not come out — he is at a home on the other side of the river and not far from a gentleman who is well acquainted with his father, he will not want for attention. Dr. Neely and John Hayne is staying with him. J. H. came to camps this morning and says Walter is doing as well as could be expected. Capt Kyle will go to see him this morning. Walter suffered a good deal as he had to be brought some distance to be secure from the Yankees. We all hope he will soon recover, he is one of our best and bravest soldiers."

A week later, Sergeant John W. Hill wrote home, "Some of the boyes went to see W. H. Caldwell yesterday He is getting along very well I hope that he will bee well again and that his wound will prove nothing serious." Will Nicholson was one of the boys who visited Walter, and his letter to his sister Ruth sounded half-envious, "Yesterday I went to see Walter Caldwell and was rejoiced to see him doing so well. His wound is not so serious as was at first supposed. He is at a very nice place — a Mr. Jackson's — one mile from Florence. There are four young ladies there and a piano also. Walter anticipates a pleasant time as soon as he gets able to get about."

That pleasant time was long coming, though, for Walter was confined to bed for five months. When he was able to get up, he learned that he would require crutches the remainder of his life. Somehow, he made it back to Bastrop, Texas, where he became a successful farmer and stockman. Later he moved to Austin, where he died on March 5, 1910, at the age of sixty-eight, an honored citizen.

—*Confederate Military History,* XI
(Atlanta: Confederate Publishing Company, 1899), pp. 234-235.

Cay, Raymond
Private, Company G, Fifth Georgia Cavalry

Private Cay came back to Georgia with General Robertson, later to recall: "from the day we left Social Circle, Ga., with Gen. Wheeler until our return to him I had ridden 14 different mounts and came out with the best little mule in the regiment." Such ability to transcend adversity probably forecast Cay's future, for the boy (he had not attained his majority when the war was concluded) moved to Florida and flourished, By the sime of the Spanish-American War he had become wealthy and well-known; he was appointed assistant adjutant general of the state of Florida during the period when state regiments were being activated for national service. His rank as colonel entitled him to a position on the staff of the governor; he was therefore among the party welcoming General Wheeler to Tampa before his departure for Cuba. The two old Rebs had done right well for themselves. Colonel Cay continued to thrive, remembered later as being driven around Jacksonville in a Chrysler Imperial by a black chauffeur. He probably outlived all of his regimental comrades, for he did not die until November 28, 1938, in his ninety-first year. He had the high honor of eulogizing General Felix H. Robertson as "The Last General Officer," *Confederate Veteran,* XXXVI (October, 1928), 365-366.

—Personal communication from
Richard C. Cohan, Hinesville, Georgia;
James D. Birchfield, Tallahassee, Florida;
J. Porter McCall, Sarasota, Florida

Coffin, James P.
Adjutant, Ashby's Brigade

Adjutant Coffin found East Tennessee uncongenial to him after the war, so he moved, first to Memphis, later to Batesville, Arkansas, where he prospered. Having graduated from the University of North Carolina before the war, he was qualified to direct his own affairs; he was active in real estate and insurance, later in banking. A man of strong religious conviction, James Coffin served on the Board of Trustees of Arkansas College and taught a Sunday school class for fifty years. He died near the end of his ninety-first year, on July 8, 1930.

—Personal communication, October 10, 1976, from
Mrs. H. Carter Jeffrey, Batesville, Arkansas.

Cook, Gustave
Lieutenant-Colonel, Eighth Texas Cavalry

Colonel Cook was wounded so many times that his men began to call him "their Yankee lead mine." The most serious wound was received at Bentonville, North Carolina, during the last battle fought by the Army of Tennessee. It was several months after the war before he recovered sufficiently to walk to Alabama, where friends lent him money for transportation. He arrived home in Richmond, Texas, December 1, 1865. Resuming his career as a lawyer, Colonel Cook moved to Houston in 1869. He was elected to the Thirteenth General Assembly of Texas (1873) and afterwards was appointed a judge of the criminal court. In 1892 a wartime chest wound hemorrhaged, forcing him to move to San Marcos, which has a higher altitude. There he lived on Austin Street (now LBJ Drive) until his death, June 27, 1897.

—Frances W. Johnson, *A History of Texas and Texans*
(Chicago: American Historical Society, 1914), ppp. 126-128;
Hays County Historical and Genealogical Society,
IV (June, 1972), 12, 32.

Cosby, George Blake
Brigadier-General, Kentucky Brigade of Cavalry

After Saltville, General Cosby remained in Southwestern Virginia. Although he was a West Pointer, Class of '52, his command was not composed of the most promising material in the Confederate Army, so that his presence in the department was not especially remarkable. After the war, he removed to California, where, on June 29, 1909, at the age of seventy-nine, suffering from old wounds, he killed himself.

—*Generals in Gray*

Cotton, John W.
Private, Tenth Confederate Cavalry

After the surrender, John Cotton, suffering from the measles, was paroled, to walk home in the rain. Since he was a poor farmer with a wife and seven young children, he immediately began the struggle of earning them a living. But his health had been wrecked, and he died in December, 1866, in his thirty-fifth year, at Mount Olive, Coosa County, Alabama.

—Lucille Griffith, *Yours Till Death: Civil War Letters of John W. Cotton.*

Crews, Charles Constantine
Colonel, Second Georgia Cavalry

Although Colonel Crews stayed active in his command for the remainder of the war, he never again attained the prominence that he had possessed at Sunshine Church. He was a physician after the war, in Cuthbert, Georgia.

—William J. Northen, *Men of Mark in Georgia*, II (Atlanta: A. B. Caldwell, 1911), p. 442.

Darsey, Ben W.
Private, Company I, Fifth Georgia Cavalry

Ben Darsey never did get to eat his fresh beef liver. After Colonel Dibrell's camp at Readyville was overrun, Ben and Abbot hid out in the woods for hours. Then, afraid that they would be shot as spies if they were discovered, they surrendered to the first Yanks to come near. After six days in Murfreesboro, they were taken to Camp Chase, just outside of Columbus, Ohio, for the duration of the war. Ben returned then to Bulloch County, Georgia, to a life as a farmer and Methodist preacher. He never made much money as either and wrote his pamphlet, *A War Story*, in 1891, to make a little increment. The result, at ten cents a copy, was not great. By 1900 he had sold his farm in order to pay his debts, retaining only a small house and lot for himself and his invalid wife. He died on March 18, 1921, at Statesboro, Georgia.

—Personal communication, December 6, 1976, from
Edward H. Hahn, Pittsburgh, Pennsylvania;
personal communication from Richard C. Cohan,
Hinesville, Georgia.

Dibrell, George Gibbs
Colonel, Eighth Tennessee Cavalry

Colonel Dibrell was finally given, on January 28, 1865, the brigadiership that had been rumored since the previous summer. At the end he was commanding a division which accompanied the fleeing Confederate government from South Carolina into Georgia. General Dibrell surrendered his command at Washington, Georgia, on May 9, 1865. In his old brigade, now commanded by Colonel William S. McLemore, (Starnes') Fourth Tennessee, Elbert Peacock, the brigade color bearer, decided that the flag would not be given up. One of his comrades, C. L. Nolen, describes what happened to the flag: "Peacock . . . cut it into pieces and divided them among the ten or twelve comrades composing Colonel McLemore's couriers, and also to some of the staff officers. I was given one of the stars from the flag, which I have had framed and placed among my cherished Confederate mementoes."

After the war, General Dibrell thrived as a merchant and banker, railroad operator and coal mine developer. Active in politics, he served as a Representative from Tennessee from 1874 to 1884. He died at home, in Sparta, Tennessee, May 9, 1888.

—Generals in Gray
Biographical Directory of the American Congress.

Duke, Basil Wilson
Brigadier-General, Kentucky Brigade of Cavalry

General Duke commanded the brigade of his dead brother-in-law, John Hunt Morgan, as long as there was anything to fight for; his was one of the brigades that escorted Jefferson Davis. Then he came back to Kentucky and a close friendship with W. C. P. Breckinridge. Unlike Willie Breckinridge, though, Basil Duke seemed not to suffer from an explosive temper or a tendency to rashness. He became a prominent lawyer, legislator, editor, and a writer — his wit and geniality serving him well in all these fields. On September 16, 1916, he died, in his seventy-eighth year.

—Generals in Gray

Echols, John
Brigadier-General

General Echols, who almost brought Champ Ferguson and Felix Robertson to justice, continued as departmental commander until the end of the war. After the war he was an active railroad promoter, occasionally utilizing the services of his wartime colleagues, W. C. P. Breckinridge and Basil Duke. He died at the age of seventy-three, on May 24, 1896.

—Generals in Gray

Ferguson, Champ

With his gang, Champ Ferguson went to Georgia with Robertson's force. There he ran afoul of Colonel Dibrell, who placed him under arrest. The offense must not have been serious, though, for he was soon released.

During the same period, Ferguson's actions at Saltville were being publicized. The party of Saltville prisoners reached Libby Prison, in Richmond, on October 12. It was almost immediately exchanged, for it was among five hundred Yanks exchanged at Cox's Landing, October 17. There the members of the party were interviewed by E. T. Peters, the reporter for the Philadelphia *Inquirer* covering the Army of the James.

His report, appearing in the edition of October 21, was an accurate account of the events both on the field and at Emory and Henry Hospital. It identified Ferguson by name and said that although he had long been a guerrilla, he was now incorporated into the Sixth Tennessee Regiment and regarded as a regular Confederate soldier. It acknowledged that Doctor Murphree and Major Stringfield and other surgeons and attendants were threatened for their resistance to Ferguson. The article was widely reprinted, both in Northern and Southern papers, though the Southern papers cut out the section about the atrocities and sometimes used only the two lead paragraphs:

"Headquarters Army of the James, Oct. 17 — The Rebel flag-of-truce boat William Allison brought down to Cox's Landing this morning about five hundred paroled Union Prisoners, in exchange for a bunch of paroled Rebel prisoners sent up on Saturday. The boat left Richmond about 6 A.M., and reached the landing at about half-past 9.

"A number of men (between thirty and forty I believe) belonging to Burbridge's command, captured at Saltville on the 2nd instant, were among the prisoners who arrived today. One of them, a gentleman of the Teutonic persuasion, gave me his opinion on the result of that expedition in the following somewhat laconic style: 'We gets not mooch salt, dere,' said he, 'but we gets peppered like der tuyfel.'"

The Yanks were not about to forget Ferguson's acts — or dismiss

them as a part of the inescapable cruelty of war, as General Burbridge
indicated to Basil Duke, on February 24, 1865:

"Your information that I propose to hold your command responsible
for the murder of negro soldiers under my command at Saltville in
October, 1864, is incorrect. I have ascertained what troops are responsible for the outrages referred to, and should opportunity occur
I shall hold them to a strict accountability. The murder of Lieutenant
Smith at Emory and Henry Hospitals by Champ Ferguson was one of
the most diabolical acts committed during the war, and I am surprised
at its being passed over without notice by the Confederate authorities.
Should he or any of the band that accompanied him on this occasion
fall into the hands of U. S. forces they will not be treated as prisoners."

As it happened, Confederate authorities were taking notice of
Ferguson. In February, General Echols, commanding in Southwest
Virginia, *vice* Breckinridge, requested that General Wheeler arrest
Ferguson and send him back to Wytheville. There seems to have been
some confusion when Ferguson arrived there, for Colonel Stoddard
Johnston, AAG to Echols, wrote to Wheeler to ask about Ferguson's
status as a Confederate officer, perhaps in an effort to determine
what sort of court, military or civil, in which to arraign him. Wheeler
replied that he regarded Ferguson "as a Captain in the Confederate
service." Such communications took time, though, so that it was soon
March, and the Confederacy was collapsing. General Echols released
Ferguson and restored him to his command.

Although the surrender occurred in Virginia in early April, Ferguson
did not return to Tennessee or seek a parole, for the Federal General
Stoneman reported that, as of April 28, "Champ Ferguson is in command of Southwestern Virginia." By late May he had returned to
Tennessee, for it was stated, on the 24, that his attempt to surrender
had been refused. By June 7, though, the report was that he had been
captured at his home on Calfkiller Creek, twelve miles north of Sparta.
As it turned out, he was not apprehended, but rather turned himself
in, "never dream[ing] of being arrested."

He was, though, and his trial began in July, in Nashville. By August
16, the Nashville *Despatch* opined that the proceedings were half
over. As the witnesses were identified in the press, familiar names

began to appear. General Wheeler courageously appeared as a defense witness — and was attacked in his hotel room by two Tennessee Yanks. But the other witnesses were for the prosecution: George W. Carter, Orange Sells, Harry Shocker, W. W. Stringfield.

Early on, Ferguson "remarked to the guards . . . that he knew he would have no show for his life and he did not care what became of him." Still, there were times when he despaired and hoped: "I believe that there is a God, who governs and rules the universe and that we are all held responsible for our acts in this world. I think, in fact, that the 'Old Man' has been on my side this far in life and I believe he will stay with me, and bring me out of this trouble all right. I have been mighty lucky through life and I always thought that God favored me. I place all my hopes on Him and I don't believe the 'Old Man.' will throw me now." But the conclusion was foregone, for Ferguson admitted some of the acts with which he had been charged. Indeed, he admitted the truth of the very first specification of the second charge, murder, placed against him:

"I acknowledge . . . that I killed Lieutenant Smith in Emory and Henry Hospital. I had a motive in committing the act. He captured a number of my men at different times, and always killed the last one of them. I was instigated to kill him, but I will not say by whom, as I do not wish to criminate my friends. Smith belonged to the 13th Kentucky, and operated around Burkesville. I will say this much — he never insulted my wife or daughter, as reported. He was a relative of my first wife and always treated my family with respect. He is the only man I killed at or near Saltville, and I am not sorry for killing him."

Smith's killing was justified as self-defense: "Yes I killed him but it was to save my own life; Smith had sworn to kill me if he found me. He was wounded and in the hospital. I knew he would get well, and my life wouldn't be safe, so I killed him. Had I been moved by mere cruelty I could have killed others; but I only did what was necessary to protect myself."

On September 19, the *National Intelligencer* reported that the Ferguson trial was over. And a month later, on October 20, life was over for him. Champ met his fate well — the only sign of tension was the sweat that broke out on his brow as his sentence was read. The regiment on duty around the gallows was the Fifteenth United States Colored Infantry — though it is not known whether the assignment was made by a bored adjutant or by an ironic Atropos. Champ's only concern before he was swung was that his body would not be given over to the doctors, and he was assured that his wife, who was there, would immediately receive his body. Then, in his forty-fourth year, his life ended. The body was placed in Mrs. Ferguson's wagon, and she began her trip back to Calfkiller Creek.

> —Thurman Sensing, *Champ Ferguson: Confederate Guerrilla.*

Fletcher, William Andrew
Private, Company E, Eighth Texas Cavalry

Although wounded twice and imprisoned once, William Fletcher survived the war, returning to Beaumont, to pick up his father's carpenter's tools, working at first for $1.50 a day. Hard, steady, honest effort brought him success, though, for in time he accumulated a worth of over a half million dollars, primarily derived from forestry and wood products manufacturing. In his retirement he directed Park Farm, a twenty-two hundred acre tract some ten miles outside of Beaumont. He found the time, too, to write *Rebel Private, Front and Rear,* which was published in 1908. When the news that Captain Fletcher, as he was known, had died, on January 4, 1915, a little short of his seventy-sixth birthday, the Beaumont public schools were dismissed to observe his passing. A delegation of prominent citizens rode out to accompany his body into town to the undertakers: such a ceremony was exactly appropriate for the old cavalryman.

> —Beaumont *Enterprise,* January 6, 1915.

Foard, Jo F.
Major, Eighth Tennessee Cavalry

When General Williams moved his command from Rogersville toward

Saltville, he allowed his guide, Major Foard, to remain with his wife, at her father's home, for a furlough. Perhaps he was still optimistic about recapturing his reluctant scout, Adjutant Allen. In December, 1864, still on furlough, Major Foard was captured; he was a prisoner until the end of the war. Thereafter he prospered as the owner of the Hecla Coal Mines, at Earlington, Kentucky. The response to his "Vivid Prison Experience" from his old comrades cheered his last illness: "many letters came in answer to the article, and they gave the family much pleasure. When conscious he would smile, and seemed to understand some of the messages." Major J. Foard died, December 10, 1913, at the age of seventy-seven.

—Confederate Veteran, XXII (February, 1914), 89.

Fussell, Joseph H.
Second Lieutenant, Company E, First Tennessee Cavalry

Although he was in seventy battles, Lieutenant Fussell only came within a whisker of being wounded — he was shot through the beard at Franklin, December, 1864. He returned to Columbia to practice law, having been graduated in that profession by Jackson College. Lieutenant Fussell was very active in community life. He served as district attorney from 1870 to 1886. He was a lifelong prohibitionist and a force in the Tennessee Prohibitionist Party. He culminated his lengthy service in the Cumberland Presbyterian Church by serving as Moderator in 1910. He died at the age of seventy-nine, on November 4, 1915.

—Confederate Veteran, XXIV (August, 1916), 366.

Giles, Leonidas Banton
Private, Company D, Eighth Texas Cavalry

Leonidas Giles returned to farm life in Travis County, Texas, after the war. In time he became active in Confederate veteran affairs, belonging to both the Laredo and Austin U.C.V. camps. In 1893 he was appointed   immigrant inspector at Laredo. His regimental memoir, *Terry's Texas Rangers,* dedicated to Will Nicholson, his partner during the Tennessee raid, was published in 1911. In his eightieth year, he died on July 11, 1922.

—*Confederate Military History,* XI, pp. 419-420.

Giltner, Henry Liter
Colonel, Fourth Kentucky Cavalry

Colonel Giltner returned to his plantation in Hunter's Bottom, near Carrollton, Kentucky, after the war. He died in Murfreesboro, Tennessee, the summer of 1892.

—*Kentucky Cavaliers in Dixie.*

Graber, Henry W.
Private, Eighth Texas Cavalry

Private Graber returned to Hempstead after the war, to engage first in a small mercantile business and then a plantation. But the war was not through with him, for the plantation was raided by some soldiers stationed nearby. In the ensuing fight two of the soldiers were killed, and Graber and his partner forced to flee Texas until the end of the Reconstruction Period. At that time he returned, gradually to become a leading citizen of the state. He published his *Life Record* in 1916, shortly before his death, February 12, 1917, at the age of seventy-five years.

—*Confederate Veteran,* XXIV (April, 1917), 170.

Grimsley, G. K.
Private, Company C, Eighth Tennessee Cavalry

Despite his crippling, G. K. Grimsley did return to his regiment. He was with the command that provided an escort for the fleeing

Jefferson Davis, and he proudly kept his parole, dated Washington, Georgia, May 9, 1865, all his life. He spent the remainder of that life as a farmer in Oakley, Overton County, Tennessee, where he died in 1907, at the age of seventy-two.

                    —Soldier's Application for Pension, Number 2028;
                    Widow's Application for Pension, Number 1399W2.
                                              State of Tennessee.

Guerrant, Edward Owings
Adjutant, Fourth Kentucky Cavalry

The witty Captain Guerrant revealed a postwar seriousness. He studied medicine, then practiced it, during the years, 1867-1873, in Mount Sterling, Kentucky. In 1868 he went back to Leesburg, Tennessee, to marry the girl who had come to the gate to give a dipper of milk to a Confederate captain on a hot day in 1863. Dr. Guerrant became a seminarian in 1873, studying until 1876, when he became a Presbyterian minister. During the next nine years he served several pastorates, including one in Louisville. In 1885 he founded the American Inland Mission to serve the Appalachian mountain folk whom he had met during the wartime thrust and counterthrust through Southwest Virginia and Eastern Kentucky. He became a powerful revivalist in the Southeast, often visiting with old Confederate comrades on his tours. In 1903 he conducted a ten-day service in Abingdon, with visits to Saltville and other spots remembered from forty years past — his letter to Colonel W. C. P. Breckinridge's Lexington *Observer* must have been a treat for many an old Kentucky cavalryman. The reverend Dr. Guerrant died in 1916, at the age of seventy-eight.

                    —Guerrant Papers, University of Kentucky.

Guild, George B.
Adjutant, Fourth Tennessee Cavalry

Adjutant Guild became a successful lawyer in Nashville after the war. From time to time he was called upon for political responsibilities. He was a member of the Thirty-Seventh General Assembly of Tennessee, 1871-1873, and he served as Mayor of Nashville, 1892-1895. He was also active on the State Pensions Board. Like his old leader, Joe Wheeler, Guild put on the blue uniform for the Spanish-American War; he was commissioned a major in the Army Paymaster Department. Death came in his eighty-third year, on April 21, 1917.
—*Biographical Register of the General assembly of the State of Tennessee.*

Hagan, James.
Colonel, Third Alabama Cavalry

The Hagens had established businesses in both Mobile and New Orleans and plantations in Louisiana and Mississippi, since their arrival in the South about 1800. Colonel Hagan spent his postwar years managing the family estate.
—*History of Alabama,* III, 719.

Hannon, Moses Wright
Colonel, Fifty-Third Alabama Cavalry

Colonel Hannon got the drove of fifteen hundred cattle back to Confederate lines, then remained around Atlanta while Wheeler's Raid continued. When Sherman began his march to the sea, Hannon's Brigade was a part of the small force that attempted to keep the swath as narrow as possible. After the war, Hannon became a merchant in Montgomery, then practiced the same occupation in New Orleans, and later became a farmer in Freestone County, Texas.
—Thoms M. Owen, *History of Alabama*
(Chicago: S. J. Clarke, 1921), pp. 740-741.

Hargis, Othinel Pope
Private, Company I, First Georgia Cavalry

Although O. P. Hargis survived the war, there must have been times in his later years when he reflected upon his complete subjugation by the Yankees. He became a guide at the Cyclorama, in Grant Park, Atlanta, when it opened in 1898. That huge panorama of the Battle of Atlanta had been created by a crew of German painters and erected by a crew from Milwaukee.

—Lucille Cuyrus, *History of Bartow County*
(n.p.: Tribune Publishing Company, 1933), p. 63.

Harrison, Thomas
Colonel, Eighth Texas Cavalry

Perhaps no one in the Confederate Army more deserved a brigadiership than Harrison, who received his rank the last spring of the war, to date from January 14, 1865. With the surrender, he returned to Waco and the profession of law. Later he was elected a district judge. Esteemed by all who knew him, he died in Waco, July 14, 1891, at the age of sixty-seven.

—*Generals in Gray.*

Hendrix, W. W.
Chaplain, Fourth Tennessee Cavalry (Anderson's)

Chaplain Hendrix returned to College Grove, to minister to the Cumberland Presbyterian Church there. As the years went by, his fame as a revivalist grew, recalling the success that he and Chaplain Bunting had had in those long past cavalry camps. For several years he labored as a home missionary in Cincinnati. Then he was called to serve as the seventh president of Bethel College, McKenzie, Tennessee. Although he had not had the opportunity for formal education, having gained his theology in the saddle as a circuit rider, he became a student of the Book highly admired by his colleagues. His last pastorate was in Franklin, but he was forced by ill health to resign that position on January 1, 1893. Although his health did not improve, his death, on August 16, was sudden, probably as the result of a heart attack. Chaplain Hendrix was just into his seventy-second year. There was a very large assembly for the funeral at his home, on August 18, from which he was taken to his rest. The pall-bearers, all members of his regiment, included Adjutant George B. Guild, then Mayor of Nashville, and Colonel Baxter Smith, who had been commander of the regiment until his wounding caused his succession by Old Paul Anderson.

—Nashville *Daily American,* August 17, 18, 1893;
Nashville *Banner,* August 16, 17, 1893;
Cumberland Presbyterian, LII (August 24, 1893), 4.

Hill, John W.
Sergeant, Company D, Eighth Texas Cavalry

After the Tennessee raid, Sergeant Hill seemed to realize that he couldn't hope to survive many more such dangers. His letters home convey an unspoken desire for peace; he wrote his sister, Mary Scott Hill, on October 29, 1864: "Bro Tom left the Regt in North Ala And as we have not heard a word from him sinse I supose that He has gone to Texas. Tell him iff he is there that I Did not think he would go off without letting me know where he was going. We have made aplication for furlows for the whole Regt to go home this winter. I do not have mutch hopes of ever getting to Texas untill the war is over which I am affraid will bee a long time from present prospects. Iff we do get off I want you to have plenty to eat. And tell all the young Ladies to look out for the Boyes all say they are goiing to marry that is of course iff they can get the Girls consent. Scott I heard that there was a young Conscript going to see you. Have you lost all your patriotism Send him off to the war and tell him to wait untill the war is over For I could not give a cent for a man that would not serve his country. I also heard that Bro Mid wanted to go into service. Tell him for me that He had better stay at home and go to school and trye to improve his time the best he can untill He getes a year or two older. As the most of Boyes of his age do not stand the service like older men. . .'." Somehow Sergeant Hill toughed it out to the end, watching the company that he had recruited to one hundred sixty dwindle away to about thirty at its surrender. After the war, Hill prospered in milling, farming, and finally store keeping, in Smithville. Eventually he created a ranch of 2,300 acres, three hundred of which were cultivated. He died the day after Christmas, 1928, twenty-three days after his ninety-second birthday.

—Personal communication, October 29, 1976, from
Ms Linnet Shade, Librarian, Smithville, Texas;
Reminiscences of the Boys in Gray, p. 334.

Hobson, Anson W.
Colonel, Third Arkansas Cavalry

Will Nicholson was wrong in his letter when he wrote that Colonel Hobson had lost an arm at Franklin. The Arkansan may have been wounded, but if so the wound wasn't sufficient to keep him from riding. For a few days later, when the command forded the Tennessee, Hobson's horse fell, breaking his rider's leg. The fracture never did heal properly and may account for Hobson's postwar nickname, "Legs." After the war, Colonel Hobson, who was a physician, became a newspaper publisher in Camden. In 1866 he was elected to the House of Representatives, but was denied his seat. Thereafter he edited a succession on newspapers. In addition, he served one term in the state legislature, 1878-1880. He died in Washington, Arkansas, February 9, 1882, in about his fifty-seventh year.

—Personal communication, January 3, 1977, from
R. P. Baker, Archivist,
Arkansas Historical Commission, Research Project, 77-004

Holman, Daniel Wilson
Colonel, Eleventh Tennessee Cavalry

After the war, Colonel Holman returned to Fayetteville, Tennessee,
where in time he formed a partnership in law with his brother, Colonel
James H. Holman. That firm continues within the Holman family.
Daniel W. Holman died September 22, 1885, at the age of fifty-two,
from the effect of typhoid.

—Personal communication, Janury 15, 1977,
from Hubert T. Holman, Fayetteville, Tennessee.

Humes, William Young Conn
Brigadier-General, Division of Cavalry

Remaining one of Wheeler's most dependable lieutenants, General
Humes fought on through the Carolina campaign. With peace he resumed his career as a lawyer in Memphis. He died at the age of fifty-
two, on September 11, 1882.

—*Generals in Gray.*

Hunter, Hy
Captain, Company K, Eighth Texas Cavalry

Although he led the charge at McMillan's Ford without getting a
scratch, Captain Hunter was not so lucky at Farmington, one of the
skirmishes during the retreat toward the Tennessee River. There he
was fatally wounded, apparently. No one in the regiment really remembered, so that John M. Claiborne could offer only the most ten-
tative statement about him, when he created the roll for the Rangers'
Reunion, February 20, 1882, in Galveston. Thus Captain Hunter
suffered the soldier's second death — his surviving comrades could
not properly celebrate him.

—Ranger Reunion Papers, University of Texas.

Ingram, August John
Major, Twelfth Alabama Cavalry Battalion

Somehow Major Ingram's crushed leg healed, and he returned to his home in Murphree's Valley, Blount County, Alabama, after the war. There he prospered in real estate and by 1888 had founded the Ingram Land Company. His firm sponsored the settlement of Oneonta in 1891, and it was only fitting that Major Ingram served as Mayor before his death, March 15, 1901, at the age of seventy-one.

—*The Heritage of Blount County*
(Blount County [Alabama] Historical Society, 1972).

Iverson, Alfred
Brigadier-General, Georgia Brigade of Cavalry

After the war's end, General Iverson pursued a career in business, eventually becoming an orange grower in Kissimee, Florida, where he died on March 31, 1911, in his eighty-second year.

—*Generals in Gray*

Jackson, Alfred Eugene "Mudwall"
Brigadier-General

General Jackson, a generation older than the generals with whom he served, was placed on light duty soon after Saltville. He was, nevertheless, active in the defense of Saltville, when it was captured in December of 1864. After the war, he was for a time in jail at Wytheville, and then reduced to framing rented land in Washington County, Virginia. Having been a wealthy man before the war, he was subjected to suits to the amount of $390,000.00 by East Tennessee Unionists and also indicted for treason in both state and federal courts. It was ten years before he had cleared himself of postwar harassment. Never a very dynamic leader, he seems nevertheless to have had his special qualities; Jefferson Davis said of him, in 1873: "when we have chopping to do iron is better than gold." He died on October 30, 1889, in his eighty-third year, at Jonesboro, Tennessee.

—William S. Speer, *Sketches of Prominent Tennesseans*
(Nashville: Albert B. Tavel, 1888), pp. 509-511;
Generals in Gray.

Jordan, Stephen H.
Private, Company D, Ninth Tennessee Cavalry

At the age of forty-two, Stephen Jordan must have felt that he was getting a little old for war, anyhow. But he hung on to the end and got his parole, May 10, 1865, at Washington, Georgia. Then he went home to Carter's Creek, Maury County, Tennessee, and remained there, as far as history knows, until his death, February 2, 1893, in his sixty-ninth year.

—United Confederate Veterans, Tennessee Division, Bivouac Records.
State Library and Archives, Manuscripts Section;
personal communication, November 12, 1976, from
Ms Margaret Sparks, Spring Hill, Tennessee.

Kyle, Ferg
Captain, Company D, Eighth Texas Cavalry

Soon after he visited the wounded Walter Caldwell, Captain Kyle left his company (and his four younger brothers who were in it) for Texas, where he was to round up deserters. He was at this task when the war ended. Captain Kyle then engaged in farming and stock raising, moving in 1867 to Hays County, where a town grew up around his settlement. In 1882 the town was named Kyle in his honor. He was active in politics, being elected to the Twelfth General Assembly and serving as the Sergeant-at-Arms of the Seventeenth and Eighteenth General Assemblies. He was later elected to the General Assembly twice more and died in 1906, at the age of seventy-four, while campaigning for another term.

—Thomas Fletcher Harwell, *Eighty Years Under the Stars and Bars* (Kyle, Texas, 1947), p. 54.

Lewis, James Henry
Lieutenant-Colonel, First Tennessee Cavalry

After the war Colonel Lewis engaged in the practice of law in Lewisburg, Tennessee. He was sufficiently regarded by his fellow Tennessee Democrats to be chosen a presidential elector in 1872. In 1895 he removed to Birmingham, Alabama.

Lewis, Thomas W.
Major, Second Kentucky Cavalry

Major Lewis became prominent as a wealthy farmer in Stewart County, Tennessee, after the war. He died there, June 27, 1915, in his seventy-fourth year.

—Whitson, *Personal Sketches*

McKenzie, George Washington
Colonel, Fifth Tennessee Cavalry

Crusty old Colonel McKenzie survived the war, to return to Meigs County, where he farmed and kept store. He died peacefully, in September, 1906, in his eighty-eighth year.

—Stewart Lilliard, *Meigs County.*

McLemore, William S.
Colonel, Fourth Tennessee Cavalry

Colonel McLemore returned to Franklin, Tennessee, and to the practice of law. In his later years he was Judge of the Circuit Court. He died on August 7, 1908, in his seventy-eighth year.

> —Personal communication, January 14, 1977, from
> Mrs. Joe Bowman, Williamson County Historian.

Martin, William Thompson
Major-General

General Martin's military career never recovered after he was arrested by General Wheeler. Sent to command the District of Northwest Mississippi, he spent the last months of the war in a backwater. Then he entered into a feverish postwar career. He was a lawyer in Natchez, but served twelve years in the Mississippi senate, as well. He was a delegate to every postwar Democratic convention through 1880. During the same years he founded the Natchez, Jackson, and Columbus Railroad. Yet he had the time to act as a trustee of the University of Mississippi and of Jefferson College, Washington, Mississippi. He died on March 16, 1910, shortly before his eighty-seventh birthday.

> —Generals in Gray;
> Personal communication, December 9, 1974, and April 3, 1975,
> from Everette Truly, Natchez, Mississippi;
> personal communication from
> Mrs. Will C. Martin, Baton Rouge, Louisiana.

Miller, George Knox
Captain, Eighth Confederate Cavalry

Before the war Captain Miller had graduated from the University of Virginia and had been enrolled in the Department of Law. After the war he resumed his study of law. Returning to Talladega, he entered its civil life with zeal; he was Register of chancery Court from 1868 to 1884 and Mayor from 1874 to 1884, with the exception of one year. In 1884 he was appointed Judge of Probate Court. During his idle hours he corresponded with old Confederate comrades and wrote regimental sketches that were considerably less skeptical about Joe Wheeler than his wartime letters to his wife. Judge Miller died in 1916, at the age of eighty.

—*Nothern Alabama, Historical and Biographical* (Birmingham: Smith and Deland, 1888), p. 456.

Mims, Aaron Lemuel
Captain, Company E, Fifth Tennessee Cavalry

Captains Mims and Mullendore never were able to return their men to Wheeler's command. Adjutant W. G. Allen indicated that they were still absent, on January 10, 1865, when he, finally safe from General Williams, had the time to make out a quarterly report for the regiment: "Three companies and Seven Officers (7 Officers and 17 Enlisted men) was Sent on a Scout by order of Genl Humes Aug 23ᵈ 1864 — Said companies was cut off and unable to rejoin there Regt. have since that time been on duty in East Tenn by order of Brigadier Genl J C Vaughn."

Captain Mims had studied at East Tennesse University, in Knoxville, before the war and had spent five years at Emory and Henry College as a student and instructor. He was able, then, to assume a career as a school teacher, when the war was over. It was a good thing, for he had heavy family responsibilities. He took care of his mother, until her death at the age of ninety-two. And during the war, his brother Jervis, living in Morristown, Tennessee, had been mistaken for his Confederate brother by Union partisans, who killed him. Assuming the responsibility for the loss, Captain Mims took care of his dead brother's family all of his life. He never married.

Becoming Principal of Edgefield Academy, near Nashville, in 1866, Captain Mims held that position for twelve years. He then became a farmer near Antioch and engaged in politics, rising to the position of state president of the Farmers' Alliance. At first he advised Populists to support the Democratic presidential candidate, saying, "Conservative but determined forces at the helm are both the safest and the best." He could accept Democrats, he said, if they wanted "the citizen, not the dollar /to/ rule in this country." By 1893, though, disillusioned with Democratic conservatism, Mims spoke out for a graduated property tax, governmental housing projects for the poor, free coinage of silver. To the Populist faithful, he became so highly regarded that in 1894 he was nominated their candidate for governor by acclamation. Captain Mims had no better success with the wealthy than he had had with the Yankees, so he retired to his farm, where he lived until 1909. Then he was taken into the home of a niece, where he died in 1913, at the age of seventy-nine.

—Ruth Webb Odell, *Over the Misty Blue Hills: The Story of Cocke County* (1950), p. 119;
Roger O. Hart, *Redeemers, Bourbons and Populists* (Baton Rouge: Louisiana State University Press, 1975), p. 208.

Minor, John
Major, Tenth Tennessee Cavalry

Major Minor returned to Sailor's Rest, the large estate on the Cumberland River owned by his mother's relatives, the Wests. In time he married and fathered a family of five children. He was active in the iron industry, farming, and merchandising.

—Personal communication, January 10, 1977, from
Mrs. Ursula S. Beach, author of *Along the Warioto,*
A History of Montgomery County (Nashville: McQuiddy Press, 1964).

Morgan, David Boston, II
Private, Company I, Fifth Georgia Cavalry

Dave Morgan recovered from his fall out of the saddle on August 10, 1864. Since his command had gone on the raid, he was assigned to work in supply until it returned. Hearing that the Fifth Georgia was coming back, Private Morgan left to meet it: ". . . about sundown of the second day, I was waiting by the roadside as they marched along and spying my old company coming at a gallop I raised my hand and Lieut Brewer in command recognized me, and it was the meeting of long parted brothers which in fact it was, he yelled to me Dave there is a lead horse behind without either saddle or bridle take him and follow us as best you can. . . ." He must have found out then about Ben Darsey and his other comrades who were missing from his company. Like so many other privates, Dave achieved rank in the United Confederate Veterans by outliving most everybody. In time he became the Commander of the Georgia Division; he died in Savannah, May 10, 1926, in his eightieth year.

—David B. Morgan Papers, State Archives of Georgia;
Atlanta *Constitution*, May 11, 1926.

Mosgrove, George Dallas
Private, Fourth Kentucky Cavalry

Private Mosgrove, Adjutant Guerrant's clerk, went home to Kentucky after the war. There he became a school teacher, a kind and decent man, never successful, but fondly thought of by his wartime comrades. With the aid of his captain's diary and conversations with other survivors, Mosgrove published *Kentucky Cavaliers in Dixie* in 1895. He never was able to overcome a disposition to drink too much. On the night of February 21, 1907, he left some friends in Carrollton, Kentucky, to walk the six miles home to Locust Grove. He was found on the road the next morning, dead in his sixty-first year.

—Introduction to *Kentucky Cavaliers in Dixie.*

Mullendore, William Wallace
Captain, Company H, Fifth Tennessee Cavalry

Like Captain Mims, Captain Mullendore fought under General Vaughn during the last months of the war. Afterwards, he practiced law in Alabama and in Sevierville, Tennessee. He was highly regarded, and was spoken of as a candidate for governor, "but," in the words of a relative, "he would at times take too much whiskey. . . ." He died in his sixty-fifth year, on November 29, 1899, and is buried in Shiloh Cemetery, near Sevierville.

—Personal communication, January 10, 1977, from Miss Adah Mullendore, Sevierville, Tennessee.

Nicholson, William
Private, Company D, Eighth Texas Cavalry

When Will Nicholson's time came, he didn't get the four young ladies and a piano that Walter Caldwell was enjoying. A letter dated October 19, 1864, reached Will's Texas relatives:

"Henry Crocheron, Esq.

"My Dear Sir —

"I have just received a letter from my brother informing me of the death of your nephew, William Nicholson.

"He was killed in Coosaville, Ga., and there decently buried by his friends. I am not informed of the date of his decease. His arm was broken by a ball which entered his breast killing him almost instantly.

"You, Sir, and your family have my warmest sympathies. No one in that regiment was more highly esteemed for all those good and noble qualities that constitute the soldier and the Gentleman than Billy, and his untimely death is to be deplored, not only on account of the deep sorrow and grief that will thereby occasion his relatives and friends, but in his fate the country has lost a soldier and citizen of the most faultless character in every respect. Brave in battle, prompt to discharge his duties, however dangerous and laborious they might be; kind and attentive to his comrades in their sickness and misfortune. Billy was beloved by all and his death is regretted by all.

"I again assure you of my deepest sympathy and with you, your Lady, his sisters, and other relatives in their, your great bereavement. And as soon as the Campaign ends, will use every effort to procure his effects and should I succeed will hold them in careful keeping until they can be forwarded you by a safe opportunity.

"I am, Sir

"With much respect

"Your friend and Obt. Servant,

"Joseph D. Sayers"

Will Nicholson was twenty-five years old at the time of his death.

—James Nicholson Papers, University of Texas Library.

Pitts, J. F.

Private, Company F, Ninth Tennessee Cavalry

Private Pitts survived the fight that cost General Kelly his life and the remainder of the war. Then he returned to Hardin County, Tennessee, to resume the life of a farmer. He died on April 26, 1894, at the age of seventy-one, and was buried in Montague Cemetery, among his wife's people.

—Personal communication from
Charles D. Gallaher, President, Wayne County Historical Society.

Prather, John Smith

Lieutenant-Colonel, Eighth Confederate Cavalry

Colonel Prather settled in the ashes of Atlanta after the war. Having had prewar experience as a newspaper publisher in Chambers County, Alabama, he established the *Daily New Era,* which he used as a Democratic voice from 1865 to 1870. Thereafter he was employed by printing companies until his death. A charter member of Wheeler Camp, UCV, and Fulton County Confederate Veterans, he had been at work on a poem to present at the next meeting of Wheeler Camp, when death intervened, March 12, 1920, in his eighty-sixth year.

—Atlanta *Constitution,* March 13, 14, 1920;
Death Certificate, Number 8458-20, State of Georgia;
personal communication, January 6, 1977, from
Miss Nell Orr, La Fayette, Alabama.

Preston, Robert Taylor
Colonel, Preston's Battalion of Virginia Reserves

Colonel Preston returned home to Smithfield, there to curse and chew tobacco and cherish his wife, until his death in 1880, in his seventieth year.

> —Personal communication, June 6, 1973, from Mrs. Reginald A. Kenney, Blacksburg, Virginia.

Pridemore, Auburn Lorenzo
Colonel, Sixty-Fourth Virginia Cavalry

Although his regiment did not have a great deal of potential, Colonel Pridemore served creditably until the end of the war. Having had a meager education as a youth, he studied law and was admitted to the bar in 1867, at the age of thirty. Active in politics, he was a member of the Virginia senate, 1871-1875, and a Democratic representative to the United States House for the Forty-Fifth Congress, 1877-1879. He then resumed his practice in Jonesville, Lee County, Virginia, where he died, May 17, 1900, at the age of sixty-two.

> —*Biographical Directory of the American Congress.*

Reagan, Alvin Alexander
Lieutenant, Company C, Eighth Tennessee Cavalry

Lieutenant Reagan was a patient at Emory Hospital for a month. His wound healed quickly enough, but he caught erysipelas and chronic diarrhea in the ward and nearly died. Rejoining his command for the Carolina campaign, he was captured, March 16, 1865, at Averysboro, North Carolina. The Yankees sent him to Johnson's Island, from which he was released, June 17, 1865. Then he returned to Cookeville, Tennessee, to live his life. In his later years he was the proprietor of Hotel Richelieu there. In 1908, at the age of sixty-four, he admitted, "Naturally a man of my age and undergone what I did in the sixties will feel

like he is about knocked out of the box." Finally his feebleness caused
him to sell the hotel and buy a home on Dixie Avenue, where he
died on December 31, 1917, in his seventy-fifth year.

—Soldier's Application for Pension, Number 10008;
Widow's Application for Pension, Number 1929. State of Tennessee;
personal communication, January 17, 1977, from
Mrs. Jesse T. Heard, Putnam County Historian.

Reese, Warren Stone
Colonel, Twelfth Alabama Cavalry Battalion

Colonel Reese returned to Montgomery, Alabama, after the war
and became a successful farmer. Later, from 1885 to 1889, he served
as mayor of Montgomery; he was also active in sportsmen and veteran
affairs. In 1896 he was a candidate on the fusion ticket for the United
States Senate, but he was defeated by another Alabama cavalryman,
General John T. Morgan. Colonel Reese died in Montgomery, December 16, 1897, early in his fifty-sixth year.

—*National Cyclopedia of American Biography*, X, 455.

Reeve, George R.
Colonel, Eleventh Texas Cavalry

Colonel Reeve stayed until the end in Carolina and then returned
home to Grayson County, Texas. He had been a member of the state
legislature before the war, and he was reelected afterwards. He was
serving as Speaker of the House when he died, September 5, 1882,
at the age of fifty-six. Reeve County, in West Texas, was named
in his honor.

Harold B. Simpson, ed., *Texas in the War*
(originally compiled by Marcus Wright)
(Hillsboro, Texas: Hill Junior College, 1965), p. 115.

Renfrew, Henry Clay
Private, Company E, Second Kentucky Cavalry

Private Renfrew followed his new commander, General Basil Duke, who was appointed to the position formerly held by the dead John Morgan. Thus Renfrew wound up as a part of the escort cavalry for the Davis party. When the surrender came, Renfrew, unlike his close friend Dallas Mosgrove, decided not to return to Kentucky. Rather, he took the regimental colors, hid them under his clothing, and left for the southwest. He crossed into Mexico, gradually drifted down the west coast of South America. In time, 1875 or so, he landed in the Navigator Islands (now the Samoas), where he settled "on an island about five miles long and three miles wide," with a native fisherman as a friend. His possessions were few: He had the diary that he had kept during the war, an ambrotype of "a little girl about five years old, marked, in faded letters, 'Lela Giltner the daughter of the regiment,' probably Henry Giltner's daughter, and the Confederate flag, which he always flew in front of his island home. About 1900 he died and was buried by his friend, who faithfully kept Renfrew's few possessions and flew the Confederate flag from his own fishing boat. It was seen there by Captain Martin Schuyler, Company C, Seventh Ohio Cavalry, who was returning to the United States after serving in the Philippines during the Spanish-American War. Captain Schuyler, astonished by the sight of the flag that he had fought so often over three decades before, got the native to tell him its story, show him Renfrew's estate, and take him to Renfrew's grave, "situated on a rocky headland of the island, overlooking the sea. The body lies with the feet to the east, and the grave is marked with substantial stones at both the head and the foot, and the grave is kept in most excellent order. . . ." But that description was made about 1900; it is unlikely that any trace remains of Henry Clay Renfrew — a recent inquiry about him elicited this reply from Ms Hannis S. Smith, Supervisor of Library Services, Library of American Samoa: "The island which most nearly corresponds to your description is Taū in the Manu'a group in American Samoa. We will inquire of people there to see if his personal effects are still in existence, and let you know if we learn anything.

"Since 1900, there have been several severe storms, one of which virtually destroyed everything man-made on Taū, including personal effects. The likelihood of the survival of a diary is remote."
—Theodore F. Allen, "The Lost Flag of the Confederacy," *Trotwood's Magazine,* II (July, 1906), 556-559; personal communication, August 25, 1976, from Ms Hannis S. Smith.

Robertson, Felix Huston
Brigadier-General, Confederate Brigade of Cavalry

General Robertson took Williams' men from Saltville down to Carter's Station, below Bristol. There he wired Richmond, seeking permission to rejoin General Wheeler by way of Cleveland, Tennessee, and Dalton, Georgia. The War Department denied his request and ordered him to cross the mountains, by way of Asheville. At the same time General Vaughn requested Robertson's help in a move against the Yanks still fronting him. Robertson refused, saying that he had orders to report to General Hood and replying, further, that he had been relieved of duty in the department by General Breckinridge. Indeed, Robertson not only failed to be a positive force, but proved a negative force; Vaughn soon telegraphed Breckinridge: "I regret to say that General Robertson, commanding Williams' force, has positively refused to co-operate or lend me any aid whatever, and the sooner they are ordered from the department the better, as they are straggling all over the country, destroying a large quantity of supplies and forage around Jonesborough, in my rear." When he arrived in Georgia, Robertson turned the command over to General Anderson, who had recovered from the wound he had received at Newnan. Then he became Chief of Staff for his patron, General Wheeler.

Thus Robertson escaped the supervision of General Breckinridge. Who was to blame? Perhaps no *person,* perhaps that most modern of phenomena, the system of paperwork that clogs up human performance like fat in the arteries. Perhaps Breckinridge did not want just anybody reading his allegation, if he sent it over the telegraph; perhaps he was afraid that if the communication went through the telegraph office in Richmond, it might be seen and pulled from the traffic by General Bragg, Robertson's most influential patron. Whatever the reason, he mailed his charges to General Lee, who, whatever the date he received them, did not reply until October 21. But General Lee reacted with decisiveness when he did reply, a decisiveness that would argue a promptness, as well. The culprit, then, may have been — simply — the Confederate postal system. Colonel Charles Marshall, ADC, wrote:

"General Lee directs me to acknowledge the receipt of your letter of the 5th instant, and to repeat the gratification the handsome success at Saltville afforded him, and his satisfaction with the arrangements and dispositions made by you. He hopes your efforts to promote the efficiency of the troops in your department will be soon attended with the success they deserve.

He is much pained to hear of the treatment the negro prisoners are reported to have received, and agrees with you in entirely condemning it. That a general officer should have been guilty of the crime you mention meets with his unqualified reprobation. He directs that if the officer is still in your department you prefer charges against him and bring him to trial. Should he have left your department you will forward the charges to be transmitted to the Department, in order that such action may be taken as the case calls for.

"Very respectfully, your obedient servant,"

By October 21, though, Robertson was out of the department and, within a few days, back into action. The next sizeable encounter was at Waynesboro, as Wheeler endeavored to frustrate Kilpatrick's cavalry, which hoped to raid Augusta. Years later, Robertson recalled his participation in that action: "During the night at Waynesboro Wheeler directed me to take command of the advance guard, and force Kilpatrick to a fight. From daylight, we crowded Kilpatrick, and at Buckhead Creek, forced him to a halt and to form line of battle across the road, which line I promptly charged with such soldiers as I could assemble from the skirmish line; we broke the line, and went with it through the swamp of Buckhead Creek, pell mell. As I rode into the column, with my revolver in hand, I looked for some insignia of rank, with the purpose of bestowing my attention upon the highest officer then present. Kilpatrick passed within five feet of me, but had his back to me, was wearing a blouse, and no insignia of rank whatever, exposed to view. I did not shoot him, but turned my attention to a lieutenant, who seemed to be in command. I fired at him with, I supposed, fatal effect. I spurred my horse and passed him, but in a little while he came whipping by me, and when I gave attention to him again, he called out that he had surrendered, but continued to whip his horse, in the vain hope to ride by me. I stuck my pistol in his face, felt the muzzle touch something, and fired. He did not fall off as I expected, but I leaned over and pushed him off his horse, into the water. I then continued to fire, until I had emptied my pistol, and then drew my sabre, and began some sabre practice. Although my sabre had been well ground a few days before, the long gallop had dulled its edge against the mettle scabbard; and I found it impossible to force the point through the Yankee jackets while the wearers were travelling the same direction in which I rode. I then endeavored to thrust the sabre into the exposed part of the neck, and I succeeded very well, in that way, in doing some execution. As soon as I would finish disposing, with my sabre, of one man, I would spur my horse forward and reach another. This process had continued a little while, but unfortunately, my sabre strokes made no noise, and some Yankee on my left gathered sufficient presence of mind to shoot me. The bullet struck me in the left elbow, and carried away pieces from two bones and left me useless for further fighting. When I felt the shot, I raised myself in my stirrups for the purpose of cutting down the man who had shot me, and delivered with my full force a swinging blow on the head of my adversary. So great was the force of my blow that my stirrup leather broke, and I was about to fall to the ground; but caught, with my right heel, on the cantle of my saddle, and succeeded in regaining my upright position. By this time my horse was in full gallop, carrying me along with my fleeing enemies, my left hand useless and my sabre in my right hand; but by taking the reins of my bridle in my teeth, I was enabled to get a fresh hold with my right hand, bring my horse to a stop, and as soon as the rush of fugitives had passed by, I turned and rode to the rear."

Later on in the same letter, for he was writing to Captain George Knox Miller, in 1895, he confided, "When I look back on our experience in the army, I am glad to say that I have, to a great extent, lost the memory of the things that were most disagreeable in that life." Perhaps the lapse of memory included the part of the Buckhead Creek affair that George Guild remembered:

"After this we came up with Kilpatrick at Waynesboro, Ga. It was a dense, foggy morning, so much so that you could hardly discern the form of a man fifty feet ahead. We at once attacked them in a large field near the town in a very mixed-up fight, in which we killed and wounded many and took many prisoners, losing quite a number ourselves. In the midst of the battle, with balls whizzing in every direction, I came across a squad of our men who had taken as prisoners four of the enemy. They were threatening to kill them, when I remonstrated and told them to turn them over to the rear guard near by. Just then an officer of higher rank rode up. I appealed to him, telling that the soldiers proposed killing them. His only reply was: 'They know best what to do with them.' As I rode off into the fight, I heard the popping of the pistols, and I could see the prisoners tumbling over into the high sage. I had not proceeded far when I noticed this officer reel from his saddle with a shot in his arm. I could not help saying to myself: 'I wish it had been your head shot off.' It would be proper here to say that many most outrageous transactions were done by the Federals as they passed through Waynesboro, and these were told to the men. It was enough to excite to vengeance; but nothing can excuse the killing of prisoners after capture, as was done in this case."

Guild hints at the identity of the officer, but a reader of his book named him. In the copy of *A Brief Narrative of the Fourth Tennessee Cavalry Regiment* possessed by the Virginia State Library, the statement "an officer of higher rank rode up" is preceded by an *x* and underlined. At the bottom of the page (107) there is the statement "X Gen. _____ Robertson of Tex." in handwriting. The hand is the same as that which dated and signed the book inside the front cover: "May 22/13 Thos. E. Matthews."

The surgeons were able to save Robertson's arm, though the damage to the elbow permanently destroyed his use of it. He spent the next few months in the home of Mrs. William Eve, in Augusta, recovering from the operation. Meanwhile, he had not been forgotten in Virginia. General Lee had been confirmed as General in Chief of the Armies of the Confederate States, so that his authority was no longer restricted to his own department. General Bragg had lost his position of influence with President Davis. And on February 4, 1865, John C. Breckinridge was appointed Secretary of War.

Then Breckinridge could set in motion his attempt to bring Robertson to justice. (After I had finished the narrative of my book, William C. Davis very kindly sent me this additional piece of evidence that he had located in the General Sam Jones Papers, Record Group 109, National Archive.) On November 27, Breckinridge had ordered the Post Commander at Saltville, Colonel Robert Smith, to locate any witnesses among the militia who had seen Robertson kill a negro or who had heard him order others to kill. The order is docketed with information that Robertson ordered others to kill, but contains no proof that he killed a negro, himself. The docketed material is not dated, but presumably Smith's response was very quick. There may have been additional information, which was lost or which was misfiled, as this piece was. At any rate, this move by Breckinridge found by William Davis falls into the pattern of events that followed Robertson's behavior at Saltville.

On February 22, General John Echols, commanding the Department of Western Virginia and Eastern Tennessee, addressed the following letter to General Samuel Cooper, Adjutant and Inspector General:

"I have received the order of the Hon. Secretary of War directing that a Court of Inquiry be convened to investigate certain charges informally preferred against Brig. Gen. F. H. Robertson touching his conduct at Saltville on October 3, 1865 ④.

"As Brig. Gen. Robertson is not serving in this Dept, comd'g a Brigade in Wheeler's Corps of Cavalry I have the honor to request that he be directed to attend the sittings of the Court ordered to convene March 15th at Wytheville."

Once again the system creaked into motion. On Echols' letter is the endorsement, dated March 3, from Colonel Palfrey to Colonel Withers, both AAG's: "F. H. Robertson was appt^d Brig. Genl. but the appm't having been rejected by the Senate on the 22^d Feby/65 he ceased to be an officer of the P.A.C.S. on that day, as none of the other appmts held by him had been confirmed. He is however a 2' Lieut in the C.S.A." There apparently had existed a hostility to Robertson in the Senate for quite a while, perhaps because it was known that he was an errand boy for Braxton Bragg. Even so, a special coincidence seems to occur between the date of Echols' request and the rejection of Robertson by the Senate.

On March 7, A Special Order was issued by the Adjutant and Inspector General's Office: "Second Lieutenant F. H. Robertson, C.S. Army, will report without delay to Brigadier-General John Echols, commanding, &c., Wytheville, Va., that he may attend the sittings of a court of inquiry to be held at that place on the 15th day of March, 1865."

Whether or not Robertson ever received the order is not known. But he continued to exercise command as a general officer, leading a detachment of cavalry in the defense of Macon against Wilson's Raid, late in April. And he signed his parole as a Brigadier.

Then, late in the summer, he took his wife and went home to Texas. He maintained his attitude toward blacks and, much later, supported the Klan. At the same time, he began the practice of law, ultimately in Waco, where for many years he was the dean of the bar. He was very prominent in veteran activities, and there was much sadness when he died on April 20, 1928, a little over eighty-nine years old, the last of the Confederate generals.

—Generals in Gray.

Rogers, Benjamin Duggan
Private, Company B, Fourth Tennessee Cavalry

Ben survived his wounding at Saltville, living to provide the best account of life at Emory Hospital during the last months of the war: "Remained at Emory & Henry until about March 15th, 1865, was sent to Montgomery White Sulphur Springs, was beginning to go about on crutches. Winter had been very severe, snow 18 to 30 inches for several weeks. During this period Stoneman had cut the railroad east, burned the bridges and destroyed the saltworks. Surgeons and nurses kind and attentive, but they had no supplies, either medical or commissary. We suffered intensely from cold and hunger. We lived for a long time on bread made from sorghum seed, ground on a corn-mill, and sorghum molasses. After R.R. was temporarily repaired, I was sent to White Sulphur Springs on first train."

Montgomery White Sulphur Springs had, before the war, been a great resort for the planter aristocracy. Then, earlier in the war, President Davis and the Confederate establishment had summered there, sometimes viewing ring tournaments conducted by John Mosby's men, in recapitulation of the chivalric obsession that had so much contributed to Southern desire for a war. Its period as a military hospital was Montgomery's one brush with reality. After the war, it once again became a resort for the chivalry. At one time twenty former Confederate generals were registered. It is fitting that both the Southern Historical Society and the Lee Memorial Association were founded there.

Ben Rogers said that he "remained there until Lee surrendered. Surgeon in charge gave me an unlimited furlough, 'with privilege to return to Lebanon Tenn, there to remain until called for by the C.S. Authorities'." In his old age, Ben wrote, "*I am still waiting.*" The trip to Lebanon would have been tortuous even for a man with two sound legs: "Took up my tramp (on crutches) and first day waded Roanoke River and was taken in for the night by Col Daniel Hoge, next day I was picked up by some negroes driving an ox team and carried to Blacksburg. I was cited to Col Bob Prestons for lodging. Mrs. Preston kept me like a mother for four weeks, then sent me away with her blessing. I named my first baby Alice Preston for that noble woman."

Nor was Ben alone in his regard for Mrs. Preston. Young John Wise, who served under her husband at Saltville, also remembered the saintliness of the woman: "Mrs. Preston was known far and wide as the most devout woman in all the countryside. She often wept at the unregenerate profanity of her husband, whose only fault was that inveterate habit."

When Ben left Mrs. Preston's roof, he seemed to have left civilization: "Tramped down the E.T. & Va R.R. to Saltville. There I caught a salt train for Watauga Tenn. Tramped to Jonesboro, there was sent to Detention Camp at Strawberry Plains. Was sent from there to Chattanooga Prison. On 26th May I took oath of allegiance and secured transportation on a frt to Nashville; got off at Wartrace and tramped to Beech Grove where my uncle (Dr M M Chandler) lived, rested two days and he brought me in buggy to my Father's May 29th 1865." On the road home Ben had been forced to exchange shoes and hat with a Yankee homeguard. When he got to his father's he exploded: "The first thing I did when I reached my father's door was to sit down and remove those shoes and throw both shoes and hat as far as I could."

After his wound finally healed, Ben farmed and taught school. When he married, he and his wife located in Arkansas, where they went broke trying to raise cotton. Then they returned to Tennessee, where Ben became a successful farmer and an esteemed citizen and, later, a commercial traveler. He was active in veteran affairs and served in the Forty-fourth General Assembly, 1885-1887. On his deathbed, Ben dictated his account of the Champ Ferguson murders. He died July 27, 1927, at the age of eighty, in Lebanon, from whence he had left school to begin his education that summer day in 1864.

—Confederate Questionnaire, State of Tennessee;
Charles W. Crush, *The Montgomery County Story, 1776-1957*
Jamestown, Virginia, 1957);
Dixon Merritt, *The History of Wilson County*;
*Biographical Register of the General Assembly of the
State of Tennessee.*

Rogers, Henry Jordan
Private, Company B, Fourth Tennessee Cavalry

Unlike his brother Ben, Henry survived the war without a wound.

He was paroled at Washington, Georgia, May 9, 1865, after serving in the Jefferson Davis escort. He then returned to Lebanon, Tennessee, traveling part of the way on the top of a train, courtesy of the United States government. Settling down on a farm, he lived quietly until his death, May 11, 1912.

—Confederate Questionnaire, State of Tennessee.

Russell, Alfred A.
Colonel, Fourth Alabama Cavalry

A bitter-ender after the surrender, Colonel Russell went to Mexico. He bought a coffee plantation there and did not return to the United States until 1880. He never did take the oath of allegiance, hence he never again exercised his civil rights.

—John Robert Kennamer, *History of Jackson County* (Winchester, Tennessee: Southern Printing and Publishing Company, 1935), p. 50.

Shaw, Joseph
Major, Allison's Squadron

Colonel Dibrell took his boys back to Georgia from Saltville, there to begin at once to obstruct Sherman's movement toward the seacoast. Those fights between Wheeler's cavalry and Kilpatrick, Garrard, and Sherman's other cavalry commanders were relatively small affairs, perhaps, but the Southern casualties represented a physical loss that could not be replaced and a spiritual loss that deadened the survivors. Adjutant William Gibbs Allen describes one such skirmish outside Augusta: "we were in that lonely pinery when General Dibbrell came in command we had a hard battle we lost 7 men killed amongst them Lt. Col. Shaw of the 18th Battalion. One of General Dibbrells most trusted friends, we dug a ditch wraped their old blankets around them, laid them in the ditch. Genl Dibbrell stood with uncovered head with Tears streaming down his cheeks gave orders to fire the Salute.

there we left these gallant boys in that lonely pine land and nothing
but the singing wind song of the wind."
                        —William Gibbs Allen, "War Reminiscence,"
                                State of Tennessee Archives.

Sloan, William Erskine
Private, Company D, Fifth Tennessee Cavalry

When he reached the Biblical limitation, William Sloan decided to
add a concluding statement to the diary which he had kept during
the war, nearly fifty years before:

"In closing this little book, the pages of which pertain chiefly to
such part of the great civil war as I and my four brothers were actively
engaged in, I do not deem it necessary to add more than a few words
regarding myself individually. By the blessing of God and a reasonably
temperate life I have been enabled to pass my three score and ten,
being now 70 years and nearly 4 months of age, which is a good long
life, but I have accomplished next to nothing as the world looks at it.
I have lived what the world is willing to call an honest upright life,
and even as a Christian my life bears the inspection of the world very
well, but it is far from satisfactory to myself, and not what I would
like to make it if I had my time over again. As a money maker I have
been a failure, and that is about the only point on which the world
is disposed to judge a man; however I am not at this time worrying
over my failure as a money maker, for I am fully convinced that wealth
confers no advantage or enjoyment on a man as he approaches the
end of life, and the humblest burying place has as many attractions
to me as the costliest mausoleum.

"After my return to the old family home in 1866 . . . I remained
in that community for 12 years, being engaged chiefly at farming,
but also tried my hand at teaching school, selling hardware and im-
plements, selling furniture and assisting in furniture works, but in
1878 I came to San Francisco, Cal , and was there employed by the
North Pacific Coast R.R. as passenger agent. Early in 1882 I went to
Eastern Oregon and undertook pioneer wheat farming, but a year

and a half satisfied me with that country. January 1884 found me in Southern California, where I took up some public land in what was then part of San Bernardino Co., but is now Riverside Co.

The wild boom of 1887-8 and the financial crash that followed left me hopelessly struggling under a mortgage which I had been induced to give in the development of a water right. After many years of rigid economy and hardship to keep up my interest and save my property I at last developed some valuable clay on that land from which I realized enough to keep the wolf from my door for a few years, and that will perhaps be all that I will need until I take my departure. I never undertook to speculate in my life that I did not lose, and the money that I made on that ranch land seemed to be thing of accident rather than effort or business skill on my part, and came too late in life to enable me to assume the responsibility of a family. I now have a comfortable little home in the City of Los Angeles, and another home where I am now living here in Santa Monica, which can be made very comfortable and desirable, being beautifully located by the sea, so that I have the choice of two homes, either of which is plenty good enough for me, for all of which I owe a great debt of thanks and gratitude to the Father and Giver of all Good and Perfect Gifts."

William Sloan died of cerebral embolism, April 3, 1915, in California Hospital, Los Angeles, in his seventy-third year.

—William E. Sloan Diary, State of Tennessee Archive;
Death Certificate, Number 1711, April 5, 1915,
Los Angeles County, California.

Stormfeltz, George
Lieutenant, Company G, Eighth Texas Cavalry

Although George Stormfeltz had come to Texas from Pennsylvania as a grown man, he was one of the most gallant of the Rangers, as his action before Strawberry Plains proved. Despite his risk-taking, he survived the war; he had several horses killed under him, but his only wound was a slight one caused by the deflection off his pocket watch of a probably fatal ball. After the surrender he returned to Goliad, where in time he held several minor political offices, such as deputy clerk and deputy sheriff. At the time of his death, in 1912, at the age of seventy-nine, he was an esteemed elder citizen, a Texan.

—Solider's Pension Application, State of Texas; personal communication from Goliad County Library, Goliad, Texas.

Ulmer, Isaac Barton
Private, Third Alabama Cavalry

Despite his lack of confidence in General Allen, Private Ulmer was spared by the war, perhaps through the competence of Allen and no doubt through luck. Returning to Alabama, Private Ulmer became a farmer. Additionally, he clerked in the Customs House in Mobile and in the Marengo Land Equity Court, Demopolis. In his spare time, he wrote brief sketches of the Confederate Alabama cavalry regiments. He died November 23, 1925, at the age of eighty-three.

—T. M. Owen, *History of Alabama*, IV, p. 1698.

Walthour, Robert Howe
Private, Company G, Fifth Georgia Cavalry

Private Walthour survived the surprise at Readyville and the remainder of the war. He returned to Walthourville, where he died on August 15, 1905, at the age of sixty.

—Personal communication from Richard C. Cohan.

Walthour, Taylor
Private, Company G, Fifth Georgia Cavalry

The fourteen-year-old Taylor had followed his sixteen-year-old brother, Robert, into Liberty Independent Troop in 1861, but he

preceded him in death, on November 15, 1897, at the age of fifty.
—Personal communication from Richard C. Cohan.

Wheeler, Joseph
Major-General

General Wheeler did not resign after the failure of his Tennessee
raid. Soon he was ordered back to the Atlanta area, to shadow the
Yank lines. while Hood began his own Tennessee adventure. Then it
was Wheeler's few thousand and a few pick-up militia to confront
Sherman on his march to the sea. Thus it continued to the end. Brave
almost to the point of rashness, Wheeler was perhaps an ideal company
commander. But he could never maintain effective discipline among
his men, and after the Tennessee raid, when his command had been
supplemented by such recruits as Champ Ferguson's men, *Wheeler's
Cavalry* became a synonym for devastation and thievery for Georgia
and Carolina civilians. After the war, General Wheeler was briefly
imprisoned, then located in New Orleans. In 1868 he returned to
Wheeler, Alabama; in 1881 he was elected to the House of Representatives, a seat which he held for eight terms. Serving as a major-
general of the Volunteers in the Spanish-American War, he was said
to have confused the Spanish with the Yanks fought so long ago and
to have rallied his men to chase the blue-coats. He retired as a brigadier
general of the regular army on September 10, 1900, and died, in his
sixty-ninth year, on January 25, 1906.

—*Generals in Gray*;
Biographical Directory of the American Congress.

Whitsitt, William Heth
Private, later Chaplain, Fourth Tennessee Cavalry (McLemore)

The Nashville *Despatch* of September 4, 1864, reported the capture
of Chaplain Whitsitt, and a regimental roll lists him a deserter as of
December 2, 1864. But somehow he returned to the regiment and was

with it to the end, at Washington, Georgia. He was one of the men who received the famous $26.00 in gold from the Confederate Treasury, and he was able to retain a portion as a memento all his life. Before the war Whitsitt had studied at Union University, Murfreesborough, from which he graduated in 1861. He was ordained to the ministry in 1862. After the war he embarked upon further theological studies. He attended the University of Virginia, 1866-1867, and the Southern Baptist Theological Seminary, 1867-1869. Thereafter he studied at the University of Leipzig, 1869-1871. Soon after his return to the United States he became an assistant professor at the Southern Baptist Theological Seminary. After a distinguished career of over twenty years as a member of the faculty, he became chairman of the faculty, in 1895. That same year he became President of the Seminary, but his tenure as President was far from tranquil. Back in 1886 Professor Whitsitt had published an article in *Johnson's Universal Cyclopedia* which provoked doctrinal controversy. When it would not abate, Whitsitt was compelled to resign his position, in 1899. He afterwards became a professor of philosophy at Richmond College, Richmond, Virginia, where he taught until his death, on January 20, 1911, in his sixty-ninth year.

—J. Stoddard Johnston, *Memorial History of Louisville* (Chicago: American Biographical Publishing Company), II, 546-548.

Encyclopedia of Southern Baptists (Nashville: Broadman Press, 1958), p. 1496.

Williams, John Stuart
Brigadier-General, Kentucky Brigade of Cavalry

After his arrest, General Williams obediently returned to Georgia to face charges. He went first to Augusta, before reporting to General Hood. While he was there, Williams' friends began a campaign to achieve his vindication. Back in Virginia, Judge Theodore Burnett published in a newspaper his account of the battle at Saltville, which praised his fellow Kentuckian:

"It is to Colonel Giltner, who held the enemy in check, and kept

him back from the Salt Works for a period so long and to General
Williams, who placed the troops and did the fighting on the day of
the battle at Saltville, on the second instant, that the credit is due
for saving the Salt Works, and incidentally, the country. It is to him,
and the valor of the troops under him — Brigadier-general John S.
Williams — that the credit of this glorious and important victory is
due.

"There was not a general present ranking him or one that assumed
the responsibility of that important engagement, until the last gun
was fired. And yet, strange to say, from the published accounts, made
by telegraph and otherwise, no one would suppose that this gallant
and distinguished officer was even present."

When Williams' command returned to Georgia late in October, it
voted a resolution stressing his leadership at Saltville and asked that
newspapers give the resolution publicity. Williams' men were fond of
him; he was, as George Ewing put it, "a born fighter, if not a tacti-
cian."

Williams also had other friends in the Confederate Congress. While
visiting Richmond in December, 1863, after his misadventure in East
Tennessee, he was, by a resolution offered by Representative H. W.
Bruce (Kentucky), tendered a guest seat in the House chamber. He had
been able the following spring to secure another brigade command,
this one in the Army of Tennessee. His Congressional friends stood
by him after his Saltville arrest; the Augusta *Chronicle & Sentinel* of
November 3 contained this item: "COMPLIMENTARY SERENADE
— On Tuesday evening last [November 1] a large number of the friends
of Gen. J. S. Williams, better known by the soubriquet of Cerro Gordo
Williams, secured the services of the Palmetto Band, and proceeding to
the Planters Hotel, serenaded the above well known gentleman and
gallant soldier." On this occasion, Williams was lauded by Thomas
Menees and James S. Chrisman, both representatives, the former
from Tennessee, the latter from Kentucky.

Soon after, on November 8, the second day of the new Congressional
session, Judge Burnett introduced a joint resolution "of thanks to
Brigadier-General John S. Williams and the officers and men under
his command for their victory over the enemy at Saltville, Virginia,

on the second day of October, eighteen hundred and sixty-four."
With the support of Humphrey Marshall (Kentucky), under whom
Williams had served earlier in the war, the resolution made its way
through the legislative process, keeping Williams' name before the
House and the Senate. Then, failing to get the response that he wanted,
Judge Burnett, on January 20, 1865, offered additional resolutions:

"*Resolved*, That the Committee on Military Affairs be instructed
to report what additional legislation is necessary to prevent arbitrary
and malicious arrests by generals in the Army.

"Second. To report a bill fixing an adequate punishment for failing to prefer charges within a reasonable time after arrest."

These latter resolutions seem to have had their impact, for President Davis, on February 3, signed the original resolution of praise.
In the meantime, Williams had reported to General Hood at Columbia,
Tennessee. Since Hood was in the midst of conducting his desperate
invasion of Tennessee, he referrred the case, on November 23, to General Beauregard, for disposition. On January 4, 1865, General Beauregard referred the case to General Hardee, commanding in South
Carolina, where the accusing officer was now stationed. To that authority Williams requested that the case be investigated, so that he
or his accuser might be exonerated; having "been dragged across the
country for more than 2,000 miles as a public prisoner," Williams
was surely justified in seeking public vindication, in the event that
he was found innocent of charges. The same day Hardee referred
the case to the Adjutant-General, Samuel Cooper, who made inquiries
of the various commands to determine the facts of the matter. On
February 2, he recommended to the Secretary of War that Williams
be restored to his command and that the "course pursued to him"
be condemned.

Williams did resume his command and was soon cussing and argu-
ing with his superior officers in defense of his men. He became so
provoked with the apparent mistreatment of his men by Wade Hamp-
ton that he cried in frustration. His thoughts seem to have turned to
the plight of individuals, now that it was obvious that the war was
soon to end. When he was presented with some deserters from North
Carolina infantry that his men had apprehended on their way home,

Williams listened to the reason offered by the deserters, that their families were starving, broke into tears, and released them. When the surrender came, Williams took his parole with General Joseph E. Johnston's command, while his own command formed a part of Jefferson Davis' escort.

Then Williams began his journey home to Kentucky. Basil Duke recalls one incident from that trip: "Just after the final surrender Gen. Frank Cheatham, of Tennessee, and Gen. John S. Williams — better known as 'Cerro Gordo' Williams — of Kentucky, were wending their way northward in the hope of sometime regaining their antebellum homes. They were, of course, sore and dejected, and notwithstanding the personal friendship which existed between them, found matter for acrimonious discussion in every topic which either broached. Finally they got upon the causes of Confederate failure. Cheatham asserted that it was due entirely to the timidity and irresolution of Kentucky. Had Kentucky joined and assisted the Southern movement, he claimed, it would have been successful. This Williams stoutly denied. On the contrary, he contended, the reason why Kentucky did not cast her lot with the South was that she was prevented by the incertitude and hesitation of Tennessee. Moreover, there were, he insisted, other and serious objections to the Tennesseeans. 'If I had nothing else against your people, Cheatham,' he said, 'I'd avoid them because the're always singing that infernal heartbreaking song, "Lorena."' Then Cheatham swore by all that he held holy that the song had never been heard in Tennessee, and that no Tennessean ever had sung or ever would sing it. The dispute waxed hot and finally culminated in a bet, proposed by Williams, that the very first Tennesseean they met with would either be singing 'Lorena' or would sing it before he got out of hearing. Cheatham promptly accepted. Each had about two dollars in silver and they put it up.

By that date the woods and the roads were full of disbanded Confederate soldiers, and they soon came upon one. He was a tall, stalwart young fellow, seated on a log and evidently resting after a long tramp. Williams at once accosted him.

"'Where do you hail from, soldier?'

"'Well,' responded the soldier, 'that's hard to say. For four years gone I've been in the Confederacy and belonged to the army. But now I feel as if I didn't hail from anywhar'. However, I came originally from Tennessee so I may say I hail from thar; but —

   '"It matters little now Lo-ree-na."'

"'Cheatham!' said Williams, 'hand over that money.'"

Williams' command had surrendered at Washington, Georgia, then ridden as an organized body up to Chattanooga, where the Yankee commander, in violation of the terms of parole, made them surrender their horses. By that time Williams caught up with his men, and he immediately went up to Nashville, to demand the restoration of the horses. He got the order, too, from General Thomas, so that he was in a state of satisfaction when Ben C. Truman, a correspondent for the New York *Times,* interviewed him on the train back to Chattanooga:

"Our train brought down nearly a thousand paroled rebels, most of whom belong in Georgia. I had a seat with, and made the acquaintance of Gen. WILLIAMS, better known as 'Cerro Gordo Williams,' who was on the way to Chattanooga to recover some horses which he had left there. He is not quite as big as all out doors, but he is the hugest specimen I have ever seen born of woman. He must be six foot six and built in proportion. He has a head like a lion, a heart like a country fire-place, and a belly like a boiler. His legs would make good underpinnings for a water tank, while his feet looked like miniature gunboats, constructed upon the same plan that canal-boats are built in Maine — by the yard and cut off to suit purchasers. He seemed to be a pretty clever fellow, and smacked his legs with great satisfaction after a tremendous pull at my debilitated pint of traveling fluid. . . . He is very profane in conversation, and describes the Mexican war as a skirmish compared with the battles of the rebellion."

By the time that Williams got back to Chattanooga, though, most of the horses had been disposed of, and Williams' men had to settle for railroad transportation provided by the Yankees. Even so, the local Yankee commander, angered at being countermanded, added insult to injury: "As a revenge for Williams's interference in this matter, the Yankee despot at Chattanooga ordered all the officers of the brigade to remove from their uniforms the insignia of their rank.

Of course the order was obeyed, and Gen. Williams, with his pocket knife, removed his well-earned wreath and stars, while the other officers cut or tore off their stars and bars."

General Williams finally made it back to Winchester, to resume farming. Uncontrollably gregarious, though, he was soon back in politics. He was a member of the State house of representatives in 1873 and 1875, was an unsuccessful candidate for governor in 1875, and served as a Democratic presidential elector in 1876. He was elected to the United States Senate for the term 1879 to 1885, but was unsuccessful in his bid for reelection. He then retired to his farm, where he died on July 17, 1898, at the age of eighty.

—Generals in Gray;
Biographical Directory of the American Congress;
Duke;
Benjamin C. Truman, "The South," New York *Times,* June 4, 1865;
Dyer; Andrew Dickson White, *Autobiography* (New York: The Century Company, 1922), I, 215;
Henry Watterson, *Marse Henry* (New York: George W. Doran, 1909), II, 26.

Williamson, John Coffee
Sergeant, Company E, Fifth Tennessee Cavalry

That accomplished prowler, Sergeant Williamson, returned to Benton, Polk County, Tennessee, after the war, to become a prominent lawyer. In 1893 he was recognized as a citizen of unimpeached integrity by being appointed United States Commissioner for Lower East Tennessee. He held that position at the time of his death, December 19, 1898.

—John C. Williamson, "The Civil War Diary of John Coffee Williamson."

Wise, John Sergeant
Second-Lieutenant, Preston's Battalion of Virginia Reserves

When the war ended, John Wise entered the Law School at the University of Virginia. Upon his graduation in 1867, he entered practice in Richmond, joining his father in a partnership in 1869 which lasted until his father's death in 1876. During these years Wise was becoming active in Republican politics, and he was elected to the House of Representatives for the term of 1882-1884. There he was noted by the famous Washington newspaperman "Carp" as a man "with a big heart." In illustration of Wise's courage, Carp wrote: "The Wise family is accustomed to dueling. Henry A. Wise fought a number of duels, and was second in others, notably the one between Graves and Cilley, which created such excitement some fifty years ago. The blood of John S. Wise also is hot. I am not surprised to hear that he struck with his fist the face of a man who called him a liar not long ago." In 1885 Wise was the unsuccessful candidate for governor of Virginia, and in 1888 he moved to New York City, where he became a very prominent representative for General Electric and telephone and trolley interests. The Spanish-American War marked the return of the Wise family to the old flag: three of his sons fought in the hostilities. His eldest, Captain Hugh D. Wise, Ninth United States Regular Infantry, a West Point graduate, distinguished himself in the assault on San Juan Heights at Santiago. Wealthy and genial, respected by a multitude of friends, Wise died on May 12, 1913, in his sixty-sixth year.

> —*Biographical Directory of the American Congress;*
> *Carp's Washington;*
> *National Cyclopedia of American Biography,* XII.

Witherspoon, James Green
Sergeant, Company F, Ninth Tennessee Cavalry

With his uncle, J. F. Pitts, Sergeant Witherspoon toughed out the war, arriving home just about the date of his twenty-first birthday. He returned to Wayne County, Tennessee, to become a successful merchant and farmer in Clifton. In the 1870s he and his younger brother, Philip, went to Texas, where they created a huge ranch that sprawled over parts of five counties, employing such brands as *Three Nines, Ula, Teaspoon, Hip C, and Turkey Track.* J. G. Witherspoon was a leader in the founding of Foard County, living in the southern part of the county on Ula Ranch. In 1887 he moved to Quanah, in what is now Hardeman County, deciding to live there since he had to ship his cattle from that point anyhow. He died there in 1926, in his eighty-first year.

> —Bailey Phelps, *They Loved the Land* (Wichita Falls, Texas:
> Nortex Publishing Company, 1969);
> J. W. Williams, *The Big Ranch Country* (Wichita Falls, Texas:
> Nortex Publishing Company, 1971).

Witt, William Pleasant
Private, Company H, Fifth Tennessee Cavalry

W. P. Witt left Tennessee after the war. By 1876 he had arrived in McGregor, Texas, where he married and sired a family. In 1902 he bought land in Ochiltree County as a speculation. One of the stipulations to ownership was that the land had to be lived on so many months a year for three years, so Witt built a house and dug a well. Then he brought his wife and daughter to spend part of the time necessary to meet the stipulation. The farm wasn't all that a young girl could hope for; his daughter confided to a friend: ". . .fifty-eight miles from a railroad and eight miles from [town]. I have plenty of health, breath, grass, room and lonesomeness. I will be here, I think, until October. This is a country of beauty and delight, sunrises and sunsets are indescribable, but I wish somebody besides Papa would find it out. I never did want to monopolize good things. If Papa decided to live here, I suppose I will necessarily have to, which I wouldn't mind if I could only hear a train squall or whistle. . . ." Such a wide open space must have given Private Witt time to recall his Confederate past, for he sent in his contribution to the *Confederate Veteran* in

1912. He died the following year, August, 1913, at the age of sixty-
seven.

—Mrs. Clarence Neufeld, "A. C. Witt," in
(The Ochiltree Country Historical Survey Committee, 1969),
pp. 385-387.

Bibliography

Newspapers Cited

Arkansas *Gazette,* September 14, 1878.

Athens *Southern Watchman,* August 10, 1864.

Atlanta *Constitution,* March 13, 14, 1920; May 11, 1926.

Atlanta *Intelligencer,* August 21, October 21, 1864.

Augusta *Chronicle and Sentinel,* November 1, 1864.

Augusta *Southern Watchman,* August 3, 1864.

Baltimore *Sun,* December 10, 1905.

Beaumont *Enterprise,* January 6, 1915.

Charleston *Daily Courier,* August 6, 8, October 18, 1864.

Charleston *Mercury,* August 8, 1864.

Chattanooga *Gazette,* August 26, 1864.

Chattanooga *Rebel,* September 8, 1864.

Cincinnati *Daily Commercial,* August 27, 31, 1864.

Cincinnati *Daily Gazette,* August 27, 1864.

Dallas *Daily Times Herald,* August 9, 1920.

Dallas *Morning News,* August 9, 1920.

Dayton *Journal,* September 15, 1864.

Detroit *Advertiser and Tribune,* October 20, 1864.

Detroit *Free Press,* August 16, October 20, 1864.

Houston *Telegraph.*

Knoxville *Daily Press and Herald,* July 11, 1868.

Knoxville Whig and Rebel Ventilator, August 31, September 7, 21, 28, 1864.

Louisville *Journal,* September 3, November 20, 1964; August 23, 1866.

Lynchburg *Viginian,* September 24, October 8, 1864.

Macon *Daily Telegraph,* August 9, 1864.

Maryville *Enterprise,* March 3, 1932.

Memphis *Appeal,* June 25, 1864.

Monroe *Commercial,* September 1, 1864.

Montgomery *Daily Advertiser,* June 27, August 8, 11, 1864.

Nashville *Banner,* September 19, 20, 1891; August 16, 17, 1893; April 27, 1944.

Nashville *Daily American,* September 20, 1891; August 17, 18, 1893.

Nashville *Daily Press and Times,* August 23, 1864.

Nashville *Daily Times and True Union,* September 1, 1864.

Nashville *Dispatch,* September 4, 1864; July 6, 1865.

New York *Herald,* September 6, 1864.

New York *Times,* August 12, 14, 26, 1864; June 4, 1865.

New York *Tribune,* August 25, 1864.

Niles Republican, February 4, 1865.

Philadelphia *Inquirer,* August 24, 26, September 22, October 21, 1864.

Richmond *Dispatch,* October 12, 1864.

Richmond *Enquirer,* August 27, October 4, 18, 19, 1864.

Richmond *Sentinel,* October 10, 1864.

Richmond *Whig,* October 7, 1864.

Savannah *Republican,* August 18, 20, October 4, 1864.

Unpublished Materials

Allen, William Gibbs, Papers. Tennessee State Archives.

Ammen, Jacob, Papers. Illinois State Historical Soceity.

Ash, John H., Papers. Emory University.

Black, James Conquest Cross, Papers. Southern Historical Collection, University of North Carolina.

Bragg, Braxton, Papers. Houghton Library, Harvard University.

Breckinridge, John C. Papers. Chicago Historical Society.

Breckinridge, John C. Papers. Huntington Library.

Breckinridge Family. Papers. Library of Congress.

Dail, Fletcher. Interview with author, August 15, 1973.

Farmer, Wayne. Interview with author, August 15, 1973.

Fifth Tennessee Cavalry Papers. Western Reserve Historical Society.

Fifty-first Alabama Cavalry Papers. Alabama State Archives.

Grimsley, G. K., Soldier's Application for Pension, 2028, and Widow's Application, 1399W2. Tennessee State Archives.

Guerrant, Edward Owings. Diary. Southern Historical Collection, University of North Carolina.

Guerrant, Edward Owings. Papers. University of Kentucky.

Henderson, W. M. Recollections. Georgia State Arvhices.

Hill, John W. Papers. Barker Texas History Center, University of Texas.

Inman, Myra. Diary. Southern Historical Collection, University of North Carolina.

Jordan, Stephen. Application for Membership, United Confederate Veterans, Tennessee Division, Bivouac Records, Tennessee State Archives.

Lathrop, Stanley E. Papers. State Historical Society of Wisconsin.

McKenzie, Mrs. Oscar. "When Sherman Marched Through Georgia," *Reminiscences of Confederate Soldiers and Stories of the War,* III, United Daughters of the Confederacy, Georgia State Archives.

Miller, George Knox. Papers. Southern Historical Collection, University of North Carolina.

Minor, John. Diary. Tennessee State Archives.

Morgan, David B. Papers. Georgia Historical Society.

Nicholson, James. Papers. Barker Texas History Center, University of Texas.

Questionnaires, Civil War, compiled by John Trotwood Moore. Tennessee State Archives (Benjamin Duggan Rogers, Henry Rogers)

Reagan, A. A. Soldier's Application for Pension, 10008, and Widow's Application, 1929. Tennessee State Archives.

Register. Emory Hospital. United Daughters of the Confederacy Museum.

Sloan, William E. Diary. Tennessee State Archives.

Stringfield, William W. Papers. Alabama State Archives.

Ulmer, Isaac Barton. Papers. Southern Historical Collection, University of North Carolina.

Ulmer, Isaac Barton. Reminiscences of the Third Alabama Cavalry. Alabama State Archives.

Vance, Z. B. Papers. North Carolina State Archives.

Wheeler, Joseph. Papers. Alabama State Archives.

Wheeler, Joseph. Papers. Western Reserve Historical Society.

Wynn, J. A. Reminiscence. Georgia State Archives.

Books and Periodicals Cited

Alderman, Edwin A., and J. C. Harris, eds. *Library of Southern Literature*. Atlanta, 1907.

Allen, Theodore F. "The Lost Flag of the Confederacy," *Trotwood's Magazine*, II (July, 1906), 556-559.

Allen, Valentine C. *Rhea and Meigs Counties in the Confederate War*. Dayton, Tennessee, 1908.

Allen, William Gibbs. "Incidents of Wheeler's Raid," *Confederate Veteran*, XIX (June, 1911), 288.

Andrews, J. Cutler. *The South Reports the Civil War*. Princeton, 1970.

Augusta Bar Association. *Memorial Exercises in Honor of J. C. C. Black*. n.p., n.d.

Austin, J. P. *The Blue and the Gray*. Atlanta, 1899.

Barron, Samuel B. *The Lone Star Defenders*. New York, 1908.

——. "Wheeler's Cavalry in the Georgia Campaign," *Confederate Veteran*, XIV (February, 1906), 70.

Beach, Ursula. *Along the Warioto, A History of Montgomery County*. Nashville, 1964.

Beers, Mrs. Fannie A. *Memories*. Philadelphia, 1888.

Belfield, Henry H. "My Sixty Days in Hades," in *Military Essays and Recollections*, MOLLUS – Illinois, III. Chicago, 1899.

Biographical Register of the General Assembly of the State of Tennessee.

Bird, Hiram T. *Memories of the Civil War*. n.p., n.d.

Blair, Walter, ed. *Native American Humor*. San Francisco, 1960.

Blount County Historical Society. *The Heritage of Blount County*. n.p., 1972.

Boatner, Mark Mayo. *The Civil War Dictionary*. New York, 1959.

Bunting, Robert Franklin. *Letters of Robert Franklin Bunting*. Naples, Florida, 1944.

Burnett, T. L. "The Battle of Saltville," *The Southern Bivouac*, II (September, 1883), 20-22. (Original appearance, Richmond *Enquirer*, October 18, 1864).

Butler, John Campbell. *Historical Record of Macon and Central Georgia*. Macon, 1958.

Carpenter, Frances, ed. *Carp's Washington*. New York, 1920.

Carter, W. B. *History of the First Regiment of Tennessee Volunteer Cavalry*. Knoxville, 1902.

Clark, Champ. *My Quarter Century of American Politics*. New York, 1920.

Clark, Walter. *Under the Stars and Bars*. Augusta, Georgia, 1908.

Coffin, James P. "Col. Henry M. Ashby," *Confederate Veteran*, XIV (March, 1906), 121.

Coleman, Kenneth, ed. *Athens: 1861-1865*. Athens, 1969.

Colgin, James H., ed. "The Life Story of Brig. Gen. Felix Robertson," *Texana*, VIII (Spring, 1970), 154-182.

Confederate States of America. *Special Orders of the Adjutant and Inspector General's Office, Confederate States, 1865*. Washington, 18___?

Connelly, Thomas Lawrence. *Autumn of Glory*. Baton Rouge, 1971.

Crush, Charles W. *The Montgomery County Story, 1776-1957*. Jamestown, Virginia, 1957.

Cullom, Shelby Moore. *Fifty Years of Public Service*. Chicago, 1911.

Cuyrus, Lucille. *History of Bartow County*. n.p., 1933.

Darsey, Ben W. *A War Story*. Statesboro, Georgia, n.d.

Davis, W. H. "Cavalry Expeditions in Georgia," *Confederate Veteran*, XVI (June, 1908), 250-251.

——. "Cavalry Service Under Gen. Wheeler," *Confederate Veteran*, XI (August, 1903), 353-354.

Davis, William C. "The Massacre at Saltville," *Civil War Times Illustrated*, IX (February, 1971), 4-11, 43-48.

Day, B. F. "Service with Col. George R. Diamond," *Confederate Veteran*, XXVIII (March, 1920), 86.

Dodson, W. C. *The Campaigns of Wheeler and his Cavalry*. Atlanta, 1899.

——. "Stampede of Federal Cavalry," *Confederate Veteran*, XIX (March, 1911), 123-124.

DuBose, John Witherspoon. *General Joseph Wheeler and the Army of Tennessee*. New York, 1912.

Duke, Basil. *A History of Morgan's Cavalry*. Bloomington, Indiana, 1960.

———. *Reminiscences of General Basil W. Duke.* New York, 1911.

Dyer, John Percy. *From Shiloh to San Juan.* Baton Rouge, 1961.

Dyer, John Will. *Reminiscences; or, Four Years in the Confederate Army.* Evansville, Indiana, 1898.

Encyclopedia of the New West.

Encyclopedia of Southern Baptists. Nashville, 1958.

Evans, Clement A., ed. *Confederate Military History,* Atlanta, 1899.

Ewing, George D. "The Battle of Blue Springs, Tennessee," *Confederate Veteran,* XXX (February, 1922), 46-48.

Fletcher, Williams Andrews. *Rebel Private, Front and Rear.* Beaumont, Texas, 1908.

Foard, J. F. "Vivid Prison Experience," *Confederate Veteran,* XXI (November, 1913), 529-532.

Fox, James D. *A True History of the Reign of Terror.* Aurora, Illinois, 1884.

Frobel, B. W. "The Georgia Campaign," *Scott's Monthly Magazine,* V (February, 1868), 37-42.

"Gallant Phil Pointer," *Confederate Veteran,* XI (March, 1903), 110.

Garrett, Jill Knigh, and Marise P. Lightfoot. *The Civil War in Maury County, Tennessee.* n.p., 1966.

Gay, Mary Ann. *Life in Dixie During the War.* Atlanta, 1894.

Giddens, Paul H., ed. "Memories of Libby Prison by Daniel N. Reynolds," *Michigan History Magazine,* XXIII (Autumn, 1939), 391-398.

Giles, Leonidas Blanton. *Terry's Texas Rangers.* Austin, Texas, 1911.

Glazier, Willard W. *The Capture, the Prison Pen, and the Escape.* New York, 1868.

Graber, Henry William. *The Life Record of H. W. Graber, a Terry Texas Ranger, 1861-1865.* n.p., n.d.

Griffith, Lucille, ed. *Yours Till Death: Civil War Letters of John W. Cotton.* University, Alabama, 1951.

Guild, George B. *A Brief Narrative of the Fourth Tennessee Cavalry Regiment.* Nashville, 1913.

Guthrey, D. M. "Wheeler's Cavalry Around Atlanta," *Confederate Veteran,* XIII (June, 1905), 267.

Hale, Will T. "General Wheeler's Last Raid," *Confederate Veteran,* XXIII (January, 1915), 30.

——. *History of DeKalb County.* McMinnville, Tennessee, 1969.

——, and Dixon L. Merritt. *A History of Tennessee and Tennesseans.* Chicago, 1913.

Hardy, D. *Historical Review of South-east Texas.*

Hargis, O. P. "A Georgia Farm Boy in Wheeler's Cavalry," *Civil War Times Illustrated,* VII (November, 1968), 36-41.

——. "We Kept Fighting and Falling Back," *Civil War Times Illustrated,* VII (December, 1968), 37-42.

Harrison, James L., comp. *Biographical Directory of the American Congress.* Washington, 1950.

Hart, Roger O. *Redeemers, Bourbons and Populists.* Baton Rouge, 1975.

Hartpence, William R. *History of the Fifty-First Veteran Volunteer Infanty.* Cincinnati, 1894.

Harwell, Richard B., ed. *Kate: The Journal of a Confederate Nurse.* Baton Rouge, 1959.

Harwell, Thomas Fletcher. *Eighty Years Under the Stars and Bars.* Kyle, Texas, 1947.

Hays County Historical and Genealogical Society, IV (June, 1972).

High, Edwin W. *History of the Sixty-Eighth Regiment Indiana Volunteer Infantry.* Metamora, Indiana, 1902.

Hinman, Wilbur F. *The Story of the Sherman Brigade.* Alliance, Ohio, 1897.

Hoehling, A. A. *Last Train from Atlanta.* New York, 1958.

Hood, John B. *Advance and Retreat.* Bloomington, Indiana, 1959.

Inge, M. Thomas, ed. *Sut Lovingood's Yarns.* New Haven, 1966.

Johnson, Francis W. *A History of Texas and Texans.* Chicago, 1914.

Johnston, J. Stoddard. *Memorial History of Louisville.* Chicago, n.d.

Jones, J. B. *A Rebel War Clerk's Diary.* New York, 1958.

Kennamer, John Robert. *History of Jackson County.* Winchester, Tennessee, 1935.

Kent, William B. *A History of Saltville.* Radford, Virginia, 1955.

King, Edward. *The Great South.* Hartford, Connecticut, 1875.

Lambright, James T. *History of the Liberty Independent Company.* Brunswick, Georgia, 1910.

"The Last General Officer," *Confederate Veteran*, XXXVI (October, 1928), 365-366.

Lathrop, Edward S. "Gossipy Letter from Georgia," *Confederate Veteran*, XX (November, 1912), 520.

Lilliard, Stewart. *Meigs County, Tennessee*. Sewanee, Tennessee, 1975.

Lindsley, John Berrien, ed. *Military Annals of Tennessee*. Nashville, 1886.

Long, Mrs. Myrtie Candler. "Reminiscences of Life in Georgia," *Georgia Historical Quarterly*, XXXIII (December, 1949), 303-313.

"Maj. W. G. Allen," *Confederate Veteran*, XXXIII (January, 1925), 25.

"Major Gen. Joseph Wheeler, Jr.," *Southern Literary Messenger*, XXXVIII (April, 1864), 222-232.

Mason, Emily V., ed. *The Southern Poems of the War*. Baltimore, 1867.

Mason, Frank H. *The Twelfth Ohio Cavalry*. Cleveland, 1871.

Massey, Mary Elizabeth. *Bonnet Brigades*. New York, 1966.

Memoirs of Georgia. Atlanta, 1895.

Merrill, W. E. "Block-houses for Railroad Defense in the Department of the Cumberland," in *Sketches of War History, Ohio Commandry*, Series Three, MOLLUS — Ohio. Cincinnati, 1890.

Merritt, Dixon. *The History of Wilson County*. Lebanon, Tennessee, 1961.

Michigan. Adjutant General's Office. *Record of Service of the Michigan Volunteers*. Kalamazoo, 190_.

Miller, James Cooper. "We Scattered the Rebels," *Civil War Times Illustrated,* VIII (August, 1969).

Mims, Wilbur F. *War History of the Prattville Dragoons*. Thurber, Texas, n.d.

Moore, Frank, ed. *The Rebellion Record*. New York, 186_.

Mosgrove, George Dallas. *Kentucky Cavaliers in Dixie*. Jackson, Tennessee, 1957.

National Cyclopedia of American Biography. New York, 1898 +.

Nisbett, James Cooper. *Four Years on the Firing Line*. Chattanooga, 1914.

Nolen, C. L. "Dibrell's Old Flag Was Not Surrendered," *Confederate Veteran,* XIV (November, 1906), 510.

Northen, William J. *Men of Mark in Georgia.* Atlanta, 1916.

Northern Alabama, Historical and Biographical. Birmingham, Alabama, 1888.

O'Dell, Ruth Webb. *Over the Misty Blue Mountains: The Story of Cocke County.* n.p., 1950.

Overley, Milford. "Williams Kentucky Brigade, C.S.A.," *Confederate Veteran,* XIII (October, 1905), 460-462.

Owen, Thomas M. *History of Alabama.* Chicago, 1921.

Phelps, Bailey. *They Loved the Land.* Wichita Falls, Texas, 1969.

Pittard, Homer Peyton. *Legends and Stories of Civil War Rutherford County.* Unpublished M.A. Thesis, George Peabody College for Teachers, 1940.

Price, Richard N. *Holston Methodism.* Nashville, 1913.

Roach, Hattie Joplin. *The Hills of Cherokee.* n.p., n.d.

Robertson, Felix H. "On Wheeler's Last Raid in Middle Tennessee," *Confederate Veteran,* XXX (September, 1922), 334-335.

Robertson, James I., ed. *The Diary of Dolly Lunt Burge.* Athens, Georgia, 1962.

Robertson, John, ed. *Michigan in the Civil War.* Lansing, 1880.

Romeyn, Henry. "With Colored Troops in the Army of the Cumberland," *War Papers,* MOLLUS – DC, LI.

Rose, Victor M. *Ross's Texas Brigade.* Louisville, 1881.

Schroeder, Albert W., Jr., ed. "Writings of a Tennessee Unionist," *Tennessee Historical Quarterly,* IX (September, 1950), 244-272 (December, 1950), 344-361.

Sensing, Thurman. *Champ Ferguson: Confederate Guerrilla.* Nashville, 1942.

Simpson, Harold B., ed. *Texas in the War.* Hillsboro, Texas, 1965.

"Skitt," "Duck Town," *Southern Literary Messenger,* XXI (November, 1860), 337-342.

Smedes, Susan Dabney. *Memorials of a Southern Planter.* New York, 1965.

Smith, Charles H. *Bill Arp, So Called.* New York, 1866.

Smith, Frank N. *History of Maury County, Tennessee.* n.p., 1969.

Speer, William S. *Sketches of Prominent Tennesseans.* Nashville, 1888.

Stegeman, John F. *These Men She Gave,* Athens, Georgia, 1964.

Stringfield, W. W. "The Champ Ferguson Affair," *The Emory and Henry Era,* XVII (May, 1914), 300-302.

Summers, Lewis Preston. *History of Southwestern Virginia, 1746-1786, Washington County, 1777-1870.* Baltimore, 1966.

Tarrant, Eastham. *The Wild Riders of the First Kentucky Cavalry.* Louisville, 1894.

Thatcher, Marshall P. *A Hundred Battles in the West — The Second Michigan Cavalry.* Detroit, 1884.

Thomas, H. H. "Personal Reminiscences of the East Tennessee Campaign," in *Military Essays and Recollections,* MOLLUS — Illinois, III. Chicago, 1907.   ;

Townsend, William H. *Lincoln and the Bluegrass.* Lexington, Kentucky, 1955.

Vale, Joseph A. *Minty and the Cavalry.* Harrisburg, Pennsylvania, 1886.

VanMeter, B. L. "General Burbridge in Kentucky," *Confederate Veteran,* XXII (November, 1914), 512.

Vaughter, John B. *Prison Life in Dixie.* Chicago, 1880.

"W. W. Hendrix," *Cumberland Presbyterian,* LII (August 24, 1893), 4.

Wallace, Lee A. *A Guide to Virginia Military Organizations, 1861-1865.* Richmond, 1964.

War of the Rebellion: A Compilation of the Official Records of the Union and Confederate Armies. Washington, 1880-1901.

Warner, Ezra J. *Generals in Gray.* Baton Rouge, 1959.

——, and W. Buck Yearns. *Biographical Register of the Confederate Congress.* Baton Rouge, 1975.

Watkins, Sam R. *"Co. Aytch": A Side Show of the Big Show.* New York, 1962.

Watterson, Henry. *Marse Henry.* New York, 1909.

Weaver, Richard M. *The Southern Tradition at Bay.* New York, 1968.

Wells, James Monroe. *With Touch of Elbow.* Philadelphia, 1909.

Wheatheart of the Plains: An Early History of Ochiltree County. n.p., 1969.

White, Andrew Dickson. *Autobiography.* New York, 1922.

Whitenack, Daniel S. "Reminiscences of the Civil War: Andersonville," *Indiana Magazine of History,* XI (June, 1915), 728-743.

Whitson, *Personal Sketches.*

Williams, Carolyn White. *History of Jones County.* Macon, Georgia, 1957.

Williams, J. W. *The Big Ranch Country.* Wichita Falls, Texas, 1971.

Williamson, John C., ed. "The Civil War Diary of John Coffee Williamson," *Tennessee Historical Quarterly,* XV (March, 1956), 61-74.

"A Winter in the South," *Harper's Magazine,* LXXVIII (September, 1857), 444-448.

Wise, John S. *The End of an Era.* Boston, 1899.

Witherspoon, J. G. "Confederate Cavalry Leaders," *Confederate Veteran,* XXVII (November, 1919), 414-417.

Witt, W. P. "After M'Cook's Raid Below Atlanta," *Confederate Veteran,* XX (March, 1912), 115-116.

Wooten, Dudley G. *Comprehensive History of Texas,* Dallas, 1898.

Yeary, Mamie, ed. *Some Recollections of the Boys in Gray.* Dallas, 1912.

Younger, Edward, ed. *Inside the Confederate Government: The Diary of Robert Garlick Hill Kean.* New York, 1957.

Index to Names

This book is almost entirely about individual experience. It does not study the preparation for or execution of a campaign or even a single battle, except as an event in someone's life.

This index, therefore, contains nothing but the names of individuals. The names of places through which these individuals passed may be learned from the Table of Contents and the headings within the text. The location of these places may be learned from the map which accompanies each segment of the raid.

Almost every name in the text is cited in this index. Every name of a Confederate or Union soldier is given, with unit identification if it is known. Where a name recurs with some frequency, a set of inclusive page citations is given: for example, Williams, John S., Gen., 271-343 — with the understanding that that name is often cited in connection with a particular event. The Table of Contents will indicate the event.